Language Teachers Studying Abroad

FSC
www.fsc.org
MIX
Paper from
responsible sources
FSC® C013604

PSYCHOLOGY OF LANGUAGE LEARNING AND TEACHING

Series Editors: Sarah Mercer, *Universität Graz, Austria* and Stephen Ryan, *Waseda University, Japan*

This international, interdisciplinary book series explores the exciting, emerging field of Psychology of Language Learning and Teaching. It is a series that aims to bring together works which address a diverse range of psychological constructs from a multitude of empirical and theoretical perspectives, but always with a clear focus on their applications within the domain of language learning and teaching. The field is one that integrates various areas of research that have been traditionally discussed as distinct entities, such as motivation, identity, beliefs, strategies and self-regulation, and it also explores other less familiar concepts for a language education audience, such as emotions, the self and positive psychology approaches. In theoretical terms, the new field represents a dynamic interface between psychology and foreign language education and books in the series draw on work from diverse branches of psychology, while remaining determinedly focused on their pedagogic value. In methodological terms, sociocultural and complexity perspectives have drawn attention to the relationships between individuals and their social worlds, leading to a field now marked by methodological pluralism. In view of this, books encompassing quantitative, qualitative and mixed methods studies are all welcomed.

All books in this series are externally peer-reviewed.

Full details of all the books in this series and of all our other publications can be found on http://www.multilingual-matters.com, or by writing to Multilingual Matters, St Nicholas House, 31-34 High Street, Bristol, BS1 2AW, UK.

PSYCHOLOGY OF LANGUAGE LEARNING AND TEACHING: 17

Language Teachers Studying Abroad

Identities, Emotions and Disruptions

Edited by
Gary Barkhuizen

MULTILINGUAL MATTERS
Bristol • Jackson

DOI https://doi.org/10.21832/BARKHU9943

Library of Congress Cataloging in Publication Data
A catalog record for this book is available from the Library of Congress.
Names: Barkhuizen, Gary Patrick, editor.
Title: Language Teachers Studying
Abroad: Identities, Emotions and Disruptions/Edited Gary Barkhuizen.
Description: Bristol; Jackson: Multilingual Matters, [2022] | Series: Psychology of Language
  Learning and Teaching: 17 | Includes bibliographical references and index. | Summary:
  "This book focuses on the study abroad experiences of pre-service and in-service language
  teachers and language teacher educators, discussing their psychological experiences in
  cognitive, affective and social terms"— Provided by publisher.
Identifiers: LCCN 2021061129 (print) | LCCN 2021061130 (ebook) | ISBN 9781788929936
  (paperback) | ISBN 9781788929943 (hardback) | ISBN 9781788929950 (pdf) | ISBN
  9781788929967 (epub)
Subjects: LCSH: Language teachers—Training of. | Language teachers—In-service training. |
  Foreign study—Psychological aspects. | Foreign study—Social aspects. | Multicultural
  education.
Classification: LCC P53.85 .L373 2022 (print) | LCC P53.85 (ebook) | DDC 418.0071—dc23/
  eng/20220125
LC record available at https://lccn.loc.gov/2021061129
LC ebook record available at https://lccn.loc.gov/2021061130

British Library Cataloguing in Publication Data
A catalogue entry for this book is available from the British Library.

ISBN-13: 978-1-78892-994-3 (hbk)
ISBN-13: 978-1-78892-993-6 (pbk)

Multilingual Matters
UK: St Nicholas House, 31-34 High Street, Bristol, BS1 2AW, UK.
USA: Ingram, Jackson, TN, USA.

Website: www.multilingual-matters.com
Twitter: Multi_Ling_Mat
Facebook: https://www.facebook.com/multilingualmatters
Blog: www.channelviewpublications.wordpress.com

The policy of Multilingual Matters/Channel View Publications is to use papers that are
natural, renewable and recyclable products, made from wood grown in sustainable forests. In
the manufacturing process of our books, and to further support our policy, preference is
given to printers that have FSC and PEFC Chain of Custody certification. The FSC and/or
PEFC logos will appear on those books where full certification has been granted to the
printer concerned.

Typeset by Nova Techset Private Limited, Bengaluru and Chennai, India.
Printed and bound in the UK by the CPI Books Group Ltd.

Contents

Acknowledgements ix

Contributors xi

1 Language Teachers Studying Abroad 1
Gary Barkhuizen

Part 1 Identities and Professional Development

2 Emotionality in Field Trip Narratives: Confronting Deficit
Perspectives 23
*Julia Menard-Warwick, Enrique David Degollado and
    Shannon Kehoe*

3 Japanese English Teachers' Professional Development in a
Canadian University: Perceptions of Self and Imagining Practice 35
Steve Marshall

4 Study Abroad as a Site of Transformative Learning: Post-Sojourn
Knowledge and Identity Change of Two Cambodian Teachers 47
Rosemary Wette and Gary Barkhuizen

5 Life and Learning through Study Abroad: Trajectories
Connecting Identity and Communicative Repertoires 60
Donna Starks and Howard Nicholas

6 'They Say My Job is Propaganda': Professional Identities of
Pre-Service Chinese Language Teachers in Overseas Schools 71
Danping Wang

Part 2 Interculturality and Intercultural Learning

7 Re-Imagining Immersion for Teachers: Exploring the
Seedlings of Decolonial Roots within Ecuadorian/United
States Partnerships 87
*Rachel Shriver, Magda Madany-Saá, Eleanor Sweeney,
    Elizabeth Smolcic, Sharon Childs, Ana Loja Criollo and
    Yolanda Loja Criollo*

8   The Experience of Pre-Service Language Teachers Learning
    an Additional Language through Study Abroad   100
    Roswita Dressler and Colleen Kawalilak

9   Border-Crossing and Professional Development of Taiwanese
    EFL Teachers in a Study-Abroad Program   111
    Chiou-lan Chern, Angel M.Y. Lin and Mei-Lan Lo

10 'I Thought it was Really a No!': A Narrativized Account
    of an L2 Sojourn with a Homestay   123
    Sin Yu Cherry Chan and Jane Jackson

11 Language for the Heart: Investigating the Linguistic
    Responsiveness of Study Abroad   135
    Erik Jon Byker and Natalia Mejia

Part 3   Emotions and Personal Growth

12 Dreams Cut Short but Heads Held High: Study Abroad in
    Times of Coronavirus   151
    Takaaki Hiratsuka

13 No Ordinary Time: Language Teachers Abroad in an
    Extraordinary Year   163
    John Macalister

14 When Teachers Become 'the Other': Studying Abroad in the
    Dominican Republic   174
    Shondel Nero

15 Study Abroad as Subjection: Doctoral Students' Emotions
    during Academic Short Stays   191
    *Harold Castañeda-Peña, Carmen Helena Guerrero-Nieto
       and Pilar Méndez-Rivera*

16 Emotional Aspects of Online Collaboration:
    Virtual Exchange of Pre-Service EFL Teachers   202
    Diana Feick and Petra Knorr

Part 4   Relationships and Careers

17 From Language Teaching Assistant Abroad to Language
    Professional: A Longitudinal Study of Career Entry   219
    Rosamond Mitchell and Nicole Tracy-Ventura

18 Understanding Pre-Service Teachers' Study-Abroad
    Experiences through Duoethnography: Challenges, Emotions
    and Developments   233
    Christine Biebricher and Yue You

19 From ESL Student to Teacher Educator: Reflections
    on Transnational and Transcultural Professional Identity
    Development   245
    Michael Burri

20 Transformative Learning and Professionalization through
    Uncertainty? A Case Study of Pre-Service Language Teachers
    During a STIE   256
    Anja Wilken and Andreas Bonnet

21 The Impact of a Two-Week Study-Abroad Teacher
    Development Program on Pre-Service L2 Teachers   269
    Meredith D'Arienzo and YouJin Kim

    Index   283

Acknowledgements

There are many people involved in putting together a book such as this one. I am grateful to all of them, especially the chapter contributors for their interest and perseverance. I would particularly like to acknowledge Rosemary Wette at the University of Auckland for her initial input into the book – from conceptualizing it to working on (multiple drafts) of the proposal. Thanks also to Sarah Mercer for her guidance, support and enthusiasm from the very earliest stage of the project. The idea for the book was sparked by the collaborative work, disrupted by the Covid-19 pandemic, of a group of interested researchers at the University of Auckland. Our fruitful discussions and research activity, funded by a Faculty Research Development Fund grant, inspired the focus and aims of this book in the first place. Thank you to both the Faculty of Arts and the research hub.

Contributors

Christine Biebricher is a teacher educator and works as Senior Lecturer in the Faculty of Education and Social Work at the University of Auckland. Christine is a trained teacher, who has worked in pre- and in-service language teacher education in several countries. Her academic work draws on her background in Language Didactics, Applied Linguistics, and on her expertise in Teaching English as a Second Language. Her research interests focus on teacher education and teacher professional development in languages and literacies.

Andreas Bonnet is Professor of TEFL at the Universität Hamburg, Germany. He has done extensive research in the areas of content and language integrated learning, co-operative learning and multilingualism in the foreign language classroom. His empirical research comes from a qualitative angle and uses interpretative techniques, such as the documentary method. He is particularly interested in research on teachers and holds broad expertise as a teacher trainer, having run professional development courses in Germany, Switzerland and other European countries.

Michael Burri is a Senior Lecturer in TESOL in the School of Education at the University of Wollongong, Australia. Born in the United States and raised in Switzerland, he has taught and conducted research in a variety of contexts in Australia, Japan and Canada. His professional interests include pronunciation teaching, teacher education, Mind Brain Education, context-sensitive/innovative pedagogy, and non-native English-speaking teacher issues.

Erik Jon Byker is an Associate Professor in the Cato College of Education at the University of North Carolina (UNC) at Charlotte and serves as UNC Charlotte's Resident Director at Kingston University in London, United Kingdom. Erik has a PhD Degree in Curriculum, Teaching, and Educational Policy from Michigan State University. His research agenda is comparative and international in scope as he has conducted ethnographic field studies in Cuba, England, Germany, India, South Africa, South Korea, and across the United States.

Harold Castañeda-Peña is currently the Director of the Doctorado Interinstitucional en Educación at Universidad Distrital Francisco José de Caldas (Bogotá, Colombia) where he also teaches on the ELT Education major. He has published articles where the interphase between gender and language learning and teaching is explored. He is part of the research group Information Society and Learning.

Sin Yu Cherry Chan is a Lecturer in the English Language Teaching Unit (ELTU) at The Chinese University of Hong Kong, where she is teaching EAP and ESP courses including Intercultural Communication. Her current research interests include intercultural communication, language and identity, and education abroad. With the support of a University teaching development and learning enhancement grant, Dr Chan is leading a project which develops e-learning tasks and materials in two alternative communication-intensive courses at ELTU.

Chiou-lan Chern received her PhD from the University of Queensland, Australia. She is a Professor of English at National Taiwan Normal University (NTNU), where she teaches courses on TEFL methodology at undergraduate levels and reading seminars at the graduate level. Her research interests include L2 reading instruction and critical thinking, English language policies and English teacher education. She has conducted various research projects sponsored by the Ministry of Science and Technology and teacher development projects commissioned by the Ministry of Education in Taiwan.

Sharon Childs is Associate Teaching Professor and Chair of the MA TESL Program in the Department of Applied Linguistics, The Pennsylvania State University. Dr Childs prepares undergraduate and Master's level students to work with English language learners. Her research interests focus on language teacher professional development, the knowledge-base of language teacher education, and language teacher cognition from a sociocultural perspective.

Meredith D'Arienzo taught EFL in Italy and Thailand for a number of years before returning to the United States, where she has taught Italian as a foreign language, ESL and applied linguistics courses. She has developed research interests in the areas of second language acquisition and pedagogy, particularly in the study-abroad context, as well as L2 teaching approaches and L2 teacher education. She hopes to return to teaching students abroad when it is more feasible.

Enrique David Degollado is an Assistant Professor of Multilingual Education at the University of Iowa in the Department of Teaching and Learning. David earned his PhD in Curriculum and Instruction-Bilingual/

Bicultural Studies at The University of Texas at Austin. His research focuses on how the life stories of bilingual teachers illuminate their language and literacy ideologies and inform their pedagogical practices in relation to biliteracy, bilingualism and anti-racist education.

Roswita Dressler is an Associate Professor in the Werklund School of Education, University of Calgary. She holds an MA in German and a PhD in Education. Her research examines pre-service and in-service teachers' understandings of second language teaching and learning. Her research in K-12 school settings looks at Canada's bilingual programs in international languages and global competencies of teachers and students. Her higher education work examines the formal and informal learning of students on study abroad.

Diana Feick is a Senior Lecturer in German and Applied Linguistics/Language Teaching in the School of Cultures, Languages and Linguistics at the University of Auckland. She worked as a lecturer of German as a Foreign Language and German Teacher Education at Universities in Colombia, Germany and Austria before joining the University of Auckland. Her research interests include digital and mobile media in language learning, learner autonomy and multimodal interaction. Diana leads a research hub on language education in New Zealand.

Carmen Helena Guerrero-Nieto is a Full Professor in the PhD program in Education and in the MA in Communication Education from the Universidad Distrital Francisco José de Caldas (Bogotá, Colombia). Her research interests and publications are in critical pedagogy, bilingualism and teacher education. Her work has aimed at voicing English teachers' concerns, experiences and interests. She is the main researcher of the group Critical Studies on Educational Policies.

Takaaki Hiratsuka is an Associate Professor at Ryukoku University in Kyoto, Japan, where he teaches a range of applied linguistics courses at both undergraduate and postgraduate levels. He received his PhD in language teaching and learning from the University of Auckland, New Zealand. His research and teaching interests lie in the areas of teacher education, teacher research and qualitative research methods (in particular, narrative inquiry and classroom-based research).

Jane Jackson (PhD, University of Toronto) is Professor Emerita at the Chinese University of Hong Kong. Her research centers on education abroad, intercultural communication and eLearning/intercultural pedagogy. Her Routledge books include *Online Intercultural Education and Study Abroad* (2019), *Interculturality in International Education* (2018), *Intercultural Interventions in Study Abroad* (2018, co-editor Susan

Oguro), *Introducing Language and Intercultural Communication* (2014/2020) and *The Routledge Handbook of Language and Intercultural Communication* (2012/2020, editor). She authored *Intercultural Journeys* (Palgrave Macmillan, 2010) and *Language, Identity, and Study Abroad* (Equinox, 2008).

Colleen Kawalilak, Full Professor and Associate Dean International in the Werklund School of Education, University of Calgary, provides leadership in negotiating international partnerships and developing initiatives that support internationalization at home and abroad. Her research, teaching and graduate supervision span formal and informal adult learning in diverse work and learning contexts; internationalization; and building intercultural capacity, lifelong learning and relational epistemologies that inform teaching and learning.

Shannon Kehoe has an MA in Bilingual Education from University of Texas Austin and has worked as a bilingual educator for 10 years. Currently she is a bilingual teacher-librarian and has recently obtained a Masters of Library & Information Science from the University of North Texas. Her research interests include transnational and cultural identities, critical teacher education, and study abroad.

YouJin Kim is Professor in the Department of Applied Linguistics and ESL at Georgia State University where she is involved with second/foreign language teacher training. Her research focuses on second language acquisition, task-based language teaching and assessment, and classroom-based research. She has co-authored *Pedagogical Grammar* (2014) and also co-edited *Task-Based Approaches to Teaching and Assessing Pragmatics* (2018). She is currently the associate editor of the *Journal of Second Language Writing*.

Petra Knorr is a lecturer and researcher in the Department of English Studies at Leipzig University, Germany. She trained as an EFL teacher and did a PhD on student-teacher collaboration in lesson planning scenarios. Current research projects focus on the potential of virtual exchange projects, the development of multilingual awareness and video- and classroom-based learning in the context of foreign language teacher education.

Angel M.Y. Lin is Professor and Tier 1 Canada Research Chair in Plurilingual and Intercultural Education in the Faculty of Education, Simon Fraser University, Canada. She is well-respected for her interdisciplinary research in Content and Language Integrated Learning (CLIL), classroom interaction analysis, bilingual and multilingual education, academic literacies, and language policy and planning in postcolonial contexts. She has published over 90 research articles and six research books including *Language Across the Curriculum & CLIL in English as an Additional Language (EAL) Contexts*.

Mei-Lan Lo is an Associate Professor in the Department of English, National Taiwan Normal University. She served as Director of the Foreign Language Education Division, Common Core Education Committee at the National Taiwan Normal University from February 2018 to July 2019, and August 2020 to January 2021. Her research interests include bilingual education, teacher professional development, reading and writing instruction, and English as a medium of instruction.

Ana Loja Criollo is an English instructor at the Universidad de Cuenca, Ecuador. She also has been responsible for the development and coordination of Spanish and service-learning programs with various foreign universities. Ana has taught Spanish and Latin American Culture in the United States. Her research interests include developing intercultural competence with L2 learners and the role of interaction in foreign language learning.

Yolanda Loja Criollo is an English instructor at the Universidad de Cuenca, Ecuador. She coordinates the conversation partner program offered by the Spanish for Foreigners Program. She has been in charge of the design of specific English courses for college students, and has been part of the team of translators in the Language Department. Her research interests include the development of speaking skills in second language learners.

John Macalister is Professor of Applied Linguistics at Victoria University of Wellington, New Zealand. He has a long-standing interest in 'abroad'. Two recent co-edited books are *Multilingual Memories* (with Robert Blackwood, Bloomsbury, 2020) and *Family Language Policies in a Multilingual World* (with S. Hadi Mirvahedi, Routledge, 2017).

Magda Madany-Saá is a PhD Candidate in Curriculum & Instruction in College of Education, and TESL Instructor at The Pennsylvania State University. She teaches Language and Culture for practitioners, Teaching Methodologies, and Socio-politics of Applied Linguistics. Her research interests are decolonial theory and methodology, critical interculturality, language policy and translingualism. Magda has experience teaching Spanish in Poland and English in Ecuador, as well as training in-service English teachers in Latin America. She translanguages between Polish, English and Spanish.

Steve Marshall is a Professor in the Faculty of Education at Simon Fraser University, in Vancouver, Canada. Steve's main research focus is on issues related to plurilingualism and academic literacy across the disciplines in Canadian higher education. He is also currently researching the experiences of pre-service and in-service language teachers participating in study-abroad programs at Canadian universities.

Natalia Mejia graduated with honors from UNC Charlotte's Cato College of Education with a major in Elementary Education and a double minor in Reading and Teaching English as a Second Language. She has received numerous awards for her international scholarship including the Benjamin A. Gilman International Scholarship. She has applied to join the Peace Corps and anticipates such experience will provide deeper appreciation for her culture while equipping her with global competencies to create responsive learning experiences for diverse students.

Julia Menard-Warwick has taught at the University of California Davis since 2004. Her research explores power and identity in language learning and teaching. She began her career teaching English to university students in Nicaragua and adult immigrants in Washington State. More recently she conducted research with English teachers at a Chilean university; researched a study-abroad program in Guatemala; and served as a visiting professor in Mexico. Recent articles appear in *Applied Linguistics* and *The Modern Language Journal*.

Pilar Méndez-Rivera is a Full-time Professor at Universidad Distrital Francisco José de Caldas (Bogotá, Colombia). She has worked as a teacher educator in undergraduate and graduate programs for over 18 years. She currently coordinates the Research Committee of the Faculty of Science and Education. Her research interests revolve around teachers' struggles, resistance practices and subjectivity. She is passionate about understanding the power-knowledge relations and affirmative discourses of English language teachers in the negotiation of their identity construction.

Rosamond Mitchell FAcSS is Emeritus Professor of Applied Linguistics at the University of Southampton, United Kingdom. She has longstanding research interests in language in education, including development of several open-access L2 corpora (FLLOC, SPLLOC and LANGSNAP). Her recent research focuses on study abroad and its consequences for linguistic and identity development. She is lead author of *Second Language Learning Theories* (with Florence Myles and Emma Marsden, Routledge) and co-editor (with Henry Tyne) of *Language, Mobility and Study Abroad in Contemporary Europe* (Routledge, 2021).

Shondel Nero is Professor of Language Education in the Department of Teaching and Learning at New York University's Steinhardt School of Culture, Education, and Human Development. She has written and published extensively on the politics, challenges and strategies of educating speakers of Caribbean Creole Englishes, World Englishes and vernacular varieties of English, as well as related issues on language and identity, and language education policy. She also directs a study-abroad program for pre- and in-service teachers in the Dominican Republic.

Howard Nicholas is an Adjunct Professor in the School of Education at La Trobe University, Australia. His research focuses on additional language development, including approaches to teaching additional languages. Recent publications include the edited volume *Widening Contexts for Processability Theory*, as well as contributions to the *AILA Review* and the *Journal of Language Identity and Education*.

Rachel Shriver is a practicing ESL teacher at a middle school in Virginia. She graduated from The Pennsylvania State University with a degree in Secondary English Education. She participated in Penn State's TESL certificate program, and later received an Erickson Discovery Grant to research reciprocity within the program. She was a Fulbright scholar at la Universidad Industrial de Santander in Bucaramanga, Colombia from 2019–2020 and will return to complete a second scholarship year in Colombia in 2021.

Elizabeth Smolcic is Teaching Professor at The Pennsylvania State University. She prepares educators to teach multilingual learners in K-12 contexts. Her research explores teacher learning about additional language learning, as well as the development of interculturality. She coordinates Penn State's TESL certificate program which offers a cultural/linguistic immersion and field teaching experience in the Andean highlands of Ecuador. She has taught teachers and English language learners in bilingual schools in Ecuador, Mexico, Spain and the United States.

Donna Starks is an Adjunct Associate Professor in the School of Education at La Trobe University, Australia. Her research focuses on language and identity. Recent publications include articles in the *International Journal of Multilingualism*, *Language Policy*, the *Asia Pacific Journal of Education*, *Social Semiotics* and *Applied Linguistics Review*.

Eleanor Sweeney recently earned her PhD in Curriculum & Instruction, Second Language Education, at The Pennsylvania State University. Her research interests included using music for second language learning, supporting the development of intercultural competence with L2 teachers, and Sociocultural Theory applied in the classroom. Before graduate school, she taught World Languages K-12 and English as a Second Language K-16 for 20 years.

Nicole Tracy-Ventura is Assistant Professor of Applied Linguistics at West Virginia University where she teaches in the TESOL Master's program. Her research focuses on second language acquisition, study abroad, task-based language teaching, and corpus linguistics. She is co-author of *Anglophone Students Abroad* (with Rosamond Mitchell and Kevin McManus, Routledge) and co-editor of *The Routledge Handbook of Second Language Acquisition and Corpora* (with Magali Paquot). She is also a founding member of the Languages and Social Networks Abroad Project (LANGSNAP).

Danping Wang is Senior Lecturer in Chinese at the University of Auckland. She was awarded the Early Career Research Excellence Award in 2020. In her last job as Assistant Professor in Hong Kong, she received the Teaching Excellence Award. She is currently leading a Marsden Fund project supported by the Royal Society of New Zealand. She also serves on the Special Expert Group for the Chinese subject by the New Zealand Ministry of Education. Her research focuses on multilingualism in language education and Chinese language education.

Rosemary Wette is an Associate Professor in Applied Linguistics and Language Teaching at the University of Auckland. Her main teaching and research interests are the second language curriculum and the development of academic literacies by graduate L2 writers. She has published in the *Journal of Second Language Writing, Journal of English for Academic Purposes, System* and *ELT Journal.* She is currently an associate editor of the *Journal of Second Language Writing.*

Anja Wilken is a post-doc researcher in the Teaching English as a Foreign Language team at the Faculty of Education, Universität Hamburg, Germany. Her research interests are located in the fields of individual teacher professionalization and study-abroad research, using a qualitative approach as well as interpretative methods (such as the documentary method) in empirical studies. She is project coordinator of the Faculty's exchange program Tricontinental Teacher Training (TTT).

Yue You has been involved in Chinese language teaching for eight years. She earned an MA degree in Teaching Chinese to Speakers of Other Languages (TCSOL) at Shanghai Jiao Tong University, China. Yue is currently completing her PhD at the University of Auckland, New Zealand. Her PhD project explores Chinese teachers' beliefs and practices with regard to grammar teaching in New Zealand secondary schools. Her research interests include teachers' beliefs, teacher education and Chinese as a second/foreign language.

1 Language Teachers Studying Abroad

Gary Barkhuizen

Introduction

In 2019, funding was made available from my university to establish a research network with the aim of identifying researchers who had an interest in the experiences of language teachers who study abroad. The plan was for the network to develop ideas for possible research projects, recruit further network participants, and eventually to apply for external research funding. The long-term goal of the proposed network was to bring together these researchers to engage over time in common research projects focusing on aspects of language teachers studying abroad and to publish findings in relevant outlets. The collaboration and the research would also benefit the network members, since we work in an institution that hosts and enrols study-abroad teachers in many capacities, including formal Master's and doctoral programs in TESOL and applied linguistics.

A meeting time was scheduled and invitations sent out to targeted researchers in the university. At this meeting it was discovered that an interest in *language teachers studying abroad* indeed existed as a research focus; some recruited network members were in fact already engaged in their own research, others were formally involved in organizing study-abroad programs for teachers, and almost all taught or supervised the research of teachers enrolled in university degree programs. And, of course, all had studied or worked abroad themselves, either in pre-service or in-service positions. The concept of *study abroad* was familiar to us all.

The network kicked into gear. We scheduled a second meeting. The funding allowed for a pilot research project, which was begun (see *Rosemary Wette* and *Gary Barkhuizen*, Chapter 4). Funding also covered the costs for an international study-abroad expert to visit the university to conduct workshops, consult with researchers and present seminars to academics in related disciplines (e.g. language teaching, global studies), and flights and accommodation were booked. We began planning a one-day colloquium with invited colleagues from across the university and New Zealand. We even had a catering budget! But this was all happening at the start of 2020.

It wasn't long before most of our plans fell through. Meetings were cancelled, no international visitor arrived, and the colloquium became a distant, unattainable goal as the Covid-19 pandemic began to sweep the world and we went into lockdown. Although our academic lives were severely disrupted, like so many researchers and teachers across the world, our independent work continued. For example, in November 2020, a number of network members collaborated to present their study-abroad research at the annual symposium of the Applied Linguistics Association of New Zealand, a welcome face-to-face conference after periods of lockdown. By this time, I had secured a book contract with Multilingual Matters to edit the book you are now reading. Members of the research network have contributed as authors, and so too have many others, reporting from a range of international backgrounds and about varying study-abroad program types, teacher characteristics and study-abroad outcomes.

In the sections that follow, I begin by explaining what *language teachers studying abroad* (LTSA) means within the context of the book, breaking down the components of this concept. I then provide a rationale for the book and describe its aims, including a summary of some of the topics covered, the research methods used and the implications of the research presented. Twelve salient topic themes are then presented, weaving in quotes from the chapters. These are the main themes covered across the chapters in the book. Finally, I describe how and why the book has been divided into four sections, representing four crucial areas of experience in the psychological and social lives of language teachers who study abroad.

Language Teachers Studying Abroad

Study abroad has been defined as 'a temporary sojourn of pre-defined duration, undertaken for educational purposes' (Kinginger, 2009: 11). This general definition obviously applies to a wide range of study-abroad arrangements, and includes the essential ingredients of engaging in some form of *study* in a different *location* for a specified period of *time*. These three aspects (study, location and time) can mean very different things across study-abroad experiences. For example, the following definition of study abroad fills in some details that are applicable to pre-service teachers:

> Any internationally based program or experience including exchange, clinical placement, field study, internship, co-op placement, practicum or voluntary service/work placement, which are offered by a post-secondary institution, and for which academic credit may or may not be granted. (Bond *et al.*, 2009: 9)

Here, options regarding the type of international program are provided and a potential authorized outcome is indicated. This definition works quite well for the purposes of this book, which focuses on language teachers, but falls short in a number of ways. In indicating how this is so, I outline the scope of the book in more detail: (1) The participants in some of the chapters are in-service teachers, who may or may not be working towards a further (accredited) qualification. The chapters in the book, therefore, include the study-abroad experiences of teachers who are seeking further or continuing professional development, either in short exchange programs, extended visits to institutions, or as part of formal qualifications (e.g. Master's or doctoral degrees). The teachers may also be involved in some sort of 'work abroad'; an internship, formal teaching practice, paid employment or volunteer work for a fixed period of time. (2) Some sojourners are not attached to any program at all in their home countries; in other words, they are not enrolled in a program or qualification in an institution but have traveled abroad independently to study further or for some other form of professional development. (3) Some may identify more as teacher researchers or language teacher educators than as language teachers, although they could be all three. (4) The abroad location might be virtual (e.g. online exchange) rather than study abroad involving physical movement across international borders. *Language teachers studying abroad* (LTSA) in this book, therefore, encompasses a wide range of possibilities, but central to all these is that those doing the sojourning, over time, in a physical or virtual location, are language teachers.

Aims, Rationale and Topics

In the current (post-) Covid-19 era, Beck (2021: 134) comments that 'there are signs that universities are still thinking about internationalization in practice as being primarily about mobility'. This intriguing comment, although targeted specifically at the internationalization of universities, also raises questions about the nature of future study-abroad practices more generally. Since the start of the Covid-19 pandemic there have been drastic changes to the way teachers engage with international study initiatives, if they do at all. The cessation of international travel and the emergence of regional lockdowns have meant that study abroad in its traditional sense has not been able to take place as before. Consequently, the shift to easy online connectivity has seen alternative practices and platforms such as webinars, virtual conferences, and online courses and qualifications proliferate. But what does this mean for the future of LTSA? Surely, things can't return to the way they were before. Will there be a 'new normal' we hear so much about? And what will this look like?

Critical internationalization studies is an area of study that 'problematizes the overwhelmingly positive and depoliticized approaches to internationalization in higher education' (Stein, 2019). Stein and McCartney

(2021: 2) add that scholars working in critical internationalization studies 'draw attention to the risks of reproducing uneven global power relations, colonial representations, and extractive resource flows in mainstream approaches to internationalization'. They have noted a number of purposes of internationalization, including business as usual (internationalization for a global knowledge economy), making the existing system more efficient and inclusive (internationalization for the global public good), and denaturalizing the enduring uneven colonial flows of knowledge, resources and people within the existing system (internationalization for global equity) (Stein & McCartney, 2021). Internationalization in higher education and LTSA are not exactly the same thing, of course, though there is considerable intersection in terms of the ideologies that drive their practices. For example, Stein and McCartney (2021: 3) point out that a business-as-usual model of internationalization incentivizes 'individual competition for limited positions within the global middle class'. This raises questions about which language teachers study abroad, and why, and what are the outcomes for them. And also, questions about who does not study abroad.

In the midst of these macro ideological concerns, uncertain futures and disrupted professional lives are the personal experiences of the language teachers who do study abroad, whether virtually or by physically crossing international borders. The chapters in this book focus on those experiences, paying particular attention to their psychological and social aspects, as reflected in the subtitle of the book: *Identities, Emotions and Disruptions*. This book is about the people who study abroad, as well as those they interact with along the way; prior to, during and after the study-abroad sojourn. These include home-country program organizers, teacher educators, homestay host families, host school teachers and students, members of the local populations, and many others too.

Crucially, however, the central characters in these stories – at least for the purposes of this book – are the language teachers. I have used the term *narrative knowledging* (Barkhuizen, 2011) to capture how, in the process of sharing stories about life experiences, narrators make sense of them. As we tell (or write) stories about our past and imagined experiences we understand and learn about those experiences, and so too do those who listen to (or read) them. Narrative knowledging is thus a cognitive activity. But it is also a social activity. Narratives are discursively constructed with others in particular spatiotemporal contexts and during the process life experiences are shared and interpreted. There is much sharing of experiences and stories in the chapters of this book.

Although not all framed as narrative inquiries, the studies reported all delve deeply into the personal and professional study-abroad experiences of the main characters – the language teachers – focusing particularly on the psychological and social aspects of these experiences. In other words, the book is less about the organization and management of study-abroad programs, their goals and outcomes, and more about the people – the teachers – at the center of the action. All these areas are obviously very much interrelated, however, and are addressed to varying degrees in the chapters. Some of the questions the book addresses include:

- Who exactly are the language teachers who participate in LTSA?
- How and why do they change – as people and as professionals?
- What do language teachers do on study abroad and how does this contribute to their identity and professional development?
- How does the LTSA experience affect them emotionally, before, during and after study abroad? What do these emotions mean and how do they influence the teachers' (and others') perceptions of who they are and what they do as teachers?
- What do the language teachers learn about themselves and about the people they interact with during the entire LTSA process, even years post-sojourn?
- What do they learn about their place in the world – the world of language teaching and of education more broadly, a rapidly changing world where everyone's place in it is questioned and uncertain.

why imp?

Answers to questions such as these are certainly useful for those who plan, manage and host LTSA programs, including teacher educators, curriculum developers, professional development facilitators and program leaders, but they are vital for the language teachers themselves. Reflecting on the above questions at all stages of LTSA (prior to departure, during study abroad, and then post-sojourn) will enable participating teachers to interpret their lived study-abroad experiences in relation to what happens or happened during their time abroad. As many of the chapter contributors suggest in the implications of the studies they report on, teacher educators and program organizers could take responsibility for organizing such reflective activities by embedding them in coursework or research projects, for example, but teachers too can work independently through self-reflective narrative writing, action research projects or ongoing virtual communications with their LTSA hosts. Further innovative suggestions are provided within the chapters.

inquiry approach

The studies employ a wide range of inquiry approaches to explore the teachers' experiences, including narrative inquiry, duo- and autoethnography, case studies, and other mainly qualitative approaches. Data is collected and analyzed using many different methods, from interviews and observations, to reflective writing tasks, questionnaire surveys, blog writing, program evaluations, emotiograms, narrative frames, Zoom conversations, email communications, teaching philosophy statements and collaborative or dialogue writing. These methods not only serve as the research instruments in the reported studies but are potentially valuable exemplars for approaches to teacher self-reflection or course activities. Each chapter provides sufficient details of its methods to be useful in this regard.

Table 1.1 Selected themes drawn from topics in all chapters

Selected themes	
– LTSA challenges	– professional growth
– teacher resilience	– confidence with online teaching
– teacher empathy	– becoming politically aware
– self-confidence	– critical reflexivity
– self-awareness	– critical awareness
– self-efficacy	– confronting ideologies and the media
– teacher identity	
– imagined future identity	– emotional dissonance
– identity repertoires	– emotional struggles
– new professional roles	– managing feelings
– culture shock	– emotions in the face of disaster
– interculturality	– Covid-19 disruptions
– cross-cultural sensitivity	– making sense of disruption
– intercultural understanding	– becoming a language teacher
– building intercultural capacities	– affirming a future teacher career
– language learning	– career entry
– multilingualism in the classroom	– professionalization
– social relationships	– decolonial teacher education
– personal relationships	– postcoloniality
– collaborating with host partners	– Indigenous worldviews
– personal growth	– transformative learning

A rich array of topics is covered in the chapters; these topics are captured in the 12 themes discussed in the next section. I have categorized the 12 topics from an even larger group of themes, a selection of which I list in Table 1.1 both for interest and for the record. In many cases I use the words of the authors to describe the themes; these will be explained and exemplified in the chapters.

Twelve LTSA Themes

1. *Disruption*

Studying abroad – anticipating it, doing it, and re-settling after the experience – inevitably entails a certain amount of tension or instability in the teachers' lives. This psychological and social *disruption* is a result of what Ingersoll *et al*. (2019: 42) refer to as *encounters with difference*; the 'contrasting nature of the [study abroad] experience'. Bateson (1972) refers to instability in life in general, saying that people are self-corrective systems. By this he means that people adjust to instability or disruptions in order to achieve equilibrium. In other words, when people experience 'disequilibrium' in their lives, they strive to self-correct in order to once again achieve stability. This theme of disruption, or encounters with difference, or disequilibrium, is a major one running through all of the chapters, even though it may not be explicitly articulated as such. Perhaps the most obvious and devastating example of disruption is Covid-19, which deserves its own theme (see below). In all cases, I am using disruption here less by its negative connotations and more to refer to change or difference. But important in this theme is that dealing with disruption, working towards equilibrium or overcoming challenges involves not only cognitive effort, but also emotion work and identity work. It can also lead to transformational learning (Mezirow, 2000) and professionalization, as the following extract from Chapter 20 explains:

> The students experienced disorienting dilemmas and ways of processing them, which means that transformative learning and thus professionalization can be initiated by certain elements of study-abroad programs. Furthermore, our results show that disruptions cause students to notice and focus on uncertainty … Different ways of dealing with disruption (being paralyzed or taking it as a prompt for decision-making) thus call for an analysis of personal causes for these differences, which may include factors such as individual tolerance of ambiguity. (*Anja Wilken* and *Andreas Bonnet*, Chapter 20)

2. Covid-19

> 'In the first semester, I was lonely, felt homesick, and lost confidence. However, I finally started to get used to life in Sweden, and I was determined to take advantage of the remaining months by meeting new people, embracing new experiences, and enjoying the university. Then, Covid-19 invaded my life. It hit Europe and hit us all. I could not believe it. I felt a void in my heart'. (*Takaaki Hiratsuka*, Chapter 12)

This extract from a Japanese study-abroad student stranded in Sweden during the early stages of the Covid-19 pandemic illustrates the 'large impact of Covid-19 on both lifestyle and well-being' (Giuntella *et al.*, 2021: 1). Together with disruptions to social and professional activity, shifts to online teaching and learning and residential lockdowns resulted in enormous emotional (and even physical) trauma for some study-abroad participants. For some, plans were cancelled pre-departure, and yet others were urgently called back to their home countries. For some returnees who arrived home shortly before the Covid-19 pandemic began or escalated, their LTSA experiences were productively drawn on; see, for example, the following about a post-sojourn teacher in Cambodia:

> In the interview with Lina in 2020, during a period of lockdown … she reflected that she had volunteered to advise colleagues about online teaching because 'I'm still confident with myself, even now when – suddenly, like everything turned from physical to online. Because I took two online

courses in NZ, I learned faster than the other teachers, so I became a trainer for online teaching'. (*Rosemary Wette* and *Gary Barkhuizen*, Chapter 4)

The focus of this book, however, is not specifically on the Covid-19 disruption; it is one of the disruptions experienced by LTSA participants, as discussed in the theme immediately above. The book also does not make predictions regarding how the future of LTSA programs and personal study-abroad experiences will unfold post-Covid-19. It is impossible to tell. However, being optimistic, in the words of *John Macalister* (Chapter 13), 'presumably – hopefully – international education will recover and opportunities for language teachers to study abroad will not become an historical artefact'.

3. Identity work

Block (2014) explains how study abroad may threaten one's sense of identity because crossing geographical and social borders unsettles the stable self and leads one into 'a period of struggle to reach a balance' (2014: 24). Again, we see here the theme of disruption, but this time related to changes to the sojourner's identity. Drawing on his own multiple experiences of studying and working abroad, *Michael Burri* (Chapter 19) reflects on the lessons he has learned:

> Thinking about my own journey of living, studying and working abroad, educators should view their students as multilinguals and multicultural beings with prior learning experiences and a fluid identity. Educators should also keep in mind that language learning and identity construction occur at the same time, and the process often includes struggles, tension, and positive as well as negative emotions.

Identity is a salient theme running through the chapters, and its intersection with emotions, beliefs, and professional development is often explored. Identity change or development is typically the main concern, reinforcing previous research in LTSA (see Kinginger, 2015). As Donato (2017: 25) says, when crossing 'major life boundaries', such as spending time studying abroad, identities are disrupted, sometimes contested, and certainly changed in the process. Some of these changes are imagined – being in other places or social spaces or future times; as evident in this comment about a Japanese teacher participating in an LTSA program in Canada:

> Akira referred to being promoted to a higher teaching position when considering his ideal future self. In his case, he linked it not only to more effective teaching, but also to the instrumental goal of getting paid more. He saw the professional development program as a stepping-stone to meeting this goal: 'My ideal self is to continue to teach in the same high school and to be a teacher with high English skill; not only using it but also teaching it effectively. And at the same time, I want to be promoted as a chief teacher so that I can get paid more'. (*Steve Marshall*, Chapter 3)

4. *Emotion work*

I use the term *emotion work* to mirror the previous theme, *identity work*, and to emphasize their close relationship; as Song (2016: 633) says, 'Emotions are a critical element in the dynamic process of negotiating and constructing teacher identity'. The chapters in the book examine, whether explicitly or not, emotions in the personal LTSA stories of the teachers (as all the illustrative extracts in this section covering the 12 themes show). Studying abroad is inevitably an emotional experience, on so many levels; *encounters with difference* (Ingersoll *et al.*, 2019) – being away from home and family, confronting unfamiliar cultures and educational practices, participating in new social and professional activities, dealing with disasters – means that emotions are implicated. For example, the following excerpt regarding a US teacher:

> a final type of emotionality was less clear-cut – perhaps best described as *conflicted* – as when Annie admitted to feeling like a 'cynic' given her own lack of clear answers about how to improve the lives of Guatemalan families struggling with poverty. (*Julia Menard-Warwick et al.*, Chapter 2)

As this and the next extract exemplify, teachers can respond emotionally to events, conditions and difference, on both intimate, personal levels as well as macro ideological levels. As expressed by an experienced English teacher from Colombia on an overseas doctoral internship in Spain and the United Kingdom:

> 'Why did I cry? Because they talked about the injustices done to Latin America about … and I started to cry and I remember well that Professor One realized that I was crying and he spoke of crying as the first way to protest, so it seemed to me that they understood very well the emotions and the things going on in the classroom'. (*Harold Castañeda-Peña et al.*, Chapter 15)

5. *Professional development*

What makes language *teacher* study abroad different from other forms of study abroad (e.g. language learning programs, cultural exchanges) is that LTSA always includes a professional development component. Some form of professional development is the goal of LTSA, and may be articulated in a variety of ways, including language enhancement (Roskvist *et al.*, 2015), pedagogical knowledge (Plews *et al.*, 2010), intercultural competence and academic success, as the following extract illustrates:

> It is worth mentioning that this teacher was motivated by academic success. She had received a very good grade on her first piece of submitted work, which had made her feel 'very excited inside' and wanted to repeat the feeling, so she was 'sad' when the next grade was a little lower. She wanted to do well academically because 'I'm so excited to see myself grow'. (*John Macalister*, Chapter 13)

Professional development has different meanings for pre-service and in-service teachers (and novice and experienced teachers, etc.) and their professional development (goals, activities and outcomes) reflect these differences. But in common is that teachers grow professionally in some way during study abroad and then transfer the new knowledge to their domestic environment. The following extract from a Taiwanese teacher is an example of this happening:

> 'Our new curriculum requires us to adopt competency-based learning. I always reflect on my teaching and see if it is related to students' daily life. I always remember how touched I was when I was sitting and learning in the US classroom. Whenever I feel down, I remember those touching moments and encourage myself to continue making an effort and trying different approaches'. (*Chiou-lan Chern et al.*, Chapter 9)

6. *Intercultural learning*

Many of the chapters address *culture* in some way; sometimes broadly in terms of a national culture or cultures of the host or home country, or the culture of an educational system, or more particularly the culture of a host family or classroom life. Studies explore how teachers learn about unfamiliar cultures, are challenged (or 'shocked') by cultural differences, or develop intercultural communicative abilities or competences. The following extract, reporting on the experiences of US teacher candidates in South Africa, is an example:

> The teacher candidates recognized how multilingualism was a strength of the South African education system as well as a way to better understand the diverse cultures within South Africa. One teacher candidate put it this way, 'I have seen how English is used as a common way to communicate in South Africa and gives me access to the things I want to buy at the store. But it doesn't give me full access to cultural understandings'. This quote is a reflection of how the teacher candidates recognized that language is a form of communication and expression as well as a means to be culturally responsive. (*Erik Jon Byker* and *Natalia Mejia*, Chapter 11)

I am using the term *intercultural learning* for this theme (see Jackson, 2018) in a very broad sense to index a plethora of related concepts such as intercultural adaptation (Gu *et al.*, 2010), interculturality (Beaven & Borghetti, 2016), and cultural understanding (Çiftçi & Karaman, 2019), among others. These will become clearer when explained and used in context within the relevant chapters. Important in these discussions on culture is the associations made with professional learning. In a critical literature review of study abroad for pre-service teachers, 'fostering intercultural competence and/or skills to work with diverse students' (Morley *et al.*, 2019: 11) was the highest ranked reported purpose of study-abroad trips for pre-service teachers. Here is an example of such learning:

In Canada, there are 'so many rules' that keep teachers 'far away from [students]'. In Andrea's current teaching, students 'are always really fascinated'. She believed this serves to heighten engagement because 'as soon as you get kids interested, then it's a shoe in'. As mentioned in Andrea's reflections, the emphasis on relationships and the flexibility to focus on student interests were the two strongest aspects of her professional learning about the culture of Brazilian education. (*Roswita Dressler* and *Colleen Kawalilak*, Chapter 8)

7. *Language enhancement*

Sometimes the only or main articulated purpose of LTSA programs is language enhancement (Allen, 2010); for example, improving the language proficiency of the language that teachers will or do teach, acquiring or improving proficiency in an additional language, experiencing what language learning is like (in instructed or natural learning environments), or developing a particular language skill (speaking or writing, for example). Even when language enhancement is not the primary goal of LTSA, it is often included as an expected outcome, as are language-related issues, for example in this observation about a pre-service teacher from Hong Kong about to embark on a sojourn to the United Kingdom:

> In the pre-sojourn interview and pre-immersion reflective essay, Kelvin disclosed his study-abroad goals, which included the enhancement of his academic writing skills, grasp of English language pedagogy, and intercultural knowledge. He believed that he was well-prepared for informal use of the language and could handle interactions at a basic level. He also expected to encounter some awkward situations due to lack of familiarity with local communicative norms. (*Sin Yu Cherry Chan* and *Jane Jackson*, Chapter 10)

None of the chapters in the book focuses exclusively on teacher language enhancement. In terms of the LTSA program organization or LTSA activities described, language learning is usually embedded in a wider program that includes educational site visits, TESOL courses, and practice teaching, for example. And in terms of how language enhancement is examined by the authors of the chapters, it is usually related to teacher professional development or identity changes. The following excerpt shows such a connection:

> This case study was able to illustrate how one Vietnamese teacher who had studied abroad drew on his existing identity repertoire to metalinguistically analyze communicative features around him to gain control over those communicative features. We have shown how his processes enabled him to align and elaborate a new identity as an Australian-trained Vietnamese EFL teacher, an identity construct compatible with his existing multiple identities as a language teacher, as an English language speaker, and as a professional. (*Donna Starks* and *Howard Nicholas*, Chapter 5)

8. *Personal growth*

Personal growth and professional development as a language educator are clearly very much interrelated. However, *personal growth* is often discussed as a separate theme in the chapters. Çiftçi and Karaman's (2019) review of study abroad in language teacher education identifies personal growth as an important theme in the research literature, and describes it as more independence, increased self-confidence, and increased adaptation and survival skills. Expanding this list somewhat, the research by Ingersoll *et al.* (2019) categorized the following features of personal growth: self-awareness, empathy, flexibility/risk-taking, self-confidence, tolerance for ambiguity, and perseverance. Many of these characteristics are addressed in the chapters. Here is an example from Cambodian teachers after their LTSA experience in New Zealand:

> Lina and Vin returned home with more motivation and confidence, having become more resourceful and autonomous. They reported a changed perception of themselves and a more resilient sense of self overall. Both teachers spoke in their interviews and reflections more than once about growth in confidence, and Vin believed he had also learned how to work through challenging tasks. He reflected that 'perseverance is the biggest thing that is valuable for me, also living in a different environment where I did not know how to cope and I learned how to cope and how to live on my own'. (*Rosemary Wette* and *Gary Barkhuizen*, Chapter 4)

In their duoethnography, *Christine Biebricher* and *Yue You* (Chapter 18) reflect on a number of personal growth characteristics (especially in relation to emotions). Their extract below ends with a reference to career choices. This is another illustration that personal growth, which may or may not be an expressed goal of any particular study-abroad sojourn, is a salient theme in LTSA closely associated with probably all of the 12 themes discussed in this section.

> We had found we had become more resilient as a result of the study-abroad experience. Leaving our familiar context forced us to deal with the problems we encountered. In the process, we became aware of our thoughts, actions and emotions and developed a new skillset to cope with challenges, which resulted in a feeling of resilience and higher self-confidence. As Christine reflected, the study-abroad experience taught her what her personal strengths and her challenges were … Studying and living abroad enabled us to discover different options for our lives, which further influenced our career choices.

9. *Relationships*

Mercer and Gkonou (2020: 164) maintain that 'Positive social relationships can give teachers strength and support to cope with the daily challenges in the classroom and they represent a key contributory factor to teachers' overall well-being, which is vital for effective and creative teaching'. I would suggest that positive relationships also support teachers

during study abroad – relationships with fellow LTSA participants, homestay families, host country teachers and students, local friends – and are
vital for successful professional development and new intercultural understandings, as the following extract involving LTSA participants from the
United States in Ecuador shows.

> A central theme begins with and recurrently points towards *relationships*
> being of equal importance not only for program staff, homestay families
> and local communities but also among participating students. Meaningful
> relationships seem to be a necessary element to move towards the 'inter'
> of intercultural and to dismantle object-based traditions (of 'us' and
> 'them'). (*Rachel Shriver et al.*, Chapter 7)

Not all relationships turn out to be positive and productive, however,
which is probably to be expected when a group of people travel together
for a period of time. Intercultural misunderstandings and miscommunications may also occur with hosts, and the result may lead to some significant emotion work. In the extract below, the LTSA participants are
engaging in a *virtual* exchange program involving universities in New
Zealand and Germany.

> At the product level, unsuccessful collaboration was attributed to fewer
> contributions of artefacts, more superficial analysis of artefacts, lack of
> consultation on creation of the project product, or individual instead of
> joint product creation. Less successful collaboration was also linked to
> negative emotions, which these participants referred to as frustration,
> regret, disappointment, anger, annoyance, despair, sadness, unhappiness
> and helplessness. (*Diana Feick* and *Petra Knorr*, Chapter 16)

LTSA relationships may also evolve into the non-professional type, even
though they might have lingering professional or career implications:

> When asked what she was going to miss about Mexico, [she] mentioned
> her Mexican boyfriend. Because of him, she planned on returning after
> graduation and already had a prospective job teaching English at a private
> language school. Once back in Mexico she completed a CELTA course
> and taught first of all in the private school and later in a state school, also
> marrying her partner and having her first child in 2017. (*Rosamond
> Mitchell* and *Nicole Tracy-Ventura*, Chapter 17)

If one thinks about it, relationships – good or bad, short-term or long-
term, professional or otherwise – are at the very heart of LTSA. Every
chapter in the book deals in some way with relationships, with the focal
character in all relationships being the language teacher.

10. Political awareness

I have called this theme *political awareness* because it relates to teachers coming to realize or understand or question the ideologies underlying
and sometimes confronting their living and working circumstances while
studying abroad. These ideologies may be evident in local discourses and

related practices in schools and communities in which the teachers are located and interact with others. For example:

> In my class the next day, they shared their emotions that ranged from 'sadness' at seeing such poverty to 'appreciation for their own privilege' to 'anger' at me, for 'not preparing them properly' for the trip (although I thought I did). Many participants said they felt 'helpless' in the market or felt it was an exercise in 'poverty tourism'. Students from international education raised questions about the purpose of the United States sending frivolous items as 'aid' to developing countries when Haitians really needed food and the tools to be agriculturally self-sufficient (an example of critical thinking in action); other students suggested more debriefing time for such an emotional experience. (*Shondel Nero*, Chapter 14)

Ideologies may also operate more explicitly at macro levels, including, for example, the colonial power dynamics between the North and the South (Morley *et al.*, 2019). Or East and West – the following extract describes the experience of a Chinese language teaching assistant in New Zealand:

> She introduced herself as a 'teacher', but it was immediately rejected by one of the guests. The teacher commented as follows: 'They say my job is propaganda. I didn't know propaganda is such a negative word in English at that time. I thought it meant promotion'. Clearly, her demand for recognition of her professional identity was met with resistance. The experience shows that their English ability was inadequate for them to apprehend the ideological and political discourses surrounding their work. (*Danping Wang*, Chapter 6)

The relationship between local and global discourses is bidirectional, as both these examples show. Language teachers who study abroad are at all times involved in negotiating their feelings, identities and development in the midst of these ideological concerns.

11. *Critical reflexivity*

I have already pointed out (citing Ingersoll *et al.*, 2019) that some ideological frameworks underpinning study abroad are supported by notions of economic competitiveness and positional advantage, and Stein and McCartney (2021) express similar notions in terms of econominism, eurocentrism, racism and ethno-nationalism. The theme immediately above, *political awareness*, illustrates how language teachers during their study abroad may become aware of these ideologies. But *critical reflexivity* takes the process of working towards awareness even further. It involves a deliberate, critical, deep questioning of encounters with difference (Ingersoll *et al.*, 2019), or a decolonial critique, a critical self-reflection of one's place and the place of others, and their interrelationship, in new worlds confronted. For example:

> [R]ather than construct an experience abroad whose benefits focus squarely on participants of the Global North, we can work to incorporate

models of decolonizing teacher education that ask students from both the visiting and host countries to collaboratively engage in self-reflection, and work to develop awareness of colonial perspectives and histories. An emerging awareness of *decoloniality* and ownership of one's cultural identity and histories are the first moves to developing dispositions that endure past the program's end date, following participants into their post-program professional lives. (*Rachel Shriver et al.*, Chapter 7)

The following extract illustrates one of the potential outcomes of such self-reflective engagement – in this case, an opportunity for teachers from the United States to imagine a future time and place as well as the students who will be a part of their professional lives:

> The exposure to the Dominican education system, including conversations with current Dominican teachers (albeit brief) is meant to facilitate the intercultural development of pre-service teachers. It provides a space for them to think about their future students' prior educational experiences more critically, how to harness that knowledge to interact with them more empathetically, and instruct and assess them more equitably when they inhabit new identities as immigrant children in classrooms. (*Shondel Nero*, Chapter 14)

12. Careers

Ultimately, LTSA relates to the careers of the language teachers who embark on an international sojourn. Whether they be pre-service or in-service language teachers, LTSA activities and the resultant personal and professional development, new levels of awareness, and political understandings, all contribute to their careers as language educators – how they unfold, how meaningful they are to the teachers, and whether or not they do indeed eventuate. In some cases the effects may be immediate and in others they may become evident well into the future. We have seen numerous examples in the chapter extracts above, and the chapters themselves are filled with many more, of how LTSA has led to role and identity changes post-sojourn, how teachers have become leaders directly as a consequence of their LTSA experiences, how others have moved out of teaching and returned to it later in life, and so on. LTSA also presents an opportunity for those considering a language teaching career to 'test the waters'. As the following two examples show:

> Prior to study abroad, Chobi stated that she had wanted to teach EFL for a long time but had never had the chance to try it out. She was anxious to find out if she enjoyed teaching as much as she thought she would. Study abroad affirmed her passion for TEFL: 'This was kind of the determining trip for me, like, "Am I doing the right thing?" And once I got there, and it felt so natural and so good, I was like, "it's the right thing. I'm on the right career path"'. (*Meredith D'Arienzo* and *YouJin Kim*, Chapter 21)

To sum up, the prospect of a teaching career was not prominent among the motivations of LTAs [Language Teaching Assistants]. When weighing up an LTA-ship over other options, the break from study, the intercultural nature of the experience (especially prominent for those heading to Mexico), financial considerations and possible limitations on social opportunities and opportunity to speak their priority target language, were all more salient than an interest in 'tasting' teaching. However, of those participants who later did actually work in education, almost all had previously been LTAs, either during their year abroad or post-graduation. (*Rosamond Mitchell* and *Nicole Tracy-Ventura*, Chapter 17)

The Structure of the Book

In this section, I briefly describe the overall structure of the book. Following this introductory chapter are a further 20 chapters. They all touch on the 12 themes discussed above, some being addressed more explicitly and saliently than others. This, therefore, makes ordering or grouping the chapters somewhat challenging. What I have done is to group the themes into four main categories, and these form the four parts of the book. Figure 1.1 attempts to illustrate and emphasize their interconnection.

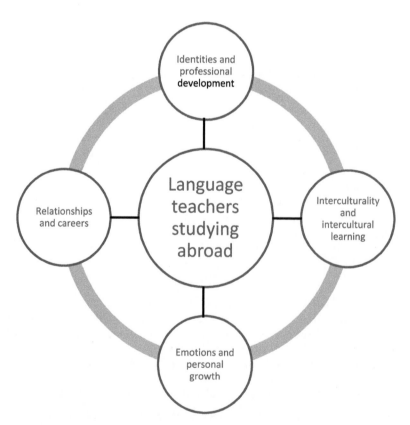

Figure 1.1 The interrelationship of four main categories

Part 1: Identities and Professional Development: Themes in this category reflect the intersection of identity, particularly identity negotiation and identity changes, and professional development. Norton (2013) has consistently stated that an investment in language learning is an investment in identity. In a similar vein, investment in professional development (through a commitment to LTSA) is an investment in identity. As the chapters in this section show (as do chapters in other sections), identities change both short term while abroad and in the longer term (e.g. over time post-sojourn) as a result of participation in LTSA.

Part 2: Interculturality and Intercultural Learning: Various aspects of culture and culture learning related to LTSA experiences are the focus of this category. Again, although most of the chapters in the book deal with culture in some way, the chapters in this section tend to address culture more explicitly or say something particularly interesting about culture, intercultural learning or interculturality.

Part 3: Emotions and Personal Growth: Gkonou *et al.* (2020) claim that 'emotions are at the centre of all human behaviour' (1) and that emotions can fluctuate over time and across settings, with some settings, such as those encountered during LTSA, generating intense emotions. Some chapters in this section examine emotions head-on, while others allude only to the emotion work of the LTSA participant teachers. But they all make connections with how their emotion work leads to personal growth, with more or less connection to professional growth.

Part 4: Relationships and Careers: This grouping of themes tends to focus more on careers than relationships. However, some aspects of relationships are included in the chapters; for example, involvement of significant or influential people, good relationships or bad, the psychological effects of establishing or breaking off relationships, and the consequences for career choices or trajectories.

Conclusion

This chapter has introduced the focus of the book; that is, the psychological and social personal experiences of pre-service and in-service language teachers who study abroad. The growth in the numbers and diversity of those traveling abroad to study and learn temporarily in new environments highlights the need for considerable depth and breadth in understanding what this mobility means for individuals and the language teaching and learning communities they encounter and return to post-sojourn. The chapters in the book acknowledge the need to 'recognize the heterogeneity of the study abroad environment' (Coleman, 2013: 26), particularly given the recent increase of new study-abroad programs that differ considerably in terms of length, goals and features, including moving from physical to online or virtual environments. At the same time, the chapters take up Coleman's (2013) call to account for *whole people and whole lives* in study-abroad research; in other words, the stories of their whole embodied and lived experiences in full psychological and social terms. In the case of this book, this means pre-service and in-service language teachers, teacher educators and researchers with histories, identities, imaginations, emotions, motivations and intentions. It also means the nature of communities they live and work in, the relationships they form and the environments they inhabit socially, geographically and digitally (both abroad and at home), particularly in times of radical disruption such as bushfires, protests and, more recently and catastrophically, Covid-19 and the post-Covid-19 era.

References

Allen, L.Q. (2010) The impact of study abroad on the professional lives of world language teachers. *Foreign Language Annals* 45, 93–104.

Barkhuizen, G. (2011) Narrative knowledging in TESOL. *TESOL Quarterly* 45 (3), 391–414.

Bateson, G. (1972) *Steps to an Ecology of Mind.* New York: Ballentine.

Beaven, A. and Borghetti, C. (2016) Interculturality in study abroad. *Language and Intercultural Communication* 16 (3), 313–317.

Beck, K. (2021) Beyond internationalization: Lessons from post-development. *Journal of International Students* 11 (S1), 133–151.

Block (2014) *Second Language Identities.* London: Bloomsbury.

Bond, S., Girgrah, A., Burrow, J., Ingersoll, M., Vander Meulen, C., Spaling, M. and Areepattamannil, S. (2009) *World of Learning: Canadian Post-secondary Students and the Study Abroad Experience.* Ottawa: Canadian Bureau of International Education.

Coleman, J.A. (2013) Researching whole people and whole lives. In C. Kinginger (ed.) *Social and Cultural Aspects of Language Learning in Study Abroad* (pp. 17–44). Amsterdam: John Benjamins.

Çiftçi, E.Y. and Karaman, A.C. (2019) Short-term international experiences in language teacher education: A qualitative meat-synthesis. *Australian Journal of Teacher Education* 44 (1), 93–119.

Donato, R. (2017) Becoming a language teaching professional: What's identity got to do with it? In G. Barkhuizen (ed.) *Reflections on Language Teacher Identity Research* (pp. 24–30). New York: Routledge.

Giuntella, O., Hyde, K., Saccardo, S. and Sadoff, S. (2021) Lifestyle and mental health disruptions during COVID-19. *Proceedings of the National Academy of Sciences* 118 (9), e2016632118.

Gkonou, C., Dewaele, J.-M. and King, J. (2020) Introduction to the emotional rollercoaster of language teaching. In C. Gkonou, J.-M. Dewaele and J. King (eds) *The Emotional Rollercoaster of Language Teaching* (pp. 1–12). Bristol: Multilingual Matters.

Gu, Q., Schweisfurth, M. and Day, C. (2010) Learning and growing in a 'foreign' context: Intercultural experiences of international students. *Compare* 40 (1), 7–23.

Ingersoll, M., Sears, A., Hirschkorn, M., Kawtharani-Chami, L. and Landine, J. (2019) What is it all for? The intentions and priorities for study abroad in Canadian teacher education. *Global Education Review* 6 (3), 30–48.

Jackson, J. (2018) Intervening in the intercultural learning of study abroad students: From research to practice. *Language Teaching* 51 (3), 365–382.

Kinginger, C. (2009) *Language Learning and Study Abroad: A Critical Reading of Research*. Basingstoke: Palgrave Macmillan.

Kinginger, C. (2015) Student mobility and identity-related language learning. *Intercultural Education* 26 (1), 6–15.

Mercer, S. and Gkonou, C. (2020) Relationships and good language teachers. In C. Griffiths and Z. Tajeddin (eds) *Lessons from Good Language Teachers* (pp. 164–174). Cambridge: Cambridge University Press.

Mezirow, J. (2000) Learning to think like an adult: Core concepts of transformation theory. In J. Mezirow (ed.) *Learning as Transformation: Critical Perspectives on a Theory in Progress* (pp. 3–32). San Francisco, CA: Jossey Bass.

Morley, A., Braun, A.M.B., Rohrer, L. and Lamb, D. (2019) Study abroad for preservice teachers: A critical literature review with considerations for research and practice. *Global Education Review* 6 (3), 4–29.

Norton, B. (2013) *Identity and Language Learning: Extending the Conversation* (2nd edn). Bristol: Multilingual Matters.

Plews, J.L., Breckenridge, Y. and Cambre, M.-C. (2010) Mexican English teachers' experiences of international professional development in Canada: A narrative analysis. *Electronic Journal of Foreign Language Teaching* 7, 5–20.

Roskvist, A., Harvey, S., Corder, D. and Stacey, K. (2015) Teacher language learning and residence abroad: What makes a difference? Perspectives from two case studies. In R. Mitchell, N. Tracy-Ventura and K. McManus (eds) *Social Interaction, Identity and Language Learning during Residence Abroad* (pp. 185–198). Amsterdam: The European Second Language Association.

Song, J. (2016) Emotions and language teacher identity: Conflicts, vulnerability, and transformation. *TESOL Quarterly* 50 (3), 631–654.

Stein, S. (2019) Critical internationalization studies at an impasse: Making space for complexity, uncertainty, and complicity in a time of global challenges. *Studies in Higher Education*, https://doi-org.ezproxy.auckland.ac.nz/10.1080/03075079.2019.1704722

Stein, S. and McCartney, D.M. (2021) Emerging conversations in critical internationalization studies. *Journal of International Students* 11 (S1), 1–14.

Part 1

Identities and Professional Development

2 Emotionality in Field Trip Narratives: Confronting Deficit Perspectives

Julia Menard-Warwick, Enrique David Degollado and Shannon Kehoe

> 'When we arrived at the Guatemala City dump, standing in a grave-yard, and listening to an NGO worker discuss the conditions of life for people living in the dump, it was a lot for me to handle. A lot for all of us to handle, I am sure'. (Annie, blog post)

Introduction

Annie[1] wrote the above blog post in July 2015, while studying to become a teacher at a Texas university and participating in an education-themed summer study-abroad program in Guatemala. Her blog reflects on what she and her classmates observed in their trip to Andar Juntos, a non-governmental organization (NGO) that served families who live and work around the main Guatemala City garbage dump. This visit followed upon an earlier field trip to another NGO, Pajaritos del Volcán, which aided impoverished indigenous families living on the slope of a volcano. As documented in our data, together these trips had a strong impact on many students in the study-abroad program. Evident in Annie's blog are the emotions they collectively experienced, 'it was a lot ... to handle'; similarly her classmate Delia said in an interview, 'it was a lot for us to take in'. We found, nevertheless, that the Texas students *did* strive to 'handle' and even more to 'take in', affectively and conceptually, the lessons inherent in the (somewhat different) ways the two NGOs addressed families in economically desperate situations.

In this chapter we discuss the potential of planned field trips within study abroad to evoke affective reactions and engage prospective teachers more deeply with concepts from their Education coursework. To analyze the intertwining of emotional response and academic learning, we focus on participants' contrasting reactions to the two NGOs.

23

Review of Literature

In this section, we review previous research on narrative and emotion, especially in study-abroad settings. As Benson *et al.* (2013) emphasize, narratives are particularly useful when researchers explore within them 'processes of identity development that are inseparable from their narration' (2013: 25). In White's (2018) narrative research with teachers, she found that talking of emotions led to 'collaborative acts of affective stancetaking ... construct[ing] wider, shared discourses about their ideals [and] constraints' (2018: 595). We follow up on these insights in our analysis of narratives told by prospective teachers from the United States studying in Guatemala.

Prior's (2016) work with refugees illustrates how *emotionality*, the linguistic representation of emotion, can become a form of social action, through evaluating, interpreting and potentially transforming social realities. In study-abroad research, students' strong emotional reactions to unfamiliar cultural contexts are a common finding (Goldoni, 2017; Kinginger, 2008; Marx & Pray, 2011). Although affect is sometimes viewed as antithetical to analysis, contemporary researchers in language and education emphasize 'the mutual entailment of the cognitive, the social, and the emotional' (Douglas Fir Group, 2016: 21).

Study-abroad research has traditionally measured language acquisition (Kinginger, 2008), but this is not the central goal of many students or educational programs. Teacher educators now recognize that even short-term abroad experiences can positively influence the dispositions and worldviews of prospective teachers (Marx & Pray, 2011; Kasun & Saavedra, 2016), especially by affording them greater insight into the struggles of language learners. In research on such programs, novice teachers' emotional reactions to unfamiliar cultural phenomena are often viewed as key to the developmental process.

Programs for teacher education through study abroad (hereafter TESA) align with theoretical currents in teacher education that emphasize reflexivity and sociocultural consciousness over technocratic, one-size-fits-all, best practices (Philip *et al.*, 2019). From this perspective, experiential learning in community contexts can help pre-service teachers better understand families and communities: 'the challenges they face and the resources they bring to those challenges' (Lucas & Villegas, 2013: 104). However, Lucas and Villegas stress that simply encountering culturally-different Others in community settings is insufficient, and can even reinforce stereotypes.

Uneven study-abroad research findings (Kinginger, 2008) suggest that simply sending students across international borders does not guarantee any particular result, whether language learning or cultural understanding (Jackson, 2018). Research instead demonstrates that study-abroad success often depends upon individual students finding contexts of local engagement where they can participate linguistically and culturally (Jackson, 2011; Kinginger, 2008); nevertheless, local residents do not always recognize sojourners as worthy participants (Goldoni, 2017).

Although cultural disequilibrium has been theorized to facilitate transformative learning (Rowan-Kenyon & Niehaus, 2011), this kind of shock treatment does not guarantee learning outcomes either, and can cause students to give up on intercultural experiences.

Thus, educators in charge of study-abroad programs increasingly build in reflection activities (Jackson, 2018) to scaffold participants' learning and help them 'develop the skill of viewing themselves from others' perspectives' (Pasterick, 2019: 132). Indeed, many TESA researchers argue that the experience of cultural and linguistic Otherness, along with systematic reflection, can set in motion developmental processes that prepare novice teachers to work thoughtfully with cultural and linguistic Others in their classrooms (Isabelli-García et al., 2018; Marx & Pray, 2011; Pasterick, 2019).

To maximize the perceived benefits of immersion, most TESA programs additionally build in experiential activities. For example, in Sharma et al. (2013), teacher candidates on a short-term program in Honduras conducted arts and crafts activities with children in rural schools, while in Kasun and Saavedra (2016), TESA participants studied Spanish, observed classes at indigenous schools, attended a talk by a Mayan shaman, toured the local ethnobotanic garden and visited the municipal market. However, since these activities are not described in depth, their pedagogical value remains undertheorized. Researchers' inattention to what students gain from specific activities follows trends in the larger study-abroad literature to ignore issues of curricula, learning approaches, materials and course assignments (Isabelli-García et al., 2018; for an exception, see Ruiz Bybee et al., 2018), implying that really, it is the general immersion in the abroad environment that either brings about desired outcomes, or not.

Therefore, further research is necessary on study-abroad program activities designed to promote specific learning objectives. For example, Marijuan and Sanz (2018) suggest that study-abroad programs oriented toward social justice could build in activities aimed at 'raising awareness of the "global marketization of doing good" … and uncovering its negative consequences' (2018: 198). Program activities such as listening to a Maya shaman (Kasun & Saavedra, 2016) potentially support equity-oriented pedagogical goals (Philip et al., 2019). However, few study-abroad studies offer analysis of the affective and academic impacts of specific activities (but see Menard-Warwick & Palmer, 2012). To explore these issues, we focus on narratives recounted by prospective teachers from the United States in Guatemala, which contrast TESA program field trips to two NGOs serving families in poverty. In this regard, we ask the following research questions:

(1) How did prospective teachers discursively construct their emotions about the field trips to the two NGOs?
(2) How did they draw upon course concepts in talking about the NGOs? What did they learn from these two field trips?

Methods

The qualitative data for this analysis is drawn from a larger research project which examined the experiences of students who participated in one or both six-week sessions of a faculty-led transnational critical education program sponsored by a Texas university in Guatemala during the summer of 2015 (Ruiz Bybee *et al.*, 2018; Menard-Warwick *et al.*, 2019). The current chapter focuses on five second-session focal participants, all of whom were female undergraduate students in their early twenties who had graduated from Texas high schools. Delia, Nicole and Xochitl grew up in Spanish-speaking families and were thus fully bilingual in English and Spanish; Jane and Annie were L1 English speakers and Spanish learners. All were majoring in education-related fields and looking forward to teaching careers: Delia and Nicole were planning to become Spanish/English bilingual teachers, while Xochitl, Jane and Annie aimed to teach in linguistically-diverse schools where every teacher must be prepared to work with English learners. Thus, all five focal participants had joined the TESA program to gain linguistic and cultural insights that could inform their future pedagogical practice at home in Texas.

Our qualitative data analysis is based on participant observation, with permission of the students: we documented all field trips through ethnographic field notes; we interviewed focal students during and after the program; we collected and analyzed biweekly blogs and other course assignments; we audio-recorded and transcribed all Education classes (see Figure 2.1 for transcription conventions). Through our own participation in the TESA program, we had observed students' emotional reactions to field trips, as well as their resultant learning, and we thus decided to explore these issues in this chapter. During our initial round of analysis, we selected all data relevant to the field trips and collectively reflected on data patterns. Through this process we agreed that students had reacted most strongly to the two NGO field trips in July, and we thus narrowed our focus to those visits.

This data was subjected to a round of inductive, *in Vivo* coding, which uses direct quotes from participants as codes. *In Vivo* coding roots the data in the language of the participants (Saldaña, 2015), allowing us to

text	clear construction of emotionality
?	rising intonation, sounds like a question
...	trailing off, not completing
[comment]	note from author
[...]	text omitted
(italicized)	translation of preceding

Figure 2.1 Transcription conventions

center and honor participants' voices (Miles *et al.*, 2014). Patterns emerging from the *in Vivo* coding were used to generate new codes, which were then used for a subsequent round of coding. In particular, our *in Vivo* coding thematized explicit mention of emotions and emotional responses, as seen in Annie's blog quoted in our epigraph. In the same blog post, Annie commented that she was 'way more emotional' on that visit, and that she had an 'emotional heart to heart [with classmates] about the greatness of [that] NGO'. After reading this account and others which mentioned affective responses and which reflected on the experience of visiting the garbage dump, the codes 'emotion' and 'dump' were created and subsequently used in another round of coding. Codes for negative and positive comments were also created and used to find patterns in students' narratives about their emotional reactions to the NGOs. In this regard, we define *narratives* as individual and collective accounts which evaluate experiences.

Our identities and roles as researchers shaped the data collected. First author, Julia and third author, Shannon, identify as White women, and second author, David, as a Mexican-American man. All three of us are bilingual in Spanish and English. We all collected data in Guatemala during the first session of the program. This chapter focuses on the second session, during which only Julia collected data. Shannon participated in the second session as a teaching assistant (TA), so she did not engage in program research again until after submitting her students' grades. However, she additionally conducted the post-program interviews included in this chapter and found that her TA experience shaped how the focal participants reconstructed (or co-constructed) their experiences in these interviews. David's involvement in data collection during the first session as well as post-program shaped his understanding of our findings. Since Julia and Shannon attended the two focal field trips,[2] and David did not, his contribution to the data analysis offered a level of objectivity. We mutually discussed our perspectives and the ways our varying roles had shaped them.

Findings

In this section we introduce three themes that illustrate how the excursions reinforced classroom learning. Firstly, many students stated that they found these trips to be metaphorically *eye opening*, that is, bringing global poverty into their conscious awareness. Secondly, students' negative reactions to the first of the two NGOs gave them a concrete context in which to apply the course concept of *deficit perspective*. Thirdly, their collective questions about how to respond to these experiences pushed at least some participants toward *critical reflexivity*: a recognition of how they themselves are connected to the systems that perpetuate poverty along with a growing sense of responsibility to promote positive change.

Together, these themes build on one another and highlight developing levels of understanding and interpretation among the participants. In recounting these narratives about their own emotional responses to global injustice, study-abroad participants constructed identities (Benson *et al.*, 2013) as future educators dedicated to equity (Philip *et al.*, 2019).

Eye opening

When Julia asked Delia in an interview about her most memorable TESA experiences, she immediately brought up the Andar Juntos trip, specifying, 'that was definitely a real big eye opener for me'. She added, '<u>it was a lot to take in</u>', repeating that phrase twice. When Julia asked for specifics, Delia first mentioned her emotions, and next the resultant learning: she repeated twice that she was '<u>shocked</u>' then explained, 'I knew that there was poverty, but I didn't know that it was to that extreme'. Annie's blog, quoted above, similarly repeated, '<u>a lot for me to handle, a lot of all of us to handle</u>'. To support this statement, and evoke similar emotions for the reader, she listed visual images: '<u>the literal mountain of trash, the hundreds of vultures that dotted and circled the entire area, and the garbage trucks being called and competed over</u>'.

Furthermore, the trips caused students to reflect emotionally on their own past experiences with poverty, as demonstrated in Delia's blog post:

> When I thought of the poverty those kids experienced, I thought about my family. I thought about when I was young and <u>my family didn't have food to eat</u> so we depended on the donations of generous charities and organizations ... It was then that I realized I could be like [NGO founder], I had the thought which is what she began with, the idea and <u>compassion</u> for others, and the drive and willingness to help ... I called my parents and told them <u>I love them</u> because I knew that if we were ever in the situation as the families from here, they would also <u>risk their health working in the dump</u>.

In this post we see how Delia began to make emotional connections to her own life – having experienced poverty herself – to the extent that she called her parents that night. She empathized with the people who work in the garbage dump, feeling sure that her parents would do the same under similar circumstances; this sense of identification inspired her to work with impoverished families in the future.

Similarly, in her post-program interview, Nicole cited the trip to Andar Juntos as having raised her awareness of poverty:

> I know we hear about it all the time. I know that it exists, but actually going to that dump that they had in the ciudad (*city*), it was something that was ... You get to see, and there's <u>children and there's families who are trying to live their life from picking trash and stuff</u>.

She added that visiting Andar Juntos had given her the desire to 'work as a teacher in a non-profit, in a ... country that needs more resources like that'.

Significantly, part of Nicole's new awareness of poverty included insights about the causes of poverty, based on the NGO visits as well as TESA classroom learning. As she stated: 'These people work hard. They don't have the resources. They come from a background where there's too many barriers to help them get to there'. These remarks put into perspective the realities that she observed in Guatemala. The trips for the students proved to be a turning point in how they understood poverty but also (to some extent) the systemic perpetuation of poverty and the need for action to overcome the 'barriers' faced by so many families. Thus, the trip resulted in a call to action to do better and be better.

Defining 'deficit'

Being able to compare two NGOs' approaches to the same issues was invaluable in clarifying what it means 'to do better'. According to Annie's blog, 'we all agreed we really <u>liked</u> Andar Juntos and that Pajaritos was the epitome of the <u>nightmare</u> NGO. Why? ... It was the attitude!' The TESA program included excursions so participants could apply theories about schooling and society from their Education coursework. In subsequent classes, the students discussed their observations in relation to theoretical concepts.

Specifically, the contrast in 'attitude' that students perceived between the two NGOs afforded them a much clearer conceptual understanding of *deficit thinking*, defined within the field of Education as 'positing that the student who fails in school does so because of internal deficits or deficiencies' (Valencia, 1997: 2). More widely, deficit perspectives draw on negative stereotypes to characterize groups of people, for example families in poverty, as both pitiful and blameworthy (Gorski, 2011). As the participants talked and wrote about the first NGO, Pajaritos del Volcán, they ascribed this perspective to the tour guides there.

At the beginning of the classroom discussion following the Pajaritos field trip, Delia recalled an NGO staffer's claim that their clients did not know where babies came from. For her this comment exemplified the organization's condescending approach and thus the reasons for the students' negative emotional response: 'We agreed that the tours had like this deficit thinking that we were talking about? And we were just <u>kind of upset</u> about how she <u>kind of belittled</u> the community'. As a further example of this mentality, Delia quoted their guide's comment about trash lying on the ground: 'She said "oh yeah, they just walk by the trash and this is how it is ... They don't know any better"'.

After more students repeated similar criticisms of the NGO, one of their classmates (not a prospective teacher) extolled the nutrition classes offered by Pajaritos, including cooking instruction. Xochitl immediately objected: 'Okay, <u>that threw me off – that threw me for a loop a little bit</u>'. The expression to be 'thrown for a loop' involves a negative emotional reaction to confusing or unpleasant information. Xochitl clarified her response by stating, 'I understand the diet of coffee and tortillas, it isn't the best. But sometimes that's the only thing those families can offer. And it's like you're just <u>putting that down</u>'. For Jane, this attitude stemmed from a lack of attention on the part of the NGO to getting feedback from the people they served: 'It's like, then, you're not talking to people'.

In all this attention to deficit thinking on the part of the tour guides, students demonstrated mastery of the course material. Once the students could identify deficit thinking, however, they then had to wrestle with questions about better approaches to helping others. As Annie summarized the classroom discussion in her blog:

> A lot of what we talked about was 'victim blaming' and only looking at the problems in this micro community, not looking at the macro, systemic problems that exist within the country and the world … However, it's easy to let this over-analysis of deficits convince you that helping others is detrimental, because you will never understand how to help them 'perfectly'.

Through these musings, Annie clarified her understanding that deficit thinking (Valencia, 1997; Gorski, 2011) as a conceptual tool could be useful for identifying inequities in society but should not impede efforts to help people in need. Overall, participants concluded that despite the dilemmas raised by the trips, they should still prioritize social engagement.

Critical reflexivity

Throughout their Guatemala sojourn, as students reflected on what they had learned and observed (Pasterick, 2019), they began, in some cases, to engage in critical reflexivity: recognizing their own roles, not only within inequitable systems, but also within initiatives for positive change. As prospective teachers, with interests in language and culture, they began most specifically to interrogate *voluntourism*, the process by which people from wealthier countries go to developing countries to volunteer, especially as English teachers. This questioning was partly sparked by the NGO trips, given that both emphasized English instruction within their educational programs. Both Jane and Annie raised this issue during the class discussion and considered it further while writing their blogs.

Strikingly, Annie highlighted her own emotions when she told the class that Pajaritos' emphasis on English teaching was 'the thing that <u>angered</u> [her] the most'. Language instruction at the NGO connected with another Pajaritos' initiative, training youth for hotel jobs. This aspiration reminded Jane of the overemphasis on English within the Texas school system:

> Like when you're teaching kids English that are coming in like, you're teaching them how to operate in the United States. Like that's how you're

gonna be successful in the United States, like it sucks ... They're working to like bandaid it. So they're like, 'here, work in a hotel for rich, white people' ... and that's wrong.

In this classroom discussion, Jane shared her emotional reaction ('like it sucks') to the ethics of assimilating children into the current inequitable system, whether in the United States or Guatemala ('that's wrong'). In using the metaphor 'working to bandaid', Jane implied that conditions for poor children in both countries were a bleeding wound not easily stanched. Because her teachers and classmates knew of her existing plans to teach in Texas schools, this affective response put her on record as seeking more radical solutions.

Annie's blog post, composed later, responded to the NGO's efforts in a more measured way. After making the case that Pajaritos del Volcán served its purpose in doing good for others, she again questioned the need to teach English there: 'they live in a Spanish speaking country with a significant indigenous population ... Shouldn't those languages be of first priority to the school?' In the class discussion, Xochitl had likewise deprecated the low priority the Pajaritos' school placed on the community's indigenous heritage. While acknowledging that the field trips were pedagogically designed to highlight NGO dilemmas, Annie concluded this post with a significant confession: 'I felt like the ultimate cynic, though, because I was questioning and criticizing everything, but had no idea of how to solve any of it'.

These final thoughts reveal Annie's struggles to reconcile ideas from coursework with the very real needs of Guatemalan youth. In doing so, this young prospective teacher from the United States questioned not only the motives of Guatemalan NGOs but her own motives, attempting to make sense of everything. This type of inner dialogue, deliberately sparked by the field trips, was not meant to have resolution but rather to incite consideration of theory and practice within concrete contexts. That is, critical reflexivity was most evident when participants began to see nuance in their own arguments and to talk themselves out of being simplistically 'critical' while grappling with course concepts and their own experiences.

Discussion

Over their time in Guatemala, the Texas student teachers who participated were impacted in many ways by individual experiences of travel, of language learning, of getting to know host families. However, these two back-to-back field trips to NGOs seemed to involve the most intense emotion and most intense learning. In our analysis, the heart of this experience was the encounter with 'extreme' poverty, however brief and carefully scaffolded. While the group collectively struggled with what they perceived as belittling attitudes at the first NGO, it was the tension between the students' 'shock' at poverty and their negative reactions to certain NGO staffers that most seemed to propel them in the direction of critical reflexivity. Since this entire process was both emotional and conceptual, we next tease out the role of affect in conceptual learning by summarizing the answers to our research questions.

First, we review here the emotionality (Prior, 2016) constructed by the prospective teachers in regard to the NGO field trips. One approach taken by participants was to tie emotion directly or metaphorically to physical experience, as in the common expression 'eye opening', used by a number of participants to emphasize the vividness of their first-hand encounters with poverty. The word 'shock', also widely used in our data, suggests a powerful bodily experience, as in receiving a jolt of electricity. Another approach involved the use of details with widespread emotional associations, for example, the common mention of *vultures*, a bird whose presence connotes death. More straightforward affective vocabulary appeared in critiques of NGO staffers, including verbs such as 'angered' or adjectives such as 'upset'. Another common strategy was to quote negative comments made by staff members about their clients; for example, 'they don't know any better'. However, a final type of emotionality was less clear-cut – perhaps best described as *conflicted* – as when Annie admitted to feeling like a 'cynic' given her own lack of clear answers about how to improve the lives of Guatemalan families struggling with poverty.

To answer our second research question, we list what students seemed to have learned from their field trip experiences. First, even students who had themselves grown up in poverty reported 'shock' at the 'extreme' poverty in Guatemala; the NGO trips made this real to them in a way they had not previously experienced. Second, it was abundantly clear that students had learned the meaning of the word 'deficit' (Valencia, 1997; Gorski, 2011) and how to identify *deficit thinking* on the part of NGO staffers. Much of the classroom discussion around the visit to Pajaritos del Volcán involved listing the guides' negative comments toward the families they served. Indignation at these dismissive remarks fueled students' recognition that many NGO program offerings, such as cooking classes (when families could not afford food), English classes (in a Spanish dominant country), or training for low-skilled tourism jobs, had little potential to change families' lives for the better. Some students additionally realized that these situations of 'extreme' poverty are the result of an unjust economic system that is not amenable to 'bandaids', as Jane pointed out.

As previous research indicates, study-abroad programs have the potential to immerse students in unfamiliar cultural settings, and in some cases to change their views of themselves and the world (Kasun & Saavedra, 2016; Kinginger, 2008; Marx & Pray, 2011; Rowan-Kenyon & Niehaus, 2011; Sharma *et al.*, 2013). This has been particularly true for students who find ways to invest personally in 'local engagement', often away from the main group (Jackson, 2011; Kinginger, 2008). However, previous studies have primarily attempted to measure the effects of entire study-abroad sojourns, and thus have rarely examined particular study-abroad activities (e.g. field trips) and what students actually learned from them (for an exception, see Menard-Warwick & Palmer, 2012).

Insofar as the study-abroad literature has explored participants' emotions, these have primarily been viewed as reactions to the overall immersion experience (Rowan-Kenyon & Niehaus, 2011), with the danger that too intensely negative experiences will reinforce stereotypes (Marx & Pray, 2011) or lead to disengagement (Goldoni, 2017). In our exploration, as in White (2018), we found participants collaboratively constructing affective stances toward their aspirations and perceived obstacles. Through further analysis, we found that students' strong feelings tended to reinforce their engagement with course content and program objectives (Douglas Fir Group, 2016); however, more research is needed in this regard.

As Kinginger notes (2008: 105), study abroad can foster 'an appreciation of global diversity and of human solidarity' – but this is not guaranteed. Similarly, Lucas and Villegas (2013) advocate that new teachers deepen their understanding of how families are challenged, and how they surmount those challenges. The Guatemala program strove to set these developmental processes in motion through experiential learning. To this end, course discussions and reflective assignments impelled participants' (co)construction of highly emotional narratives, which connected intimately to their simultaneous process of developing identities as new teachers committed to equity (Benson *et al.*, 2013; Philip *et al.*, 2019). In our analysis, these study-abroad narratives illustrate the key role that emotionality can play in reinforcing awareness not only of global injustice, but also of human resilience, along with a deeper commitment to global solidarity.

Notes

(1) All names of students and NGOs are pseudonyms.
(2) Like the students, we had strong emotional reactions, both positive and negative; unlike the students, we saw more similarities than differences between the NGOs.

References

Benson, P., Barkhuizen, G., Bodycott, P. and Brown, J. (2013) *Second Language Identity in Narratives of Study Abroad*. New York: Palgrave Macmillan.

Douglas Fir Group (2016) A transdisciplinary framework for SLA in a multilingual world. *Modern Language Journal* 100 (S1), 19–47.

Goldoni, F. (2017) Race, ethnicity, class and identity: Implications for study abroad. *Journal of Language, Identity & Education* 16 (5), 328–341.

Gorski, P.C. (2011) Unlearning deficit ideology and the scornful gaze: Thoughts on authenticating the class discourse in education. *Counterpoints* 402, 152–173.

Isabelli-García, C., Bown, J., Plews, J.L. and Dewey, D.P. (2018) State of the art: Language learning and study abroad. *Language Teaching* 51 (4), 439–484.

Jackson, J. (2011) Cultivating cosmopolitan, intercultural citizenship through critical reflection and international, experiential learning. *Language and Intercultural Communication* 11 (2), 80–96.

Jackson, J. (2018) Intervening in the intercultural learning of study abroad students: From research to practice. *Language Teaching* 51 (3), 365–382.

Kasun, G.S. and Saavedra, C.M. (2016) Disrupting ELL teacher candidates' identities: Indigenizing teacher education in one study abroad program. *TESOL Quarterly* 3, 684–707.

Kinginger, C. (2008) Language learning in study abroad: Case studies of Americans in France. *The Modern Language Journal* 92 (S1), 1–124.

Lucas, T. and Villegas, A.M. (2013) Preparing linguistically responsive teachers: Laying the foundation in preservice teacher education. *Theory into Practice* 52 (2), 98–109.

Marijuan, S. and Sanz, C. (2018) Expanding boundaries: Current and new directions in study abroad research and practice. *Foreign Language Annals* 51 (1), 185–204.

Marx, S. and Pray, L. (2011) Living and learning in Mexico: Developing empathy for English language learners through study abroad. *Race, Ethnicity and Education* 14 (4), 507–535.

Menard-Warwick, J. and Palmer, D.K. (2012) Eight versions of the visit to La Barranca: Critical discourse analysis of a study-abroad narrative from Mexico. *Teacher Education Quarterly* 39 (1), 121–138.

Menard-Warwick, J., Ruiz Bybee, E., Degollado, E.D., Jin, S., Kehoe, S. and Masters, K.A. (2019) Same language, different histories: Developing a 'critical' English teacher identity. *Journal of Language, Identity, & Education* 18 (6), 364–376.

Miles, M.B., Huberman, A.M. and Saldaña, J. (2014) *Qualitative Data Analysis* (3rd edn). Thousand Oaks, CA: Sage.

Pasterick, M.L. (2019) Language and (inter)cultural learning: Supporting language teacher candidates' development of interculturality during study abroad. In D. Martin and E. Smolcic (eds) *Redefining Teaching Competence through Immersive Programs* (pp. 127–153). Cham: Palgrave Macmillan.

Philip, T.M., Souto-Manning, M., Anderson, L., Horn, I., Carter Andrews, D.J., Stillman, J. and Varghese, M. (2019) Making justice peripheral by constructing practice as 'core': How the increasing prominence of core practices challenges teacher education. *Journal of Teacher Education* 70 (3), 251–264.

Prior, M.T. (2016) *Emotion and Discourse in L2 Narrative Research*. Bristol: Multilingual Matters.

Rowan-Kenyon, H.T. and Niehaus, E. (2011) One year later: The influence of short-term study abroad experiences on students. *Journal of Student Affairs Research and Practice* 48 (2), 213–228.

Ruiz Bybee, E., Menard-Warwick, J., Degollado, E.D., Palmer, D.K., Kehoe, S. and Urrieta, L. (2018) Curricula without borders: Integrating multicultural and multilingual preservice teacher education coursework. In C. Sanz and A. Morales-Front (eds) *The Routledge Handbook of Study Abroad Research and Practice* (pp. 344–358). New York: Routledge.

Saldaña, J. (2015) *The Coding Manual for Qualitative Researchers*. Thousand Oaks, CA: Sage.

Sharma, S., Rahatzad, J. and Phillion, J. (2013) How preservice teachers engage in the process of (de)colonization: Findings from an international field experience in Honduras. *Interchange* 43, 363–377.

Valencia, R.R. (ed.) (1997) *The Evolution of Deficit Thinking: Educational Thought and Practice*. London: Routledge.

White, C.J. (2018) Agency and emotion in narrative accounts of emergent conflict in an L2 classroom. *Applied Linguistics* 39 (4), 579–598.

3 Japanese English Teachers' Professional Development in a Canadian University: Perceptions of Self and Imagining Practice

Steve Marshall

> 'As a role model for my students, I believe to continue my journey is very important. To explore new places and get to know new people would help me to broaden my horizons'.
>
> While participants may have been able to freely perceive their practice and sense of self, mentions of past, present and future performance were often tied to constraints in the school systems in which they work due to powerful social/institutional discourses.

Introduction

Japan is currently in the grips of its own version of internationalization in education, a process through which competence in English plays a key role. Japanese school boards have been looking for ways to improve, and perhaps move on from, traditional approaches to English language teaching that prioritize rote learning, grammar translation, vocabulary memorization and preparation for standardized examinations through prescribed curricula and textbooks. Such approaches, it has been said, have resulted in students who are unable to, or lack confidence to, communicate effectively in English after many years of study. Regarding the goals of English language education in Japanese schools, Bouchard (2017) cites Kubota (2011) when raising questions such as why young Japanese learners need to learn English considering many will not work in future jobs that require the language. Bouchard sums up some of the answers as

35

follows: English is the world's lingua franca; English speakers today are less bound by geography in terms of crossing borders; and competence in English can offer increased linguistic, cultural and economic capital.

When English language teachers leave Japan for professional development in countries such as Canada, they may be required to re-imagine their practice through reflective writing and to write action plans about who they are as teachers and where they want to go with their teaching. Reflective writing tasks such as these involve reflecting on past and recent practice, as well as re-imagining a future self, all of which is done during an identity switch from being a teacher to re-becoming a student. Engaging in such multilayered reflection also involves considering goals, opportunities and perceived constraints that may come with applying new knowledge in the future, as well as changes in beliefs and identities. This is the context of the study I present in this chapter.

The Study

I present selected data from a broader study of 16 Japanese English teachers who took part in a 10-week professional development program at a university in western Canada in collaboration with an urban school board in Japan. In this chapter, I focus on six participants and two key questions:

(1) How did the teacher-students express their perceptions of professional identities through reflective writing?
(2) How did the teacher-students conceptualize their future practice and application of knowledge learned during the program?

The program took place at a university in western Canada that I have called Western Metropolitan University (WMU; pseudonyms are used to refer to names of institutions and individuals). A feature of the program was homestay with a local family, which aimed to give teachers a chance to learn how local families live and to immerse themselves as much as possible in English-speaking environments. During the first five-week period, the teacher-students joined English language classes at the university's English Language Centre four days a week and did one day a week of TESOL study, during which they reflected on the classes they attended, writing reflective texts, which would culminate in an action plan on completion of the program. During the second five-week period, the teacher-students attended classes on approaches to education and TESOL, also visiting local schools and observing undergraduate education classes at the university.

After gaining ethics approval to carry out the study as the principal investigator, approximately one year after completing the program I emailed potential participants, inviting them to participate in semi-structured interviews via Zoom and/or to provide samples of texts written during the program. The six who agreed to participate were English language teachers in urban junior and senior high schools: Eiji, Mika, Tamiko, Toshi, Yuji and Akira. To guarantee confidentiality, I do not provide further information about their backgrounds, age, teaching experience and where they teach. In this chapter, I will analyze the reflective writing samples of the six participants, focusing on issues that relate to the two research questions above. Data excerpts have been selected from five writing tasks done during the program:

- Task 1: Review of professional development goals.
- Task 2: Reflection on experiences so far as a student and on TESOL.
- Tasks 3–5: Action plan: Exploring topics through to completion.

Study Abroad and Professional Identities

The focus of much of the study-abroad literature has been on the experiences of undergraduate and graduate university students, focusing on intercultural awareness, language learning, and impacts of post-study abroad (see, for example, recent studies by Amadasi & Holliday, 2018; Badwan, 2017; and Mocanu, 2019). The study-abroad experiences of teachers has also been the focus of various studies: for example, Rapoport's (2008) study of international exchange programs for educators from the United States and Russia; Santoro and Major's (2012) analysis of 15 Australian pre-service teachers who attended programs in Korea and India; Santoro, Sosu and Fassetta's (2016) examination of Scottish student teachers' attitudes to study abroad; and Bodycott's (2015) work on intra-group conflict between members of co-national groups studying abroad.

The experiences of pre-service and in-service teachers of English as a foreign language, attending professional development programs in Anglophone countries, has also been the subject of study. For example, Barkhuizen and Feryok (2006) analyzed the experiences of pre-service English teachers from Hong Kong participating in a short study-abroad program in New Zealand, highlighting the lessons learned by the researchers and the host institution. Devlin (2014) focused on learners' language contact experiences during study abroad, different loci of learning, and how learners' language developed over time, while Garbati and Rothschild (2016) studied the experiences of two study-abroad students, analyzing their reflective narratives and email communications for issues related to language, culture, identity, and the impacts of their experience. The focus on narratives, identities and impacts is also taken up by Barkhuizen (2017), who carried out follow-up interviews with one study-abroad participant from a program in New Zealand after a year of undergraduate study, and five years later after returning to Hong Kong.

Finally, a few studies have analyzed the experiences of Japanese pre-service and in-service teachers of English during study abroad in

Canada. Cook (2010) focused on a program in Canada designed for junior and senior high school Japanese teachers of English and how the program impacted participants' teaching practices six months after the program, then one year later. Cook found that the effective incorporation of content learned in Canada depended on the extent to which teachers were constrained by several factors, including grammar or translation-based entrance examination pressures, the perceived need to conform to colleagues' teaching practices, and whether teachers were teaching communication-oriented classes. Later, Cook and Gulliver (2014) addressed the challenges that Japanese teachers of English face when engaging with the theories and practices of communicative language teaching (CLT) in overseas teacher development programs. The authors highlighted some common constraints that Japanese teachers of English face, for example, 'entrance examination pressures, time constraints, fixed curricula, and mandatory government approved textbooks' (2014: 24), and offered recommendations for teaching such programs. With a focus on third-year teacher candidates from Japan, Douglas *et al.* (2018) analyzed the potential of narrative inquiry as a tool to gain insight into the students' 'storied experiences' (2018: 127) in a study-abroad program in western Canada that aimed to develop English language competence and content knowledge. Similarly, Moore *et al.* (2019) analyzed the experiences of Japanese secondary school teachers of English who took part in a program in western Canada, and the effectiveness of the program.

With a focus in this chapter on aspects of professional identity formation during study abroad, my analysis is based on the following understanding of identity/identities. I view the identity formation of participants in the study as fluid, not static; as perception as well as performance; as moving between essentialism, fixity, multiplicity and hybridity; as identities that are national, cultural, linguistic, professional, individual, collective; and as identities that are professional, teacher identities.

Kinginger (2015) and Barkhuizen (2017) have theorized identity in the specific contexts of study abroad, suggesting that 'student soujourners abroad may encounter challenges not only to their language skills but also to their identities' (Kinginger, 2015: 6, as cited in Barkhuizen, 2017). Accordingly, the identities of the participants in this study will inevitably have been impacted in different ways by changes in place (from Japan to Canada), changes in role (from practicing expert teachers to learning students), changes in setting in terms of local language(s) (from Japanese to English and other languages), and in terms of perceptions of a present and imagined future self. It is worth noting that a common feature of professional development programs such as the one that the participants took may be a shift from a relatively stable view of identity in terms of who you are (Edwards, 1985; Joseph, 2004; Marshall, 2010) to an identity, or identities, of what you might become (Hall, 1996). As teachers of English language who are taking a professional development program in a multi-lingual, yet Anglophone-dominant, province of Canada, language also plays a fundamental role in the participants' identity formation (Joseph, 2004; Marshall, 2009; May, 2000): for example, linguistic competence, the status of English in Japan and internationally, among other factors. Moreover, with the focus of this chapter on participants' written reflective texts as representations of evolving identities through mobility, Giddens' (1991) take on identity as 'a reflexively organised endeavour, involving a dialectical interplay of the local and the global' (1991: 5) and on 'the capacity to keep a particular narrative going ... the ongoing story of the self' (1991: 53–54) is also of relevance. That said, it is likely that partici-pants' identities tend to be not just about the self, but also the product of discursively constructed and negotiated practices, molded by social con-text and discourses (Benwell & Stokoe, 2006; Butler, 1993).

In the following section, excerpts of participants' reflective writing will be presented with mainly descriptive analysis. This will allow readers to engage with the data as a whole followed by a more theoretical analysis in the Discussion and Conclusion section.

Perceptions of Teacher Identity

Excerpts from five of the reflective texts written by participants during the program were analyzed for representations of factors relating to the two research questions. It should be noted that the writing tasks did not contain any explicit instructions to discuss identity as a concept. I thus present selected excerpts that illustrate factors that relate to the complex processes of identity formation during professional development abroad.

Eiji presented a complex professional identity in Task 1, in which he reviewed his professional development goals:

I don't want to change much.
I love teaching everyday conversation with authentic materials.
I can challenge myself.
I'd like to learn much more about the newest theories.
I feel the students there [in Japan] are slaves of system and they have to do the tasks they were imposed. It's not learning at all. I don't want to teach in that environment. To me, teaching English is teaching a way to communicate with people.

Eiji combines a stable sense of who he is as a teacher with aspects of imagining his future. He begins by describing a stable core identity of a teacher who knows who he is and who does not want to change much, with a passion and love for teaching his students, albeit with a willingness to take on new ideas. In doing this, he positions himself as a teacher who will put communication between himself and his students at the center of learning.

Mika also describes a complex sense of self as a teacher in the following excerpts from Tasks 1 and 2:

> I made my mind to go abroad and study English more there before I became a teacher. My English skill needed to be improved and I didn't have enough confidence to stand in front of students. [Task 1]

> As a role model for my students, I believe to continue my journey is very important. To explore new places and get to know new people would help me to broaden my horizons. [Task 1]

> As a junior high school teacher, I believe it is my responsibility to make my students be aware who they really are. [Task 1]

> I realize that I still have a kind of student's mind that teachers give us a lot of information. I'm standing between student's side and teacher's side. [Task 2]

In the excerpts from Task 1, Mika describes herself as a reflective teacher, aware of the need to study more and improve her English skills to gain confidence. She also self-identifies as someone who needs to be a role model to her students, and as a traveller on a journey, needing to go to new places and broaden horizons. She extends her self-identification to the importance of developing self-awareness and identity development among her students. In Task 2, Mika addresses the shift that teacher-students go through on professional development programs from being a teacher to re-becoming a student, explaining that she is standing between her teacher's side and her student's side, and is still able to enact her 'student mind'.

A strong feature of Kohei's writing was his aspiration to become a change-maker: 'I want to be a leading teacher because I want to devote my school life to teaching English and change the English teaching style in Tokyo. It's not because I want to raise my reputation' [Task 1]. Of note here is Kohei's explicit rejection of being a higher ranked teacher for personal reward, instead linking it to the desire to effect change in schools. In relation to this goal, Kohei was speaking from the experience of having failed to make change after a previous professional development experience outside of Japan: 'I have already tried to change our teaching style in my school, but it failed' [Task 1].

Like Eiji above, Tamiko, self-identified as a teacher who loves her job as an English teacher: 'I love teaching languages ... Also I love to learn some theories and methodologies by reading books regarding to SLA, Learning Skill Development, and of course TESOL' [Task 1]. And like Kohei, the stated aspiration to become a better teacher, based on idealism rather than personal benefit through promotion, was central to Tamiko's perception of purpose in participating in the program: 'I am very eager to be an expert to inspire my students' [Task 1]. Tamiko also described her process of re-becoming a student in a positive light:

> It has been a great experience being a student again. I can experience how students would feel when they are taking lessons. Furthermore, I can also

reflect on the things I felt and learned in my lessons by observing other teachers' lessons. [Task 2]

> As a student, it was hard for me to get motivated when teachers did not give lessons that I expected ... That discouraged me to try harder in class. On the other hand, I thought it was a very fascinating experience to nego-tiate our course syllabus in [teacher's name] class, who gave us a chance to go through and revise what we would be taught. [Task 2]

Tamiko's critical reflection of her revisiting the student experience com-bines positivity, insight into how it feels to be a student again, and learning (as a language student) through observing teachers during the first month of the course. She also refers to the challenges that come with attending classes, highlighting the positives and negatives of her experience.

Unlike some of the other participants, Akira referred to being pro-moted to a higher teaching position when considering his ideal future self. In his case, he linked it not only to more effective teaching, but also to the instrumental goal of getting paid more. He saw the professional develop-ment program as a stepping-stone to meeting this goal:

> My ideal self is to continue to teach in the same high school and to be a teacher with high English skill; not only using it but also teaching it effec-tively. And at the same time, I want to be promoted as a chief teacher so that I can get paid more ... So this TESOL program is the first step to be the ideal self in the future. [Task 1]

Finally, Toshi described himself as a novice, struggling to keep up in the early stages of his career:

> Perhaps, so far, I may have been just surviving days without setting any goals as a teacher. In that sense, I have been a novice. It does not mean I have been lazy not making any effort to improve myself. It was as if I had been drowning not capable of prioritizing all the things to do ... So, we are stabilizing our career, making experiments, and taking stock. We are experimenting by adopting certain theoretical methods, making trial and error. [Task 1]

In the excerpts above, participants write about their perceptions of self as a teacher (past, present and future) after becoming teacher-students during the program. Their responses encompass perceptions of what they are and what they may become, conceptualized during the process of re-becoming students. The identities they describe are multiple, complex, linking the present and the future, representing the desire to make a change, have an impact, and to develop and progress professionally. Summing up, a stable core identity was described by Eiji, a love for teaching by Eiji and Tamiko, being an intermediary between teachers and students (Eiji and Mika), being a change-maker (Mika and Kohei), lacking in English language skills (Mika and Akira), being a role model to students and a traveller (Mika), a self-aware student (Mika and Tamiko) and a novice (Toshi).

Applying New Knowledge: From Past to Imagined Future

The reflective writing tasks also asked the teacher-students to think about their practice – in particular, to look forward to how they might apply ideas studied during the program after returning to their schools in Japan. Eiji discussed his future teacher self in terms of letting go, thus allowing his students to develop more: 'I would like to be a teacher who can hand over the language learning to learners more' [Task 5]. Tamiko provided detailed explanations of how she envisaged applying knowledge learned on the program, first by describing how she used to teach:

> I did not give choices for them to choose what they want to learn. I tended to spoon-feed them from time to time; I fell into being a lawnmower teacher who didn't give them opportunities to make mistakes nor embraced their mistakes. I simply followed the textbooks and focused on teaching test-taking skills. I often asked them only one-answer questions instead of open-ended questions for them to think about the issue deeply and critically. I have to admit that I need to improve my critical pedagogy and teaching style. First, I would like to incorporate inquiry-based learning into my lessons. Inquiry-based learning will inspire students' questions and interests and enable them to make choices during their learning process. [Task 5]

> It is important to educate students to obtain autonomous learning ability. [Task 1]

> I also strongly desire to educate our students to be global mindset individuals who have a critical thinking skill to realize that they have the power to change the world that they are living in ... I know clearly now the reason why I teach English. I teach English for world peace. [Task 1]

> Although I listed various doable changes to establish better English education in my school in Japan, I can easily anticipate that it will not be so easy. Especially, it might be unacceptable for some teachers to change the way we assess students. In our school, we share the same test when we teach the same English class. If we have a very different view of the way to assess our students, there will be conflicts. [Task 5]

Tamiko's imagined future as a change-maker involves moving on from being a 'lawnmower teacher' to one who embraces inquiry-based learning. Through those two lenses, she imagines her future teacher self in terms of promoting learner autonomy, developing a global mindset that promotes world peace, while recognizing the constraints she may face in a system that requires a strong focus on standardized assessment.

Mika also mentioned the dominance of entrance exams as constraints, the need for more learner autonomy, and a desire to implement inquiry-based learning:

> Students are slaving away at their studying not only at school but also activities after school and they tend to obtain only useful knowledge

which they could use for exams [entrance exams]. On the surface, they look smart and obedient; however, their imagination would not be built up. [Task 5]

I would like to encourage students to analyze what they are interested in and why they have to study English ... Setting their goals to study English by themselves could help them to be motivated when they confront their difficulties. [Task 5]

I would like to try inquiry based learning such as a field work in a park. Students would be required to find their interests through the field work and to solve their questions within groups. [Task 1]

Having previously taken a professional development program in North America, Kohei reflected on past experience while looking forward, referring to the failed attempt (mentioned above) to change the assessment at his school. He thus aspires to becoming a leading teacher who will be able to make changes:

But it was refused and changed to 'memorization test' because they would stick to their experiences and never leave their familiar ways of teaching. I was disappointed and wished if I could have been very persuasive and convincing enough to make them understand based on the theories of English teaching ... In order to change the current English teaching style from old fashion teacher-centered lecture style to up-to-date communicative student-centered style, I think it's better for me to be a leading teacher in the future. [Task 1]

Finally, a constraint mentioned by Toshi in realizing his imagined future self as a teacher is not assessment, but the textbooks used in his classes:

It seems reasonable to set the goal in a statement like *to make the textbook interesting enough to engage students in the lesson* ... So, a teacher's role here is to bridge between the textbook and students. [Task 5]

Summing up the excerpts above, in which the participants, during the program, wrote about how they imagined their futures as teachers, and how they might apply knowledge from the program, the following aspects came to the fore: promoting learner autonomy (Tamiko), inquiry-based learning (Tamiko, Mika), the constraints posed by a rigid assessment framework and entrance exams (Tamiko, Mika, Kohei), the limitations of textbooks (Toshi) and the need to gain promotion to a position of authority to effect meaningful change (Kohei).

Discussion and Conclusion

In the excerpts of reflective writing above, the six participants in the study described their sense of self as teachers and a number of factors that relate to future applications of knowledge learned on the program. These reflections were written in the contexts of a professional development program that asked teachers to re-imagine their practice in terms of who they are and who they want to become (Hall, 1996) as English language teachers in Japanese junior and secondary high schools. The first research question asked the following: How did the teacher-students express their perceptions of professional identities through reflective writing? The answer to the question is: with considerable complexity and in an ongoing way, an ongoing narrative of the self, as described by Giddens (1991). In liminal spaces between Japan and Canada, teacher and student, Japanese and English language, old self and new self as a teacher, some participants stressed the importance of language as a key marker of identity (Joseph, 2004; Marshall, 2009; May, 2000) in their roles as language teachers, notably the need to improve their English language abilities, and described aspects of identities that relate to both *perception* and future *performance* as change-makers. While participants may have been able to freely perceive their practice and sense of self, mentions of past, present and future performance were often tied to constraints in the school systems in which they work due to powerful social/institutional discourses. It is in such contexts that teachers may become more likely to reproduce rather than challenge dominant discourses and structures (Archer, 2003; Benwell & Stokoe, 2006; Butler, 1993). And in the case of Kohei's stated failure to effect change, or Tamiko's cautioning that change in the assessment of courses could lead to conflict with colleagues, constraint can evidently over-ride the potential for teachers to exercise their agency as change-makers. Nonetheless, as stated by Pennycook (2007) in his work on global Englishes and transcultural flows, performance is not just about being able to perform what has been prescribed; it can also be about fashioning futures, or I would suggest, finding openings and spaces for change, thus engendering change, one step at a time, agentively and recursively, within educational structure (Giddens, 1984).

In conclusion, the study has illustrated the multilayered complexity of the imaginings of self and practice that six Japanese English language teachers experienced during a study-abroad professional development program in Canada. In doing so, it has perhaps raised as many questions as it has answered. Many of these remaining questions are beyond the scope of this chapter, for example, questions about effective content delivery, the balance between English language learning and TESOL on study-abroad programs, among many other issues. Answers to these and other questions lie in ongoing research, involving follow-up interviews with participants one year after taking the program as they take stock and reflect on what they have been able to achieve as teachers and how their teaching has developed post-program.

References

Amadasi, S. and Holliday, A. (2018) 'I already have a culture': Negotiating competing grand and personal narratives in interview conversations with new study abroad arrivals. *Language and Intercultural Communication* 18 (2), 241–256.

Archer, M.S. (2003) *Structure, Agency and the Internal Conversation*. Cambridge: Cambridge University Press.

Badwan, K.M. (2017) 'Did we learn English or what?': A study abroad student in the UK carrying and crossing boundaries in out-of-class communication. *Studies in Second Language Learning and Teaching* 7 (2), 193–210.

Barkhuizen, G. (2017) Investigating multilingual identity in study abroad contexts: A short story analysis approach. *System* 71, 102–112.

Barkhuizen, G. and Feryok, A. (2006) Pre-service teachers' perceptions of a short-term international experience programme. *Asia-Pacific Journal of Teacher Education* 34 (1), 115–134.

Benwell, B. and Stokoe, E. (2006) *Discourse and Identity*. Edinburgh: Edinburgh University Press.

Bodycott, P. (2015) Intragroup conflict during study abroad. *Journal of International Students* 5 (3), 244–259.

Bouchard, J. (2017) *Ideology, Agency, and Intercultural Communicative Competence*. Singapore: Springer.

Butler, J. (1993) *Bodies That Matter: On the Discursive Limits of 'Sex'*. New York: Routledge.

Cook, M.L. (2010) Outsourcing in-service education: The effects of a Canadian pedagogical programme on Japanese teachers of English teaching practices. Doctoral thesis, Macquarie University.

Cook, M. and Gulliver, T. (2014) Helping Japanese teachers of English overcome obstacles to communicative language teaching in overseas teacher development programs. *Asian EFL Journal Professional Teaching Articles* 79, 24–46.

Devlin, A.M. (2014) *The Impact of Study Abroad on the Acquisition of Sociopragmatic Variation Patterns: The Case of Non-Native Speaker English Teachers*. Bern: Peter Lang.

Douglas, S.R., Sano, F. and Rosvold, M. (2018) Short-term study abroad: The storied experiences of teacher candidates from Japan. *LEARNing Landscapes* 11 (2), 127–40.

Edwards, J. (1985) *Language, Society, and Identity*. Oxford: Basil Blackwell.

Garbati, J.F. and Rothschild, N. (2016) Lasting impact of study abroad experiences: A collaborative autoethnography. *Forum Qualitative Sozialforschung/Forum: Qualitative Social Research* 17 (2). https://doi.org/10.17169/fqs-17.2.2387

Giddens, A. (1984) *The Constitution of Society: Outline of the Theory of Structuration*. Berkeley: University of California Press.

Giddens, A. (1991) *Modernity and Self-Identity: Self and Society in the Late Modern Age*. Stanford, CA: Stanford University Press.

Hall, S. (1996) Who needs identity. *Questions of Cultural Identity* 16 (2), 1–17.

Joseph, J. (2004) *Language and Identity: National, Ethnic, Religious*. New York: Palgrave Macmillan.

Kinginger, C. (2015) Student mobility and identity-related language learning. *Intercultural Education* 26 (1), 6–15.

Kubota, R. (2011) Questioning linguistic instrumentalism: English, neoliberalism, and language tests in Japan. *Linguistics and Education* 22, 248–260.

Marshall, S. (2009) Languages and national identities in contact: The case of Latinos in Barcelona. *International Journal of Iberian Studies* 22 (2), 87–107.

Marshall, S. (2010) Re-becoming ESL: Multilingual university students and a deficit identity. *Language and Education* 24 (1), 41–56.

May, S. (2000) Uncommon languages: The challenges and possibilities of minority languages. *Journal of Multilingual and Multicultural Development* 21 (5), 366–385.

Mocanu, V. (2019) A mixed methods approach to identity, investment, and language learning in study abroad: The case of Erasmus students in Finland, Romania, and Catalonia. Doctoral dissertation, Universitat de Lleida.

Moore, A., Kubota, R., Balyasnikova, N. and Takeda, Y. (2019) Exploring the effectiveness of overseas professional development for EFL teachers. Presentation at the Canadian Association of Applied Linguistics, Vancouver, Canada.

Pennycook, A. (2007) *Global Englishes and Transcultural Flows*. New York: Routledge.

Rapoport, A. (2008) Exchange programs for educators: American and Russian perspectives. *Intercultural Education* 19 (1), 67–77.

Santoro, N. and Major, J. (2012) Learning to be a culturally responsive teacher through international study trips: Transformation or tourism? *Teaching Education* 23 (3), 309–322.

Santoro, N., Sosu, E. and Fassetta, G. (2016) 'You have to be a bit brave': Barriers to Scottish student-teachers' participation in study-abroad programmes. *Journal of Education for Teaching* 42 (1), 17–27.

4 Study Abroad as a Site of Transformative Learning: Post-Sojourn Knowledge and Identity Change of Two Cambodian Teachers

Rosemary Wette and Gary Barkhuizen

> *Transformative learning involves the alteration of people's frame of reference, which refers to the expectations, beliefs, feelings, attitudes and judgements that shape how they make sense of their experiences.*
>
> *'I now have new teachers coming up to me and asking me a lot of things about my experience in New Zealand, and I share a lot with them'.*

Introduction

For language teachers, studying abroad as international graduate students is invariably an intense personal and professional experience. It requires them to develop a number of personal qualities such as independence, resourcefulness and flexibility in an educational environment that may be quite different from their home countries, and is therefore likely to be a time of disorientation and fast learning (Kinginger, 2019). This chapter analyzes the plans, actions and reflections of two recently qualified EFL teachers from Cambodia in just this kind of situation. The teachers completed a graduate language teacher education qualification (MTESOL) on a one-year study-abroad program at a university in New Zealand, and then returned to Cambodia to continue their careers as English language educators. The study reported in this chapter responds to calls to increase the diversity of participants, sources and destinations in research on language teachers studying abroad (Plews & Jackson, 2017) and particularly their post-sojourn experiences in order to achieve a more holistic understanding of language teacher study abroad (LTSA). The study also explored Plews' assertion (2019: 158) that 'the greatest social consequence of LTSA is the transfer of new linguistic, cultural, intercultural and pedagogic knowledge to the domestic classroom'.

Professional and personal learning through a year of study abroad for a language teacher education qualification is significant and attained relatively rapidly. The type of professional knowledge gained by experienced teachers through in-service teacher education of this kind is likely to blend disciplinary or content knowledge with an understanding of learners' needs and teacher roles and draw on the teachers' prior experience to modify their existing knowledge base (Clandinin, 1985; Shulman, 1987). Opfer and Pedder (2011) advise that this kind of change is more likely to take place when a professional development initiative, such as study abroad, is intensive and sustained over a long period of several months, rather than brief or sporadic. A likely consequence of this shift in professional knowledge is personal growth and change in a teacher's identity. Research in teacher identity has recently tended to follow a poststructuralist agenda whereby identities are perceived to be 'socially constructed, self-conscious, ongoing narratives that individuals perform, interpret and project' (Block, 2014: 32) in interaction with others and objects in particular sociocultural contexts. When these contexts involve crossing 'major life boundaries' (Donato, 2017: 25), such as spending time studying and undertaking further teacher education abroad, identities are disrupted, sometimes contested, and certainly changed in the process.

In a number of publications over the past two decades, Jack Mezirow and associates (e.g. Mezirow, 1997, 2000; Taylor, 2000) have described a specific type of learning which they call transformative. It involves the alteration of people's frame of reference, which refers to the expectations, beliefs, feelings, attitudes and judgments that shape how they make sense of their experiences. The stages of transformative learning (a theory originally proposed to account for changes in women returning to education after a lengthy period in the home) report changes that affect emotional and cognitive aspects of learning and are influenced by the sociocultural contexts in which the learning takes place. Transformative learning comprises five main stages:

(1) A crisis event: It is usually initiated by some kind of significant personal event or crisis, described by Mezirow (2000: 22) as a 'disorientating dilemma'. Provided the person is able to acknowledge and process their own feelings and preconceptions, and is willing to change, this event leads to a second stage of critical reflection.
(2) Critical reflection: At this stage, previously held beliefs and taken-for-granted ways of thinking and acting are scrutinized.
(3) Planning and trialing of new options and roles: Exploration and planning of options for new roles, relationships and actions emerge as the

third phase of transformative learning, and the person independently considers and selects from available options.

(4) Professional and personal knowledge gains: Acquisition of requisite knowledge and skills to implement plans is the next priority, followed by some provisional trialing of new roles.

(5) A revised or transformed personal frame of reference: The final stage and outcome of transformative learning is an enhanced sense of self-efficacy, confidence and self-worth as the new perspectives are reintegrated into the revised frame of reference.

This account of the phases of transformative learning resonated strongly for us with the accounts Lina and Vin (both pseudonyms) gave of their during- and post-sojourn study-abroad experiences. We therefore planned to explore the effects of their experiences as transformative learning, and how the experiences continued to impact on their lives and work in classrooms and the workplace after they returned home. We asked the following research questions about these two teacher participants who had completed a postgraduate language teacher education qualification during their year of study abroad:

(1) What did they learn about themselves, personally and professionally?
(2) What was the impact of study abroad on their post-sojourn experience?

The Study

We used qualitative research methods (guided reflective writing, interviews and classroom observations) common to the study of social, emotional and cultural aspects of study abroad (Opfer & Pedder, 2011; Smolcic, 2013) to understand the two teachers' experiences and learning processes. The study took place over several months in two sites: the first was the university in New Zealand where the teachers completed eight courses in subjects such as computer-assisted language learning, language analysis for teachers, language testing and assessment, task-based language teaching, curriculum design, academic literacies development, and sociolinguistics as part of a one-year taught Master of TESOL (MTESOL) degree. The second was a language teaching center in Phnom Penh where both Lina and Vin took up positions (at different branches) on their return to Cambodia.

Lina and Vin each had three years' English teaching experience prior to studying abroad in New Zealand and had just successfully completed (Lina achieved an average GPA of 8.0 and Vin 8.5 out of a best-possible GPA of 9.0) their MTESOL qualification when the first interviews took place in Auckland. Data collection took place over a four-month period (plus a further interview with Lina eight months post-sojourn). The first round comprised a written reflection of two to three pages in response

Table 4.1 Data sources

	Interview themes	Written reflection themes	Observation
Immediate post-sojourn *Auckland*	• Personal history • Expectations and initial experiences • Professional learning • Support and assistance	• Significant new learning • Professional identity changes • Effecting change: constraints and opportunities	*Neither participant had teaching duties in Auckland*
4 months post-sojourn *Phnom Penh*	• Professional identity changes post study abroad • Further comment on implementing change and reflections on study abroad • Changed perspective on Cambodia • New professional roles	• Professional identity changes • Plans for change • Effecting change: constraints and opportunities	*Vin only; Lina had no teaching duties in February 2020* • Flipped learning • Communicative tasks and learner engagement
8 months post-sojourn (*via Zoom – Lina*)	• Online teaching and teacher training during lockdown in Cambodia • Reflections on new professional roles and study abroad as a personal experience		

to prompts provided by the researchers and an open-ended semi-structured interview of approximately 40 minutes with each participant in Auckland in November 2019. Another written reflection and interview were completed in Phnom Penh in February 2020, and we also observed a class session taught by Vin (Lina did not have teaching duties at that time). A third interview with Lina took place in July 2020. Interviews, which were audio-recorded and transcribed, were the primary data source for this study, supported by the written reflective comments and field notes taken by the researchers during the lesson and school observations. Each participant was interviewed by only one of us in order to establish and maintain a good rapport. A summary of the main themes explored at each time point and through each data-collection method can be seen in Table 4.1. Data was analyzed following the steps typical of thematic content analysis (Miles *et al.*, 2014). This process involved coding for themes common to both participants and that pertained particularly to transformative learning in relation to the two research questions.

Findings

As well as the prerequisite of a significant new event (such as study abroad), both Mezirow (1997) and Cushner and Mahon (2002) state that teachers need to be open to modifying current perspectives – both personal and professional – through critical reflection, and be able to integrate new learning into existing attitudes and beliefs. In reporting the findings, we drew on the two participants' readiness and ability to reflect on their study-abroad experiences in order to answer the research questions and to explore study abroad as a site of contextualized learning constructed by the teachers through their personal reflections and social interactions inside and outside the classroom (Putnam & Borko, 2000).

Transformative personal learning

Although professional knowledge changes were significant consequences of the teacher education qualification completed by Lina and Vin, as Taylor (2000: 303) asserts, personal changes such as 'the affective dimension of knowing, such as developing an empathic viewing of other perspectives and trusting intuition' also occur and are significant. These were evident in their reports of discomforting emotions of homesickness, alienation, anxiety and fear of failure that they had experienced in New Zealand (the 'disorientating dilemma' stage), which are said to initiate transformative learning. Lina's and Vin's descriptions revealed another prerequisite for transformative learning, namely, an ability to recognize and articulate their feelings and beliefs about their study-abroad experience. They reported that their feelings of disequilibrium in the first few weeks of study abroad resulted from the many and striking differences in thinking, social behavior and the environment they had noticed – not only in the educational arena but also in the management of everyday life experiences such as the weather, food, urban life and social customs.

As with other study-abroad students (e.g. Gu & Maley, 2008; Jackson, 2018), this sudden exposure to a very different environment had marked psychological, cognitive and emotional consequences, which were described by the teachers in the first interview. In their lives outside the university, both of them remarked on how much more independent they had become. Before coming to Auckland, they had lived at home with their parents or had been in very close contact with their first families. They also had well-established social networks of friends and colleagues. Lina contrasted her life at home, where 'I lived with my parents so a lot of the things they would do for me', with the experience of study abroad which obliged her to quickly learn to cook (guided by YouTube clips), as well as managing grocery shopping and other household chores. However, she reflected on this experience with a sense of satisfaction on her achievement: she felt that she had become a 'more confident, independent, and less stressed' person. Vin commented similarly, saying that he felt he had become 'very independent' in his thinking and actions and less likely to simply follow what others thought and did.

In the third stage of transformative learning where new options and actions are explored, the two teachers reported having sought out academic and personal support from a number of sources in the first semester of studies in New Zealand. Although contact with classmates outside the classroom had been limited and they had mixed mostly with other international students, and while they had found their classmates to be sympathetic and helpful during collaborative classroom tasks, they had envied local students' comparative confidence and assertiveness. Other sources of initial support included (for Lina) a student counsellor and former study-abroad student who advised about study techniques, and (for Vin) a course lecturer who provided clarification of the requirements of an assignment.

Transformative professional learning

Both teachers reflected on differences in educational practices between Cambodia and New Zealand, such as the expectation that in New Zealand students are capable of adopting a critical perspective on theories and of learning independently without substantial guidance from academic staff. These particular study skills were unfamiliar to the teachers and initially caused them much anxiety and stress. Lina had felt 'very afraid I might not do well because it was just very different', explaining that instruction in Cambodia followed a traditional lecture format, with assessment through examinations that tested students' ability to memorize information. As MTESOL students on fully-funded scholarships, in their first semester they both felt the weight of expectations from their funding bodies, but also from parents, colleagues and friends. However, they reported that the sudden realization that studying abroad at graduate level would be difficult and very different from their undergraduate studies at home was followed by a period of critical reflection about several beliefs and practices that they had previously considered the norm. From their interview interactions it appears that both were not only willing but resolute about learning the new disciplinary content and methodologies and adopting more independent ways of studying. Their determination and hard work helped them to overcome their initial anxiety and timidity and to learn how to communicate the kinds of clear arguments and critical perspectives that earned them very high course grades.

The two teachers' critical reflections, as recorded in written comments and their interviews, related to changes in their professional identities as a result of professional knowledge gains over the year and revealed an awareness of how their own culture had shaped their ways of thinking and acting. Their views on appropriate teacher classroom management had shifted from a teacher-centered approach with the teacher an authoritarian 'rule imposer' (Lina) who did not seek out students' perspectives and who used a blend of traditional and communicative methods of instruction, to a more constructivist-based philosophy with the teacher as facilitator, motivator and information source. They also saw students' needs as being at the center of classroom instruction. After study abroad, the teachers envisioned a new type of classroom instruction with new roles for themselves as teachers, based on their new perspectives and specific learning from the MTESOL program. Plans that they articulated for the post-sojourn period included the following:

- To incorporate a wider variety of accents and English varieties in their teaching materials, in the belief that this would help their learners communicate with other non-native speakers in Cambodia using English as a lingua franca, and also because of initial difficulties experienced by Vin in New Zealand with different non-native English accents.
- To supplement the global coursebooks they were obliged to use at home with authentic materials that would engage their learners' interest and allow a wider variety of characters and Englishes to be included, again with the aim of fostering awareness of cultural differences and intercultural competence (Lina and Vin).
- To use and allow learners to use their first language during lessons when appropriate (Lina).
- To be more flexible, 'more open to new ideas' (Lina) and willing to accommodate learners' needs and wishes in their general approach to instruction (Lina and Vin) rather than following conventional and traditional practices.
- To experiment with task-based/flipped learning approaches (where students spend most of the lesson time on collaborative, communicative tasks, with limited explicit instruction), leaving exercises from the coursebook to be completed during independent study (Lina and Vin).
- To develop learners' ability to question what they read and hear (Lina) and to convey a clear textual voice in their writing (e.g. IELTS[1] essays) (Vin).
- To provide their students with detailed and constructive feedback which they had found most useful on their MTESOL courses, rather than just a numerical mark or grade (Lin).
- To use technology for instructional and assessment purposes, for example, 'playful' quizzes that provide immediate feedback on errors (Vin).

While Lina and Vin still viewed themselves primarily as teachers (in fact, Vin asserted in a written reflection that 'I'm still the kind of teacher who wants to help each and every individual student reach their respective potentials. I want to make a difference as a teacher'), study abroad gave them the confidence and knowledge to state an intention of moving into management and academic leadership roles. Through the study-abroad experience they had clearly developed an enhanced sense of self-efficacy, defined by Bandura (1977: 3) as 'belief in one's capabilities to organize and execute the courses of action required to produce given attainments'. Vin reflected that he had developed understanding about life and ways of calmly finding solutions to any challenges he faced, and also that, with this new-found confidence, he was able to envision a future that included plans for more senior roles for himself in the teaching profession. However, his feelings were mixed: he realized that he had grown in confidence and had gained important knowledge and insights into second language teaching and learning, but admitted to also 'feeling anxious because my co-workers will look up to me for answers regarding teaching, with the expectation that I am a know-all person, while in fact, I am not, and no one is'. He was also concerned that his colleagues, family and friends 'seem to have high expectations of what I have learned … they also expect that I will get a really good job with a good salary, better than before I went to New Zealand'. Lina expressed no such reservations: she believed that the study abroad had 'built my confidence, self-esteem and resilience; it has toughened me up and taught me many useful life lessons'.

Post-sojourn transformative learning

Cushner and Mahon (2002) elicited reflective comments from 50 study-abroad student-teachers from the US about the impact of their experiences when they returned to work and live in their home country. Many of their comments had much in common with what we heard from Lina and Vin in their post-study-abroad interviews and written reflections. Topics on which there was agreement included gains in independence, a more positive self-image and a sense of authority, an interest in sharing new knowledge with colleagues and the acquisition of a more sophisticated, theory-based professional knowledge. They also developed a professional identity that enabled them to seek out opportunities for professional advancement post-sojourn and an ability to hold views that mediated between home and host cultures with respect to approaches to second language teaching and learning.

In common with a group of British undergraduate year-abroad students (Tracy-Ventura et al., 2016), Lina and Vin returned home with more motivation and confidence, having become more resourceful and autonomous. They reported a changed perception of themselves and a more resilient sense of self overall. Both teachers spoke in their interviews and reflections more than once about growth in confidence, and Vin believed he had also learned how to work through challenging tasks. He reflected that 'perseverance is the biggest thing that is valuable for me, also living in a different environment where I did not know how to cope and I learned how to cope and how to live on my own'. In the interview with Lina in 2020, during a period of lockdown due to the Covid-19 pandemic, she reflected that she had volunteered to advise colleagues about online teaching because 'I'm still confident with myself, even now when – suddenly, like everything turned from physical to online. Because I took two online courses in NZ, I learned faster than the other teachers, so I became a trainer for online teaching'. Like the students in the Cushner and Mahon study (2002), her worldview had expanded as a result of transformative learning, and she commented that 'the experience of going to study abroad has made me much more mature. I've learned to be more humble, more grateful and to tolerate different changes in general because I've seen the world much bigger than when I was in Cambodia'.

Lina and Vin also reported changes in how they were perceived by others. This was something of a concern for Vin, who expressed dismay about differences in the way some people related to him after he returned from study abroad. He gave the example of colleagues who used to relate to him as 'just another teacher ... they would talk to me normally like friends; they were not afraid to talk to me'; however, he had noticed on his return that 'a few people, when they talk to me, they're really nervous and very polite talking to me. The relationship is kind of distant'. Despite feeling disappointed about the social distance that had developed between themselves and some colleagues, Lina and Vin were pleased about having developed a stronger sense of authority and self-efficacy, as well as a willingness to share their new knowledge within their institutions. Their desire for professional advancement seems to have been realized very soon after they returned to their jobs in Cambodia. Within three months, Lina reported that she had (i) taken on a number of academic management duties (in addition to teaching one class) that included being part of a team to select a new coursebook and to incorporate communicative language teaching into the curriculum, (ii) planned to enrol in a course to become a CELTA trainer, and (iii) advised the next group of scholarship students who were about to travel to New Zealand. Four months after that, in the middle of a Covid-19 lockdown, she reported that she was training teachers who had minimal experience in online teaching, mentoring other teacher trainers in her institution, as well as devising an interactive course that would help high school students prepare for the traditional (grammar-based) national school-leaving exam. She reflected that 'I now have new teachers coming up to me and asking me a lot of things about my experience in New Zealand, and I share a lot with them'. Vin was using what he had learned about computer-assisted language learning to assist colleagues, and commented that he was now regarded as 'somebody who is a point of contact for any questions regarding teaching. And I'm also seeing myself as part of a larger group, which is a management team'. He declared a long-term plan of becoming 'an academic coordinator – or maybe a campus manager'.

The teachers' accounts provided evidence on which they drew from and applied what they had learned from their studies in New Zealand. Lina reported that she 'used what I learned from the courses in New Zealand: I go back to my notes and take materials from them'. In comments by Vin in an interview after we had observed him teach an intermediate-level class, he referred to his MTESOL studies, saying that he felt he was now able to 'develop a sense of purpose for each activity that I'm using', and to connect his instruction with the theories of second language learning he had learned about. He had shifted from relying on traditional, teacher-centred methods to more inductive, task-based teaching, and included in the lesson we observed were a group jigsaw task, a collaborative writing task and personalized examples for present simple vs. continuous contrasts to engage students' interest. Drawing on a 'flipped learning' approach, he assigned preparatory learning and exercises from the core textbook for out-of-class work.

The final change that Lina and Vin most evidently share with other study-abroad teachers (Cushner & Mahon, 2002) was to reveal that their thinking involved critical distancing from the norms and practices of both home and New Zealand cultures. Although in her teaching Lina endeavored to fit Anglo-Western practices into the traditional curriculum and the quite conservative global course textbook she was obliged to use, she commented (with some feelings of remorse) that 'I tend to get quite frustrated when things are different from New Zealand. Just a little bit. I complained a lot when I came back, which is not good, because I used to live here'. She also reported a personal source of frustration – that she had not been able to maintain the independence she had been so proud to achieve in New Zealand: 'I miss the lifestyle in general. I was independent. Kind of all by myself there and I enjoyed it a lot. Now I've come back I live with my family. There is something going on at home again – a curfew – parents calling to ask me where I am'. Vin's comment on this topic was one of personal longing: 'Some of my friends are now in New Zealand on 2020 scholarships. They've been posting photos of New Zealand nature and I'm starting to miss it'.

Implications

We can see implications of this investigation of the study-abroad and post-sojourn experiences of two teachers from south-east Asia for the following groups of people: (a) teachers and those providing an orientation course for prospective study-abroad teachers, and (b) course lecturers and those responsible for providing pastoral care and educational support in the host country. Lina and Vin were of the opinion that the pre-departure course for study-abroad teachers needed to give realistic advice about the heavy workload of the MTESOL, and the very different, more independent way of studying that would be expected of them. Vin also felt that he would like to have known more about the host academic culture and to have had a basic course in Anglo-Western academic writing practices. When Lina talked to prospective study-abroad teachers on her return to Cambodia, she advised them to 'prepare mentally for the workload, work very hard from the beginning, seek support if they need to, and be confident'. These statements support Mezirow's (1997) assertion that it is important for educators preparing sojourners for the kind of transformative learning that is likely to occur during study abroad to foster the development of critical reflection and autonomy through inter- active tasks such as problem-solving, group projects, role play and simu- lations that 'help learners [become] aware and critical of their own and others' assumptions' (Mezirow, 1997: 10).

The findings of this study also carry a message for managers of study abroad, both in the home and host countries, with regard to giving realis- tic information about what can be expected in terms of academic work- load, the nature and evaluation of assignments, and personal and student lifestyle, drawing on the experiences of those who have recently completed the study-abroad program. Study-abroad teachers need to be provided with opportunities to reflect on and acknowledge the inevitable identity negotiations and changes that will take place in their academic institu- tions and activities, and in life beyond their university courses. They should be prepared for changes to the ways they see themselves and how others see them with respect to their linguistic self-concept (how they see themselves as language learners and language users), their current and future professional roles, and their personal growth (Benson *et al.*, 2013).

There is also a need for close personal support, especially during the initial period in the host country. 'Take-home' points for teachers of study-abroad students (or teacher educators working with study-abroad teachers) include the need to attend to the relational aspects of teaching and learning in their classrooms (Mercer & Dörnyei, 2020) and, more specifically, the affective as well as language and learning needs of newly arrived study-abroad students. Encouraging peer support and a bonded class group through collaborative in-class activities and assignment tasks, and peer feedback on drafts of writing, for example, would be helpful strategies.

Conclusion

This study has provided evidence in support of Plews' (2019) claim that it is in the transfer of professional, intercultural and personal learning to the post-study-abroad classroom that significant benefits of study abroad are to be found. Study abroad is clearly a profound experience that is likely to initiate a transformation of a teacher's professional identity and knowledge base, and its impact on the self-perceptions and instructional practices of our participants appeared to be enduring. It is therefore an immensely valuable, worthwhile investment for educational providers with the potential for significant, long-lasting benefits for their institu- tions. Reflecting on our discussions with Vin and Lina and their written comments, we can see their progression through the stages of transforma- tive learning as outlined by Mezirow during and after their study abroad: phases of confusion and resolution to succeed that had eventually resulted in taking on new academic and professional roles and a fresh sense of themselves as independent adults and skilled professionals. However, Lina and Vin had also made some wistful comments about moving away from their previous identities and social/professional roles. This reservation notwithstanding, study abroad is clearly an immensely worthwhile investment for educational providers with the potential for significant, long-lasting benefits for their employees and institutions.

administrat
Stakeholder
Ministry of edu-
Somali. E. teachers

Note

(1)   International English Language Testing System.

References

Bandura, A. (1997) *Self-Efficacy: The Exercise of Control*. New York: W.H. Freeman.

Benson, P., Barkhuizen, G., Bodycott, P. and Brown, J. (2013) *Second Language Identity in Narratives of Study Abroad*. London: Palgrave Macmillan.

Block, D. (2014) *Second Language Identities*. London: Bloomsbury.

Clandinin, D.J. (1985) Personal practical knowledge: A study of teachers' classroom images. *Curriculum Inquiry* 15, 361–385.

Cushner, K. and Mahon, J. (2002) Overseas student teaching: Affecting personal, professional and global competencies in an age of globalization. *Journal of Studies in International Education* 6, 44–58.

Donato, R. (2017) Becoming a language teaching professional: What's identity got to do with it? In G. Barkhuizen (ed.) *Reflections on Language Teacher Identity Research* (pp. 24–30). New York: Routledge.

Gu, Q. and Maley, A. (2008) Changing places: A study of Chinese students in the UK. *Language and Intercultural Communication* 8 (4), 224–245.

Jackson, J. (2018) 'Breathing the smells of native-styled English': A narrativized account of an L2 sojourn. In C. Borghetti and A. Beaven (eds) *Study Abroad and Interculturality: Perspectives and Discourses* (pp. 20–36). New York: Routledge.

Kinginger, C. (2019) Four questions for the next generation of study abroad researchers. In M. Howard (ed.) *Study Abroad, Second Language Acquisition and Interculturality* (pp. 263–278). Bristol: Multilingual Matters.

Mercer, S. and Dörnyei, Z. (2020) *Engaging Language Learners in Contemporary Classrooms*. Cambridge: Cambridge University Press.

Mezirow, J. (1997) Transformative learning: Theory to practice. *New Directions for Adult and Continuing Education* 74, 5–12.

Mezirow, J. (2000) Learning to think like an adult: Core concepts of transformation theory. In J. Mezirow (ed.) *Learning as Transformation: Critical Perspectives on a Theory in Progress* (pp. 3–32). San Francisco, CA: Jossey Bass.

Miles, M.B., Huberman, A.M. and Saldaña, J. (2014) *Qualitative Data Analysis* (3rd edn). Thousand Oaks, CA: Sage.

Opfer, V.D. and Pedder, D. (2011) Conceptualising teacher professional learning. *Review of Educational Research* 81, 376–407.

Plews, J. (2019) Language teacher education in study abroad contexts. In G. Barkhuizen (ed.) *Qualitative Research Topics in Language Teacher Education* (pp. 155–160). New York: Routledge.

Plews, J. and Jackson, J. (2017) Introduction to the special issue: Study abroad to, from, and within Asia. *Study Abroad Research in Second Language Acquisition and International Education* 2, 137–146.

Putnam, R. and Borko, H. (2000) What do new views of knowledge and thinking have to say about research on teacher learning? *Educational Researcher* 29, 4–15.

Shulman, L. (1987) Knowledge-base and teaching: Foundations of the new reform. *Harvard Educational Review* 57, 1–22.

Smolcic, E. (2013) 'Opening up to the world'? Developing interculturality in an international field experience for ESL teachers. In C. Kinginger (ed.) *Social and Cultural Aspects of Language Learning in Study Abroad* (pp. 75–99). Amsterdam: John Benjamins.

Taylor, E.W. (2000) Analyzing research on transformative learning theory. In J. Mezirow (ed.) *Learning as Transformation: Critical Perspectives on a Theory in Progress* (pp. 285–328). San Francisco, CA: Jossey Bass.

Tracy-Ventura, N., Dewaele, J.-M., Köylü, Z. and McManus, K. (2016) Personality changes after the 'year abroad'? *Study Abroad Research in Second Language Acquisition and International Education* 1 (1), 107–127.

5 Life and Learning through Study Abroad: Trajectories Connecting Identity and Communicative Repertoires

Donna Starks and Howard Nicholas

This chapter outlines how the processes of noticing and selecting features to fill lexical holes led one Vietnamese EFL teacher to notice, connect and align communicative features with identity constructs in response to selected moments of communicative challenge during his study abroad.

'i didn't understand him . to say i just understood for ... { + } "twenty per cent or thirty per cent"/ yeah so . it was . a little bit terrified/ i was a little bit terrified at that time actually'.

Introduction

Individuals imagine belonging to the worlds associated with their additional language (Norton & Pavlenko, 2019) in complex ways. Consequently, additional language learning journeys involve building complementary communicative and identity repertoires through engagement with lived experiences. In this chapter we consider the consequences of communicative challenges faced during study abroad by one Vietnamese EFL teacher who had returned to Vietnam after completing an in-service language teaching program in Australia.[1] We unpack his responses to communicative challenges and how these connect with how he assembled and aligned features within his communicative repertoire as part of building his identity repertoire. In this specific instance, many of the challenges and features are associated with vocabulary.

To access individual language-related experiences, we draw on personal narratives, as they provide insights into events in ways that highlight participants' voices and their lived experiences. Narratives are a particularly apt choice as a method for considering how an individual's identity changes and the reasons behind those changes (Benson *et al.*, 2012). One reason for this is because of how narratives connect participants' decisions/actions to their experiences. The selected narratives that we consider in this chapter focus on communicative challenges and their resolution. This thematic choice enables us to analyze how particular communicative features are used in enacting unfolding identities. In this way, narratives offer insights into imagined belongings, the important events that affect these imaginings, various connections between how communicative repertoires are built, as well as illuminating the complex and varied constructions within identity repertoires.

Identity and Communicative Repertoires

Research on study abroad has documented diverse evidence of identity transformation as well as a change in the communicative repertoires of the individuals involved in study abroad. For example, Du (2015) reported how American study-abroad students in China created 'opportunities to use [Mandarin]' and through this process made 'critical discoveries about their identity' (2015: 262). Karakas (2020) detailed how Turkish scholars' experiences abroad contributed to personality changes and a new awareness of self. From a slightly different perspective, Song (2016) reported how Korean teachers of English shifted their teacher identity constructs to reveal 'different models of curriculum, identity and practice' (2016: 651) when responding to the perceived English proficiency of their students who had studied abroad.

Although identities are widely accepted as multiple, interacting and changing, there has been very little discussion of how facets of identities combine and interact in the process of change. Several researchers have shed some understanding on this issue through the idea of an 'identity repertoire' (see Nagel, 1995; Varis *et al.*, 2011; Valle, 2020). In one example of engagement with identity repertoires, Amara and Schnell (2004: 191, n. 1) have written about the need to consider the complex interrelations among identities as each facet of the repertoire takes its turn in 'the centre of the identity field as a response to everyday practices' (2004: 191, n. 1). Still other researchers who have explored the notion of identity repertoires have engaged with the ways in which language features interact with identity repertoires. In this view of complex wholes, Halwachs (1993) makes use of Wandruszka's (1981) idea of a polysystem and Gregory's (1967) concept of a diatype, in relation to recognizable clusters of diverse language features that form a whole for a (group of) speaker(s). From this perspective, Halwachs (1993: 88–89) sees identity repertoires and communicative repertoires as inter-related and identity choices as co-existing with choices about particular linguistic/language varieties in 'identity revealing acts' in specific situations.

We see an identity repertoire as being established through features that are connected and aligned in ways that reference particular norms (see Nicholas & Starks, 2014). This perspective makes the notion of an identity repertoire particularly useful in advancing the connection between identity and the building of communicative repertoires. We draw on the concept of identity repertoire to explore multiple inter-related individual identity constructions. We focus on how features, that are assembled in the communicative repertoire, cluster and overlap to enable new identities to be created in ways that align with or alter the existing identity repertoire and the growing communicative repertoire.

We see the emergence of identities through the selected alignment of communicative and identity features as an inherent part of language learning. The selection of features for identity purposes can come from existing features that are reinterpreted or reconfigured or from newly discovered features. To understand the processes that drive language internalization, including how communicative features get noticed, we take as our beginning point Schmidt's formulation of the noticing hypothesis (Schmidt & Frota, 1986; Schmidt, 1990, 1995, 2001), where noticing leads to learners paying attention to features of input such that they are able to internalize and use the feature attended to.

From this base, more recent research into vocabulary acquisition has considered whether/how vocabulary holes are noticed (De Vos *et al.*, 2019). De Vos *et al.*'s experimental study asked learners to refer to something whose name was unknown and then investigated their subsequent learning of the relevant word. They found that noticing a hole had a significant benefit for subsequent implicit vocabulary learning.

Their research on vocabulary acquisition suggests that L2 learners are able to notice the complete absence of a resource and this kind of noticing appears to allocate 'more attentional resources to the input' (De Vos *et al.*, 2019: 511) to support filling a hole in their vocabulary. If learners function in this way in their vocabulary learning, we contend that it may also be possible to consider that learners can notice a hole in their identity repertoire. We believe that this research agenda can potentially offer up a way to understand how the processes of identity building are configured to enable exploration of what is involved in understanding and expanding identity repertoires and their complementary communicative repertoires. By introducing the issue of total absence of knowledge (holes), De Vos *et al.* created a way of understanding contexts of incomplete knowledge, that they refer to as 'gaps'. We use these concepts of holes and gaps to explore how holes in the communicative repertoire are filled in relation to holes and gaps in identity construction.

This idea is of importance because in Nicholas and Starks (2014, 2019) we argued that the learner needs to notice a communicative feature to select it into their communicative repertoire. In this work, we contended that as a feature is brought within the communicative repertoire, it is able to be connected with an array of other features that can be drawn on in the deployment of a communicative act. What is currently underdeveloped in the field (including in our own research) is an analysis of how selected features are connected within a communicative repertoire and how these communicative features align with features of the identity repertoire. This chapter outlines how the processes of noticing and selecting features to fill lexical holes led one Vietnamese EFL teacher to notice, connect and align communicative features with identity constructs in response to selected moments of communicative challenge during his study abroad.

Methodology

Personal narratives offer a multitude of insights into events, the importance of these events in the lives of the narrators, and the narrators' positioning of themselves (Depperman, 2015). As such they offer potentially rich insights into the nuancing of how identity can be seen as multiple and multifarious, fluid, intersecting, and subject to change over time.

The narratives considered here came from written responses to a series of emailed prompts and oral follow-ups of those responses in an 80-minute face-to-face interview. They were provided by a participant who we will refer to as Minh. Minh had been part of a two-year postgraduate in-service teacher program in Australia (Starks & Nicholas, 2020) and at the time of the interview had returned to Vietnam to work in the tertiary context he had worked in prior to his study abroad.

We selected Minh as our case study as both authors had taught him and knew him well. We knew that if he agreed to participate, he would be invested in the task and that he would be honest enough to report his perceptions of his actual experiences, good and bad. His narratives were about past experiences in Australia and the later reporting of these events in Vietnam enabled more time for critical reflection, a key contributor to identity construction (Li, 2011). The portions of Minh's stories that we analyzed drew on narrations related to three time periods in Minh's life: (a) his future imagined views of self from the time prior to departure for Australia, (b) his lived experiences in Australia, and (c) his reflections on his identity after he had returned home to Vietnam. Stories about his imagined future self prior to study abroad provide understandings of pre-existing linguistic capital and the associated ideologies. This information sets the scene for understanding change. Stories about his lived experiences in Australia provide understandings of how encounters in his daily life during his study abroad connect with his imagined self. These reported experiences introduce critical moments during Minh's journey where he noticed particular features that he later drew on to nuance his identity. Narratives about his life after return help in understanding the long-term impact of the study-abroad experience for the construction of his identity and communicative repertoires. In analyzing the data, we considered where Minh mentioned features of language, and what they reveal about how facets of his identity shaped the selection, connection and alignment of communicative and identity features.

Minh's Imagined Trajectory

Minh's comments about his imagined experiences in Australia suggested that he was heavily invested in learning some form of native speaker English, but not one associated with any specific national identity. He listed his options as Australia, the US or the UK, three locations that Minh felt had large numbers of native English speakers and education systems that he considered to offer similar opportunities for a prestigious education:[2] 'i intended to do a Master of TESOL or Applied Linguistics in either Australia, US or UK [an English-speaking country with a prestigious education system] in 2010 when i was a young teacher of English at …'. From this starting point, we might expect Minh to seek to engage in activities related to his profession as an English language teacher and that he might have no particular investment in any specific regional or local form of English. In his words:

> before arriving in Australia, i had many dreams about communication and work experience in Australia. i hoped to be as proficient at English as a native speaker. i hoped i could understand every word when i watched English movies, for example. i hoped to work part time at an English language centre for refugees or international students to gain teaching experience.

In his narrative, he envisaged an ideal world that would enable him to be 'as proficient at English as a native speaker' so that he would be able to 'understand every word' and have improved teaching skills. In other words, his imagined communicative journey was one that encompassed a development of linguistic and professional identity.

Minh's Initial Experiences

While the stories of his imagined experiences positioned Minh as confident and knowledgeable, events after his arrival challenged this imagining. In describing an early trip to a former gold mine in Ballarat (a historical site in the Australian state where he studied), he recounted that he had had difficulty understanding the tour guide, assessing the amount of his comprehension as 20–30%. He described his reaction to his perception of his language competence, as a 'little bit terrified'. In this excerpt, he repeated this emotion a second time, 'I was a little bit terrified', and finally in his summary statement about the event, he reiterated it but this time without the qualifier, 'the man from the ballarat terrified me ((laughs))', with a laugh that seemed to us to reflect the unease he felt at the time of the experience about the hole in his communicative repertoire.

> after few days we were taken to a trip to ballarat . to the mine gold . gold mine/ and the er the guide i thought he was local people there/ i couldn't understand him/ i hardly . i didn't understand him . to say i just understood for .. { + } 'twenty per cent or thirty per cent'/ yeah so . it was . a little bit terrified/ i was a little bit terrified at that time actually.

In describing this experience, Minh did not explain his reactions at the time but the absence of explanation in his story suggested that the nature of the experience left him feeling he had few options to communicate. In later stories, he recounted similar trepidation. In describing his experiences at a local market, Minh expressed a lack of confidence that we associate with his earlier feelings of fear at not understanding. In this reporting, he described this encounter as creating a feeling of uncertainty, 'when i went to the market with the farmers. local farmers i was not confident at all', where he talked 'very little'. In a classic Labov and Waletzky (1997) narrative, the initial experiences that Minh reported constitute a series of complicating events that reveal a hole in his communicative repertoire and a perceived gap in his identity repertoire: he did not feel that he was someone 'as proficient at English as a native speaker'.

This gap in his identity is entangled with a professional identity that was distant from the identities evoked by his experiences with the tour guide in Ballarat and the traders in the market. Minh initially dealt with the associated hole in his communicative repertoire by referring to features of his identity repertoire. He categorized the varieties of the tour guide and the traders as ones that he 'was not invested in'. He separated the identities associated with these varieties from his own, describing them as 'very different' and as ones that he did not 'really care about'.

> i talk very little but i was not invested in this aspect of social life umm the english was very different for the market/ most of them were local farmers and er i didn't really care about what they say or they call out at the market i was just looking and very . i talked to them very little yeah i was not very confident about my english within the . the market yeah

Minh reported on how his experiences with the tour guide and traders contrasted sharply with his prior construction of his identity as someone who had done quite well on IELTS and was already familiar with the associated Australian accent.

> i say oh aussie that was too difficult strange for me/ even i took the ielts i got quite well a good score and in the ielts test there were aussie australian voice as well . accent as well but the man from the ballarat terrified me ((laughs)).

The facet of his identity repertoire that was foregrounded in the study-abroad context of Australia was also challenged in social interactions in informal academic contexts. When he tried to socially interact with his peers in informal academic contexts, he found fellow international students living in Australia spoke Englishes that he sometimes found difficult to understand.

> the difficulty was listening to fellow students coming from Indonesia, Papua New Guinea, and Muslim people from Iraq, Iran, Sri Lanka, etc. admittedly, i sometimes just nodded my head without understanding when i talked to [name of student], [a] student from Papua New Guinea

These initial experiences impacted on Minh's sense of self and presented a perceived obstacle to his goal of becoming as proficient as a native speaker. At this point in his journey, these social encounters served to consolidate his attention to his identity as a professional English language teacher and the communicative features associated with that identity: 'my first week at [ ] University was with IAP course. in the classroom or in the library, Australian English was not too difficult'. Thus, while this particular sense of self as a proficient English speaker was challenged by experiences associated with social uses of Australian English, Minh was able to maintain an identity as a professional English language teacher and align that identity with features of English that he perceived as 'not too difficult'. These alignments within his identity repertoire came into play in subsequent communicative encounters that Minh experienced that contributed to expansions of his communicative repertoire that we present next.

Connecting the Communicative and Identity Repertoires

Minh narrated how throughout his study-abroad experience he regularly encountered new vocabulary. He talked about these encounters in ways that were consistent with his identity as an English language teacher. In the following three excerpts from his narratives, he reported on how he analyzed communicative features that he encountered in various events to build new knowledge. In the first example, he reported on a use of the word 'beautiful' as an interjection for 'approval, delight, enthusiasm' (Macquarie Dictionary and Thesaurus, 2020) that was new to him. In reporting on his analysis of the communicative feature that he encountered during the event, he recounted how he took note of the context of the interaction, the question-answer-response sequence that occurred, alternative vocabulary options, and how this newly encountered use of this lexical item had been absent in curriculum materials that he had previously encountered.

> and i was surprised with the word beautiful in the . in [ ] bank for example . the staff always said ↑ **beautiful** when they ask me to fill in the form they said ↑ **beautiful** they asked question and i answer and they said ↑ **beautiful/** and we never use that word for . with comment before/ we say very good or great but we didn't say **beautiful/** and even in the . in the

materials for learning or on the website we didn't . really experience that word . that comment/ they said **beautiful** we said great or good or excellent

In his reflection, he positioned himself as a professional English language teacher. In reporting on the use of the word 'beautiful', he articulated the word '↑ *beautiful*' confidently, with the intonational contour characteristic of its use in Australian English.

The professional facet of his identity emerged a second time when he reported on the value of mistakes he made in understanding Australian vocabulary. In this particular excerpt, the unknown word (the vocabulary hole) is 'aussie', a colloquial term for a person from Australia.

ah i think for .. the most funny experiences for the very first few days i i was in australia . i was . at that time i was looking for the . for apartment for for for rent [D: um hm] yes and i went to the residential services at latrobe/ and i saw some **adverts** and i i was interested in <u>one</u> that says er a three bed room flat [D: ok] **and two aussie girls** [D: um hm] = i did er i **asked people aussie aussie girls where are they from and they laughed at me they say aussie australia** i didn't know that slang that that **aussie word** ((laughs))/ and that was quite funny/

In relation to this example, he recounts how this encounter with the word 'aussie' prompted him to recognize that this was a word that he didn't know. In his detailing of how he had responded to what he had noticed, he did so in ways that were reminiscent of his identity as an English language teacher. He actively asked about the meaning of the lexical item and reflected on what others said in response to his query.

Minh used 'aussie' five times in this part of his narrative. In the first three uses, he replicated what was written on the advertisement, 'aussie girls'. Then he moved beyond this usage, using 'aussie' as a noun, 'aussie Australia' and later as an adjective 'aussie word'. In other words, his repeated uses of the word demonstrate that he has filled a hole that he had noticed in his communicative repertoire, selected that feature into his communicative repertoire, and built connections to other features of his communicative repertoire.

Thus far in our analysis, we have shown how Minh engaged with newly encountered lexical items in ways that aligned with his identity as an English language teacher. The excerpts themselves were of interest for another reason. Minh's use of these two Australian expressions performed membership of an Australian English community. Other vocabulary that he used in his story also added to this facet of his identity repertoire. In the above excerpt, he used the shortened form of the word 'advertisement'. This shortening also positioned Minh as a member of an Australian English community.

Although these lexical items created an alignment with a general (national linguistic) identity rather than an academic one, Minh embraced these vocabulary items. One potential reason for this is because both were appropriate for selection in formal contexts, a bank and a university housing office, and were able to perform the identity of an Australian-trained EFL teacher.

When we conducted the interview after his return to Vietnam, Minh acknowledged that he was now easily identified as having been trained in Australia and that this identity as an Australian-trained EFL Vietnamese language teacher was now part of his identity repertoire. In reporting on this, he commented, 'I feel quite happy with that'.

Discussion

In this chapter we have focused on the narrated experiences of one Vietnamese teacher of English to focus on how the two parallel constructs, identity repertoires and communicative repertoires, engage with one another in shaping trajectories of learning. We have built on the finding by De Vos *et al.* (2019) that once learners notice a hole/gap in their communicative skills, they are better positioned to acquire communicative features to fill in what is missing. We draw on (in this case) the concept of a hole in one's communicative repertoire and the concept of holes and gaps in one's identity repertoire to show how individuals select, connect and align communicative features to nuance their communicative and identity repertoires.

This case study illustrates how one Vietnamese teacher who had studied abroad drew on his existing identity repertoire to metalinguistically analyze communicative features around him to gain control over those communicative features. We have shown how his processes enabled him to align and elaborate a new identity as an Australian-trained Vietnamese EFL teacher, an identity construct compatible with his existing multiple identities as a language teacher, as an English language speaker, and as a professional. In this way, the case study shows how multiple events from multiple contexts interact. This interaction is an important process in the parallel development of communicative and identity repertoires and the creation of new identities to build on existing identities. This is especially important for teachers of additional languages whose professional identity needs to align with their other identities, including their identity in their first language and culture, their identity as a teacher, and their identity as a speaker of an additional language.

Practical Implications

This case study has reinforced how study-abroad experience nuances the connections between communicative and identity repertoires. In particular, it has shown how the interweaving of communicative and identity repertoires contributes to the process of language acquisition through noticing, selecting, connecting, aligning and ultimately deploying communicative features. The findings show how identity repertoires are not shaped by what is encountered, but rather by how the learner connects what has been encountered with other features of the identity and communicative repertoires. For this participant, these connection processes were conscious ones articulated through personal narratives. Our understanding of the processes of selecting, connecting and aligning clusters of features and how they help build communicative repertoires is still under-developed. While this study has revealed that these issues can be brought together through lived experiences that challenge and cause additional language learners and teachers to reflect on their performed identities, we still need to know much more about:

- the nuanced decisions involved;
- how selected communicative features are connected;
- how and when communicative features are discarded and deployed in future interactions;
- the ways in which others may perceive what they have done; and
- how this in turn (re)builds identities and communicative repertoires and heightens the potential for gaps and holes to be noticed.

Such issues need to be complemented by pedagogic innovations that make identity-related work not only part of an overall curriculum design but also part of the design of experiences that are intended to generate additional language learning opportunities in learning contexts at home and abroad. This requires preparing teachers and their students to understand how to teach vocabulary in ways that connect with identity construction. The embracing of clusters of features that come together as identity constructs has far-reaching consequences for teachers and students who plan to study abroad and for helping them to re-enter their home country post-sojourn. To this end, in relation to vocabulary teaching, we suggest that teachers and language program designers consider not only meanings, collocations and style but also how individuals draw on various features associated with vocabulary for their own and others' identity construction.

Notes

(1) This study was funded by La Trobe Asia and approved by the La Trobe University College of Arts, Social Sciences and Commerce Human Research Ethics Sub-Committee (E15/69). We thank Minh for his extensive collaboration.
(2) The comment hints that he might have had a special place for some native varieties of English as there is no mention of Canada or New Zealand.

References

Amara, M. and Schnell, I. (2004) Identity repertoires among Arabs in Israel. *Journal of Ethnic and Migration Studies* 30 (1), 175–193.
Benson, P., Barkhuizen, G., Bodycott, P. and Brown, J. (2012) Study abroad and the development of second language identities. *Applied Linguistics Review* 3 (1), 173–193.

De Vos, J., Schriefers, H. and Lemhöfer, K. (2019) Noticing vocabulary holes aids incidental second language word learning: An experimental study. *Bilingualism: Language and Cognition* 22 (3), 500–515.

Depperman, A. (2015) Positioning. In A. de Fina and A. Georgakopolou (eds) *The Handbook of Narrative Analysis* (pp. 369–387). New York: John Wiley.

Du, H. (2015) American college students studying abroad in China: Language, identity, and self-presentation. *Foreign Language Annals* 48 (2), 250–266.

Gregory, M. (1967) Aspects of varieties differentiation. *Journal of Linguistics* 3 (2), 177–198.

Halwachs, D. (1993) Polysystem, repertoire und identität. *Grazer Linguistische Studien* 39&40, 71–90.

Karakas, A. (2020) Disciplining transnationality? The impact of study abroad educational experiences on Turkish returnee scholars' lives, careers and identity. *Research in Comparative and International Education* 15 (3), 252–272.

Labov, W. and Waletzky, J. (1997) Narrative analysis: Oral versions of personal experience. *Journal of Narrative and Life History* 7 (1–4), 3–38.

Li, W. (2011) Moment analysis and translanguaging space: Discursive construction of identities by multilingual Chinese youth in Britain. *Journal of Pragmatics* 43, 1222–1235.

Macquarie Dictionary and Thesaurus online (2020) Macmillan Publishers Australia, https://www.macquariedictionary.com.au/ (accessed March 2, 2021).

Nagel, J. (1995) American Indian ethnic renewal: Politics and the resurgence of identity. *American Sociological Review* 60 (6), 947–965.

Nicholas, H. and Starks, D. (2014) *Language Education and Applied Linguistics: Bridging the Two Fields*. London and New York: Routledge.

Nicholas, H. and Starks, D. (2019) Using the multiplicity framework to reposition and reframe the hypothesis space. In A. Lenzing, H. Nicholas and J. Roos (eds) *Widening Contexts for Processability Theory: Theories and Issues* (pp. 157–183). Amsterdam: John Benjamins.

Norton, B. and Pavlenko, A. (2019) Imagined communities, identity, and English language learning in a multilingual world. In X. Gao (ed.) *Second Handbook of English Language Teaching* (pp. 703–718). Cham: Springer International Publishing.

Schmidt, R. (1990) The role of consciousness in second language learning. *Applied Linguistics* 11 (2), 129–158.

Schmidt, R. (1995) Consciousness and foreign language learning: A tutorial on the role of attention and awareness in learning. In R. Schmidt (ed.) *Attention and Awareness in Foreign Language Learning* (pp. 1–63). Honolulu, HI: University of Hawai'i, National Foreign Language Resource Centre.

Schmidt, R. (2001) Attention. In P. Robinson (ed.) *Cognition and Second Language Instruction* (pp. 3–32). Cambridge: Cambridge University Press.

Schmidt, R. and Frota, S. (1986) Developing basic conversational ability in a second language: A case study of an adult learner of Portuguese. In R. Day (ed.) *Talking to Learn: Conversation in Second Language Acquisition* (pp. 237–326). Rowley, MA: Newbury House.

Song, J. (2016) Emotions and language teacher identity: Conflicts, vulnerability, and transformation. *TESOL Quarterly* 50 (3), 631–654.

Starks, D. and Nicholas, H. (2020) Reflections of Vietnamese English language educators on their writer identities in English and Vietnamese. *Journal of Language, Identity and Education* 19 (3), 179–192.

Valle, A. (2020) Second generation Central Americans and the formation of an ethnoracial identity in Los Angeles. *Identities: Global Studies in Culture and Power* 27 (2), 133–152.

Varis, P., Wang, X. and Du, C. (2011) Identity repertoires on the Internet: Opportunities and constraints. *Applied Linguistics Review* 2, 265–284.

Wandruszka, M. (1981) *Die Mehrsprachigkeit des Menschen*. München: Deutscher Taschenbuch Verlag.

6 'They Say My Job is Propaganda': Professional Identities of Pre-Service Chinese Language Teachers in Overseas Schools

Danping Wang

> *Study-abroad teachers do not only enter a new geographical land or a new embodied cultural dimension, but also an invisible discursive territory that has long been shaped culturally and politically.*
>
> *The teachers revealed they were more tolerant about the ubiquitous negative comments about China than when they first arrived. They experienced as much hostility as hospitality during the one-year sojourn.*

Introduction

This chapter aims to enrich our understanding of teacher study-abroad experiences under an increasingly intensified global political environment. Despite drastic sociopolitical changes experienced by teachers and students, discussions of the impact on language teaching remain absent in teacher education (Peña-Pincheira & De Costa, 2020), let alone training of practical skills to address sensitive topics surrounding the language they teach. This background knowledge and communication skills are vital for language teachers to succeed in politically challenging circumstances and are becoming especially urgent for pre-service teachers to adapt to their study-abroad programs in a new environment with unfamiliar social values and confronting political ideologies. These skills are particularly relevant for the growing number of Chinese postgraduate students in the programme of Master of Teaching Chinese to Speakers of

Other Languages completing practicums as Mandarin Language Assistants (MLAs) in overseas contexts. This chapter will focus on MLAs' professional identity development during their one-year study and teaching experience in overseas schools.

The recently heightened United States–China rivalry has witnessed the re-emergence of a cold war mentality since the second decade of the 21st century. In many aspects, confrontations between the two superpowers are making the world increasingly divided by geopolitics and ideologies. The recent closure of Confucius Institutes in the United States, Europe and Australia has made Chinese language teaching unprecedentedly politicized (e.g. Green-Riley, 2020). Controversies surrounding Confucius Institutes have inevitably complicated the professional work and identities of teachers and volunteers from Confucius Institutes. Studies in general view Confucius Institutes as a foreign agent and a propaganda tool of the Chinese Communist Party (Hartig, 2018; Luqiu & McCarthy, 2019). Chinese teachers associated with Confucius Institutes are often viewed as representatives of the Chinese government recruited to instill students in the West with a pro-China viewpoint. In English-language news media, Chinese language learning is frequently reported in provocative ways that reflect and reshape broader sociopolitical discourses and public attitudes in and beyond Anglophone countries (Duff *et al.*, 2015). However, in China, teaching Chinese to speakers of other languages is regarded as 'a national cause' that is associated with patriotism and pride (Wang & Adamson, 2014). On both sides, the ideological discourses and media representations of Chinese language teaching are produced and reproduced through amplified and recurring media coverage. When Chinese language teachers study abroad, their professional identities will inevitably become highly contested. It is imperative to adopt a political framework to understand the lived experience of cross-border language teachers. Against this macro political context, this chapter explores the increasing complexity of language teachers' identities within these challenging political contexts.

Teacher Study Abroad

Study-abroad experiences are highly complex and multi-faceted, making a wide range of positive and negative impacts on sojourners' personal and professional lives. An extensive body of literature has reported study abroad as a transformative experience for teachers whereby they challenge their prior knowledge about being a teacher and reflect on their assumptions and beliefs. The study reported in this chapter recognizes Coleman's (2013) call to account for 'whole people and whole lives' in study-abroad research. It focuses on what is actually experienced by sojourners instead of only what is positively achieved. In addition to the well-exemplified positive effects of study abroad, sojourners' experiences are often embodied or confronted by sexism, racism, stereotypes, prejudices and various kinds of conflicts at the foreign site (Bodycott, 2015; Nishimuta, 2008). Such encounters can regretfully curtail their engagement in local activities and thereby reduce their learning and networking opportunities. Negative experiences cause emotional distress and affect sojourners' perceptions of the home and host culture, the nature of their journey, and themselves as social beings. For example, Goldoni (2017) found study-abroad experiences can be highly 'disconcerting' (2017: 328), challenging sojourners' sociocultural identities, values, learning objectives and expectations. For some, study-abroad experiences are isolated and unfair, and for others, they are shocking and humiliating. Nonetheless, sojourners are often silent about their negative experiences and the research paradigm on study abroad tends to ignore the unpleasant episodes experienced by individual sojourners.

One goal for study abroad is for teachers to improve their intercultural competence and understanding of student diversity (Marx & Moss, 2011). Previous studies on teacher study abroad have largely focused on pre-service teachers who are 'white, middle class, and monolingual speakers of English' (Sharma et al., 2011: 10) with little exposure to diverse backgrounds of non-white students. Another focus of teacher study-abroad research is on English language teachers traveling to Anglophone countries for English immersion or field experience (see e.g. Barkhuizen & Feryok, 2006). However, studies on the lived experiences of *teachers of other languages* in study-abroad programs remain under-researched.

This chapter is concerned particularly with the experiences of non-white and non-English teacher sojourners who enter a new sociopolitical environment where powerful and contradicting ideologies exist. The study takes account of the fact that in this post-truth era, people refuse to listen to evidence but instead resort to emotion and prejudices. Public knowledge about a particular culture, people or event is perpetuated as a power game (Fuller, 2018). Existing bias and prejudices among individuals are fueled by social media fraught with fake news and conspiracies, a situation that has posed long-term serious challenges to education and cultural exchange (Peters, 2017). Fears and ill-intentioned commentaries affect one's personal, professional and political identities. Studies on multicultural education have been cautious about the role of mass media in the construction of people's perceptions about particular cultures and identities (see e.g. Cortes, 1995). Study-abroad teachers do not only enter a new geographical land or a new embodied cultural dimension, but also an invisible discursive territory that has long been shaped culturally and politically. The second decade of the 21st century has seen the re-emergence of ideological competitions, trade wars, as well as the Covid-19 pandemic crisis. The intensified global political environment has made it imperative for study-abroad research to examine sojourners' whole-people experience from a more macro global political environment and move beyond analyzing county-to-country cultural differences.

The Program

The Mandarin Language Assistants (MLA) program was launched in 2010 as part of the 2008 New Zealand–China Free Trade Agreement between the two countries. A maximum of 150 Chinese students per year are placed in New Zealand primary and secondary schools as teaching assistants for one year, and this quota increased to 300 in 2019 when the agreement was renewed. In its first decade, the program has received over 800 MLAs in New Zealand.

The three Confucius Institutes in New Zealand organize the MLA program. MLAs are selected, trained and supported by Confucius Institutes; they arrange their homestay, locate schools for their placements and provide teaching materials and professional development. Because of their close ties with Confucius Institutes, MLAs are viewed predominantly through a political lens in the local media: 'They aren't qualified as teachers, and they're hired and employed, not in New Zealand, but by an arm of the Chinese government' (MacNamara, 2020). A recent study in New Zealand found school students' views about China and Chinese people seemed to have been significantly affected by the macro ideological environment. In Kennedy's (2020) research, a 15-year-old girl studying Chinese in a New Zealand secondary school shared her disinterest in traveling to China: 'They've always got military bases in different countries and it's like I don't know, hopefully they are not trying to take over the world!' (2020: 435). This comment is strikingly political.

Two review reports were explicitly prepared for the MLA program by local educational and policy experts in New Zealand. Eriksen (2018) found that MLAs are in high demand as Chinese has become the fastest growing language in New Zealand. The New Zealand government has no plans to increase the capacity of Chinese teaching in schools and the shortage of Chinese teachers will remain a problem. Eriksen also noted that MLAs were made 'responsible for developing and delivering the Chinese programme' even though they are intended only to be assistants to teachers (2018: 12). In another report, East (2018) identified cultural adaptations as the most crucial barrier for MLAs to survive their one-year field experience. They were expected to 'embrace changes and integrate learner-centred experiential approaches to language teaching' (2018: 10).

Requirements of cultural adaptations for Chinese teachers are a common issue, and not only a New Zealand phenomenon (Moloney & Wang, 2016). Chinese teachers are often found incapable of genuinely understanding the Western way of teaching and thus need to be 'educated' (Singh & Han, 2014; Wang & Ma, 2009). Studies on Confucius Institute teachers are primarily concerned with improving Chinese language teachers' intercultural competence and transforming their teaching beliefs and approaches to become more Westernized (Wang, 2015; Ye & Edwards, 2018). To date, there appears to be little research on the whole-person experiences of Chinese language teachers teaching and studying abroad.

There are two exceptions. Ye's (2017) in-depth analysis of the lived experiences of Confucius Institute Chinese teachers in the United Kingdom has provided an excellent example of the whole-person approach in study-abroad research. Drawing on Bourdieu's concepts, the study explored Chinese language teachers' self-development and the impacts of the overseas environment on their professional identity and agency. Secondly, taking an ecological perspective, Jin *et al.* (2020) explored Chinese language teachers' well-being and resilience, also in the United Kingdom. Jin *et al.*'s study goes beyond 'educating' Chinese language teachers. Instead, it shows empathy to these temporary sojourners, who were working under a heavy workload, enduring low social respect and low salary and yet managed to remain positive in the face of all kinds of challenges and adversity.

Language Teacher Identity

This chapter highlights the importance of examining the impact of the macro political environment on study-abroad teachers' experiences and professional identities. The political framework views language teacher identity as 'a complex matter of the social and the individual, of discourse and practice' (Zembylas & Chubbuck, 2018: 188). Power and resistance are at the center of understanding teacher identity and emotion. Power produces a discourse of truth and particular forms of knowledge in teaching practice and teacher development. Power can deconstruct and reinstitute the curriculum and even resist the legitimacy of the teaching profession. This chapter draws on Mockler's (2011) framework that highlights the political impacts on teacher identity. The framework includes three domains: personal experience, professional context, and the external political environment. Personal experience relates to 'personal lives, framed by class, race and gender, that exist outside the professional realm' (2011: 520), and the professional context refers to 'the located professional experiences of particular schools or educational contexts' (2011: 521). The political environment 'comprises the discourses, attitudes and understandings surrounding education that [are] external to the profession, experienced by teachers largely through media' (2011: 521). The three domains operate reflexively, are constantly shifting, and impact each other.

Research has shown that pre-service Chinese language teachers enter the profession primarily due to altruistic purposes and a strong national identity. In China, Zhang *et al.* (2020) investigated 411 first-year, pre-service Chinese language teachers from ten universities. The study found that the participants' professional identities are explicitly linked to intrinsic and altruistic values. The altruistic values include participants' desires to 'communicate Chinese culture to the people in other countries and to contribute to a deeper and better understanding of China around the world' (Zhang *et al.*, 2020: 11). Despite there being chances to work abroad, most are volunteer jobs organized by Confucius Institutes where there are no full-time teaching positions. Interestingly, the findings resemble the experience of Peace Corps volunteer teachers from the United States in the 1960s. Guthrie and McKendry (1963) found altruism was one of the major motivations for young Americans to join the Peace Corps. In a recent study, based on interviews with 140 current and returned Peace Corps volunteers, Kallman (2020) found that many of them, after their overseas experience, had seen their political idealism transformed to apolitical professional identities. Due to political spats, the Peace Corps terminated its China program in 2020. Finally, Ye (2017) found that sojourning Chinese language teachers demonstrated a strong national pride and identity. Their national identity is interlocked with their professional identity which is committed to promoting Chinese language and culture. Ye (2017: 126) pointed out that the overseas experience had an impact 'on their ways of doing things, but less on their ways of being'.

The Study

The study explores the professional identity formation of pre-service Chinese language teachers in a one-year study-abroad program in New Zealand. The qualitative research design stresses the socially constructed nature of reality: it is locally situated, participant-oriented, holistic and inductive (Barkhuizen, 2019). The researcher is a university lecturer who coordinates Chinese courses at tertiary level. There are no personal or professional relationships between the researcher and the participants.

Data collection included a descriptive questionnaire survey and in-depth interviews for each participant. The purpose of the questionnaire survey was to understand the participants' personal background as a group. The survey included 12 questions. The first two aimed to understand their willingness to come back to New Zealand for work or further studies, and the rest were related to the changes in their professional identities during the sojourn, including their professional, home and host contexts, and themselves as a person, their professional knowledge, teaching approaches and their professional identities. The questionnaire was distributed to one of the cohorts in the middle of their sojourn. It used a 5-point Likert scale with 1 being *strongly disagree* and 5 being *strongly agree*. Due to the close relationship among the MLAs, the specific year the survey was distributed will not be indicated in order to protect the identities of the participants. In total, the study surveyed 62 MLAs, covering 42.2% of the total MLAs for that year. Five participants volunteered for interviews (one interview during sojourn and one post-sojourn) to further interpret the survey data and to offer new insights to enrich the researcher's understanding of their professional identity formation in the study-abroad context.

Findings

A short profile of MLAs in New Zealand

The majority of MLAs in New Zealand are native speakers of Chinese enrolled in a postgraduate Master's program in Teaching Chinese as a Foreign Language in a prestigious Chinese university. They are mostly young female students who have a high proficiency in English. Survey data for the participants in this study show that 87% were between 21–25 years of age and 95% were female. Eighty-two percent have passed College English Level 6 (roughly IELTS band 6).

Their pre-sojourn experience was competitive and intensive. MLAs are selected through highly rigorous testing. The selection process includes a Competence Assessment (e.g. Chinese language knowledge, teaching demonstration, cultural adaptability test and a Chinese talent show), an interview in English and a psychological test. The cultural adaptability test is worth noting due to its direct relevance to sensitive topics such as stereotypes and racism against Chinese overseas. MLA candidates are asked questions such as 'How do you respond to the claim that the toilets in China are not clean and there's no paper?' and 'How do you respond to students who think it's disgusting that Chinese eat dogs and century eggs?'. This shows that the study-abroad organizers are aware of the cultural bias and stereotypes about China and Chinese culture in overseas contexts.

The study shows that MLAs' willingness to return to New Zealand after graduation for teaching and further study was low. As shown in Table 6.1, only 11.3% of MLAs indicated an interest in returning to New Zealand for teaching or further studies. The post-sojourn interviews revealed that participants were mostly concerned with three issues: (a) female teachers in their 20s under family pressure to get married and have a stable job near home, (b) the financial burden to study overseas and get certified as a teacher, and (c) limited job opportunities (even after earning PhD degrees) and low teacher salaries in New Zealand.

Table 6.1 Number of participants who intended to return for teaching and study

Question (N = 62)	Yes	Not sure	No
Would you like to return to New Zealand for teaching?	7 (11.3%)	36 (58.1%)	19 (30.6%)
Would you like to return to New Zealand for a PhD?	6 (9.7%)	29 (46.8%)	27 (43.5%)

By the time of the post-sojourn interviews, the five participants were all employed. Three became full-time teachers in local schools, and two were hired by private education organizations. One participant shared her reason for deciding not to return. Her initial passion for returning was extinguished after discussing her career plans with one of her colleagues in her placement school in New Zealand, where she had felt welcomed and supported throughout the year. To her surprise, her desire to relocate from China to New Zealand was interpreted politically.

> I revealed my intention [to return] to a colleague, and was shocked to hear him commenting like 'It'd be nice for you to get out of there'. I was offended. He didn't see me as a professional but a poor Chinese student who is desperate to escape China.

Although her encounters with cognitive prejudices were covert and subtle, and expressed out of good will, it indicates how an ideological bias has been entrenched in people's views of China and Chinese students who study in the West. This episode is an example of how MLAs' professional identity development can be repressed or resisted due to the impact of macro political ideologies. It also indicates that there are deeper levels of misunderstanding among individuals and more complex reasons behind the MLAs' low willingness to return.

From idealists to realists

The study-abroad experience appears to have transformed MLAs from idealists to realists. As shown in Table 6.2, the group of teachers experienced significant changes in their personal and professional growth during the study-abroad trip.

Table 6.2 Changes in personal and professional growth during study abroad

	Question	Mean	Standard Deviation
1.	My understanding of China has changed.	3.71	0.88
2.	My understanding of New Zealand has changed.	4.14	0.77
3.	My understanding about myself has changed.	4.09	0.75
4.	My understanding of a Chinese teacher's job has changed.	3.85	0.83
5.	I find there is a gap between what I learned and what overseas teaching demands.	4.12	0.84
6.	I find the Chinese way of teaching does not work very well in an overseas context.	3.14	0.98
7.	I find English is very important for teaching Chinese.	4.46	0.71
8.	I find the immersion approach is effective.	1.95	0.81
9.	I am proud to be a Chinese language teacher.	3.79	0.80
10.	My primary job as an MLA is to promote Chinese culture.	3.34	0.89

First, their ideal expectations of living and working in a Western country were greatly challenged. They found that life was no longer comfortable and convenient, particularly due to the lack of delivery service and the inconvenience of public transportation. Many had to rely on their homestay to drive them to work and the supermarket because they did not have a driving license. MLAs placed in rural areas felt incredibly isolated. The drastic change of lifestyle pushed them to critically examine their prior understanding of China and the host country (Q1–2). They started to appreciate what they took for granted in China, such as the rich social life and the affordability of food. They discovered how different New Zealand culture is compared to what they expected, which is similar to what Barkhuizen and Feryok (2006) found with a group of English teachers from Hong Kong. The participants were also surprised by the commitment and passion shown by New Zealand schools to promote the indigenous language and culture, which was rarely seen in other Western countries.

Second, the group of teachers felt their overall understanding of the profession had greatly improved (Q4). It was their first time to put what they had learned into practice, as well as discover what they had learned was relevant to teaching Chinese in an overseas context. On many levels, they experienced an empowering process of identity formation which affirmed their professional identity as Chinese language teachers. Despite the hard work and frequent travel to multiple schools on a weekly basis, they enjoyed the opportunities to decide what to teach and how students were assessed in their courses. They exercised their agency in promoting Chinese language and culture in their workplaces. They reported a high degree of freedom to explore new or self-developed approaches. Also focusing on Chinese language teachers studying in New Zealand, Sun (2012) pointed out that all participants in his study felt the study-abroad program was an excellent opportunity to gain real experience and prepare themselves for a professional life as a Chinese language teacher in New Zealand schools.

Furthermore, the participants found there was a mismatch between their prior learning and what the workplace demanded. They reported a constant re-examination of their professional knowledge and undertook self-directed professional learning throughout the sojourn period. None of them had experience in teaching young students overseas, and this part of their knowledge was absent in their previous teacher education (Q5). Having realized the Chinese way of teaching was not suitable for New Zealand school students, they paid attention to observing and learning from their lead teachers (Q6). For example, one participant said, 'Our bookish English is not good enough for teaching. There were lots of times I lost my students because my instruction was not clear. My lead teacher had to give the same instruction again in a language that young students can understand'. Notably, they found that their beliefs about students' first language and local languages changed significantly (Q7). They found the ability to speak English was vital for successful teaching, similar to what Wang (2020) found with tertiary-level Chinese language teaching in New Zealand: 'The importance of English has been downplayed in my previous study. In real teaching here, it is impossible to make students speak in Chinese all the time'. Being proficient in the learners' first language was not well supported in Chinese language teacher education (Wang, 2019). As one participant shared, the most popular teaching approach in China is monolingual (Q8), and they were prohibited from speaking English when teaching Chinese. In her previous understanding, an experienced teacher would never need to resort to English. But this idealist professional thinking was soon scrapped when they were given the floor to manage the classroom and build rapport with their students.

From pride to propaganda

The most striking experience for MLAs was related to the macro political environment. The study found the Chinese language teachers' professional identities were inextricably linked to the political ideologies they experienced through personal contact and the mainstream media. The study reveals a contrast between the claimed identity as 'pride' and an assigned identity as 'propaganda'. Their altruistic motivation was labeled with a political agenda (Q9–10). The skepticism of the nature of their job came from both the foreign site and their fellow Chinese at home, who saw their government-funded trip as 'squandering taxpayers' money'. One participant reported a casual conversation she had at a social event. She introduced herself as a 'teacher', but it was immediately rejected by one of the guests. The teacher commented as follows: 'They say my job is propaganda. I didn't know propaganda is such a negative word in English at that time. I thought it meant promotion'. Clearly, her demand for recognition of her professional identity was met with resistance. The experience shows that their English ability was inadequate for them to apprehend the ideological and political discourses surrounding their work. Participants explained that they were not capable of making themselves well understood in English. They all reported knowing limited English vocabulary related to politics and ideologies. One participant shared her discomfort in getting involved in conversations on Chinese political topics: 'Although I have studied how to respond to such questions, I was still not able to utter a word when I heard it. I was shocked and humiliated'. Besides linguistic skills, they were also concerned with being outspoken on sensitive topics that might cause trouble or bring unnecessary attention to Confucius Institutes. They hoped to do the best that they could to bring honor to the MLA program. Their strategy to deal with sensitive topics was to avoid them and remain reticent about negative experiences such as being provoked into talking about politics. Although they all successfully completed their one-year sojourn, they did not find that they were genuinely accepted or respected.

They also encountered pejorative and racist names like 'ching chong', and sometimes confronted awkward questions such as 'Are you a spy?' As Kennedy's (2020) research pointed out, it is impossible to separate a Chinese teacher's professional identity as a teacher from their personal, national and ideological identity as a Chinese person from a communist country. The discourses that overshadow the sojourning site made the teacher participants' professional identity formation extremely complex and controversial.

In general, the teachers felt they became more independent and open-minded (Q3). They revealed they were more tolerant about the ubiquitous negative comments about China than when they first arrived. They experienced as much hostility as hospitality during the one-year sojourn. MLAs found it difficult to make local friends whose knowledge about China was either too outdated or too political to form common grounds for friendship. They were shocked by how little the outside world knew about their lives and how often their presence and profession were misinterpreted due to political influences. The study-abroad trip made them more sympathetic to China.

Conclusion

Focusing on a group of pre-service Chinese language teachers studying abroad, this study has revealed a significant gap between self-perceptions (including those prior to study abroad) of their professional identity and how they were viewed in the workplace and local communities. The teachers, for the first time, experienced difficult processes of negotiating multiple fragmented identities due to the unfavorable sociopolitical discourses and events surrounding Confucius Institutes and China. They discovered that their professional identity had become highly politicized, and its development disrupted or denied due to political ideologies.

This chapter has implications for study-abroad program organizers, teacher educators, student teachers, and researchers of language teacher education. First, it highlights the increasing impact of the political environment and media discourses on language teachers' identities during study abroad. In addition to coping with challenges in a new field, study-abroad teachers are vulnerable to being confronted with provocative questions related to sensitive topics, or questions that are offensive to one's racial, sexual, religious, political or national identities.

Second, this chapter invites practitioners and researchers to consider applying a political framework to understanding and analyzing pre-service language teacher identities. The rise of identity politics requires social science research to develop conceptual frameworks that capture the most striking changes in our times. Study-abroad language teachers need to be equipped with the knowledge and social skills to communicate in a politically charged environment. The negative impacts on border crossers cannot be ignored or kept only at the personal level. This study highlights the importance of listening to the voices of those who see their careers being affected by politics and media discourses.

Finally, an in-depth understanding of the sociocultural and socio-political dimensions of the host country is crucial for study-abroad teachers. It is suggested that pre-departure training should include the most up-to-date news about recent major social events related to critical racial, religious and political topics in the host-country media. One of the recommendations that Barkhuizen (2019: 5) gives to teacher education researchers is particularly relevant: become aware of the geo-political context and pay attention to media discussion and debates when they arrive in the host country. An in-depth and critical understanding of the global political climate is especially important for teachers whose careers are caught up in escalating political tensions between China and other nations, as well as in other forms of cultural, religious and racial confrontations.

References

Barkhuizen, G. (ed.) (2019) Introduction: Qualitative research topics in language teacher education. In G. Barkhuizen (ed.) *Qualitative Research Topics in Language Teacher Education* (pp. 1–14). London: Routledge.

Barkhuizen, G. and Feryok, A. (2006) Pre-service teachers' perceptions of a short-term international experience program. *Asia-Pacific Journal of Teacher Education* 34 (1), 115–134.

Bodycott, P. (2015) Intragroup conflict during study abroad. *Journal of International Students* 5 (3), 244–259.

Coleman, J.A. (2013) Researching whole people and whole lives. In C. Kinginger (ed.) *Social and Cultural Aspects of Language Learning in Study Abroad* (pp. 17–73). Amsterdam: John Benjamins.

Cortes, C. (1995) Knowledge construction and popular culture: The media as multicultural educator. In J.A. Banks and C.A.M. Banks (eds) *Handbook of Research on Multicultural Education* (pp. 169–183). New York: Macmillan.

Duff, P.A., Anderson, T., Doherty, L. and Wang, R. (2015) Representations of Chinese language learning in contemporary English-language news media: Hope, hype, and fear. *Global Chinese* 1 (1), 139–168.

East, M. (2018) Teaching languages in schools: Rationale, potential, constraints and recommendations with particular relevance to Mandarin Chinese. Unpublished manuscript, New Zealand China Council.

Eriksen, L. (2018) Review of the Mandarin Language Assistant Program at the Confucius Institute in Auckland: Enhancing New Zealand's capacity to teach additional languages. Unpublished manuscript, The University of Auckland.

Fuller, S. (2018) *Post-Truth: Knowledge as a Power Game.* London: Anthem Press.

Goldoni, F. (2017) Race, ethnicity, class and identity: Implications for study abroad. *Journal of Language, Identity & Education* 16 (5), 328–341.

Green-Riley, N. (2020) The State Department labeled China's Confucius programs a bad influence on U.S. students. What's the story? https://www.washingtonpost.com/politics/2020/08/24/state-department-labeled-chinas-confucius-programs-bad-influence-us-students-whats-story/ (accessed February 24, 2021).

Guthrie, G.M. and McKendry, M.S. (1963) Interest patterns of Peace Corps volunteers in a teaching project. *Journal of Educational Psychology* 54 (5), 261–267.

Hartig, F. (2018) China's global image management: Paper cutting and the omission of politics. *Asian Studies Review* 42 (4), 701–720.

Jin, J., Mercer, S., Babic, S. and Mairitsch, A. (2020) 'You just appreciate every little kindness': Chinese language teachers' wellbeing in the UK. *System* 96. https://doi.org/10.1016/j.system.2020.102400

Kallman, M.E. (2020) *The Death of Idealism: Development and Anti-Politics in the Peace Corps.* New York: Columbia University Press.

Kennedy, J. (2020) Intercultural pedagogies in Chinese as a foreign language (CFL). *Intercultural Education* 31 (4), 427–446.

Luqiu, L.R. and McCarthy, J.D. (2019) Confucius Institutes: The successful stealth 'soft power' penetration of American universities. *Journal of Higher Education* 90 (4), 620–643.

MacNamara, K. (2020) New Zealand school children have become a bargaining chip in trade negotiations. https://www.stuff.co.nz/business/opinion-analysis/300041520/new-zealand-school-children-have-become-a-bargaining-chip-in-trade-negotiations (accessed February 24, 2021).

Marx, H. and Moss, D.M. (2011) Please mind the culture gap: Intercultural development during a teacher education study abroad program. *Journal of Teacher Education* 62 (1), 35–47.

Mockler, N. (2011) Beyond 'what works': Understanding teacher identity as a practical and political tool. *Teachers and Teaching* 17 (5), 517–528.

Moloney, R. and Wang, D. (2016) Limiting professional trajectories: A dual narrative study in Chinese language education. *Asian-Pacific Journal of Second and Foreign Language Education* 1 (1), 1–15.

Nishimuta, Y. (2008) The interpretation of racial encounters: Japanese students in Britain. *Journal of Ethnic and Migration Studies* 34 (1), 133–150.

Peña-Pincheira, R.S. and De Costa, P.I. (2020) Language teacher agency for educational justice-oriented work: An ecological model. *TESOL Journal* 12 (2). https://doi.org/10.1002/tesj.561

Peters, M.A. (2017) Education in a post-truth world. *Educational Philosophy and Theory* 49 (6), 563–566.

Sharma, S., Phillion, J. and Malewski, E. (2011) Examining the practice of critical reflection for developing pre-service teachers' multicultural competencies: Findings from a study abroad program in Honduras. *Issues in Teacher Education* 20 (2), 9–22.

Singh, M. and Han, J. (2014) Educating teachers of 'Chinese as a local/global language': Teaching 'Chinese with Australian characteristics'. *Frontiers of Education in China* 9 (3), 403–428.

Sun, D. (2012) 'Everything goes smoothly': A case study of an immigrant Chinese language teacher's personal practical knowledge. *Teaching and Teacher Education* 28 (5), 760–767.

Wang, D. (2019) *Multilingualism and Translanguaging in Chinese Language Classrooms.* London: Palgrave Macmillan.

Wang, D. (2020) Studying Chinese language in higher education: The translanguaging reality through learners' eyes. *System* 95. https://doi.org/10.1016/j.system.2020.102394

Wang, D. and Adamson, B. (2014) War and peace: Perceptions of Confucius Institute in China and USA. *The Asia-Pacific Education Researcher* 24 (1), 225–234.

Wang, L. (2015) Change in teaching beliefs when teaching abroad? A case study on Confucius Institute Chinese teachers' teaching experiences in the US. In F. Dervin (ed.) *Chinese Educational Migration and Student-Teacher Mobilities* (pp. 144–165). London: Palgrave Macmillan.

Wang, Q. and Ma, X. (2009) Educating for learner-centredness in Chinese pre-service teacher education. *Innovation in Language Learning and Teaching* 3 (3), 239–253.

Ye, W. (2017) *Taking Chinese to the World: Language, Culture and Identity in Confucius Institute Teachers*. Bristol: Multilingual Matters.

Ye, W. and Edwards, V. (2018) Confucius Institute teachers in the UK: Motivation, challenges, and transformative learning. *Race Ethnicity and Education* 21 (6), 843–857.

Zembylas, M. and Chubbuck, S. (2018) Conceptualizing 'teacher identity': A political approach. In P.A. Schutz, J. Hong and D. Francis (eds) *Research on Teacher Identity* (pp. 183–193). Cham: Springer.

Zhang, H., Wu, J. and Zhu, Y. (2020) Why do you choose to teach Chinese as a second language? A study of pre-service CSL teachers' motivations. *System* 91. https://doi.org/10.1016/j.system.2020.102242

Part 2

Interculturality and Intercultural Learning

7 Re-Imagining Immersion for Teachers: Exploring the Seedlings of Decolonial Roots within Ecuadorian/ United States Partnerships

Rachel Shriver, Magda Madany-Saá,
Eleanor Sweeney, Elizabeth Smolcic,
Sharon Childs, Ana Loja Criollo and
Yolanda Loja Criollo

*To Eleanor Sweeney, our dear friend and colleague,
a bright and warm spirit we had the pleasure to encounter
in our personal and professional lives. This chapter is one of many
contributions you made to transform education and the teaching
of world languages. You'll be always in our hearts.*

*This chapter describes elements of a TESL immersion program and
uncovers how the people, landscapes and histories of two communities support or inhibit the development of a critical interculturality.
Learning to teach English learners is knowledge and skill-based, but
importantly it is relational at both institutional and personal levels.*

*In US students' reflections of their experiences, they largely miss
the differences between their voluntary and highly supported,
five-week experience in Ecuador and an English learner's
experience in a US classroom.*

Introduction

The intricacies mesmerized me. I (Rachel, first author) was trying my hardest to keep the threads separate while weaving them together. My fingers seemed foreign, the pattern puzzling. After guidance and focus, Mama Susana smiled at me with approval; I began to make progress. Four years later as a teacher of English learners, those complex threads still have evolving meaning for me; just as it took intentional, guided learning to recognize and weave each thread into a multi-colored band, it has taken reflection and practice for me to understand the ways that language, nationality, culture and so many other threads of our identities are vital to our brilliance. I cannot haphazardly jumble my students' threads of identity like I did with the threads in Saraguro. I now recognize and celebrate their countless intertwined threads, as we talk about how these make us vivid and whole.

Mama Susana sparked my epiphany while I was a student in an ESL teacher education program which unfolded on the US university campus and through a cultural/linguistic immersion experience in Ecuador. As I shift roles from student to researcher, the themes of intricacy and interwovenness remain salient in our research and my still-developing teaching practice. This chapter describes elements of the TESL immersion program and uncovers how the people, landscapes and histories of two communities support or inhibit the development of a *critical interculturality*.

With the participating students and program instructors, researchers who investigate intercultural projects must ask themselves what it means to centralize reciprocity in institutional and individual relationships, to build intercultural dispositions in practice, and to go beyond the theoretical to actions. For example, rather than construct an experience abroad whose benefits focus squarely on participants of the Global North, we can work to incorporate models of decolonizing teacher education that ask students from both the visiting and host countries to collaboratively engage in self-reflection, and work to develop awareness of colonial perspectives and histories. An emerging awareness of *decoloniality* and ownership of one's cultural identity and histories are the first moves toward developing dispositions that endure past the program's end date, following participants into their post-program professional lives.

In this chapter, we (the authors) first outline our theoretical commitments and then describe elements of the TESL immersion program and our reciprocal focus. We offer contextual details of the program demonstrating that study-abroad programs may contain important mediating factors that help or hinder intercultural development. Next, we explain the research process, highlight excerpts from qualitative data that illuminate key themes, and offer recommendations for teacher education programs abroad that work toward decolonizing their thinking and practices.

Critical Interculturality in ESL Teacher Education

Over many decades, teacher educators have worked to develop inter/multi/cross-cultural experiential learning experiences for teacher candidates. Debate continues over the conceptual meaning of these terms, and what the process of 'intercultural learning' and its assumed goal of 'intercultural competence' or 'interculturality' might involve (Smolcic & Katunich, 2017). Critical scholars argue that study-abroad or intercultural projects often follow the tradition of viewing culture as object-based learning that separates the self (knower) from the object (known) which then becomes a profoundly colonizing practice (Bernardes *et al.*, 2019; Smolcic & Martin, 2019). As Pirbhai-Illich and Martin (2019) explain:

> Object-based thinking is a way of understanding social and natural phenomena as objects that exist in isolation and possess certain properties which remain constant over time ... Interactions between cultures then become something that happens at the intersection of two entities (i.e., cultures) each of which is bounded ... and in the context of identity, can become essentialized and reified. (2019: 71)

In this way, even if culture is understood as multiple and intersecting, dimensions of identity become homogeneous when scaled up to group (national) identity and are often used as a basis for distinction, stereotyping or bias between members of one group towards another (Dervin, 2017). When we consider North-South immersive experiences, learning from an object-focused perspective leads to the visiting (usually dominant) group's norms as a basis for making racialized judgments about the ways of being within a host community, which is then often positioned as exotic and/or deficit (Pirbhai-Illich & Martin, 2019). Importantly, the societal structures that divide people by race, class, gender, religion and other categories of difference – which are historically rooted in the processes of colonization – are often obscured.

Coloniality is founded upon a hierarchical object-focused knowledge structure that creates a divided world of superior-inferior, civilized-savage along lines of race viewed as biological and thus the natural order, enabling the colonizers to justify their actions. It is 'a mindset, a way of being and knowing, that is the legacy of colonialism' (Pirbhai-Illich & Martin, 2019: 70). Decolonial scholars contend that coloniality deeply affects the way we operate in the world whether on a global or local scale. This mindset continues to act as a set of unstated norms which are mostly invisible to Euro-Western people, who assume their ways of knowing are universal. Critical theorists have drawn attention to the ongoing harm inherent in practices that devalue and further marginalize students of color or from non-English speaking backgrounds. From this critical standpoint comes the imperative to identify and disrupt the roots of the 'colonial project' and to decolonize our educational practices (de Sousa Santos, 2018; Pirbhai-Illich et al., 2017).

The need for teacher intercultural competence is increasingly recognized in order to meet learner needs in a globalized world. However, many teachers feel ill-prepared to instruct linguistically and culturally diverse learners (Lucas et al., 2018). Importantly, in school systems with high levels of immigrant learners, all teachers must have the capabilities and consciousness to be responsive to and advocate for sustaining the cultures, languages and social realities of their students' lived experiences and communities. Research that examines the effects of international teaching practicums or immersive experience on teachers' intercultural development is mixed. However, the two program characteristics that seem to be foundational to teacher learning include: (a) critical and guided reflection, and (b) opportunities for teachers to enact what they are learning (Romijn et al., 2021). While there are few studies that employ a critical perspective on teacher intercultural development (Bernardes et al., 2019; Mwebi & Brigham, 2009) our work in collaboration with colleagues of the Global South compels us to adopt such a lens.

Critical interculturality (interculturalidad) is a central element of decolonial teacher education to both expose power relationships and support more equitable relations between groups (Granados-Beltrán, 2016). Walsh (2010) describes interculturality as an effort to construct a just, plural and equitable society and explains three forms it might take: relational, functional and critical. The tenets of our work are built around critical interculturality, which seeks to transform structures and institutions so that social relations can be based on respect, legitimacy, equity and equality.

The Research Setting: An International Immersion Program in Ecuador

The Teaching ESL Immersion Program is one pathway to complete the 15-credit ESL teaching credential offered to K-12 teachers in our state. It begins with one course in the spring semester and ends with a blended course at the end of the summer; sandwiched in between are three courses offered during an immersion and teaching practicum in Ecuador. Table 7.1 presents the six main components of the summer 5-week immersion experience. Guided critical reflection in writing, individual and group discussions are ongoing, and a coached teaching practicum takes up much of the days.

As a student in 2017, my day (Rachel, first author) began with breakfast made by my host mom; she scribbled notes on my napkin like 'cafe = coffee, que te vaya bien mija! [I hope everything goes well, daughter!]' My morning included three classes: Spanish, and two courses about teaching English language learners (ELLs) and second language learning. Once a week I met with my Ecuadorian tandem partner in a course called *Global Conversations*. Each week featured an invited speaker/theme of global reach such as gender, sustainability, Indigenous knowledges. We discussed the topic in groups of US and Ecuadorian students, choosing which language we wanted to use or sometimes creatively translanguaging. We also wrote dialogue journals continuing our discussions from class, having free rein on language usage.

My classmates and I were asked to meet once a week with our tandem partners outside of class; what actually happened is that students (every year!) formed a group chat on WhatsApp and spent a lot of time hanging

Table 7.1 Components of the immersion experience

Component	Who/What's Involved?
Home stay	– Daily grappling to communicate in Spanish; 'living' another culture.
Global Conversations Course + Tandem partners	– Translingual, facilitated discussion amongst US and Ecuadorian students around weekly global topic; one-hour tandem conversation weekly. – Spontaneous hangouts initiated by students; ongoing conversation through social media. – Dialogue journals between tandem partners.
Language Courses (Spanish or Kichwa)	– Serves as a 'new language learning experience' for US students. – Journal writing to deconstruct the language learning experience.
Teaching practicum	– Co-teacher model; two student teachers per class to teach English through a cohort-wide content theme. – Coaching by experienced ESL instructor. – Ecuadorian students volunteer for course; finish with certificate rather than grades.
Weekend excursions	– Various themes and locations; spoken and written reflections in journals and in-class discussion.

out. I remember constant texts: 'I'm on Calle Larga – alguien está por allí? [is anyone near there?]' And suddenly there would be 6, 10, 20 of us playing soccer or splitting a mojito while unpacking the world around us. Our translanguaging never stopped, nor our cultural revelations and conversation. This close-knit friendship with local students was the most enriching part for me. Hearing questions like 'why do gringos leave without saying good-bye?' gave me pause, causing me to consider my own thoughts and actions and to interrogate my culture (sometimes more genuinely than class prompts did).

After morning classes, I had lunch with my host family. Their seven voices bustled as I hyper-focused, attempting to understand a full idea. I remember once I was engrossed in a very basic conversation with my 3-year-old 'niece' about her doll's favorite foods. On my walk back to class I was on cloud nine; I had had my first conversation in Spanish! This moment changed me personally and professionally; I realized my students didn't need perfect grammar or a developed vocabulary to achieve meaningful communication.

Three weekend excursions were organized: Ingapirca (an Incan temple and archeological site), Cajas National Park, Reserva Mazar (a cloud forest and conservation area) and Saraguro (a strongly indigenous, Kichwa-speaking town). In Mazar, we learned about efforts to conserve the surrounding cloud forest and planted over 500 trees. We slept in basic cabins with no service and made meals together; for some students, these experiences pushed them emotionally in all directions. In Saraguro, we participated in weaving demonstrations, dancing, shaman-led spiritual cleansing rituals, eating Indigenous foods, and blazing through mountains in jeeps. Every activity was first contextualized, involved personal engagement in some activity, and closed with discussion and reflection.

The research process

This study was launched through the initiative of the first author who was a previous student in the program and secured a university research grant. The research team includes program instructors as well as researchers who were not directly involved in the implementation of the program, and the chapter was written in collaboration with colleagues at the Ecuadorian partner university.

We (the authors) used grounded theory to analyze data and found Emerson et al.'s (2011) approach to writing up the data a helpful tool. We worked collaboratively and cross-referenced themes among the researchers in the group, discovering themes relating to cultural self-awareness, racism, language teaching and sustainability, the loss of Indigenous languages/cultures, privilege, and English as a lingua franca.

Research questions

The analysis for this study was guided by the following questions:

(1) What are the impacts of the program activities on student attitudes towards language, culture and power?
(2) What conditions help or hinder the development of critical interculturality for the students, and how does this relate to their future professional lives?

Participants

This chapter focuses on a subset of data from the larger project and is guided by the intention to be inclusive of the Ecuadorian and US student participants. Data was collected from the 2018 cohort involved in the immersion program in Ecuador. Five US and five Ecuadorian students were interviewed three times: before the program began, during the program, and six months to a year after the program had ended. All participants were university students enrolled in undergraduate programs. The US students were all pre-service teacher education majors working towards their ESL teaching endorsement. All of the Ecuadorians had intermediate to advanced English proficiency and were motivated to learn English to pass a university required English exam.

Students were interviewed individually using a semi-structured approach with a set of guiding questions that probed the following themes: (a) language awareness; (b) understandings of culture, race and decolonial ideas; (c) personal awareness or growth; (d) attitudes or beliefs about English as a lingua franca, and (e) global awareness or knowledge. The data also includes dialogue journals written by program participants in US/Ecuador pairings (44 students). Students chose which language they preferred for the interviews and the interviews conducted in Spanish were transcribed by an Ecuadorian speaker of Spanish and then analyzed by research staff proficient in English and Spanish. Pseudonyms are used in place of actual names.

Interweaving New Threads of Understanding

Focusing on the activities of the Global Conversations course, we now describe its apparent impact on student thinking. Without exception, the students stated that the experience helped them to share perspectives, develop self and cultural awareness, and become more comfortable with multilingual language use. However, we acknowledge that constructions of the cultural self and Others which stop at awareness are problematic because they ignore power relations.

We begin with a look at five students, one from the US and four from Ecuador, who embrace and question ideologies surrounding the loss of Indigenous knowledges and languages. Tiffany (US) connected language loss and cultural identity while acknowledging how important home languages are to individual learner identities, familial relationships and broader humanity. In a conversation about the loss of worldwide Indigenous languages, she remarks:

> But their language ... different ones are being wiped out and if the language was literally beaten out of you and you can't participate in that part of your life anymore, or you can't communicate with your grandma who only speaks this language, it's such a big part of somebody's life. And I don't think people view language that way. They don't think about how it has all these connections that make a person who they are. And when you take that away, like they lose the sense of identity. If you take the language away from them or it dies out, disappears, that piece of their identity is now gone.

Several Ecuadorian students echoed Tiffany's ideas, particularly the value of an Indigenous language of their home country, Kichwa. Gabriel (Ecuador) claims:

> One of the most important lessons that this program gave me, it made me feel I really should know Kichwa. I've been always aware of ... that it's not okay that Ecuadorians don't know one of their native ... their languages. But when the people from [US university] came and sometimes you were talking about that, for example my tandem asked me about Kichwa, what was the government efforts to implement it ... when I was talking about that I'm realizing, 'Oh my god, I should know Kichwa'.

Alberto (Ecuador) not only asserts he will learn Kichwa, he goes further to critique his country's educational policies around language.

> There should be something like a subject, which teach you Kichwa. So if as a kid you start learning your language because it just is also **our language**, if you as a kid start to learn in Kichwa, you are gonna have actual feelings about Kichwa ... There's something wrong there, because I think it's part of our culture, and if a language disappears, it means that ... groups of people, are gonna disappear ... for example, what about a child who just speaks Kichwa? What if this child wants to study? What if a native Kichwa speaker needs a hospital, nobody knows Kichwa?

Alberto's proposal is surprising in the face of global English dominant ideologies, whereby higher-status students learn English for career advancement, and Indigenous languages, lacking societal value, are frequently relegated to low-status minoritized groups. Alberto explained that, prior to the Global Conversations course, he had not given much thought to Kichwa and the Indigenous peoples of Ecuador.

Looking back on a talk by an Indigenous scholar from her own university, Tannya (Ecuador) recognizes significant gaps in her knowledge of her country's Indigenous cultures and, thus, her own roots.

> I felt so bad and ignorant, because, according to me, Ecuadorians only came from the Cañaris. And in this talk I found out that we can come from the Saragureños, the Cañaris, the Huancavilcas ... Kichwa must be

respected. In Ecuador we are dollarized, but I don't believe that it would be correct to decree English as our language, never! It would be a type of dictatorship. The language should be Kichwa, not even Spanish.

Tannya reports her embarrassment at the gaps in her knowledge of the Indigenous historical foundations of her country. She references Ecuador's adoption of the US dollar as national currency (in 2000) and relates the growing dominance of English (and Spanish) to colonizing forces, which she now rejects.

Concern for the loss of an Andean Indigenous worldview which values the interconnectedness of all things and rejects anthropocentric perspectives was also raised by Sandra (Ecuador) who studies environmental engineering.

> The Andean cosmovision caught my attention because it was something that I had heard, but had never known. Since there is a lot of belief that the crops depend on the moon, the sun, the mother earth. I study an environmental area, so it calls my attention that this cosmovision has to do with environmental issues.

While her major focuses on human interaction with the environment, she claims that she had not previously made connections between Indigenous agricultural techniques and success in conserving the land before hearing the speakers and discussing Indigenous knowledge with her classmates. Sandra concluded that the knowledge and awareness she gained through the talks offered by Indigenous experts in our program fundamentally enabled her to work toward solutions to environmental problems in her own country.

Limited Growth in Decolonial Thinking

Most pre-service teachers enter the immersion program with limited previous multilingual/multicultural experiences. The program provides structured opportunities for them to engage with people in another linguistic and cultural context. The data shows students adopting an accepting attitude towards multilingualism, clearly a positive move for teachers who will work with English learners. However, these positive attitudes lack criticality of power structures and societal or global inequities.

Patrick (US) drew on his struggles with Spanish in Ecuador as he considered English-only policies in US schools:

> I think [English-only] puts unnecessary stress on students. And I can say that with experience because when I was in Ecuador, there was a short period where I got very depressed … And the last thing I wanted was to hear Spanish. And on a child, I can only imagine it would be worse. So, I don't in any way support an English-only approach. Using an English-only approach is easier on the teacher and on the administration, but it is unnecessarily harder on the student.

Patrick's rebuttal shows some rejection of prevalent English-only discourses in schools. However, Patrick lacks a nuanced understanding of the powers of privilege at play that make his experience in Ecuador quite different from English learners who attend schools where English-only attitudes are predominant. Although Patrick's experience of language learning might give him empathy, the false equivalency fails to acknowledge his privilege in being able to travel and having supportive peers and program structures to bolster his language learning.

Like Patrick, Tiffany (US) remarks on the inappropriateness of English-only policies, expressed empathy for the challenges language learners face in classrooms requiring the use of English, but did not demonstrate awareness of broader power dynamics.

> Those poor kids. They would drown. I've kind of experienced that when I was there because my host mom wanted me to use Spanish only and it was so hard. I tried and then because I couldn't get out what I wanted to say quick enough or maybe she was talking too quick, it's hard for me to process so I would shut down ... I found that when I was able to translanguage, so use Spanish and then use the English where I needed it, that helped build my Spanish.

Tiffany built on her own experiences learning Spanish to suggest that incorporating home languages would be most effective for students learning English. This is a positive attitude regarding multilingualism, translanguaging and student's identities; however, her wording that 'those poor kids ... would drown' seems to further Other and disempower them. While she speaks from a deficit mindset, she grows in empathy:

> I think especially with kids, ESL kids, I can understand their frustrations so much more because I was that person in Ecuador. Like I'm able to empathize with you, so I'm not going to be so quick to make judgments like, they're not listening or they're being defiant. I think that's one of the most important things I have is experience of being the outsider.

But Tiffany goes no further. In US students' interpretations and reflections of their experiences, they largely miss the differences between their voluntary and highly supported, five-week experience in Ecuador and an English learner's experience in a US classroom.

Sarah (US), however, begins to analyze institutional post-program inequities. In a course during the semester before going to Ecuador, she partnered with a Saudi Arabian student learning English. While Sarah considers learning languages to be a positive thing, the widespread motivation to learn English is 'accommodating us rather than us accommodating everybody else'. She begins to construct the dynamic of English dominance, finding it 'mind boggling' and 'hypocritical' that her partner was learning English to be able to speak to US workers who went to Saudi Arabia for business. She extends this accommodation inequity to the Global Conversations course, pointing out that Ecuadorian students tended to accommodate to them when interacting in small groups because they (the US cohort) spoke less Spanish. These comments still fall short of making critical commentaries that are societal in scope, but are a step beyond those offered by Tiffany and Patrick.

Through lived experience, pre-service teachers can shape understandings of how deeply language, culture and identity are connected. On the other hand, critical interculturality and interrogation of colonialism in their own lives and across the globe is still mostly emergent.

Developing Critical Interculturality: Programmatic Structures and Relationship Building

We have examined our data to ask what conditions of this immersion experience have supported or hindered the critical intercultural development of our students. A central theme begins with and recurrently points towards *relationships* being of equal importance not only for program staff, homestay families and local communities but also among participating students. Meaningful relationships seem to be a necessary element to move towards the 'inter' of intercultural and to dismantle object-based traditions (of 'us' and 'them').

As institutional associations in a study-abroad experience precede student interaction, there must be a commitment on the part of program developers to create and sustain long-term relationships built on trust and friendship. In the case of the program in Ecuador, our ties have deepened over five years. Our contact began as a cooperative effort to design a study-abroad experience that would benefit students from both countries. We prioritize teamwork and create space to ask and listen. We have discussed finding common goals that might sometimes favor the Ecuadorian students over a sole focus on US students' growth. For example, we directed resources to allow greater participation of the host country students in weekend excursions rather than more comfortable lodging for US students. We have rewritten our end-of-program evaluation so that the questions do not probe US student levels of satisfaction, but instead ask ways that the student has moved outside of daily structured routines to talk with, notice and engage in localized cultural practices. Program leaders from both institutions consider and ask about potential benefits to the broader host community. Over time our relationship has moved towards collaborative research that reveals new ways we can build towards enacting decolonial thinking within the program.

Pedagogical Recommendations towards a Critical Interculturality

Over time we have come to see that we need to continually attend to decentering White, English-speaking ways of being which tend to dominate relationships and program practices, and instead explicitly give space for other ways of being. We encourage translanguaging in our classrooms as well as written and oral communications. For example, our program explicitly instructs students about the concept of translingual practices and presents ideas about how it is used in language classrooms, and we also model it in our own teaching. Since neither group of students is proficient in the language of the other group, instructors are conscious of using both languages in the classroom and translating key ideas into both languages (Spanish and English; there were no Kichwa speakers). We encourage 'playing' with language and use of either language in class and in reflective writing.

Building on the results of a recent review of the literature on efforts to improve intercultural development of teachers (Romijn *et al.*, 2021), we highlight two key elements that are visible in the program we studied: (a) guided critical reflection, and (b) sustained enactment. The extent to which pre-service teachers understand social inequities in education and recognize their own cultural biases and White privilege affects their readiness to change their beliefs. The input of new knowledge on understanding systems of power, oppression and Whiteness/privilege, and how these factors are reproduced in schools, is essential, as is detailed background knowledge regarding the history and contemporary realities of the host culture. Relatedly, not all students possess skills of reflection when they start the program, and we spend time teaching and supporting the development of reflective abilities; the chance to work with students over time and in five credit-bearing courses is a distinct advantage.

Learning about components of intercultural or translingual interaction must also be complemented with opportunities to enact them. While interculturality is knowledge and skill-based, it is most importantly relational. The explicit invitation to Ecuadorian students to join us in class and the expectation that informal connections will occur outside of class are important openings to enactment. Offering instruction in an Indigenous language along with Spanish and spending time in multilingual Indigenous communities is a way to offer openings to decolonial thinking, as well as asking our students to help set the global themes of interest to them to be discussed in the Global Conversations course. Finally, for the US pre-service teachers, making explicit links to instructional practices for English learners through the teaching practicum is vital; it allows them to translate newly addressed knowledge and skills into lesson plans and experiment with how strategies might be adapted to learners of differing language abilities.

Conclusion

International learning experiences for teachers can be constructed to center on a critical look at intercultural and global issues and offer program structures that build on binational peer collaborations and expectations for meaningful and long-term relationships. Our analysis concludes that while opportunities exist to make decolonial perspectives more visible, without intentional program supports, program participants can remain captive to entrenched deficit perspectives that are common to colonial discourses. These findings are consistent with previous work that shows that participants can grow in awareness and engage with diversity. We emphasize that enactment and relationship building are long-term goals that happen over a lifetime; intricate threads can only be made sense of with intentional, enduring commitments to listening, engagement and reflection.

References

Bernardes, R., Black, G., Otieno Jowi, J. and Wilcox, K. (2019) Teachers' critical interculturality understandings after an international teaching practicum. *Critical Studies in Education* 62 (4), 502–518. https://doi.org/10.1080/17508487.2019.1620817

Dervin, F. (2017) *Critical Interculturality: Lectures and Notes.* Newcastle-upon-Tyne: Cambridge Scholars Publishing.

de Sousa Santos, B. (2018) *The End of the Cognitive Empire: The Coming of Age of Epistemologies of the South.* Durham, NC and London: Duke University Press.

Emerson, R.M., Fretz, R.I. and Shaw, L.L. (2011) *Writing Ethnographic Fieldnotes.* Chicago: University of Chicago Press.

Granados-Beltrán, C. (2016) Critical interculturality. A path for pre-service ELT teachers. *Íkala, Revista De Lenguaje Y Cultura* 21 (2), 171–187.

Lucas, T., Strom, K., Bratkovich, M. and Wnuk, J. (2018) Inservice preparation for mainstream teachers of English language learners: A review of the empirical literature. *The Educational Forum* 82 (2), 156–173.

Mwebi, B.M. and Brigham, S.M. (2009) Preparing North American pre-service teachers for global perspectives: An international teaching practicum experience in Africa. *The Alberta Journal of Educational Research* 55 (3), 414–427.

Pirbhai-Illich, F. and Martin, F. (2019) Decolonizing teacher education in immersion contexts: Working with space, place and boundaries. In D. Martin and E. Smolcic (eds) *Redefining Teaching Competence through Immersive Programs: Practices for Culturally Sustaining Classrooms* (pp. 65–93). Cham: Palgrave Macmillan.

Pirbhai-Illich, F., Pete, S. and Martin, F. (2017) *Culturally Responsive Pedagogy: Working towards Decolonization, Indigeneity, and Interculturalism.* London: Palgrave Macmillan.

Romijn, B.R., Slot, P.L. and Leseman, P.P. (2021) Increasing teachers' intercultural competences in teacher preparation programs and through professional development: A review. *Teaching and Teacher Education* 98, 103236.

Smolcic, E. and Katunich, J. (2017) Teachers crossing borders: A review of the research into cultural immersion field experience for teachers. *Teaching and Teacher Education* 62, 47–59.

Smolcic, E. and Martin, D. (2019) Cultural/linguistic immersion in teacher preparation for emergent bilingual learners: Defining a new space for asset-based pedagogies. In D. Martin and E. Smolcic (eds) *Redefining Teaching Competence through Immersive Programs: Practices for Culturally Sustaining Classrooms* (pp. 1–36). Cham: Palgrave Macmillan.

Walsh, C. (2010) Interculturalidad crítica y educación intercultural. In J. Viaña, L. Tapia and C. Walsh (eds) *Construyendo Interculturalidad Crítica* (pp. 75–96). La Paz: Instituto Internacional de Integración del Convenio Andrés Bello III-CAB, Bolivia.

8 The Experience of Pre-Service Language Teachers Learning an Additional Language through Study Abroad

Roswita Dressler and Colleen Kawalilak

> *Andrea observed that 'Brazilians work such long days and students spend so much time in schools' so 'teachers [hold] a lot of responsibility for how students develop and who they [become]'. Andrea felt that that was the reason behind the cultural practice of referring to teachers as '"Tia" which literally means Aunt!'*
>
> *'An outside perspective can make a long-lasting impact and as more teachers both "get" and "give" support around the world, more students will be inspired to do great things'.*

Introduction

One way to prepare pre-service teachers for teaching culturally and linguistically diverse students is through international study-abroad experiences (Devillar & Jiang, 2012). Teachers who engage in pre-service study abroad are open to the immediate benefits associated with such experiences (Corder *et al.*, 2018). Many develop skills in second languages, advanced intercultural competencies and responsiveness, and deepen critical thinking and reflection skills that they can draw on in their teaching of culturally and linguistically diverse students (Anderson *et al.*, 2006; Cushner & Mahon, 2002). In addition, they are likely to enhance their understanding of their field and gain practical experience in a cultural context very different from their own (Coryell, 2011; Sharma *et al.*, 2011). However, there is a scarcity of follow-up research that specifically focuses on personal and professional learning acquired from having participated in a study-abroad sojourn (Dressler *et al*., 2022). Our intention in this chapter is to augment the discourse concerning how study-abroad programs not specifically designed to advance language learning may, nonetheless, contribute to personal and professional learning about language and culture.

The personal and professional development of pre-service sojourners can alter their sense and identity as culturally responsive educators (Arthur *et al*., 2020; Driscoll *et al*., 2014; Franklin, 2010). Notably, future teachers, upon immediate return from an international experience that involves meaningful time in a foreign classroom, often report significant personal and professional learning, highlighting an enhanced empathy toward students from diverse backgrounds in their home country classrooms. However, after completing their pre-service studies and searching for teaching jobs, the opportunity to further reflect on the personal and professional learning accrued from their study-abroad experience could be eclipsed by the day-to-day activities of their chosen profession.

Context

In this chapter, we feature two former participants from a study-abroad initiative, referred to as a pre-service sojourn, co-curricular service option, in a Bachelor of Education program. Open to all pre-service teachers in the last year of their program and regardless of content area specialization, participating students spend approximately 9–10 weeks in a host country outside of Canada to experience another culture and context by living and volunteer teaching in schools or other analogous educative centers. Additionally, in some cases, students may learn a new language either formally or informally. Broadly speaking, the primary aim of this co-curricular service option is to build intercultural capacities, such as awareness and engagement, and to inform and foster personal development and future teaching practice.

For the purpose of this study, we have chosen to focus on two participating sojourners who traveled to Brazil – Andrea in 2015 and Matthew in 2016. Although most participants in the study-abroad initiative are not second language specialists, Andrea and Matthew were both specializing in second language teaching in their Bachelor of Education degrees, so their perspectives include those of future second language teachers. Andrea's stated goal was 'to become a Spanish and French teacher'. Matthew noted that through his sojourn, he wanted to become 'a better language teacher'. Like their peers who had chosen other international destinations, Andrea and Matthew each experienced varied opportunities to teach and often found themselves with more informal than formal learning opportunities. In addition to their experiences of teaching and exploring the cultures of Brazil, they each wrote blogs while abroad and participated in a reflective writing workshop two months post-sojourn. The blogging and reflecting writing activities were a formal component of the study-abroad program. Further, Andrea and Matthew were also interviewed, post-graduation, in summer 2018 (two years post-graduation for Andrea, one year for Matthew) when both had been working as language teachers.

We present their personal and professional learning below as narratives spun from their blogs, post-sojourn reflection and post-graduation interview. Both Andrea and Matthew used these reflections to shed light on their personal learning about language learning as new learners of Portuguese. They also reflected on their personal learning about the Brazilian cultures as they encountered them through travel and forming relationships with local students and liaisons. Their professional learning focused on language teaching as well as the culture of education in Brazil. From this investigation, we can see which aspects remained salient throughout all aspects of reflection.

Personal Learning

Personal learning about language learning

Both Andrea and Matthew approached their sojourns as language and cultural learning opportunities. They set language learning and cultural participation goals, sought opportunities to practice, and documented their learning through their written reflective pieces and verbally through interviews. As successful language learners, they saw their sojourns as fertile ground for further personal learning about language and culture.

Andrea declared herself a 'language enthusiast'. She wrote in her blog that 'since [she] first started learning Spanish [she] knew [she] wanted to understand all of the Romance languages, and here [she was] now, working on number four'. She used her blog to document the ways she practiced Portuguese (e.g. using gestures, watching films, reading graffiti) and showcase her learning through headings like *Tia, me pode ayudar?* (Aunt, can you help me?). Andrea's successes in language learning were part of what she reflected on in her post-sojourn reflection when she spoke of using a positivity journal to 'write [about] all the beautiful things that happened abroad'. In a post-graduation interview, two years later, Andrea still viewed herself as 'a language nut ... [who] tried speaking Portuguese as much as possible'. She could still recall that 'it was really fun because that was a way of communicating with people ... understand what they were trying to tell me'. The experience of Andrea's personal language learning was a highlight of her sojourn and its salience extended beyond the actual sojourn into the early years of her career as a teacher.

Matthew blogged about how 'learning Brazilian Portuguese' was one of his goals for his sojourn. He mused that he could 'speak English and

French fluently and [had] studied Chinese extensively but with Portuguese [he was] back to square one'. Still, Matthew claimed that he was 'by no means a magical language learning machine'. Matthew's perspective on learning multiple languages was that 'knowing two languages [was] great, it opened [his] eyes a little wider to the world and challenged [his] perspective. Knowing three languages [was] a way for [him] to work hard and push [his] perspective a little bit further and to refine [his] understanding of the language learning process'. This learning did not come without its challenges. Matthew noted that 'it is certainly frustrating to be lost in translation, afraid of failure and embarrassment BUT rather than remaining still, intimidated by the challenge before [him] to keep MOVING and TRY, TRY and TRY AGAIN!' Since most of Matthew's personal language learning was informal, he commented that it took 'a lot of self-discipline and confidence ... but with enough determination and support anyone can learn a second language'. However, not all of Matthew's learning was informal. He profited from formal classes offered by the host university 'which [had] been so valuable because [he was] still unable to express [himself] at a comfortable level' when he started the classes. In Matthew's post-sojourn reflection, he proclaimed that he had accomplished his goal when he wrote that he could 'speak another language' which he credited to the work he put into that objective during the sojourn. When we interviewed Matthew one year later, he recalled being 'able to speak Portuguese pretty fluently near the end' of the sojourn. Matthew reported that personal language learning was 'pretty central' to the sojourn, supported by the formal classes which were small, and students were 'super motivated, so it was easy to move quickly'. While he hadn't 'been able to really keep it up ... to remain as fluent as [he] was', he credited his success to his having approached the sojourn 'on a level of mutual respect', an approach he had taken forward into his work as a teaching language assistant on a French government program.

For Andrea and Matthew, learning Portuguese while on their sojourn added to their experience of personal language learning since it was an additional language for both of them. Throughout their blogs, post-sojourn reflection, and interview, they documented and reflected upon their progress, noting post-sojourn and post-graduation that they felt they had succeeded in learning Portuguese to a level of which they were proud. From their personal experiences, they drew conclusions about language learning in general.

Personal learning about culture

In addition to personal language learning, Andrea and Matthew reflected in their blogs, post-sojourn reflections and interviews on their personal learning about culture. For Andrea and Matthew, culture involved food, travel and the experience of getting to know local

Brazilians. They sometimes made sense of that learning through comparison with Canadian culture as they saw it. While most of their reflections were positive, both shared some challenges they faced. Together, positive and negative experiences shaped their personal learning about culture.

Andrea frequently referenced Brazilian culture in her blog. She wrote of 'truly experiencing the REAL Brazil – full of warm welcoming people and waaaaay too much food' and also included 'fun facts' about the language and food. In addition, Andrea referred to close friendships formed with the Brazilians she met. She referred to herself and her host as 'a team – travelling, roaming the streets, learning Portuguese, trying new foods, going for coffee, shopping, studying'. In her final post, Andrea reflected on 'the incredible people I traveled with and met along the way' and felt that 'everyone I met was so welcoming'. During her school placement, students and the partner teacher 'shared their culture with [her] by showing [her] patience, understanding (especially with [her] broken Portuguese) and by sharing their views on their school and their way of life'. She had been invited over to dinners and family gatherings or offered rides so that she would be safe. She concluded that 'Brazilians come from a very inclusive and welcoming culture and [she felt] truly blessed to have been a part of it'. The cultural elements of people and language remained salient in her post-sojourn reflection, but Andrea admitted that some aspects of the sojourn 'mixed together made for a very isolating experience' and that she had to 'work almost every day to make sense of this exchange and find the positives in it'.

During Andrea's post-graduation interview, she reiterated the warmth she felt from her host and the Brazilian students she met. Andrea claimed that she 'never felt like [she] was a foreigner or excluded … They would tell [her] things about the culture, [and] they were so inclusive'. While Andrea avoided talking about the negative experiences she had alluded to in her post-sojourn reflection, she reflected that she 'was the Other because [Andrea] was white and because [she] was English speaking' so she 'was like a commodity' in that people wanted 'to find out more about [her] and they want[ed] to show [her] their culture'. Unlike the negative 'Othering' some sojourners might feel, she 'was completely the Other, but in the best way possible'. Warmth, curiosity and openness were the primary characteristics that Andrea attributed to Brazilian culture from her experience of her sojourn.

For Matthew, culture encompassed people and food, but also uniquely Brazilian elements such as *capoeira* (dance) and music as he arrived with a 'plan to take capoeira classes and learn a Brazilian song or two'. Once he settled, he noted that 'it took no time [at all] to feel welcome'. He described himself and his Brazilian roommate as 'similar cats from two totally different places'. Matthew claimed 'the street food here [was] miles ahead' of his home city. Like Andrea, he also related stories of his travels. These afforded him opportunities to reflect on the 'soft spot' he now had for

Brazil. Referencing a hike to a waterfall, Matthew 'spent what seemed like ages sitting under the thundering downpour of fresh water, grateful to be in Brazil'. As with Andrea, Matthew used the post-sojourn reflection to critically explore, more deeply, negative aspects of his sojourn experience. Although he had 'attempted to go into this program without any expectation of what life would be like in Brazil', Matthew had 'unfortunately succumbed to some less than ideal media representations of what it would be like (drugs, guns, violence, gangs, poverty, etc.)'. However, he 'quickly learned (or remembered) that every news story or anecdote [he] had heard before going to Brazil would not be reflective of [his] experience' and that he was 'choosing to do something that [was] intimidating and "out of [his] comfort zone"', determined to '[stick] to it right until the end'.

In his post-graduation interview, he revisited his initial nervousness about going to Brazil. He realized that 'sometimes you can't control [your fears]' because they are based on 'the only impressions that we have of whatever country'. He also recognized that it may be 'ingrained in a culture that we're surrounded by', thereby noting that his fears may be more rooted in his culture of origin than an actual picture of the host country. In the end, he felt that he could 'check [himself]' before he gave in to his fears. He recognized that he might always have 'subconscious anxieties about things that don't really matter', but that 'it takes a little experience ... to learn from that'. Through this reflection, his personal learning about culture became part of personal learning about himself.

Andrea and Matthew shared some similar cultural experiences of food, travel and friendships in their blogs and used the post-sojourn reflection to critically examine these experiences. During the post-graduation interview, both expressed that they had worked through the negative aspects of the sojourn to some degree and had emerged with personal insights into themselves as sojourners.

Professional Learning

Having the shared goal of becoming language teachers, Andrea and Matthew both reflected upon their professional learning associated with their respective sojourns. They often related aspects of language learning to language teaching, such as when Andrea commented in her blog that she would be assuming 'the role of a language student once more before [she] assume[d] the role of teacher'. They also reflected upon how culture influenced teaching, including, at times, making comparisons with their experiences in Canada to make sense of what they were observing. Their professional learning about language teaching and culture came through in all of the reflective pieces: the blogs, the post-sojourn reflection, and their post-graduation interview.

Andrea reported in her blog of 'having the mindset of an educator' by being aware of how she was 'learning best and alternative ways of learning'. She felt that through her sojourn she was 'acquiring many new strategies which will without doubt help ... future students'. She set herself the goal of 'collect[ing] as many resources and annotat[ing] as many ideas as [she could to] incorporate them into [her] practicum and ... teaching portfolio'. In reflecting upon the sojourn during her post-sojourn reflection, she noted the professional relationships and 'meaningful connections with the staff and students'. She related the anecdote that she 'even received letters saying that [she didn't] need to go home, that this [was her] home now'. Two years later, in her post-graduation interview, she compared teaching in Canada with teaching in Brazil, noting that 'being a teacher [in Canada] is quite a respectable profession [whereas] teachers aren't paid much [in Brazil]. So, they really, really do it out of love'. Her overall takeaway from her professional learning was that as a language teacher 'it was so good to go back and be able to be a learner again and kind of remember what it's like to be a beginner'. She reminded herself that she wanted to remember to 'have the student at the centre of learning'. Since the sojourn gave her the opportunity to 'be a student again, to remind yourself how to, how to teach', she felt that she had gained professional learning about language teaching which she carried into her current profession.

Matthew noted in his blog that during the sojourn he would be 'visiting a few different school systems ... and [helping] some of the teachers here come up with effective language learning lesson plans'. He mused that 'creating and sustaining international academic relationships is one of the most effective ways to improve education'. He felt that 'an outside perspective can make a long-lasting impact and as more teachers both "get" and "give" support around the world, more students will be inspired to do great things'. He referred to this long-lasting impact in his post-sojourn reflection when he revealed his future aspiration 'to return to Brazil to live and work as an educator'. One year after graduation, Matthew commented that his school visits in Brazil 'continued to inform [his] understanding of language education and language education in different countries and cultures'. While Matthew was honest that he observed 'a lot of things that didn't work', he was beginning to understand that language teachers in different countries 'have different understanding' and that the more he worked 'with different populations', the more he gained 'a much more broad understanding of what language learning tactics really work'. Thus, Matthew considered his sojourn as one opportunity where he learned about the profession of language teaching.

Both Andrea and Matthew viewed their sojourn as an opportunity to learn about language teaching through their experiences of being language learners while on their sojourn. They reflected upon strategies that they observed, resources they encountered, and the disposition of teachers. Both saw their sojourn as mutual learning for all involved.

Professional learning about culture

Professional learning about culture involved Andrea and Matthew making meaning around cultural practices in Brazil and how they were reflected in education. The culture of relationships appeared to permeate the culture of the schools. Education in Brazil has a strong tradition of educational reform, but the everyday realities demonstrate challenges. Part of their meaning-making came from comparisons with Canada.

Andrea's professional learning about culture permeated her blog posts. She often contrasted the openness and warmth of the people with the stark realities of high poverty and 'funding, supplies and resources'. When describing one school, she noted that 'the doors are always open (once you pass through security and the locked gate that is) to children, parents and whole families'. In other words, everyone is welcome, but precautions must be taken because 'it is not the safest area of the city'. Andrea observed that 'Brazilians work such long days and students spend so much time in schools' so 'teachers [hold] a lot of responsibility for how students develop and who they [become]'. Andrea felt that that was the reason behind the cultural practice of referring to teachers as '"Tia" which literally means Aunt!' She concluded that 'it changes the dynamic greatly inside of the classroom' and resulted in 'a lot more laughter, inclusion of student interests and personal involvement, hugs, and autonomy'. From Andrea's perspective, 'they treat each other as family and ... that contributes to the image that we all have of South Americans being so warm, friendly and family oriented', which, in her opinion, they were.

Andrea learned that 'the percentage of literate Brazilians is quite low and so the instructors try their best to incorporate reading and writing into the activities'. Some schools also provided specialized programs like art education, one of which she was able to teach in as a volunteer. She noted that, 'teachers aren't tied to a specific curriculum or expectations. They work with the students and fellow teachers in order to maximize learning and engagement of the students'. Andrea's contribution was to teach a unit comparing Canadian and American fashion. She observed that 'a lot can be learned through fashion'. The students were 'pleasantly engaged' and asked 'numerous questions about Canada, including how cold it is and "have you seen Sasquatch?"' Looking back, during her post-sojourn reflection, Andrea credited the sojourn as providing the 'opportunity to understand the school culture' and be 'a part of the school and representing "staff" to a certain degree'. She characterized the culture of education as 'accepting and student-focused'. As such, Andrea expressed that she 'would love to bring some Brazil into [her] classroom and make lessons more fun, more about practical learning than tests'. She felt that from her experience in Canada, although 'these are definitely qualities that exist more so in the elementary setting', she 'would strive to establish them in the secondary [setting]' in her future teaching practice.

In Andrea's post-graduation interview, she recalled that teachers would be called aunt and uncle in Portuguese and maintained it 'was really great, because it kind of just changed how you view education'. Andrea felt it was 'like you were learning from a relative, like you were from the same family'. In Canada, there are 'so many rules' that keep teachers 'far away from [students]'. In Andrea's current teaching, students 'are always really fascinated'. She believed this serves to heighten engagement because 'as soon as you get kids interested, then it's a shoe in'. As mentioned in Andrea's reflections, the emphasis on relationships and the flexibility to focus on student interests were the two strongest aspects of her professional learning about the culture of Brazilian education.

In Matthew's professional learning about culture, he began by blogging about Paulo Freire, 'a great Brazilian educator who had a role in the education reform in Brazil'. He chose to begin one of his blogs with the popular quote: 'Whoever teaches learns in the act of teaching, and whoever learns teaches in the act of learning' (Freire, 1998: 31). Matthew anticipated 'being in a variety of public and private, urban and rural schools' and getting the chance 'to interact with the students and to share with them a little Irish-Canadian culture'. As he visited schools, Matthew observed that 'it takes a while to truly understand the complexities' of education in Brazil, especially 'the difference between the public and private systems'. When he visited the same school that Andrea had taught in, Matthew considered it 'a really healthy balance of traditional "in-class" learning and a newer "artistic-approach" to education'. However, when visiting a 'public school nearby', he found that 'the atmosphere was not comparable'. He also observed that, along with a police presence, 'the classrooms were very plain and somewhat run-down'. In addition, Matthew saw 'handfuls of students "hanging-out" in cliques while a few were silently working and talking with their teacher during class'. This lack of engagement was 'shocking' to him and he was dismayed to find out that 'those who teach cannot rely on their teaching income'. In comparing the schooling systems in Canada and Brazil, Matthew felt that in Canada, 'students in the public system are not put at such a disadvantage as it would seem they are in this city in Brazil'. He also noted the 'on-going political turmoil and the fact that the population of Brazil is almost 6 times that of Canada' as possible factors. Yet, Matthew acknowledged 'a slow movement toward education reform in Brazil much like the one we are experiencing in Canada'. Matthew tempered his earlier remarks by pointing out that there was 'a lot of good happening in Brazil in terms of alternative approaches to education' and 'there are some great historical leaders in the education reform movement such as Paulo Freire'. Interestingly, Matthew's post-sojourn reflection focused on his personal learning and, as such, he did not comment on his professional learning about culture until his post-graduation interview. In the interview, he summed up his repeated comparison of public and private K-12 education in Brazil as 'you get what you pay for', noting that it was 'a shame that there are so many public schools that suffer'. The observations of the inequities between the two systems of education made a strong impact on his professional learning about the culture of Brazilian education.

Professional learning about culture emerged in Andrea's and Matthew's blogs, post-sojourn reflections and post-graduation interviews. They observed teachers, students and educational structures and chose to learn from both the positives and the negatives. They were able to take this learning into professions as language teachers with the relational aspects resonating as most salient.

Implications

While Andrea and Matthew learned Portuguese, explored the cultures of Brazil and later became language teachers, insights gained from this study have implications beyond study-abroad programming that may inform pre-service teacher education generally. Considering the demographics of student diversity in many countries, questions for future research arise which may be of interest to pre-service teacher educators and study-abroad program administrators.

(1) What is the role of study abroad in introducing non-language specialist pre-service teachers to foundations in language learning and teaching? What is the role of teacher education generally in introducing all pre-service teachers to foundations in language learning and teaching?
(2) What philosophical foundations inform and shape education in other countries? What can be gained by exploring these foundations during pre-sojourn preparation and pre-service teacher education in general?
(3) How do curricula reflect diversity of perspectives, approaches to learning and the fostering of cultural humility?

These questions may also be of interest to researchers and educators in other professional programs that work directly with diverse populations. Two examples would be social work and nursing.

Conclusion

In this chapter, we focused on two language teachers, Andrea and Matthew, who learned an additional language while participating in a pre-service teacher study-abroad sojourn in Brazil. When in their host country, they volunteer-taught in schools and explored Brazilian culture. Narratives drawn from their blogs, post-sojourn reflections and post-graduate interviews revealed personal and professional learning about language and culture. Even though this study-abroad program was not specifically designed to advance language learning, as future language teachers, Andrea and Matthew applied a lens of personal and professional learning about language and culture when revisiting and reflecting on their experiences.

Although we recognize that not all pre-service teachers have the opportunity or resources to participate in study abroad, having demonstrated the learning that is possible by reflecting on one's personal and professional learning, we invite researchers and educators to provide opportunities for learning about language and culture to student teachers in professional programs.

References

Anderson, P.H., Lawton, L., Rexeisen, R.J. and Hubbard, A.C. (2006) Short-term study abroad and intercultural sensitivity: A pilot study. *International Journal of Intercultural Relations* 30 (4), 457–469.

Arthur, N., Becker, S., Dressler, R., Crossman, K. and Kawalilak, C. (2020) Pre-service teachers and study abroad experiences: Don't forget about them when they come home. *Teaching and Teacher Education* 89, 1–11.

Corder, D., Roskvist, A., Harvey, S. and Stacey, K. (2018) Language teachers on study abroad programmes: The characteristics and strategies of those most likely to increase their intercultural communicative competence. In J.L. Plews and K. Misfeldt (eds) *Second Language Study Abroad Programming, Pedagogy, and Participant Engagement* (pp. 257–297). Basingstoke: Palgrave Macmillan.

Coryell, J.E. (2011) The foreign city as classroom: Adult learning in study abroad. *Adult Learning* 22 (3), 4–11.

Cushner, K. and Mahon, J. (2002) Overseas student teaching: Affecting personal, professional, and global competencies in an age of globalization. *Journal of Studies in International Education* 6 (1), 44–58.

Devillar, R.A. and Jiang, B. (2012) From student teaching abroad to teaching in the U.S. classroom: Effects of global experiences on local instructional practice. *Teacher Education Quarterly* 39 (3), 7–24.

Dressler, R., Kawalilak, C., Crossman, K. and Becker, S. (2022) Implementing longitudinal, reflective follow-up study abroad research: Following former pre-service teachers into professional practice. In J. MacGregor and J. Plews (eds) *Designing Second Language Study Abroad Research: Critical Reflections on Methods and Data.* New York: Palgrave.

Driscoll, P., Rowe, J.E. and Thomae, M. (2014) The sustainable impact of a short comparative teaching placement abroad on primary school language teachers' professional, linguistic and cultural skills. *Language Learning* 42 (3), 307–320.

Franklin, K. (2010) Long-term career impact and professional applicability of the study abroad experience. *Frontiers: The Interdisciplinary Journal of Study Abroad* 19, 169–191.

Freire, P. (1998) *Pedagogy of Freedom: Ethics, Democracy, and Civic Courage.* Lanham, MD: Rowman & Littlefield.

Sharma, S., Phillion, J. and Malewski, E. (2011) Examining the practice of critical reflection for developing pre-service teachers' multicultural competencies: Findings from a study abroad program in Honduras. *Issues in Teacher Education* 20 (2), 9–22.

9 Border-Crossing and Professional Development of Taiwanese EFL Teachers in a Study-Abroad Program

Chiou-lan Chern, Angel M. Y. Lin and Mei-Lan Lo

Through this intercultural professional development program, the participating teachers were able to venture out of their schools' remote locales and find a supportive community.

'*Everything I knew about America used to come from textbooks. This study abroad experience made me understand a Chinese saying, "Travelling millions of miles is better than reading millions of books"*'.

Introduction

Taiwan is a small island with a central mountain range where villages are isolated from main towns. Schools in areas with limited public transportation, poor socioeconomic resources and little cultural and technological support are designated as remote-area schools. For the sake of educational equity, various projects have been put in place to provide additional educational resources; however, it is difficult for remote-area schools to retain teachers due to a lack of professional support. In 2015, the Ministry of Education (MOE) in Taiwan initiated a program to send a group of 15 English teachers from remote-area schools overseas for their professional development. This MOE-sponsored project was commissioned to a local university with a strong background in teacher education, and cooperation with a United States university similarly strong in teacher training was established to plan a customized professional development

(PD) program. The program, 125 hours of courses that spanned five weeks in the summer, included courses on TESOL pedagogical content knowledge (PCK), cultural and educational visits, as well as online co-teaching via Google Hangouts or Zoom for the semester following this summer program. Since 2015, the program has been offered annually to English language teachers from remote-area schools. In 2020, however, the program was suspended due to the Covid-19 pandemic. Through this intercultural professional development program, the participating teachers were able to venture out of their schools' remote locales and find a supportive community. They reported their rekindled passion for teaching and for different cultures. This chapter describes the program requirements as well as the participating teachers' reflections on their experiences.

Building a Community through Professional Development

Researchers on study-abroad programs have described and theorized the impact of this sojourn experience on both pre-service and in-service language teachers. In a meta-synthesis study exploring the effects of short-term international experiences on both pre-service and in-service language teachers, Çiftçi and Karaman (2019) concluded that the outcomes documented in 25 studies published from 2000 to 2016 are three-fold: (a) professional (e.g. personal growth and pedagogical improvement), (b) linguistic (e.g. language skills and language awareness), and (c) intercultural (e.g. increased tolerance toward cultural differences, cultural awareness and respect for diversity).

Although studies on teachers' study-abroad experiences have focused more on pre-service rather than in-service teachers, since 2010, a growing amount of research has examined the study-abroad experiences of in-service language teachers (Allen, 2010, 2013; Baecher & Chung, 2020; Gleeson & Tait, 2012; He et al., 2017; Kasun et al., 2019; Li & Edwards, 2013; Roskvist et al., 2014, 2017; Wang, 2014; Zhao & Mantero, 2018). For instance, Baecher and Chung (2020), drawing on the literature on study abroad and transformative learning theory (Mezirow, 1978, 1997), as well as their own findings synthesized from ten primary and secondary teachers' international service learning experiences, developed a conceptual framework for the design of transformative teacher professional development in the context of international service learning. The key elements in the framework are experience, dissonance, community of practice and critical reflection. They argued that these elements will lead to teachers' continuous professional identity construction and reconstruction.

In terms of teacher professional development, many researchers have adopted the notion of *community of practice* (Wenger, 1998) as an underpinning for their studies (Baecher & Chung, 2020; Gleeson & Tait, 2012; He & Lin, 2018). He and Lin (2018) developed a professional development model for Content and Language Integrated Learning (CLIL) teachers, and they argued that CLIL teacher professional development should be a collaborative, dynamic and dialogic process, where both teachers and teacher educators are co-developing their knowledge and expertise in CLIL. Baecher and Chung's (2020) study on in-service teachers' international service experiences found that the teachers 'were able to build a community by traveling, living, and creating new relationships, which also contributed to their self-confidence and self-efficacy' (2020: 46). In the same vein, Gleeson and Tait's (2012) study on nine EFL teachers' five-week professional development program in New Zealand revealed that these teachers from Hong Kong formed a transitory community to support their academic and social learning while studying abroad. However, after returning to Hong Kong, the teachers no longer shared a common goal and thus the community was disbanded.

The existing literature on the effects of study abroad indicate that short-term programs can lead to language teachers' growth in personal, pedagogical, linguistic, cultural and critical awareness (Baecher & Chung, 2020). As adult learners, in-service teachers have already accumulated much experience and thus formed their own concepts, rooted values and 'frames of reference that define their life world' (Mezirow, 1997: 5). As a result, they may be reluctant to accept new ideas. To foster teacher learning in a transformative way, program designers and providers need to take the essential elements – experience, dissonance, community of practice and critical reflection – into consideration. Moreover, the relationships among the stakeholders involved in teacher professional development should not be hierarchical. Rather, teacher learning should be a collaborative, dynamic and dialogic process (Baecher & Chung, 2020; He & Lin, 2018).

Regarding professional development for EFL teachers, adding a collaborative co-planning and co-teaching component with partners from the US has hitherto been scarce. To bridge the research gap, this chapter aims to explore EFL teachers' reflections on participating in a professional development program that was blended with on-site cultural immersion and virtual real-time co-teaching modes.

Overview of the PD Program in Focus

Over the past five years, the specific course content of the MOE-sponsored PD program for remote-area school English teachers in Taiwan has varied slightly each year. However, the main structure has remained constant in outlining three phases: pre-departure orientation, on-site cultural immersion, and virtual real-time co-teaching stages.

Stage 1: Pre-departure orientation (May and June)

After the teachers from Taiwan are recruited in April each year, they are paired up with their US partners (called Cloud partners as the online project is dubbed Cloud Project) and start to meet online. Taiwanese teachers initiate three virtual meetings before they embark on their journey overseas. The purpose of the first two meetings is to introduce themselves and their classroom settings, student profiles and language learning backgrounds to their Cloud partners. The third pre-departure virtual meeting is to introduce their Cloud partners to their students and test-run the co-teaching procedures.

Stage 2: On-site cultural immersion (July to August)

During the five-week study in the US university, the Taiwanese teachers attend classes five hours a day, with their Cloud partners joining some of the classes. The Taiwanese teachers and their Cloud partners are given time to prepare lessons via face-to-face meetings. Most of them draft several units to be used in their later online teaching sessions when the Taiwanese teachers return home to their schools. The Taiwanese teachers are required to write reflections and post the highlights of their learning on Facebook on a weekly basis to document and reflect on their learning in the US.

Stage 3: Virtual real-time co-teaching (September to December)

The Taiwanese teachers conduct online teaching with their US partners for one class period every other week. They discuss the content of the lesson in advance even though some of the units have already gone through preliminary planning and discussions in the summer. During this stage, the Taiwanese teachers post bi-weekly entries on Facebook to share their online co-teaching experiences. The climax of this stage is the US partners' actual visit to Taiwanese classrooms in December and co-presentation at a conference to share their experiences on teaching collaboration.

Program evaluation

Being an integral part of the program, two program-wide surveys are conducted, one immediately following the five weeks of courses in the US and the other, four months later after the end-of-program conference in December. These surveys contain 5-point Likert scale questions and open-ended questions to explore participants' opinions toward various components of the program.

Data Sources

The data in this study came mainly from the 20 teachers who participated in the program in the summer of 2019. The first of the two program-wide surveys was conducted in August (Survey 1) as the post five-week cultural immersion course survey; the second was given out in December (Survey 2), which was the post-program survey conducted at the very end of the program. The first survey aimed to tap the participants' opinions on courses, cultural activities and school visits. The second survey consisted of three open-ended questions to investigate participants' perceptions on the online sessions and the end-of-program conference. To further explore the effects of online co-teaching, an additional open-ended survey (Survey 3) was distributed electronically in October 2020 to ask all participants, from 2015 to 2019, whether the online partnership teaching had any long-term effect on their subsequent teaching and whether it encouraged them to conduct online teaching when Covid-19 became an issue. All three surveys were answered anonymously, and the respondents could complete the open-ended questions in either Chinese or English. Most of the responses were in Chinese, which were translated into English for inclusion in this chapter.

Results

The three surveys were analyzed based on the time they were administered, from Survey 1 to Survey 2, to see if the participants' perceptions were sustained over a period of time. The third survey was analyzed to explore whether any long-term effects existed for the teachers' virtual teaching experience.

Survey 1 (Immediate effect after coursework)

The first part of this survey focused on participating teachers' opinions of the program; the second part asked for the participants' perceptions of their growth after the five-week program. Seventeen of the 20 teachers answered the survey. In the first part, most of the items received a very high ranking, with over 4.5 out of 5 points. The participants were particularly satisfied with the course content offered in the program, especially the unit *Hands-on Activities for Integrating Science into the ESL Classroom* (with a score of 4.94). This is probably due to the fact that the curriculum reform implemented in September 2019 in Taiwan introduced a new emphasis on content integration and interdisciplinary cooperation. The national policy of making Taiwan a bilingual nation by 2030 is likely another reason that raised teachers' awareness of integrating English with other subjects. In addition, an item that received an almost perfect score was the weekend cultural activities (a score of 4.94), one of which in the 2019 program was a field trip to a mountain area that was still snow-capped in July. This was a unique experience for teachers from a tropical region like Taiwan, where snow is rare and utterly unheard of in summer. Therefore, the relevance of pedagogical input to national policy and cultural novelty were reasons for the participants' unanimously positive feedback.

The second part of the survey probed participants' growth in language and professional knowledge. The 17 teachers surveyed were very positive about their growth in TESOL pedagogical content knowledge and understanding of American culture (both received an average score of 4.88). They also thought their English language skills had improved, though more on listening and speaking (with average scores of 4.82 and 4.64, respectively) and less on reading and writing (with average scores of 4.3 and 4.05, respectively). Overall, they unanimously agreed that the enrichment program had promoted their professional growth (with an average score of 5).

When asked to elaborate on the biggest change resulting from this enrichment program, many participants commented on their cultural experiences:

> The biggest impact is to know American culture. This is the first time for me to visit the USA. Everything I knew about America used to come from textbooks. This study abroad experience made me understand a Chinese saying, 'Travelling millions of miles is better than reading millions of books'. (S1-08-2019)[1]

> Thanks to our Cloud partners, we actually experienced American culture and the local people's way of life. (S1-12-2019)

Some teachers also reflected on the language used around them and how that differed from the language used in their student textbooks:

> I learned a lot about Americans' way of life, the cultural differences and the education system. I also know they don't use sentences like 'I go to school by car'. They say, 'I drive to school'. This makes me think about the lessons I will teach in the future. (S1-10-2019)

A great majority of the comments centered around teaching English in English, which has been advocated for years in Taiwan but has recently become an issue due to the goal of becoming a bilingual nation:

> Before taking courses in this program, I could not increase my use of English in class for fear that students would suffer. Now I feel more confident and will try to use more English in class. (S1-04-2019)

> I have decided to use English to teach English. I have begun to believe that it's good for students to learn English in English. (S1-11-2019)

> I think teaching English in English might work. I have been very dubious about CLIL and don't think science content can be taught in English. It's time-consuming and not effective. But after various discussions, I know I have to give it a try, and I will take the big stride bravely. (S1-12-2019)

As for the program's most impressive aspect, many respondents mentioned the online lessons, the collaboration with their partners on Cloud and the purpose of these lessons:

> Through discussions with my Cloud partners, I could understand the differences in education systems and thinking patterns. (S1-09-2019)

> In the beginning, we were very quiet in class as there were few questions raised. When our Cloud partners joined us later on, I observed how actively they participated in class and openly shared their ideas. In the following weeks, we became more active in class discussions. I did a lot of reflection on this and will create this kind of atmosphere in my own class when I return home. (S1-15-2019)

> I reflected deeply on the online Cloud lessons and realized that those classes were not intended to put pressure on students. Instead, they should immerse students in an English environment and motivate them to learn English. Therefore, I should not plan complicated activities. Let's wait and see how I implement the lessons next semester! (S1-02-2019)

The above comments represent some of the overwhelmingly positive comments revealed in the survey. The following excerpts capture the overall experience of the five-week cultural immersion program for all the participants:

> This is a very fruitful experience in many ways, including learning from taking courses, from living experiences, and from being immersed in an authentic cultural and linguistic environment. Being able to work with foreigners broadened my vision, and I learned different philosophies and methods in teaching. Cooperation is another kind of cultural experience. I look forward to teaching online cooperatively. (S1-11-2019)

The comments in the first survey seem to echo other sojourn studies regarding the increase in cultural and linguistic awareness (Baecher & Chung, 2020; Çiftçi & Karaman, 2019). The participants also encountered linguistic dissonance (language used in textbooks vs. in real life) and pedagogical approaches (using the target language as a medium of instruction) that challenged their original beliefs. However, after being immersed in an English language environment for five weeks, they re-evaluated their beliefs and gained confidence in both their teaching and language ability. Nevertheless, whether this positivity was sustained after the participants returned to their own schools in Taiwan was another issue worth exploring.

Survey 2 (Sustained effects upon completion of the program)

When asked about the biggest gain from the program, many teachers reiterated the valuable experience of cultural immersion and the interactions with their American instructors and Cloud partners. They cherished the language skills they developed through daily exposure. In addition, several teachers noted that receiving support and being able to inspire their students were important achievements:

> I met a group of passionate teachers, both from Taiwan and the US. We supported each other, which helped me build up confidence and bring about passion towards teaching. (S2-11-2019)

> When I shared my experience in the US with my students, some of them said they would want to experience this themselves in the future. I think being able to inspire students is another sense of achievement. (S2-05-2019)

Obviously, some teachers transferred their own growth and motivation to their students, who shared the sentiment with their teachers. Another important question in the December survey related to the participants' experience of online teaching. Their responses, however, were not as positive. Most of the teachers encountered technological problems such as poor network connections or inadequate equipment:

> Students' voices cannot be heard by my Cloud partner. If I ask my students to speak through a microphone, it will lower their willingness to speak up in class. (S2-04-2019)

> One time, we spent 20 minutes on solving computer problems. In the end, students had to sit around me and my notebook to continue the online lessons. (S2-05-2019)

> When technical problems occurred, it was hard to find help right away as my colleagues were also engaged with their work or classes. (S2-12-2019)

Other problems mentioned were challenges in scheduling due to the different time zones between the US and Taiwan, the amount of time spent on communicating with Cloud partners before class, and the compatibility of Cloud partners:

> The time I could work with my Cloud partner was very limited as she was busy, and finding time to co-teach with me was not easy due to the time difference between U.S. and Taiwan as well as the fixed schedule at my school. (S2-05-2019)

> I spent 2 to 3 class periods (45 minutes per period) to prepare my students for what we would cover during one online session. By doing that, students would be able to participate and interact with my Cloud partner. But that really cut down the time I could spend on teaching textbook content. I frequently pondered the pros and cons of this. (S2-03-2019)

> My American partner lacked teaching experience so she did not know how to interact with students. She could not devote her time to teaching and lesson planning ... We need more professional and passionate partners for this project. (S2-09-2019)

Even though technological problems were not uncommon, the planning of online lessons was time-consuming, and not all Cloud partners were as devoted to or as experienced in teaching as the Taiwanese teachers, some participating teachers still considered online teaching a good option and wanted the online portion to be extended from one semester to one year. For example, one teacher made the following comment:

> Actually, the effect of virtual teaching cannot compete with in-person teaching, but it is not a bad alternative. After many sessions of online classes, my students really looked forward to meeting Beth [the online teacher] in person. When Beth actually visited my class, students felt like she was already an old friend. (S2-06-2019)

The above excerpt illustrates that most of the participating teachers understood that every cloud has a silver lining and they could find value in the challenging task of collaborative teaching online. The following points raised by one of the teachers summarize the overall growth that the majority of teachers reported in Survey 2, which were in line with Baecher and Chung's (2020) pedagogical, language, personal, cultural and critical awareness.

> These are what I gained from the program: (1) became familiar with teaching methods, (2) sharpened my language skills, (3) broadened my world view, (4) met many US partners in the TESL field, (5) tasted the local way of life, (6) readjusted my teaching goals and methods, (7) experienced culture shock, and (8) refreshed myself. (S2-13-2019)

These remarks show that the participating teachers held a positive view of the intercultural enrichment program both immediately after they completed the coursework and four months later. They built a rapport among themselves and established friendships with their US partners. More importantly, they regained their confidence and rekindled their passion for teaching. However, since the participants encountered various technical problems with online teaching and therefore didn't feel very positively about it, it would be worthwhile investigating whether they subsequently continued to try teaching online.

Survey 3 (Long-term effects of online teaching)

Since virtual real-time co-teaching was a unique feature in this PD program for remote-area teachers, the researchers conducted another survey to explore whether there was any lasting impact. All the participating teachers from 2015 to 2019 were asked to complete an open-ended survey to ascertain whether they still conducted online teaching, whether they felt comfortable teaching online due to Covid-19, and whether their experience of virtual co-teaching had any impact on their teaching. Of the 92 participating teachers during those five years, 44 (47.8%) responded to the survey. Most of the respondents (39) did not adopt online teaching after the program because they had no access to international partners and did not feel comfortable bothering their Cloud partners after the program had ended. Four teachers said they either kept in touch periodically with their Cloud partners or occasionally conducted online lessons. However, one teacher ventured into another online project sponsored by the Ministry of Education:

> Since I took the summer enrichment program in 2016, I have started to participate in International Companions for Learning (ICL).[2] Through iEARN, I have also participated in projects to interact and give presentations online with teachers from different countries. (S3-03-2016)

When asked if the experience of conducting the Cloud project enabled them to feel comfortable teaching online, the respondents unanimously agreed that they were no longer afraid of teaching online, and some said they felt competent and ready to implement virtual teaching. The respondents all said they would encourage and help other teachers to teach online if necessary:

> With the Cloud teaching experience, I have no fear of teaching online, and I am more confident and very willing to teach others if necessary. (S3-01-2018)

> I have no anxiety at all if we need to teach online. I will definitely help other teachers if necessary. (S3-02-2017)

> Teaching online is a piece of cake for me now as it has become a habit. Thanks to the nine-month solid training and practice. (S3-03-2016)

When asked what major impact the experience of teaching online has had on their teaching, the participants responded with a variety of answers, but all were positive. Some of them noted their own growth in language, culture and ESL pedagogy. Many of them mentioned the improvements they had observed in their students' attitude toward learning:

> I think it is important 'to use English as a bridge to connect with the world'. It dawned on me that learning a language is learning its culture as well. The Cloud lessons allowed me to go beyond my textbooks and the classroom boundaries. It allowed my students to experience the joy of using English and gave them a motivation for learning English. (S3-09-2017)

> The best thing about teaching online with my Cloud partner is that we could broaden our students' global visions without being confined by geographical space or a limited budget to hire native-speakers. I think online teaching has had a great impact on my students' English learning. (S3-05-2016)

> What impressed me most was that my students' learning motivation became stronger, and they looked forward to the next class. After class, I frequently overheard my weaker students using the words or sentences they had just learned to talk to their classmates. I was so touched! (S3-02-2018)

Like the above teacher who felt excited to see the students' improved motivation, another teacher summed up the entire experience with the online teaching component in a very reflective and sentimental tone:

> Our new curriculum requires us to adopt competency-based learning. I always reflect on my teaching and see if it is related to students' daily

life. I always remember how touched I was when I was sitting and learning in the US classroom. Whenever I feel down, I remember those touching moments and encourage myself to continue making an effort and trying different approaches. (S3-06-2019)

The results of the third survey show that although only one teacher embarked on another virtual project to provide students with intercultural learning opportunities, most teachers were unhesitant about creating an online learning environment for their students. The virtual real-time teaching component of the program seemed to have had an effect on these participants.

Conclusion and Implications

Teachers who work in remote areas with fewer resources often feel geographically and professionally isolated and therefore tend to leave once they find a more centrally-located school. This hybrid intercultural PD program was instituted by the MOE solely for those teachers working in remote schools. The purpose has been to provide opportunities for them to grow professionally and to introduce Cloud partners as resources who could interact in English with their students. As reported in this study, the program appears to have met these goals.

When teachers, including English teachers, were placed in an environment where English is the language of communication, they experienced dissonance (cultural shock) coupled with excitement. They gained a deeper understanding of the role of the English language, beyond textbook English, and consolidated their beliefs about the value of teaching English in English. This program was tailored for the group of participating teachers and was therefore meaningful to them because of its relevance to their school curriculum and the national policy. Novelty in both the cultural and educational contexts was certainly the highlight of this study-abroad program. However, providing a clear structure to prepare in-service teachers for their sojourn experiences is essential. Like students encountering new course material, teachers also need scaffolding before they leave their familiar environment and experience immersion in a new country.

The overwhelmingly positive feedback from the participants certainly had a lot to do with the structure of the program, which provided the participants with pre-departure orientation, customized course content and a supportive learning community. However, certain aspects of this program can be further explored; for instance, how to ensure that the methods the Taiwanese teachers were exposed to during study abroad can be sustainable even after the co-partnering has ended. Longitudinal studies with more follow-up interviews, surveys or class observations might provide a more comprehensive picture of the effect of study-abroad programs.

Notes

(1) The numbers in the parentheses indicate participant ID. The first two digits indicate the survey number, with S1 referring to Survey 1. The second two digits indicate the participant's number on the survey, and the last four digits indicate the year the participants attended the program.
(2) ICL is a program that pairs international students in Taiwan with teachers who are interested in having international speakers interact with their students.

References

Allen, L.Q. (2010) The impact of study abroad on the professional lives of world language teachers. *Foreign Language Annals* 43 (1), 93–104.

Allen, L.Q. (2013) Teachers' beliefs about developing language proficiency within the context of study abroad. *System* 41 (1), 134–148.

Baecher, L. and Chung, S. (2020) Transformative professional development for in-service teachers through international service learning. *Teacher Development* 24 (1), 33–51.

Çiftçi, E.Y. and Karaman, A. (2019) Short-term international experiences in language teacher education: A qualitative meta-synthesis. *Australian Journal of Teacher Education* 44 (1), 93–119.

Gleeson, M. and Tait, C. (2012) Teachers as sojourners: Transitory communities in short study-abroad programmes. *Teaching and Teacher Education* 28 (8), 1144–1151.

He, P. and Lin, A.M.Y. (2018) Becoming a 'language-aware' content teacher: Content and language integrated learning (CLIL) teacher professional development as a collaborative, dynamic, and dialogic process. *Teacher Development for Immersion and Content* 6 (2), 162–188.

He, Y., Lundgren, K. and Pynes, P. (2017) Impact of short-term study abroad program: Inservice teachers' development of intercultural competence and pedagogical beliefs. *Teaching and Teacher Education* 66, 147–157.

Kasun, S., Trinh, E.T. and Caldwell, B. (2019) Decolonizing identities of teachers of color through study abroad: Dreaming beyond assumptions, toward embracing transnational ways of knowing. In D. Martin and E. Smolcic (eds) *Redefining Teaching Competence through Immersive Programs* (pp. 207–233). Cham: Palgrave Macmillan.

Li, D. and Edwards, V. (2013) The impact of overseas training on curriculum innovation and change in English language education in Western China. *Language Teaching Research* 17 (4), 390–408.

Mezirow, J. (1978) Perspective transformation. *Adult Education* 28 (2), 100–110.

Mezirow, J. (1997) Transformative learning: Theory to practice. *New Directions for Adult and Continuing Education* 74, 5–12.

Roskvist, A., Harvey, S., Corder, D. and Stacey, K. (2014) 'To improve language, you have to mix': Teachers' perceptions of language learning in an overseas immersion environment. *The Language Learning Journal* 42 (3), 321–333.

Roskvist, A., Harvey, S., Corder, D. and Stacey, K. (2017) Language teachers and their perceptions of the impact of 'short-term' study abroad experiences on their teaching practice. *Electronic Journal of Foreign Language Teaching* 14 (1), 5–20.

Wang, D. (2014) Effects of study abroad on teachers' self-perceptions: A study of Chinese EFL teachers. *Journal of Language Teaching & Research* 5 (1), 70–79.

Wenger, E. (1998) *Communities of Practice: Learning, Meaning and Identity.* Cambridge: Cambridge University Press.

Zhao, Y. and Mantero, M. (2018) The influence of study-abroad experiences on Chinese college EFL teacher's identity. *Indonesian Journal of English Language Teaching and Applied Linguistics* 3 (1), 53–77.

10 'I Thought it was Really a No!': A Narrativized Account of an L2 Sojourn with a Homestay

Sin Yu Cherry Chan and Jane Jackson

> *'Another night during dinner, I asked him if I could have some more food. He replied, "No, you can't". Once again, I didn't know if he's being serious'.*
>
> *Limited sociopragmatic knowledge and skills undermined his L2 confidence. He did not build a close relationship with his hosts and did not feel as if he was part of the host family.*

Introduction

In many parts of the world, pre-service English as a second language (ESL) or foreign language (EFL) teacher education programs include a short-term study-abroad component (e.g. Barkhuizen & Feryok, 2006; Benson *et al.*, 2013; Trent *et al.*, 2014). Since 2002, to enhance the quality of EFL teaching in Hong Kong, the Hong Kong government has been subsidizing overseas immersion programs for pre-service EFL teachers at local universities. All English Language Education (ELED) undergraduates are required to complete an eight- to ten-week language and culture immersion program in an English-speaking country (e.g. Australia, New Zealand, the UK). This initiative aims to enhance their language and intercultural learning and support their professional development as future English language teachers in Hong Kong.

To better understand the psychological, social and linguistic challenges that L2 student teachers may face in the host environment, this chapter centers on a case study of Kelvin (pseudonym), a young man who provided valuable insight into the multifarious internal and external factors that appeared to hamper his L2 and intercultural learning during his stay in the UK. The analysis of his narrative largely focuses on his home-stay experience as it is in this environment that he experienced significant emotional distress. Where relevant, reference is made to the journeys of his peers.

Factors Affecting Homestay Experience and L2/Intercultural Learning

Pre-service ESL/EFL teacher education programs increasingly provide L2 students with opportunities to participate in study-abroad programs in English-speaking countries (e.g. Benson *et al.*, 2013; Bodycott & Crew, 2001; Trent *et al.*, 2014). Typically, they seek to enhance L2 proficiency and pedagogical skills in an environment where English is the primary language (Barkhuizen & Feryok, 2006). As Jackson (2017) observes, student teachers who participate in these programs may have limited inter-cultural experience before the sojourn, with their English use largely confined to formal academic settings. A homestay element is often built into these programs with the expectation that this will provide more exposure to the use of English in daily life. It is widely assumed that programs of this nature will enhance students' L2 proficiency, intercultural development, L2 self-efficacy, and awareness of their language teaching and learning beliefs. Contemporary study-abroad researchers, however, have found that these gains are not guaranteed. Individual characteristics and environmental factors result in differing sojourn experiences and outcomes (e.g. Benson *et al.*, 2013; Coleman, 2013; Jackson, 2008, 2010, 2018; Kinginger, 2013). In particular, variations in the degree of reflection and meaning-making can lead to very different developmental trajectories (Jackson, 2008, 2010, 2017).

Recent qualitative and mixed-method studies have challenged the per-ception of the 'homestay advantage'. Allen (2010), for example, conducted a mixed-method study of 18 American students of French who partici-pated in a six-week study-abroad program in France and each lived with a homestay family. She found that in the pre-sojourn phase, most of the students assumed that a homestay was an optimal way to learn about the host culture and language, and experience daily life. They believed that this housing arrangement would automatically guarantee interactions with host nationals, thus ensuring their language development, especially their speaking skills. The researcher, however, found that homestay experi-ence is complex and variable due to a range of individual factors (e.g. differing language learning motives and goals, agency, capacity for risk taking, awareness and use of appropriate communicative strategies, per-ceptions of the hosts) as well as external elements (e.g. host receptivity).

Benson (2017) conducted a qualitative study of Hong Kong students who participated in a semester-long study-abroad program in an English-speaking country. Adopting a narrative approach, he analyzed the narratives of 200 students over a period of five years, paying particular attention to their homestay experience to investigate links between emotion and identity. The participants' emotional responses to interactions with their hosts appeared to be linked to their self-identities in the homestay. Those who were able to imagine themselves as members of the host family tended to make more of an effort to develop rapport with their hosts, even when facing difficulties (e.g. misunderstandings, weak host receptivity).

These studies underscore the variability of homestay experience. It is naïve to assume that meaningful host-sojourner relationships will develop and foster significant gains in language and intercultural learning. To optimize the study-abroad experience of L2 student teachers and enhance homestay life, it is important to carefully examine the perceptions and lived experiences of participants in programs of this nature. In addition to providing valuable insight into study-abroad learning, case studies can provide useful direction for pre-sojourn programming and sojourn support.

Research Design and Methodology

With the 'social turn' in applied linguistics research (Kinginger, 2013), more and more study-abroad researchers are adopting a case study design to investigate the developmental trajectories of L2 learners in the host speech community (e.g. Benson *et al.*, 2013; Jackson, 2008, 2010, 2018). In line with this development, the present study examined the journeys of pre-service English Language Education (ELED) teachers from a Hong Kong university who took part in an eight-week English immersion program. This compulsory, credit-bearing component was designed to provide them with opportunities to learn and use their L2 in an English-speaking environment and also expand their exposure to diverse L2 teaching practices.

The cohort under study took place during the summer of 2016 at a university in northeast England. Each week, 20 hours of class mainly focused on English language enhancement, intercultural learning and English language teaching methodology. The program also included visits to primary and secondary schools with social and cultural excursions on weekday afternoons. The students lived with a homestay family either individually or in pairs.

Twenty third-year students were invited to join the main study. Nine were selected as case participants based on: (a) their willingness to participate in the study; (b) the fact that they had little or no previous study-abroad experience in tertiary education, and (c) their aspiration to teach English in the future. All case participants were asked to fill in a questionnaire survey before and immediately after the sojourn. Individual semi-structured interviews were regularly conducted at four phases of the study: pre-sojourn, while abroad, immediate post-sojourn, and four months after the sojourn. All participants chose to use their native language, Cantonese, for the interviews. Their interviews were then transcribed and translated into English. During translation, efforts were made to retain the nuances and emotions of the discourse. Interview transcripts were sent to participants for member checks to ensure fair representation of their viewpoints (Grbich, 2013). With their consent, pre- and post-immersion reflective essays and reflective journals were reviewed to provide further insight into their experience. The essays and journals were written in English and excerpts are mostly in their original form except for minor amendments due to grammatical and spelling mistakes. This study adopted a recursive process of coding and analysis (Grbich, 2013), identifying potential patterns (Merriam, 1998). Qualitative data analysis software, NVivo 11, was used to process the data (Bazeley & Jackson, 2013). Coding was also open and ongoing, with codes modified when necessary (Bazeley & Jackson, 2013; Grbich, 2013).

Kelvin's Story

To better understand the internal and external variables that can affect the study-abroad experience, the remainder of this chapter centers on the experiences of Kelvin, a young man who experienced significant ups and downs in his homestay, which hampered his language and intercultural development. Where relevant, comparisons are drawn with the stories of other case participants who participated in the main study.

Pre-sojourn

Language attitudes, ability and usage

Kelvin was 21 years old when the study began. A very diligent student, he had a grade point average of 3.60 (out of 4) and was placed on the dean's honors list of the Faculty of Education. He spoke three languages: Cantonese, English and Mandarin. In the pre-sojourn questionnaire, he assessed his language ability and use, and offered further insight into his language attitudes and use in a 40-minute semi-structured interview. In the survey, using a 5-point scale, whereby 1 = poor and 5 = excellent, he rated his overall English proficiency as 'very good'. Later in the interview, when asked about his perceptions of his proficiency level, he compared himself with more fluent speakers. While he appeared to be quite confident in his conversational English, he felt ashamed when he did not understand what native speakers of English said. Instead of asking for clarifications, he would only smile and nod.

Outside of class, he actively participated in English language activities on campus. He also had daily exposure to the language through different social media platforms due to his interest in pop culture. However, in the interview he remarked that he would not speak English with his ELED peers outside of class as he did not wish to be perceived as bragging about his English skills.

Kelvin had made some international friends through a summer English language teaching program in Hong Kong and remained in contact with them on social media platforms after the program. He had never taken a course in intercultural communication. In the future, as well as being a passionate EFL teacher in a secondary school, he aspired to attain native-like English proficiency. While this belief positively motivated him to hone his English skills, it also created emotional distress when his competency to teach the language was questioned. Similar to many, Kelvin's narratives revealed that he was influenced by the myth about the superiority of native speakers in teaching English (e.g. Lee, 2015).

Pre-sojourn aims, expectations and concerns

In the pre-sojourn interview and pre-immersion reflective essay, Kelvin disclosed his study-abroad goals, which included the enhancement of his academic writing skills, grasp of English language pedagogy, and intercultural knowledge. He believed that he was well-prepared for informal use of the language and could handle interactions at a basic level. He also expected to encounter some awkward situations due to lack of familiarity with local communicative norms. However, he did not appear to have given much thought to language and intercultural learning strategies or ways to deal with intercultural misunderstandings and conflicts.

As a pre-service teacher, he wished to share his overseas experience with his future students, many of whom would likely never have travelled outside of Asia. He believed that his experience in the United Kingdom could build up his reputation as a competent language teacher.

A few days before his departure, he was informed that he would stay with a British Indian couple, along with Jack (pseudonym), an ELED classmate, while the rest of his peers were placed with Caucasian families. Kelvin appeared unaware that the UK is a multiracial country and had expected that all host families would be 'White British'. Nonetheless, he appeared to be satisfied with the arrangement.

Kelvin's homestay experience during the sojourn

Kelvin and Jack learned that their hosts had immigrated to the UK several decades ago and were now retired. As his host father was immobile, all of their interactions took place at home. At the beginning of the sojourn, Kelvin was keen to interact with his hosts and asked them culture-related questions and shared information about Hong Kong. He found his hosts to be friendly and noted that they often asked him and Jack about their activities at the university. Yet, he found it difficult to comprehend what they said and attributed this to their heavy Indian accent. Feeling too embarrassed to repeatedly ask for clarification, Kelvin only gave vague responses and simply nodded his head. In particular, he had difficulty understanding British humor and displayed a negative attitude towards it and British people.

In the first sojourn interview, he disclosed his frustration with his inability to understand his host father's jokes:

> In the middle of a conversation, I asked my host dad: 'May I jump in?' Then he said, 'No!' At that time, I thought it was really a no. Then he told me, 'Oh, it's just a joke. Don't be so serious'. Another night during dinner, I asked him if I could have some more food. He replied, 'No, you can't'. Once again, I didn't know if he's being serious.

Feeling ill at ease in situations like this, he was apprehensive that his host father would perceive him as an incompetent English speaker who could not understand jokes. Unlike some of his peers who stepped out of their comfort zone and eagerly experimented with new communicative strategies when talking with their hosts, Kelvin tended to adopt avoidance strategies. He did not initiate many interactions with his host family and made little effort to try different ways to communicate.

By the time the intercultural studies course had ended in the third week of the sojourn, Kelvin was spending the majority of his free time alone in his bedroom, except during meals. Most of the interactions he had with his hosts took place during the 30-minute breakfast time. While his hosts paid attention to major incidents in Hong Kong, he did not act on this opportunity to engage in more in-depth conversations with them. His limited interaction with them was confined to routine talk about daily events at school and his schedule. Although he stayed with his hosts for over a month, he did not develop a close rapport with them. Disappointed with this, he described himself as simply a 'sojourner staying at their residence' (Week 5, second sojourn interview). Unlike some of the other case participants, he did not see himself as a family member.

Kelvin claimed that he did not have problems understanding what his host mother said, but he could only grasp 50% of what his host father was saying and there were often misunderstandings in their conversations: 'I thought he was just saying a statement and I didn't have to give answers to him but actually he was asking me questions' (Week 5, second sojourn interview). He attributed the comprehension difficulty and sociopragmatic challenges solely to his host father's 'heavy Indian accent'. In contrast, Jack appeared to understand and communicate well with their host father and even laughed at his jokes. Kelvin found it especially difficult to understand his hosts' sense of humor: 'When I dropped something, my host mom said to me, "It's almost broken!" I was very scared at that time but then she told me she was just joking' (Week 5, second sojourn interview).

In relation to the above exchange, Kelvin was 'very puzzled' about why his hosts had responded to him like this. Even at the end of his stay, he misunderstood the intended meanings of their jokes and felt intimidated in these moments. Comprehension of humor can be challenging for L2 learners, even for advanced learners (Jackson, 2008, 2010; Shively, 2013). Kelvin's anxiety about these experiences appeared to reduce his incentive to initiate conversations and interact with his hosts. Although he gradually became more accustomed to his host father's jokes, he struggled to respond appropriately. Jack advised him not to take the jokes seriously; however, Kelvin remained tense and confused. He displayed limited sociopragmatic awareness, and an inflexible mindset, and negative perceptions of his hosts held him back from fully engaging in conversations with them. This in turn reduced his exposure to the host language and culture, hampering his L2 and intercultural development.

Close to the end of the sojourn, Kelvin still did not openly and proactively discuss his daily needs with his hosts. His notion of politeness held him back from doing so:

> There isn't a desk in my room so I've been sitting on my bed to do my assignments. Not until a chat we had a few days ago did my host mom tell me that there's a small desk available for me to use. I think you [the researcher] are right. They'll only provide the item to you if you proactively ask for it. But I feel very impolite to ask for something from them sometimes. (Week 8, third sojourn interview)

Finding it challenging to converse with his hosts, he did not appear to make much effort to push past his insecurities to interact with them. While some of the other student participants actively engaged with their hosts, Kelvin chose to keep their conversations as brief as possible throughout his stay.

Kelvin's narratives revealed that his L2 sense of self did not seem to evolve much from the middle until the end of the sojourn. While his hosts praised his advanced English proficiency level and compared him favorably with the previous international students they had hosted, Kelvin continued to view himself as an L2 learner and remarked that his aspiration to reach native-like proficiency had not been achieved. The longer he stayed in the host country, the bigger the gap he sensed between himself and native speakers, particularly in terms of the usage of idioms and daily life expressions.

After exposure to the use of English in different contexts and situations, near the end of his stay abroad he identified aspects that he needed to improve on. As he had difficulty comprehending his hosts, he pointed out that he needed to work on listening comprehension, especially with regard to different accents. Interestingly, he did not recognize the need to further his sociopragmatic awareness or intercultural competence. Also, at this stage, he still strongly believed that he needed to attain native-like proficiency to become a competent teacher of English.

Post-sojourn

Back in Hong Kong, Kelvin shared his views about his immersion experience in a 183-minute interview. He claimed that his host family was 'a source of his knowledge about British culture' and noted that they had introduced him to some aspects of the culture. Although he did not stay with a Caucasian British family, as he had expected, he said that he felt fortunate that he was able to understand British culture from an immigrant family's perspective. On reflection, he regretted that they did not interact as much as he had hoped they would. He primarily focused on the linguistic dimension and did not display much awareness of the many dimensions of intercultural competence.

The homestay was the most challenging sociopragmatic context for Kelvin. His narratives often reported on the challenges he encountered and his struggles to cope with confusing communicative events. In the interview, he revealed, 'Regrettably, I didn't build a very close relationship with my hosts'. While proactive in the beginning of the sojourn, he stopped initiating conversations with his hosts. This can be attributed to several factors including his rigid mindset, lack of mutuality between him and his hosts, and his struggle to cope with sociopragmatic failures. For instance, Kelvin compared his hosts with British Caucasians and perceived them to be more reserved and indifferent. He did not perceive them to be very hospitable as they did not offer what he needed even though he did not take the initiative to express his needs to them. In addition to linguistic and psychological barriers, differing conceptions of parenting styles and hospitality limited their intercultural communication.

Another factor that appeared to impact their relationship was the lack of mutual engagement. While meal-times were a potentially useful setting for meaningful, sustained interactions, Kelvin revealed that they usually had dinner in separate places. Unlike some case participants who actively interacted with their hosts during dinner time, Kelvin remained silent most of the time and not close to his hosts.

Thirdly, he was greatly frustrated by his inability to understand his host father's jokes and to respond to him appropriately. This led to many misunderstandings:

> He once said, 'When I said something, Kelvin started to pretend to be deaf. If you don't want to listen to me, just stay in another place'. But I really didn't know how to respond because I couldn't understand what he said. I asked him, 'Can you say that again?' Then he said, 'You aren't listening. Your brain is dead. You aren't listening to me at all'. (Post-sojourn interview)

Kelvin felt overwhelmed, intimidated and uneasy in situations like this. While he gradually sensed that his host father was teasing and not scolding him, he struggled to respond to his sense of humor. Instead, he tended to retreat from conversations:

> For instance, my host dad said, 'Oh you're doing laundry this week. You have to pay five pounds for each piece of clothes'. I knew he was joking but I didn't know how to respond. In the beginning, I said, 'No' but I didn't know how to continue the conversation. I tried to say, 'Okay I'll give you'. Then he said, 'When are you giving me money?' I didn't know how to respond next. (Post-sojourn interview)

Limited sociopragmatic awareness hampered his communication and undermined his L2 confidence. Accordingly, his conversations with his hosts did not progress much from simple and routine talk, and even by the end of his stay he had few long and in-depth interactions with them. Nevertheless, he believed that his intercultural exposure abroad had broadened his view of English learning and enhanced his confidence as an EFL teacher: 'With the rapid globalization, English learning no longer only focuses on the British culture but also cultures from other parts of the world, and my expanded world vision has made me more confident as a language teacher' (Post-immersion reflective essay). At this stage, his view of culture learning and teaching mostly focused on cultural knowledge and linguistic competence; he did not appear to have much understanding of the intercultural dimension of English language teaching and learning (Byram *et al.*, 2002).

A year after the immersion program, in a 90-minute interview, Kelvin shared his recent experience with English and reflected on his immersion experience. Commenting on the difficulty he had encountered in understanding his host father's humor, he was now able to view the experience more positively: 'At that time, I was confused although I knew that he was joking. I just didn't know how to respond. He didn't reveal his intention of joking until the very last morning. If I could do that again, I would tease him back' (Post-post sojourn interview).

Conclusion

Kelvin's development trajectory offers insight into individual factors (e.g. emotions, language attitudes, study-abroad aims, agency, willingness to participate, sociopragmatic awareness) and external elements (e.g. host receptivity, program design) that can impact homestay experience (Benson *et al.*, 2013; Jackson, 2008, 2010) and result in differing levels of satisfaction and learning. Comparisons with his peers' experiences and development raised further awareness of the impact that internal elements can have on sojourn outcomes. Differences in host receptivity and the amount of quality time spent with students also brought to light significant differences in the homestay placements.

In particular, throughout much of his stay, Kelvin encountered difficulty communicating with his hosts. Limited sociopragmatic knowledge and skills undermined his L2 confidence. He did not build a close relationship with his hosts and did not feel as if he was part of the host family. His oral account revealed negative emotions (e.g. anxiety, fear) toward his hosts and an inflexible mindset. Unlike some of his classmates, Kelvin tended to avoid interacting with his hosts and this limited his sociopragmatic and intercultural development.

External elements also played a role in how the sojourn unfolded. For example, Kelvin's hosts did not seem to make much of an effort to accommodate his language and emotional needs. They spent less quality time with him than some of the other students' hosts did with them and appeared to be unaware of his discomfort and insecurities. They were not sensitive to his struggles to understand their communication style. Thus, while some of Kelvin's classmates developed a close relationship with host family members, a complex mix of internal and external elements resulted in a rather distant host-sojourner relationship in Kelvin's homestay situation.

Pedagogical Implications

This chapter points to the potential need for language and intercultural interventions in study-abroad programs for pre-service L2 teachers. In pre-departure orientations, instructors could divide students into small groups and provide a platform for them to share their concerns and discuss possible solutions. With more awareness of their aspirations and concerns, instructors can raise students' awareness of useful resources and encourage the setting of realistic sojourn goals. In the case study, while Kelvin was excited about his homestay experience, he feared that miscommunication with his hosts might occur. For study-abroad programs that offer homestays, instructors can discuss strategies that can be adopted to facilitate relationship-building with hosts and support the development of their language and intercultural competence. Some attention should also be devoted to social discourse in English and the cultivation of useful language and culture learning strategies that could be employed in the host environment.

For Kelvin, it was his first time staying with a host family and a lack of familiarity with the living situation and social interactions were concerns. If possible, instructors could liaise with the receiving institutions and request contact information for the hosts. Instructors could then encourage the students to take the initiative to contact their host family to get to know each other before meeting in person. In their correspondence, if applicable, students could be encouraged to address such issues as both parties' expectations, their concerns about the living situation, house rules, and their plans for their stay in the host country. This may help the newcomers to adapt to their homestay more quickly.

During the sojourn, instructors can design some purposeful tasks that prompt students to actively engage in the homestay in meaningful ways. To maximize their homestay experience, students can be asked to informally interview host members about a topic of mutual interest and then report their findings in small group sharing sessions. It is important to offer regular debriefing sessions for students to unpack their language and intercultural learning. In the sessions, students could share the challenges they encounter in the host community (e.g. miscommunication with host family) and explore strategies to overcome difficulties (Deardorff & Arasaratnam-Smith, 2017; Jackson, 2008, 2010; Vande Berg *et al.*, 2012).

The study also found that affective factors played a crucial role in Kelvin's L2 learning and use. Therefore, as Jackson (2017) argues, the penning of autobiographical narratives should be encouraged in study-abroad programs to foster deeper levels of metacognition and reflection in the immersion program. Guided questions could encourage students to continuously reflect on their language and intercultural learning. Students can be prompted to identify areas of achievement as well as aspects for improvement (Benson *et al.*, 2013). Instructors can provide feedback on students' reflective essays, drawing attention to issues that have been overlooked and raise questions to stimulate deeper reflection and sociopragmatic, intercultural awareness (Hoult, 2018).

Although Kelvin became a bit more aware of the intercultural dimension of language teaching while in the UK, he did not appear to have much understanding of it and did not know how to incorporate it into his EFL lessons, which suggests that more overt attention should be devoted to this element in the ELED program.

Finally, to optimize the potential of study abroad for L2 pre-service teachers, it is important for facilitators to have an understanding of relevant intercultural development theories (e.g. Byram, 1997; Byram *et al.*, 2002; Jackson, 2018) as well as contemporary study-abroad research that centers on the individual and external factors that can lead to different developmental trajectories and outcomes (e.g. Iwasaki, 2019; Jackson, 2018). Heightened awareness of the intercultural attitudes, skills and knowledge that tend to facilitate language and intercultural learning can help educators to devise meaningful interventions at all stages of the study-abroad cycle (from pre-departure to re-entry) (e.g. sociopragmatic awareness sessions, regular debriefings during the sojourn). Informed facilitators can play a valuable role in helping pre-service EFL teachers to make the most of homestay situations and their stay in the wider host environment.

References

Allen, H.W. (2010) Interactive contact as linguistic affordance during short-term study abroad: Myth or reality? *Frontiers: The Interdisciplinary Journal of Study Abroad* 19, 1–26.
Barkhuizen, G. and Feryok, A. (2006) Pre-service teachers' perceptions of a short-term international experience programme. *Asia-Pacific Journal of Teacher Education* 34 (1), 115–134.

Bazeley, P. and Jackson, K. (2013) *Qualitative Data Analysis with NVivo* (2nd edn). London: Sage.

Benson, P. (2017) Sleeping with strangers: Dreams and nightmares in experiences of homestay. *Study Abroad Research in Second Language Acquisition and International Education* 2 (1), 1–20.

Benson, P., Barkhuizen, G., Bodycott, P. and Brown, J. (2013) *Second Language Identity in Narratives of Study Abroad*. New York: Palgrave Macmillan.

Bodycott, P. and Crew, V. (eds) (2001) *Language and Cultural Immersion: Perspectives on Short Term Study and Residence Abroad*. Hong Kong: Hong Kong Institute of Education.

Byram, M. (1997) *Teaching and Assessing Intercultural Communicative Competence* (1st edn). Clevedon: Multilingual Matters.

Byram, M., Gribkova, B. and Starkey, H. (2002) *Developing the Intercultural Dimension in Language Teaching: A Practical Introduction for Teachers*. Strasbourg: Council of Europe.

Coleman, J.A. (2013) Researching whole people and whole lives. In C. Kinginger (ed.) *Social and Cultural Aspects of Language Learning and Study Abroad* (pp. 17–44). Amsterdam: John Benjamins.

Deardorff, D.K. and Arasaratnam-Smith, L.A. (eds) (2017) *Intercultural Competence in International Higher Education: International Approaches, Assessment and Application*. New York: Routledge.

Grbich, C. (2013) *Qualitative Data Analysis: An Introduction* (2nd edn). Thousand Oaks, CA: Sage.

Hoult, S. (2018) Aspiring to postcolonial engagement with the Other: Deepening intercultural learning through reflection on a South India sojourn. In J. Jackson and S. Oguro (eds) *Intercultural Interventions in Study Abroad* (pp. 71–87). New York: Routledge.

Iwasaki, N. (2019) Individual differences in study abroad research: Sources, processes and outcomes of students' development in language, culture and personhood. In M. Howard (ed.) *Study Abroad, Second Language Acquisition and Interculturality* (pp. 237–262). Bristol: Multilingual Matters.

Jackson, J. (2008) *Language, Identity and Study Abroad: Sociocultural Perspectives*. London: Equinox.

Jackson, J. (2010) *Intercultural Journeys: From Study to Residence Abroad*. Basingstoke: Palgrave Macmillan.

Jackson, J. (2017) Second language teacher identity. In G. Barkhuizen (ed.) *Reflections on Language Teacher Identity Research* (pp. 114–119). New York: Routledge.

Jackson, J. (2018) *Interculturality in International Education*. New York: Routledge.

Kinginger, C. (ed.) (2013) *Social and Cultural Aspects of Language Learning in Study Abroad*. Amsterdam: John Benjamins.

Lee, I. (2015) Student teachers' changing beliefs on a pre-service teacher education course in Hong Kong. In T. Wright and M. Beaumont (eds) *Experiences of Second Language Teacher Education* (pp. 15–41). London: Palgrave Macmillan.

Merriam, S.B. (1998) *Qualitative Research and Case Study Applications in Education*. San Francisco: Jossey-Bass.

Shively, R.L. (2013) Learning to be funny in Spanish during study abroad: L2 humor development. *The Modern Language Journal* 97 (4), 930–946.

Trent, J., Gao, X. and Gu, M. (2014) Learning, teaching, and constructing identities abroad: ESL pre-service teacher experiences during a short-term international experience programme. In J. Trent, X. Gao and M. Gu (eds) *Language Teacher Education in a Multilingual Context: Experiences from Hong Kong* (pp. 117–135). New York: Springer.

Vande Berg, M., Paige, R.M. and Lou, K.H. (2012) Student learning abroad: Paradigms and assumptions. In M. Vande Berg, R.M. Paige and K.H. Lou (eds) *Student Learning Abroad: What Our Students Are Learning, What They're Not, and What We Can Do about It* (pp. 3–28). Sterling, VA: Stylus Publishing.

11 Language for the Heart: Investigating the Linguistic Responsiveness of Study Abroad

Erik Jon Byker and Natalia Mejia

In their reflective journals and open-ended responses on the survey, the participants ranked multilingualism in South Africa's schools as one of the most significant features they learned about the South African education system.

'It was my first academic introduction to the isiXhosa language and I will always remember how the language sounded like a song. Such is the beauty and fluidity of learning a new language'.

Introduction

We begin this chapter with two vignettes of multilingualism in the context of elementary school classroom teaching and learning in the United States, where in many states there is a scarcity of world language programs even though the schools in the country are becoming more and more diverse. Each vignette is told by the article's second author (Natalia Mejia) and written in the first person. Natalia is a multilingual educator, who was a student teacher that participated in two study-abroad programs to South Africa. The vignettes were inspired by events that occurred while Natalia was completing her elementary education teaching degree. Erik Byker is an associate professor at University of North Carolina at Charlotte and was the faculty leader and coordinator for the study-abroad programs in South Africa.

Natalia: I start the vignettes by framing my study-abroad experience in South Africa through the lens of teaching experience I had when I returned to the United States. After returning from South Africa, I was better equipped with global awareness and a deeper appreciation for multilingualism in the classroom. The first vignette captures a student teaching episode during a year-long clinical internship in a Grade 4 classroom in an elementary school in the southeastern region of the United States. This particular Grade 4 classroom had the most students identified as English Language Learners (ELL) purposely so that the classroom teacher – and student teacher – could provide targeted language support for the students. As the student teacher, I was encouraged by the classroom teacher – who I will refer to as my mentor teacher – to speak Spanish, because Spanish is my family's native language. I used Spanish vocabulary in my lessons as often as possible. During one of my math lessons on geometry, I spoke in Spanish to make a point clear for all the students. However, a couple of students in the classroom looked vexed, and one student even inquired aloud, 'Why are you speaking in Spanish?' After a few moments of silence, I responded, 'We have some students that understand Spanish because they speak it at home with their family. I want to be sure they understand this math problem. Also, think about it: you are also getting the opportunity to learn a new language. This skill will help you in life'. After this response, the students in the classroom all continued to work on their geometry problem and I continued to support the ELL students in the classroom.

Now to the second vignette. This next vignette also happened while I was student teaching, but the experience was different. I had a student who was a new arrival to the United States from Honduras. The new arrival students would spend most of the day in an ELL classroom for additional language support. However, before being pulled out for an ELL class, the newly arrived students would attend the first period homeroom class with the general classroom to which they were assigned. The newly arrived student from Honduras sat at a desk towards the front of the classroom and I would purposefully speak Spanish to her, often answering her questions, translating word problems, and just talking to her about her day. One day after translating to her what one of her peers was explaining, she turned to me and said, 'I love being able to come to your class because you speak Spanish and I understand what I am doing better'. Being responsive to this child's needs meant that I was supporting her to understand linguistically what was happening in the classroom as well as help her conceptualize the content being taught.

Both vignettes illustrate examples of what multilingualism looks like in classroom instruction in the United States, especially where there is primarily one language of instruction. While there are dedicated ELL classes for ELL students and immersive language programs in some schools, actual language support in the day-to-day instruction is often lacking or inconsistent. The inconsistencies can be manifested in the quizzical looks – like the monolingual student in the first vignette – that question the inclusion of multilingualism in the classroom. The second vignette captures how the inclusion of language support for ELL students

translates to a sense of relief among ELL students as their learning is supported with basic translation. The lessons from these vignettes became
magnified to Natalia because of her study-abroad experiences in South
Africa. Study abroad opened Natalia's mind to the power of language in
the classroom as well as ways to be responsive to the multilingual needs
of her students. In this chapter, we examine the impact of study-abroad
programs in relation to undergraduate students' perceptions of multilingualism. Specifically, we describe and report on study-abroad participants' perceptions (n = 28) of experiencing multilingualism in immersive
ways through a study-abroad program in the Western Cape province of
South Africa.

Multilingualism and Study Abroad

The literature illuminates the benefits of multilingualism and of study
abroad. For example, several studies indicate how multilingualism is a
vital asset and life-skill in today's world where global competencies are
becoming increasingly necessary (Abbott, 2018; Fox et al., 2019). Studies
also found how multilingualism is a desired skill for the current work-
force (Bartolotti & Marian, 2017; Eguz, 2019). Children who learn languages at a young age are more likely to have a greater appreciation for
cultural diversity (Shanker & Kraemer, 2014). Findings from the literature show a positive correlation between learning new languages and the
closing of achievement gaps (Fox et al., 2019; Kroll & Dussias, 2017;
Woll & Li, 2019). Researchers have found connections between active
multilingualism and the delay of cognitive decline (Klein et al., 2016).
Indeed, the findings from the literature on multilingualism show many
benefits to being a person who can communicate effectively in more than
one language.

Despite the positive findings related to multilingualism, the United
States education system – from early childhood to higher education – is
far behind and second language instruction is in decline (Loney & Lusin,
2018). Researchers explain how this decline in second language learning
relates, in part, to the country's mindset regarding how English is the
lingua franca of the business world and thus speaking English-only is
viewed as enough to get by in the world (Abbott, 2018; Diamond, 2010).
Such attitudes have unfortunately created the perception that learning
another language is too difficult or even impractical (Abbott, 2018; Kroll
& Dussias, 2017). Dewaele and Li (2012) describe how these attitudes and
perceptions on language learning affect how many US educators and
school districts resist second language learning in the curricula.

Study abroad is an experiential learning program that provides learners with opportunities to develop intercultural awareness through an
exposure to new languages (Byker & Putman, 2019). The literature shows
how study abroad has a number of benefits including the development of

global competencies (Putman & Byker, 2020) and an increase in social and emotional learning (Byker, 2019). Researchers have also found how study abroad provides learners with meaningful interactions with people and cultures in the host country (Doppen & Shahri, 2019). Often, these interactions can be fruitful ways to begin learning and practicing a new language through an authentic and immersive experience (Medina *et al.*, 2015). Likewise, researchers have found that study-abroad program participants – especially those who are practicing to become teachers – are more likely to develop empathy and confidence in speaking a second language as well as try out ways to communicate in a new environment (Byker & Putman, 2019; Pilonieta *et al.*, 2017). The high cost of study abroad, however, as well as travel restrictions related to the Covid-19 pandemic, are barriers that limit the numbers of teacher candidates who participate in study-abroad programs (Putman & Byker, 2020). More research is needed in relation to achieving equitable and affordable study-abroad programs so that learners – especially teacher candidates – can participate and reap the benefits of study abroad in relation to language learning. Likewise, there is a gap in the literature related to effective strategies and frameworks for supporting language learning while on study-abroad programs.

Theoretical Framework

One promising framework for supporting language learning is the Universal Design for Language Learning (UD2L) framework (Mejia, 2019). The UD2L blends the principles of Universal Design for Learning (UDL) with high-impact practices related to learning languages. Similar to UDL (NCUDL, 2012), the UD2L framework is founded on the notion that language learning needs to be universally accessible. Such accessibility is supported by the following components: (a) representation, (b) expression, (c) responsive, and (d) engagement. The first two components and the fourth are exactly the same as those in the UDL framework. We have added responsive as a third component to complete the UD2L framework. Figure 11.1 illustrates how the components fit together to form UD2L.

As Figure 11.1 illustrates, UD2L is made up of four components that function together as a process. The first two components are representation and expression. These components relate to the recognition of knowledge related to language learning. The gray arrow is used to show how this knowledge is connected. By representation, we mean the knowledge of how language represents and connects to culture. By expression, we mean how language is a form of expression to communicate a culture. The recognition of these two areas of knowledge related to language learning supports the skill components – being responsive and engagement – of the UD2L framework. The skill components are represented by

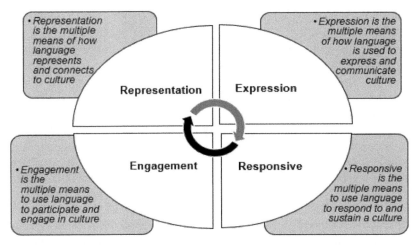

Figure 11.1 A graphical representation of the Universal Design for Language Learning (UD2L) framework

the black circular arrow. By responsive, we mean the skill of using language to respond to and sustain a culture. By engagement, we mean the skill of using language to participate and engage in a culture. Taken together, the UD2L framework is a way to conceptualize and support language learning as a process of speaking to the heart of the person. Within each of the components of the UD2L framework, we recognize multiple means for developing the knowledge and skills for language learning and for the teaching of languages. For example, the UD2L framework comprises facets that connect with ways to teach world languages through representation of the language, cultural expressions, responsiveness to language as communication, and engagement with a culture or people through language.

We posit that study abroad is one example of the multiple means of language learning. Using the UD2L framework as a theoretical lens, we investigate the following research questions:

(1) What were the participants' perceptions of the multilingual experiences in the South Africa study-abroad program?
(2) What was the impact of the South Africa study-abroad program in relation to language learning?

South Africa Context

Study abroad in South Africa provides a powerful and engaging place to examine multilingualism. South Africa has 12 official languages – including sign language. This chapter investigates the South Africa study-abroad program experiences of 28 participants (n = 28) from a large research university near a major metropolitan area in the southeast region of the United States. All of the participants were either in their sophomore or junior year of undergraduate study. Over 92% of the participants were women and there were two men who participated in the study abroad. More than two-thirds of the participants (68%) were studying to become future elementary school or primary school teachers. Of that 68%, six participants were also minoring in Teaching English to Speakers of Other Languages (TESOL) and five participants were double majoring in elementary education and special education. The other one-third of the participants were majoring in the fields of computer sciences, public health, and world languages. The duration of the study-abroad program was four weeks and primarily in the Cape Town region of South Africa. The study-abroad experience included opportunities for international teaching and over 40 hours of field experiences at Cape Town area crèches and elementary schools. The program also included lectures by South African professors about topics ranging from the history of South Africa, the legacies of apartheid that still exist in South Africa, the life and leadership of President Nelson Mandela, and the system of education in South Africa. The study-abroad program included many cultural and social excursions to places like Robben Island and the District Six Museum.

Method and Participants

To investigate our research questions, we use a case study research design. Yin (2008) explains how case study research design allows for the mixing of qualitative and quantitative data in order to investigate a phenomenon under study. For our case study, we report on data collected by way of artefact analysis of the participants' reflective journal entries as well as the open-ended responses on program surveys. Additionally, we included autoethnographic data in the form of a short narrative from the chapter's second author, who twice participated in the South Africa study-abroad program. Anderson (2006) explains how autoethnography further situates and provides an in-depth perception of an experience. Autoethnography equips researchers to connect the data collection to a first-person account of the phenomenon under study (Byker, 2014; Byker *et al.*, 2020). To analyze the data, we used Miles and Huberman's (1994) three-step interpretive approach, which includes the following steps: (a) reduction of data by reading and re-reading the data and coding the data into categories; (b) using the constant comparative method to identify themes and further organize the data; and (c) drawing conclusions from the data in order to report the findings based on the study's research questions.

Findings

We organize the case study's findings by answering the study's research questions. First, we describe the participants' perceptions of the multilingual experiences in the South Africa study-abroad program. Second, we explain the impact of the study-abroad program on the language learning of the participants. We will organize each section of the findings by first reporting the findings related to the whole group of participants and then include a second paragraph of narrative from the chapter's second author.

Participants' perceptions of multilingualism

In their reflective journals and open-ended responses on the survey, the participants ranked multilingualism in South Africa's schools as one of the most significant features they learned about the South African education system. At the same time, the participants also recognized the privileges that come with being speakers of English. They reported that they were impressed by how many of the South African elementary students they met were multilingual; speaking isiXhosa, Afrikaans and English. The teacher candidates recognized how multilingualism was a strength of the South African education system as well as a way to better understand the diverse cultures within South Africa. One teacher candidate put it this way: 'I have seen how English is used as a common way to communicate in South Africa and gives me access to the things I want to buy at the store. But it doesn't give me full access to cultural understandings'. This quote is a reflection of how the teacher candidates recognized that language is a form of communication and expression as well as a means to be culturally responsive. Knowing English provided an almost universal way to communicate in South Africa, but English did not provide access to another person's culture.

Autoethnographic findings

Natalia: During my time on the South Africa study-abroad programs, I had many opportunities to embrace the multilingualism of South African society. In this section, I share two such experiences. The first is a memory from an immersive two-week volunteer experience at a crèche. Most of the children in the crèche were Black South Africans and isiXhosa was their mother language. One of my jobs was to ride the bus, take attendance on the bus, and make sure the children were able to safely get on and off the bus. The first day, the bus driver drove to the local township to pick up the children who were waiting for the bus at a playground. The kids were playing tag to stay warm in the brisk, winter morning air in South Africa. The bus pulled up and the children quickly filed in and took their seats. The bus started its route back to the crèche and I encouraged the kids to sing. Even though the children spoke isiXhosa, they explained that they did not really know any songs in isiXhosa. I think they may have been shy to sing on their own because anytime they tried to sing an isiXhosa song it quickly faded into a shy silence. I decided to sing 'Baby Shark' and soon enough everyone was joining in. I changed the song by using Spanish and isiXhosa. Eventually the kids took over using isiXhosa in the song and the bus was filled with great laughter and song and we would sing every day until the last child waved goodbye.

The second experience happened while I had a Gatsby lunch near Cape Town. A Gatsby is a mouth-watering sandwich usually filled with meat and potato fries. It is a favorite staple in Cape Town and named after F. Scott Fitzgerald's novel *The Great Gatsby*. The menu was in Afrikaans and English. I tried reading the Afrikaans and my friend started chuckling beside me. He turned to me, 'Your American accent butchered that name'. I decided to try again using my Spanish accent, making sure to roll my 'r' the way I would if I was speaking Spanish. He turned to me, considerably impressed after that second try and said, 'That was really good. You should continue to use that accent. You didn't sound too much like a tourist that time!' We walked up to the counter to place our order, I looked up at the menu posted on the wall and placed the order in Afrikaans. I thanked the man who took the order in English. He quickly looked at me with a shocked expression and inquired, 'How did you learn that American accent?' My friend and I laughed; I then explained, 'I am an American studying in South Africa; I am originally from the USA!' I share these two experiences because I believe the experiences capture the multilingual landscape of South Africa; where at one moment there is the opportunity to sing 'Baby Shark' in isiXhosa and at the next moment there is the opportunity to order sandwiches in Afrikaans. These multilingual moments made me more aware, appreciative, and courageous to engage in these experiences on study abroad.

Impact of the study-abroad program

Our second research question inquired about the overall impact of the South Africa study-abroad program on language learning. The teacher candidates wrote about language in their reflective journals and open-ended responses on the survey. Most teacher candidates perceived the study-abroad program had a powerful impact on their understanding of the connection between language and culture. One teacher candidate explained it this way: 'Our study-abroad program opened my eyes to the importance of speaking even a few words in a new language as a way to connect to the culture. It is one thing to merely speak to someone in a language that they can understand, but have no connection to, it is an entirely different thing to speak to them in a language that they love and cherish'. Other teacher candidates explained how they had numerous occasions and interactions with South Africans who were willing to teach a few words of their native language. The impact here is that the teacher candidates had an opportunity to learn more about South African cultures through participation and engagement in language learning. Almost all teacher candidates wrote about how they committed to the inclusion of world languages in their future teaching. One teacher candidate explained, 'I had a year of Spanish and did not really have to continue learning the language. I want to change that and will introduce new languages in my teaching to be responsive to the ELL students in my class'. The impact of the study-abroad program included the recognition of how language is a connection to cultural understanding; for example, when the participants in this study-abroad program reported that they would be more likely to use basic greeting and phrases in the ELL students' home languages in order to be culturally responsive and stay engaged with the students and their families.

Autoethnographic findings

Natalia: Similar to my peers who attended the South Africa study-abroad program, the experience had a tremendous impact on me both personally and professionally. Over two years I spent almost 14 weeks in the Cape Town area of South Africa. During this time, I was able to immerse in the culture and acquire a conversational knowledge of the isiXhosa and Afrikaans languages. I saw how studying abroad was critical for future teachers, like myself, because it increased my global awareness and helped me experience the power of language. After my first time in South Africa, I wanted to make sure I was 'stepping off the veranda' (Ogden, 2008: 35). I discovered four weeks was not enough time to understand the complexities of South African cultures, languages and their education system. My second program time in South Africa was almost 10 weeks long and I learned the foundations of isiXhosa, a language spoken by 8.3 million people in South Africa. I enrolled in an isiXhosa class at the host university. On the first day of class, I remember the enthusiasm of the professor as he began his presentation by introducing himself and a short history of isiXhosa. He quickly launched into song and taught us our own part to include in the songs. With gleaming eyes and a mighty voice, the professor got the entire class – of almost 100 students – to sing and clap to different parts of the isiXhosa song. It was my first academic introduction to the isiXhosa language and I will always remember how the language sounded like a song. Such is the beauty and fluidity of learning a new language. As a future classroom teacher, the entire study-abroad experience has shaped how I would like to model and include language learning in my teaching to connect and support my students in the language that speaks to their hearts.

Discussion

Nelson Mandela said, 'If you talk to a man in a language he understands, that goes to his head. If you talk to him in his language, that goes to his heart' (as quoted in Peace Corps, 1996: vi). Language is identity and connects to a person's culture. The impact of study-abroad programs – like the South African study-abroad program examined in our study – seems to connect to an immersive experience where teacher candidates are placed as outsiders to the culture. The findings of our study reveal how teacher candidates felt culturally different and linguistically deficient in nearly all situations and contexts. Such feelings are similar to what ELL students may feel when entering a US classroom for the first time. The inclusion of multilingualism builds bridges between communities and supports a foundation for diversity which creates strong socio-emotional connections. This can be seen in the classroom such as the student in the second introductory vignette. They loved coming back to Natalia's classroom and felt relieved knowing that they were going to be supported because she was using Spanish in her lessons. Natalia recalls feeling excited and accomplished as a teacher because she was helping to meet the linguistic needs of her students. This is the strength of multilingualism: it builds a sturdy socioemotional connective bond between the teacher and student, which the mother language helps to foster. In Spanish, such a bond is captured in the word, *pana*, which means a close friend or companion that a person can be themselves around. The classroom provides opportunities to foster a multilingual environment that is responsive to diversity. In the first introductory vignette, Natalia had the opportunity to explain to a student why learning and hearing more than one language would benefit their lives. Being able to study abroad and meet more bilingual people broadened Natalia's mindset about using more than one language in the classroom and how it builds a more cosmopolitan society. Building empathy and understanding the power of multilingualism are important connections to study abroad and language learning. Another connection is the increase in teacher candidates' self-awareness and cross-cultural sensitivity for children from linguistically diverse backgrounds.

Language is the gateway to mutual understanding and it is imperative that early childhood through tertiary classrooms include a respect for multilingual communication. South Africa is a place of wide-ranging diversity of cultures, races, religions and socioeconomics. The respect for language seems to be a common denominator of unity in a land that still struggles with the legacies of apartheid. South Africa's diversity of languages – even Afrikaans and English, which have been historical languages of the oppressors – is the means to represent, express, be responsive to and engage with the humanity and culture of South African people. Nelson Mandela's quote is a reminder of the beauty of South Africa as a rainbow nation of a dozen languages that are connected to the heart of cultures.

Implications for UD2L

Our findings paint a narrative picture about how study abroad is critical for future teachers. Study-abroad programs provide an impetus for the recognition of the importance of multilingualism. We are convinced that multilingualism needs to be an essential feature of schools and classroom instruction. We believe the UD2L framework provides an instructive lens for making language accessible to all learners in the classroom. The first component of UD2L is representation or the acknowledgment that English is not the only way to communicate content in the classroom. For example, in the South Africa study-abroad experience, participants learned about including and mixing a child's home language with English in order to support the child's development of multilingualism. This was most common through music and song. The next component is expression, which is the knowledge that respect for a learner's home language is a reflection of the respect for the learner's cultural identity. For example, during the study-abroad experience, the participants connected with expression through their participation in experiences like learning and attempting to sing all the verses of the South African national anthem. The third component is being responsive, which can happen by incorporating a child's home language into the classroom through basic greetings or praise in the child's home language. For example, during the study-abroad experience, the participants were able to learn common greetings in isiXhosa as a way to show respect to the learners' cultural identity. The fourth UD2L component is engagement, which means the encouragement of home language use to maintain cultural identity. During the study-abroad experience, for example, participants engaged in a tutoring experience at the crèche with a more experienced, multilingual colleague to make the most of the engagement. This shows how the engagement component of UD2L includes a commitment to being educated about the learners' cultural norms and common greetings. This means understanding the context for engagement and supporting what the community desires and has communicated in terms of their needs.

Conclusion

In conclusion, study-abroad programs provide an immersive way to experience the power of language and culture. It provides a deeper appreciation of all cultures, equipping teachers with global competencies to create a linguistically responsive and engaged classroom for students from diverse backgrounds. Teachers will utilize the experience of going abroad to guide children towards deeper awareness of what it means to be a global citizen in a multicultural world. Reminiscing on our time leading and participating in the study-abroad program in South Africa, it continues to inspire our desire to be advocates and agents for multilingual classrooms. We believe such desire is a reflection of being global citizens who recognize the common humanity across culture, language and geographical boundaries.

References

Abbott, M.G. (2018) Beyond a bridge to understanding: The benefits of second language learning. *American Educator Journal* 42 (2), 39–43.

Anderson, L. (2006) Analytic autoethnography. *Journal of Contemporary Ethnography* 35 (4), 373–395.

Bartolotti, J. and Marian, V. (2017) Bilinguals' existing languages benefit vocabulary learning in a third language. *Language Learning Journal* 67 (1), 110–140.

Byker, E.J. (2014) ICT oriented toward nyaya: Community computing in India's slums. *International Journal of Education and Development using ICT* 10 (2), 19–28.

Byker, E.J. (2019) Study abroad as social and emotional learning: Framing international teaching with critical cosmopolitan theory. *Journal of Research in Innovative Teaching & Learning* 12 (2), 183–194.

Byker, E.J. and Putman, S.M. (2019) Catalyzing cultural and global competencies: Engaging preservice teachers in study abroad to expand the agency of citizenship. *Journal of Studies in International Education* 23 (1), 84–105.

Byker, E.J., Mejia, N. and Cruzat, M. (2020) Taking action to rewrite the world: Connecting an ubuntu of consciousness with global competencies. In E.J. Byker and A. Horton (eds) *Elementary Education: Global Perspectives, Challenges and Issues of the 21st Century*. New York: Nova Science Publishing.

Dewaele, J.M. and Wei, L. (2012) Multilingualism, empathy and multicompetence. *International Journal of Multilingualism* 9 (4), 352–366.

Diamond, J. (2010) The benefits of multilingualism. *Science Journal* 330 (6002), 332–333.

Doppen, F.H. and Shahri, B. (2019) Overseas student teachers' reflections on American national identity: A longitudinal study. *Journal of International Social Studies* 9 (1), 72–92.

Eguz, E. (2019) Learning a second language in late adulthood: Benefits and challenges. *Educational Gerontology* 45 (12), 701–707.

Fox, R., Corretjer, O. and Webb, K. (2019) Benefits of foreign language learning and bilingualism: An analysis of published empirical research 2012–2019. *Foreign Language Annals* 52 (4), 699–726.

Klein, R.M., Christie, J. and Parkvall, M. (2016) Does multilingualism affect the incidence of Alzheimer's disease? A worldwide analysis by country. *SSM-Population Health Journal* 2, 463–467.

Kroll, D. and Dussias, P.E. (2017) The benefits of multilingualism to the personal and the professional development of residents in the United States. *Foreign Language Annals* 50 (2), 248–259.

Loney, D. and Lusin, N. (2018) *Enrollments in Languages Other than English in the United States Institutions of Higher Education: Preliminary Report*. New York: Modern Language Association of America.

Medina, A.L., Hathaway, J.I. and Pilonieta, P. (2015) How preservice teachers' study abroad experiences lead to changes in their perceptions of English language learners. *Frontiers: The Interdisciplinary Journal of Study Abroad* 25 (2), 73–90.

Mejia, N. (2019) Investigating and comparing Universal Design for Learning in South Africa and the United States. Honors thesis, University of North Carolina, Charlotte.

Miles, M.B. and Huberman, A.M. (1994) *Qualitative Data Analysis* (2nd edn). Thousand Oaks, CA: Sage.

NCUDL (National Center on Universal Design for Learning) (2012) What are the features and components of UDL? http://www.udlcenter.org/ (accessed March 6, 2021).

Ogden, A. (2008) The view from the veranda: Understanding today's colonial students. *The Interdisciplinary Journal of Study Abroad* 15 (1), 35–55.

Peace Corps (1996) *At Home in the World: The Peace Corps Story*. Washington, DC: Peace Corps Publications.

Pilonieta, P., Medina, A.L. and Hathaway, J.I. (2017) The impact of a study abroad experience on preservice teachers' dispositions and plans for teaching English language learners. *The Teacher Educator* 52 (1), 22–38.

Putman, S.M. and Byker, E.J. (2020) Global citizenship 1-2-3: Educating global citizens who learn, think, and act. *Kappa Delta Pi Record* 56 (1), 16–21.

Shanker, S. and Kraemer, A. (2014) The role of higher education in raising global children. *Learning Languages* 19 (1), 6–10.

Woll, B. and Wei, L. (2019) *Cognitive Benefits of Language Learning: Broadening our Perspectives*. London: The British Academy.

Yin, R. (2008) *Case Study Research: Design and Methods* (4th edn). Thousand Oaks, CA: Sage Publications.

Part 3

Emotions and Personal Growth

12 Dreams Cut Short but Heads Held High: Study Abroad in Times of Coronavirus

Takaaki Hiratsuka

'I finally started to get used to life in Sweden, and I was determined to take advantage of the remaining months by meeting new people, embracing new experiences, and enjoying the university. Then, Covid-19 invaded my life'.

They perceived that their personal experiences with Covid-19 during study abroad (e.g. understanding the increasingly complex and fast-moving globalization first-hand) were not detrimental but rather advantageous because the experiences potentially helped them become well-rounded teachers for their future students.

Introduction

The emergence of the novel coronavirus (Covid-19) brought about a historically unprecedented and rapidly evolving situation. Since its first detection in Wuhan City, China, in December 2019, this new virus put the entire world under threat and created widespread panic and anxiety concerning the unknown illness (Lima *et al.*, 2020). The virus has continued its spread across the globe, with millions of cases and many deaths in over 200 countries (WHO, 2021). Virtually everyone on the planet has been affected and many made vulnerable to the emotional impact of Covid-19. Language teachers are no exception, and these include pre-service teacher candidates who participated in study-abroad programs during the early days of the pandemic. They found themselves in dire circumstances in which they had to make significant decisions, essentially on their own in a foreign land, in response to the pandemic. Some were forced to terminate their study-abroad experience and return home abruptly; others were stranded in their host countries due to travel bans and flight suspensions and had to shift suddenly to online classes.

The study on which this chapter is based explored the experiences of two pre-service teachers from Japan who experienced the Covid-19 pandemic during their year-long study-abroad program, one in Sweden and the other in Taiwan. Although many scholars have emphasized study abroad as a rich context for university students in general in terms of, for example, improving foreign language proficiency, increasing autonomy, raising intercultural awareness and constructing new identities (e.g. Mitchell *et al.*, 2017), largely ignored in the literature are the experiences of pre-service language teachers of English during study abroad, particularly as it relates to their raw feelings and emotions in the face of disaster, crisis or emergency. The present study therefore contributes to this area of scholarly inquiry by examining, via narrative interviews, the study-abroad experiences of two Japanese pre-service language teachers of English in the time of Covid-19.

Study Abroad for Pre-service Language Teachers of English

A number of researchers (e.g. Andrade, 2006; Smith & Khawaja, 2011) have recognized the magnitude of the unique concerns experienced by international students studying abroad and have devoted a great deal of effort to address them. They have determined several key stressors and difficulties of those students with regard to adjusting to life in the host country. These include (a) general living issues (e.g. practical concerns, such as new food and weather), (b) academic issues (e.g. educational difficulties, such as assignment overload), (c) sociocultural issues (e.g. intercultural conflicts, such as discrimination), and (d) psychological issues (e.g. personal problems, such as loneliness). Focusing specifically on *pre-service teachers* studying abroad, Morley *et al.* (2019) reviewed empirical literature covering the years 2000–2019. The review identified 47 studies and discovered that the majority of the teachers' home universities were located in the US and that the host universities were either in Europe or in Latin America (29 of 47). Noteworthy is that the review did not detect any study that included Japan as the origin or the destination of study-abroad programs for pre-service teachers. Germane to language education, the review exposed only three studies that interrogated the experiences of pre-service language teachers of English from non-English-speaking countries. Hepple (2012) traced the perspectives of 16 pre-service language teachers of English from Hong Kong, as they engaged in transnational teaching activities with primary school students in Australia during their study-abroad program. The findings demonstrated the effectiveness of both peer and lecturer feedback into the process of dialogic reflection for transformative shifts in their professional understanding. Investigating a group of student teachers from Hong Kong on study-abroad programs in the UK, New Zealand, Australia and Canada, Ma *et al.* (2015) uncovered, through the use of self-report data, various types of language and culture strategies they used before, during and after studying abroad. The focus of Macalister (2016) was on the impact of time spent studying abroad in New Zealand on the cognition and practices of Malaysian student teachers. Data gleaned from interviews, field notes and document analysis suggested that their experiences in New Zealand had an effect on their teaching practices when back in their home country (e.g. the use of a more learner-centered approach).

This small sample of studies above illustrates the impact that time abroad can have on pre-service teachers' developing teaching practices, but also exposes the lack of empirical work on the experiences of pre-service teachers from Asia studying abroad (see also Jackson, 2017), particularly Japan. Since we do not know much about the nature of stress and problems that pre-service (language) teachers encounter in a foreign country, let alone in the face of unexpected adversity and change, this study yields new insights into the field by presenting stories told by Japanese pre-service language teachers of English who grappled with the most recent catastrophic disruption, Covid-19.

Methodology

Participants and context

The participants were Hana (female) and Kouta (male) (pseudonyms). They were both third-year undergraduates from the same university in the western part of Japan. Their major was global studies and both belonged to the teaching license course in order to become public secondary school teachers. Aside from a five-day school trip to Australia during high school, Hana had never been outside of Japan and the study-abroad program was a dream opportunity for her in the sense that she could immerse herself in a linguistically and culturally different environment for an extended period of time. The rationale behind her decision for choosing Sweden as the destination was two-fold. First, the program to Sweden was a one-year program, as opposed to one semester in other countries. Second, the university in Sweden provided international students with the opportunity to learn together with local students in accredited courses (e.g. 'English for Secondary School Teachers'), rather than studying ESL/EFL only with other international students. In September 2019, she commenced studying at the university in Sweden. The autumn semester continued until the middle of January 2020, and the spring semester began the next day. Although her study-abroad program was supposed to continue until the end of the spring semester in June 2020, she returned to Japan at the end of March, due to the Covid-19 pandemic.

Kouta first studied abroad in the US for one semester when he was a second-year student at his Japanese university. After this experience, he wanted to challenge himself even more, not just by learning English in ESL courses but by studying a variety of fields in English, particularly education, with local students. Thus, he decided to study abroad again for a year, this time in Taiwan, because (a) Taiwan was financially and geographically favorable (i.e. cheap and close to Japan), (b) the university in Taiwan offered courses related to education and international studies in English, and (c) Kouta wanted to begin his study abroad from the spring semester, not the autumn semester which was the norm at European universities in which he was initially interested, because of his teaching practicum schedule in Japan. The spring semester began in February 2020. It was at the beginning of April, when the number of active cases of Covid-19 in Taiwan peaked, albeit with far fewer cases compared with other industrialized countries, that Kouta bought a plane ticket to return to Japan. However, the flight was cancelled and he could not find an alternative one. He therefore stayed in Taiwan for a while; in the meantime, the situation concerning Covid-19 in Taiwan dramatically improved. Therefore, he decided to remain in Taiwan and was taking online courses with the Taiwanese university at the time of the interview for this study.

Data collection and analysis

Human beings are storytellers by nature; conversely, telling stories makes us human: 'People shape their daily lives by stories of who they and others are and as they interpret their past in terms of these stories' (Connelly & Clandinin, 2006: 477). Narrative inquiry, a form of qualitative research that uses narratives as data and as the presentation of research findings, has been employed as a primary mode of understanding human experiences, granting research participants 'unity and coherence through time, respecting them as subjects with both histories and intentions' (Riessman, 2016: 364). In the field of language education, the popularity of narrative inquiry has gained traction particularly since the turn of the 20th century (Barkhuizen, 2013). As narrative inquiry is a potent tool with regard to transferring and sharing the knowledge and memory of participants in a verisimilitudinous fashion, as well as an effective instrument for fulfilling the desire of participants to communicate the meaning of their experiences to others (e.g. researchers) in an unprocessed way (Bruner, 1990), an increasing number of researchers now acknowledge the critical interface between narrative and interview. Concurring with those researchers, I selected narrative inquiry, specifically narrative interview, as one of the data collection methods for this study.

After gaining permission from the participants, I interviewed them in Japanese, the first language of the participants and myself, for approximately two hours each on a telecommunication application (Skype) in the middle of April 2020 with Hana, and at the beginning of May with Kouta. I began the interviews with a prompt, 'Tell me your stories, any story at all – if possible, with some examples and episodes – from your study abroad experiences. You can start wherever you like and continue however long you like'. I concentrated on the natural flow of their stories as well as the meaning from their own perspectives and priorities whilst encouraging them to speak freely using the expressions and terms they preferred. Where appropriate, I asked them follow-up questions (e.g. 'What did it mean to you to feel like that?'). In this regard, I believe that my positionality, vis-à-vis theirs, was advantageous (an empathetic, interested listener), especially when conducting research that involves trauma and can potentially expose vulnerabilities, like the present study, in that I was someone who was neither involved in the evaluation of the study-abroad programs nor had an institutional relationship with the participants. According to Morley *et al.* (2019), typically, study-abroad research is carried out by faculty members who serve as sojourn leaders (35 of 47 studies reviewed) where it is likely that an unequal power balance exists between researchers (professors) and participants (students). My hope is that our positionalities facilitated the participants being candid and open, thereby representing the co-constructed and explorative nature that this study advocates.

I transcribed and translated all the interview data whilst making every effort to maintain the essence of the participants' utterances. In terms of managing and sorting the data, I uploaded all the data into qualitative analysis software, NVivo 11, and read them chronologically (i.e. before and after Covid-19) and thematically (i.e. participants' different responses to Covid-19). In other words, the data analysis featured both a qualitative content analysis approach (Bogdan & Biklen, 2007) and a constant comparative approach (Glaser & Strauss, 1967). The dual strategies enabled me to integrate data, identify common and salient themes, and search for patterns amongst these. As a result, the data analysis elicited three inter-related emotional outcomes as primary themes. They were: (a) initial distress, (b) subsequent acceptance, and (c) dispositional optimism.

Findings

Initial distress

The first few months of Hana's study-abroad life were hectic. Not only was she juggling new experiences linguistically and culturally in a foreign country, but it was also her first time engaging in academic work at a foreign university with an enormous number of assignments as well as living on her own without her family. Around the middle point of the second semester she felt she had finally overcome the obstacles of the difficult time she had experienced in the first semester and had become accustomed to her new life abroad. Ironically, it was precisely then that Covid-19 began to engulf Europe, including her city in Sweden. On the morning of March 16 she received an email from her university in Japan, requesting that she return to Japan immediately. She was in disbelief, consumed by all sorts of feelings and emotions. She was eventually filled with deep sadness and total emptiness:

> In the first semester, I was lonely, felt homesick, and lost confidence. However, I finally started to get used to life in Sweden, and I was determined to take advantage of the remaining months by meeting new people, embracing new experiences, and enjoying the university. Then, Covid-19 invaded my life. It hit Europe and hit us all. I could not believe it. I felt a void in my heart.

Since Kouta was in Taiwan, the virus did not seem to pose an immediate threat to him. However, the situation changed drastically at the beginning of April, about one month after he arrived in Taiwan, when new confirmed cases of Covid-19 rose due to overseas returnees. He began to panic and various thoughts raced through his mind. He started to wonder whether he needed to start preparing for the teaching practicum and job hunting in Japan. His fears and anxieties mounted, too, as he weighed up the possibility of contracting the virus in a foreign country:

> Although it was not my own affair at first, I started to worry as the number of confirmed cases soared in Taiwan. It happened so suddenly, and the biggest fear I had was the possibility of having to terminate my study abroad: 'What if I have to start preparing for the teaching practicum and job hunting now instead of one year later?' I was worried about contracting Covid-19, too: 'What if I have to be quarantined in a foreign land when I don't have money and I don't speak the language?'

These comments suggest that both participants experienced severe psychological distress caused by the Covid-19 pandemic. The sheer scale and the rapidly expanding nature of the virus took them by surprise, and they were overwhelmed by a range of emotions (e.g. disbelief, anger, fear, dismay, sadness and numbness). Amid the stress, they had to make vital decisions as to what the next steps should be within a limited time. Hana immediately purchased air tickets, said cursory goodbyes to friends in Sweden, and packed her bags; while Kouta soon found out that the air tickets he had bought were cancelled and afterward negotiated with his Japanese university to let him continue staying in Taiwan rather than go back to Japan.

Subsequent acceptance

Despite her dreams being cut short, Hana told me that she did not feel regretful or upset. She suggested that the acceptance of her situation originated mainly from the following four facets: (a) she gave it her all during the six-month stay in Sweden before she had to come back to Japan; (b) she was thrilled to see her family again; (c) she was delighted to be able to learn with friends and teachers at her Japanese university again; and (d) the nature of the disruption of her study abroad was not something tangible at which she could point an accusing finger:

> I have no regret. I don't feel upset, either. The biggest reason for this is because I did everything I could while I was there … Other reasons might be that I am happy to see my family and to learn with my favorite teachers and students in Japan again. I am surprised at how calm I am whilst accepting this situation. I guess it was also because the source of the termination was external, as opposed to my fault or somebody else's.

As the situation surrounding Covid-19 in Taiwan was in fact better than the situation in Japan, Kouta successfully negotiated with his Japanese university to allow him to stay in Taiwan and take the Taiwanese university courses, albeit online. Although he experienced some inconvenience, including a lack of communication with local students and the loss of opportunity to visit local landmarks, he wished to remain in Taiwan for one year, as he had initially planned. He did not see the point of bemoaning something that was beyond his control. Rather, he accepted what had happened:

> I could continue staying in Taiwan by sheer chance and am currently taking the university courses online. There is no rich interaction with local students. Nor is there any opportunity to visit local attractions now. But I want to fully accept this situation and continue living here for one year, with or without the virus. There is no point for wishing something to be different when I have no control over the issue like this time with Covid-19, right?

Acceptance was another core theme within the participants' experiences in the wake of the Covid-19 pandemic. Given the great expectations they had about their study abroad and the significant changes they had to make to their initial plans, it was surprising to me as well as to the participants themselves that the distress caused by the virus did not appear to be long-lasting; instead, they readily accepted their circumstances with relative calmness. It seemed that Hana's acceptance derived from her contentment with her time in Sweden, her excitement about life on returning to Japan, and the cause of the disruption being external to her. Kouta's acceptance appeared to have also stemmed from the fact that the source of the disruption was not something personal over which he had control.

Dispositional optimism

Hana had an abundance of knowledge about global-related issues as a global studies major. However, the encounter with the pandemic in a foreign land made the knowledge and the concept of globalization come alive in real life. She maintained optimistically that the experience was a meaningful learning opportunity and would assist her in developing as an adept teacher with flexibility and agility:

> Because I was in a foreign country when Covid-19 began to spread, I experienced the penetration and the reality of globalization first-hand. The concept was no longer just academic or theoretical to me. As someone who experienced it, I feel I can teach English and something extra, like global environmental problems, to my students in the future. It was a steep learning curve that enabled me to be more flexible and agile.

For Kouta, the experience with Covid-19 in Taiwan accentuated the importance of carefully choosing available information, considering global issues from multiple perspectives, and empathizing with others who have different values and backgrounds from his own, all of which are arguably invaluable traits as an educator. Furthermore, since he asserted that teachers teach who they are (Farrell *et al.*, 2020), he believed that the unique experience he had during Covid-19 would in fact be an advantage, leading him down a path of being and becoming a better English teacher in the future:

> After being confronted with Covid-19 in a foreign country, I became more attentive to global issues, whether it was about selecting news responsibly, looking at world problems from diverse viewpoints, or understanding foreign people. In my opinion, what is taught is always filtered through the person who teaches it and therefore what the person experienced before would affect his/her teaching. I feel like I now have a very unique personal experience under my belt as a future teacher of English.

At first glance, the threat of the virus seemed to have a devastating and persistent impact on the lives of the participants. However, the participants accepted their circumstances, somewhat quickly, and began to see the unprecedented event in an optimistic light. As future educators, they regarded these unique experiences as developmental opportunities. Thus, they looked toward the future and did not dwell on the past. They expressed positive expectations of success as future language teachers of English, being equipped with beneficial characteristics (e.g. flexibility) and rich experiences (e.g. witnessing the global pandemic from outside Japan).

Discussion

Undeniably, Covid-19 caused a massive disruption to the study-abroad lives of Hana and Kouta. Prior to the disruption, Hana experienced a myriad of stressors, as many international students would, ranging from practical concerns, to educational difficulties, to intercultural conflicts, to psychological issues (e.g. Andrade, 2006; Smith & Khawaja, 2011). The pandemic was particularly poignant for her because it occurred when she was ready to 'take advantage of the remaining months' after overcoming the common early difficulties experienced during study abroad (see Ma *et al.*, 2015). In comparison, Kouta's concerns surrounding Covid-19 were associated with his uncertain prospects in Japan and the potential risk of contracting a potentially life-threatening virus in a foreign country. This is one of the unique findings of this study in that worrying about going back home or getting sick unexpectedly is not usually in the forefront of international students' minds while studying abroad. In fact, neither of the participants in this study imagined something like this would ever happen to them. One of the obvious practical implications for students going on a study-abroad program is therefore that they should be cognizant of the possibility of the unprecedented and the unexpected, however unlikely it might be, and keep emergency contacts and guidelines close at hand. Another is that the program organizers in their home universities should address cases and scenarios of disasters, crises and emergencies, alongside more typical stressors of studying abroad, in order to raise students' awareness so as to prepare them to deal better with distress in case any problems do arise while abroad.

Despite the initial distress, Hana and Kouta subsequently accepted their extreme circumstances without anger or complaint. This is astonishing because they had so much to lose considering the time and energy they had invested in the special opportunity of being able to study abroad. Added to this complication was the Covid-19 pandemic, which has been shown to increase psychological problems, including anxiety, depression and stress (Lima *et al.*, 2020). One possible explanation for the participants' attitudes is that, in general, we might be able to more easily reconcile ourselves to adversities when their cause and nature are external and beyond our intervention, as opposed to personal and changeable. Another is that in the cases of the participants, there might have been just enough contributory factors (e.g. positive study-abroad experiences, or anticipated future experiences) that allowed them to reach the acceptance stage. That is, Hana perceived the first half of her life in Sweden to be fulfilling and also looked forward to the reunion with her family, friends and teachers in Japan; whereas Kouta could stay in Taiwan and take online courses from the Taiwanese university and he also had already experienced a full-semester study-abroad program in the US previously. An overt lesson, then, is that students in study-abroad programs should make the most of their opportunities whilst abroad and, at the same time, strive to learn and prepare to look on the bright side of any unfavorable situation.

After the experience with Covid-19, counterintuitively, the participants expressed optimism about their current lives and exhibited positive professional dispositions towards their future teaching. Both seemed to understand that serving as a teacher entails more than just possessing the knowledge of the subject, creating lesson plans and instructing students, and believed that the extraordinary experience they had endured with the virus in a foreign country would in fact be a transformative catalyst for enabling them to become more effective teachers armed with rare, but important, experiences, viewpoints and traits (see also Hepple, 2012; Macalister, 2016). The participants realized that they could be exceptional educational agents in the future who had directly internalized globalization within the changing, complex contexts across national borders – socially, culturally, politically, economically and interpersonally – in the time of Covid-19. Since teachers' dispositions, attitudes and motivation are paramount in their teacher preparation and affect their professional behaviors significantly – hence we teach who we are (Cline & Necochea, 2006; Farrell *et al.*, 2020) – we should be encouraged to turn negative events and experiences, especially in such extreme cases as the Covid-19 pandemic, into positive outcomes, just like the participants in this study did. It might be helpful for study-abroad programs and/or teaching license programs at the home university to become familiar with and implement the concepts and applications of positive psychology (Seligman & Csikszentmihalyi, 2000), in particular relating to language learning and teaching (e.g. MacIntyre & Gregersen, 2012), as well as introduce and discuss some cases of previous students who successfully bounced back from adverse circumstances while and after studying abroad.

Conclusion

Despite initial distress, the two Japanese pre-service teacher participants not only accepted the undesired consequences due to the spread of Covid-19, but also viewed their current circumstances and future professional prospects through the lens of optimism. This study thus highlighted the importance for pre-service teachers experiencing study abroad to remain vigilant but positive in the face of disaster, crisis and emergency. One finding that merits particular attention was the participants' recognition that the foundation of teaching is teachers' individual experiences. Accompanying this thought, they perceived that their personal experiences with Covid-19 during study abroad (e.g. understanding the increasingly complex and fast-moving effects of globalization first-hand) were not detrimental but rather advantageous because the experiences potentially helped them become well-rounded teachers for their future students. This study is the first of its kind to concentrate on the study-abroad experiences of Japanese pre-service teachers who experienced hardship in the form of the Covid-19 outbreak; therefore, more research is needed that includes pre-service teacher participants from different home universities (particularly within Japan and in other Asian countries) and host universities (outside of Taiwan and Sweden) (see Çiftçi & Karaman, 2019; Morley *et al.*, 2019; Plews & Jackson, 2017). It might also prove useful to conduct a similar study with participants who experienced divergent types of disruption and trauma in a foreign country (e.g. a debilitating accident). These efforts would provide a fuller understanding of what the experiences of pre-service teachers are like under unexpected and extraordinary circumstances and events during study abroad and how they can hold their heads high and keep their dreams alive while coping with adversity.

References

Andrade, M.S. (2006) International students in English-speaking universities. *Journal of Research in International Education* 5, 131–154.

Barkhuizen, G. (ed.) (2013) *Narrative Research in Applied Linguistics*. Cambridge: Cambridge University Press.

Bogdan, R.C. and Biklen, S.K. (2007) *Qualitative Research for Education: An Introduction to Theory and Methods* (5th edn). Boston, MA: Allyn & Bacon.

Bruner, J. (1990) *Acts of Meaning*. Cambridge, MA: Harvard University Press.

Connelly, F.M. and Clandinin, D.J. (2006) Narrative inquiry. In J. Green, G. Camilli and P. Elmore (eds) *Handbook of Complementary Methods in Education Research* (pp. 477–487). Mahwah, NJ: Lawrence Erlbaum.

Çiftçi, E. and Karaman, A. (2019) Short-term international experiences in language teacher education: A qualitative meta-synthesis. *Australian Journal of Teacher Education* 44 (1), 93–119.

Cline, Z. and Necochea, J. (2006) Teacher dispositions for effective education in the borderlands. *The Educational Forum* 70, 268–282.

Farrell, T.S.C., Baurain, B. and Lewis, M. (2020) 'We teach who we are': Contemplation, reflective practice and spirituality in TESOL. *RELC Journal* 51 (3), 337–346.

Glaser, B.G. and Strauss, A.L. (1967) *The Discovery of Grounded Theory*. Chicago, IL: Aldine.

Hepple, E. (2012) Questioning pedagogies: Hong Kong pre-service teachers' dialogic reflections on a transnational school experience. *Journal of Education for Teaching* 38, 309–322.

Jackson, J. (2017) Second language teacher identity. In G. Barkhuizen (ed.) *Reflections on Language Teacher Identity Research* (pp. 114–119). New York: Routledge.

Lima, C.K.T., Carvalho, P.M.M., Lima, I.A.A.S., Nunes, J.V.A.O., Saraiva, J.S., de Souza, R.I., da Silva, C.G.L. and Neto, M.L.R. (2020) The emotional impact of Coronavirus 2019-nCoV (new Coronavirus disease). *Psychiatry Research*. https://doi.org/10.1016/j.psychres.2020.112915

Ma, A., Wong, R.M.H. and Lam, W.Y.K. (2015) Profiling language and culture strategy use patterns of ESL student teachers in study abroad by using self-reported data. *Pedagogy Culture and Society* 23 (1), 107–131.

Macalister, J. (2016) Tracing it back: Identifying the impact of a trans-national language teacher education program on classroom practice. *RELC Journal* 47 (1), 59–70.

MacIntyre, P. and Gregersen, T. (2012) Emotions that facilitate language learning: The positive-broadening power of the imagination. *Studies in Second Language Learning and Teaching* 2 (2), 193–213.

Mitchell, R., Tracy-Ventura, N. and McManus, K. (2017) *Anglophone Students Abroad: Identity, Social Relationships and Language Learning*. New York: Routledge.

Morley, A., Braun, A.M.B., Rohrer, L. and Lamb, D. (2019) Study abroad for preservice teachers: A critical literature review with consideration for research and practice. *Global Education Review* 6 (3), 4–29.

Plews, J.L. and Jackson, J. (2017) Introduction to the special issue: Study abroad to, from, and within Asia. *Study Abroad Research in Second Language Acquisition and International Education* 2 (2), 137–146.

Riessman, C.K. (2016) What's different about narrative inquiry? Cases, categories, and contexts. In D. Silverman (ed.) *Qualitative Research* (4th edn) (pp. 363–378). London: Sage.

Seligman, M. and Csikszentmihalyi, M. (2000) Positive psychology: An introduction. *American Psychologist* 55 (1), 5–14.

Smith, R.A. and Khawaja, N.G. (2011) A review of the acculturation experiences of international students. *International Journal of Intercultural Relations* 35 (6), 699–713.

WHO (2021) *Coronavirus Disease (COVID-2019) Situation Reports.* https://www.who.int/emergencies/diseases/novel-coronavirus-2019/situation-reports (accessed February 22, 2020).

13 No Ordinary Time: Language Teachers Abroad in an Extraordinary Year

John Macalister

The initial lockdown period in New Zealand was four weeks. This was extended slightly, but on 28 April the country began to move out of lockdown. It was not an immediate change, but a transition that took some adjusting to. At least two of the five participants were clearly reluctant to return to campus, but for different reasons.

'*It was* stressful at times *studying alone in a room, but when that time came,* I tried to cheer myself up *by exercising, cooking, chit-chatting with families in Cambodia digitally, or just hanging out with friends in NZ. After a month of lockdown,* I could handle *my study well*'.

Introduction

The year began in ordinary fashion. The New Zealand summer was delivering the right sort of weather; schools and universities were gearing up for the start of the academic year; and international students were starting to arrive in the country. At the same time, however, news outlets carried stories of a deadly virus outbreak in China, and neighbouring countries at least were beginning to take it seriously. While attending an international conference that February, I found that some hotels were taking temperature readings at check-in, at least one airline had suspended all cabin service, and that everywhere cabin crew were now wearing face masks. But it couldn't be too bad, could it? This was 2020 after all.

We all know now that the Covid-19 pandemic that gripped the world in 2020 was much more devastating than had been widely anticipated at the outset, and as I write this chapter much about the future remains uncertain. But presumably the vaccines now being developed and administered will be effective, the pandemic will be brought under control, and global mobility will resume. Presumably – hopefully – international education will recover and opportunities for language teachers to study abroad will not become an historical artefact.

Inevitably, this chapter focuses on a very specific time and place as it seeks to understand the experiences of a group of language teachers who were studying abroad during the Covid-19 pandemic. The pandemic, however, can be taken as a proxy for any type of unexpected upheaval or radical disruption. In this chapter, I begin by introducing the participants and the context, then tell their shared story of being abroad at the time, making use of their words and drawing attention to what they felt and experienced. From here I provide some thoughts on what was learned, what should have been learned, and what we should not forget.

This chapter adds to the study-abroad literature in two ways. Because of work, family, time and financial considerations it can be difficult for teachers to pursue a postgraduate degree in other countries, and so this chapter adds to the relatively small literature on experienced teachers undertaking postgraduate study abroad. Second, it focuses on the experience while abroad, rather than the impact of the time away from home; this could be considered a process/product distinction. Further, rather than considering the academic experience (as in, for example, Phakiti & Li, 2011) it focuses first on events and experiences beyond the classroom (see Mayumi & Hüttner, 2020).

Some Background

The participants in this study are five Cambodian teachers of English who arrived in New Zealand in early February 2020 to begin a postgraduate degree program of around 18 months' duration. When the country went into lockdown on March 25, they had already completed a two-week intensive course and had just begun their first regularly scheduled courses. The time period for this study is shown in Figure 13.1.

During the lockdown the five participants were part of a larger group who had contact with me through regular Zoom meetings. Here I was acting in a pastoral role reflecting my position at the university, and this is one of three facets of my professional identity that may have affected the data generated in this study. The participants were also aware of my long-standing involvement with English language education in Cambodia, and they knew that I would be teaching one of the courses that would be offered in the second trimester (only one of the five participants did not

Figure 13.1 Research timeline

take that course). I mention these things here as they may have affected what the participants said about New Zealand, the university and the courses they were taking. Readers should bear this in mind as they read this chapter (recalling Mann's, 2011 call for a greater focus on the interviewer).

The idea for this study actually emerged from, and was briefly discussed in, the Zoom meetings during lockdown and once the idea developed, all the Zoom attendees received an invitation to participate. The five who volunteered to participate were all asked to complete a narrative frame (Barkhuizen, 2014; Barkhuizen & Wette, 2008) and to take part in a semi-structured interview that lasted around 30 minutes. All the interviews were conducted face-to-face (although a virtual interview was also offered). Narrative frame responses provided a starting point for the interviews, which were in English, recorded and later transcribed. *from Cambodia*

More about the Participants

The five participants were a surprisingly homogenous group. All had started learning English at a reasonably young age, mainly at small private language schools, although one had begun learning at a temple and another had joined a church. The oldest age at which any had begun learning English seemed to be around 11, and this was after switching from learning another foreign language, Chinese. All saw speaking English as indexing social capital. Two of them used the word 'cool' when talking about their reasons for learning English, and one described it in her narrative frame as follows: 'At that time, I wanted to be as cool as the rich and smart city kids who went to a private English school next to my relatives' house' (P3).[1]

They also, as no doubt did the parents who had encouraged English language learning in the first place, recognized the instrumental value attached to proficiency in English with various comments along the lines of 'I thought that English is a tool to help people achieve their life goals' (P3, narrative frame). Being English teachers in Cambodia, they all used the language at work, but most reported limited use of English outside of work. The exception to this was a participant who had joined a church which was also attended by expatriates and other visitors and where, he reported, his bilingualism was often called on.

For most of the participants this was their first time abroad, other than an occasional short holiday in a neighbouring country. In other words, *same* they had not had much opportunity to use English beyond the classroom, whether as student or teacher. The exception here was one participant who had worked as a volunteer at an orphanage in Malaysia for two months (where, she said, most spoke only Chinese) and had been on exchange to Japan.

All had made the effort to obtain a scholarship abroad, and in the narrative frames three used the word 'excited', and one 'thrilled', to describe their response when they found out they had received a scholarship to study in New Zealand – conceivably the excitement was at least as much about receiving a scholarship as about the destination.

Perhaps an example of the interviewer effect is that the participants did talk about what they would learn while in New Zealand, but studying was not on the minds of all: 'So I think coming here is not about all studying but exploring and learn the lifestyle here ... it's quiet actually, especially in Wellington' (P1). Upon arriving in the country, expectations were often confirmed but there were also surprises such as:

> Um, one of the thing it's, I see people walking barefoot. [JM laughs] And I asked the Cambodian family here, they said that don't ask them why. It's rude to ask them. And another thing, it's most of people here, they said that and how it's going, Oh, how are you? Just the way to say hello. Yeah, don't expect answer from us. So we are not supposed to say oh, I'm good. A lot of things. Yeah. (P5, interview)

The way of learning seemed also to be a surprise to some, and more demanding than anticipated which is encapsulated in this comment during the interview: 'I have read, ah, in the three months more than I have read my whole life' (P1). The participants did have more to say about their experience of learning in New Zealand, as will be seen later in this chapter.

Entering Lockdown

New Zealand had 48 hours' notice of the move into lockdown. There were news reports of people rushing to return home from other parts of the country, of panic buying in supermarkets. Toilet paper seemed to be in exceptionally high demand. Most of the five participants recalled their feelings at the time with words like 'stressful', 'scared', 'anxious' and 'shocked'. They mentioned being scared of becoming infected, scared of getting depressed, and scared to go out:

> JM: And the lockdown. What did you, what did you feel when you heard about the lockdown?
>
> P1: [noticeable pause] The first feeling was that I'm gonna have a lot to tell my kids [laughter]. Yeahh, yeah. Because it, it, coming to New Zealand is something new to me. And in a lockdown in a new country in a foreign country is super strange. Like all I have to do is to stay at home, I have to be cautious all the time when I go out shopping, and then I have to rush home. Um it kind of frustrating and very stressful. It's, it was a very stressful situation for me.

Only one participant reported a different response. In her interview she said: 'I feel completely normal, I don't know why. Maybe I'm too confident that I would not be infected or that the country is doing well in protecting people' (P3).

Experiencing Lockdown

In the interview extract above, P1 draws attention to the characteristic that made the participants' experience of the pandemic, and of the lockdown, different from that of most other people in New Zealand at the time. They were 'in a new country in a foreign country', far from home and their usual support networks of friends and family. The affordances of technology, however, meant they were not out of touch. Families and friends seemed to think the participants were in a safe place and did not admit to concerns about their own safety in Cambodia: 'I think, because, you know, like, they put all the trust in the government. So I feel like they believe that New Zealand is a safe country, so they don't have anything to worry. They just feel like, okay, just take care of yourself. Don't go out. Yeah, yes, just stay indoor as much as you can' (P2, interview). The participants also seemed to feel they were in a safe place, as P3 said above, and some admitted they felt New Zealand was a safer place to be than Cambodia with comments like, 'Yeah, I'm worried about them. Because, you know, like, I don't really trust the system back there' (P2, interview).

While concerns about their own and friends' and families' safety were allayed as the lockdown continued, the participants still needed to get on with the business of living in a world where normal activities were largely curtailed. They could not go to university, they could not socialize, they could not travel. The participants reported two ways of dealing with this. The differences can perhaps best be summarized by saying that some *created* a routine, while others *fell* into a routine, as can be seen by comparing these two comments from interviews:

> But after that I tried to adopt a routine. Like in the morning, I spent some time on readings. And like, in the evening, I went for a walk. I spend some time for like, phone calls to my family members and my friends. (P5)

> And you know, we just do like normal daily routines, like chat, we meet each other in the common room, we talk. We cook, we did talk about stuff, and we watched the video and watch the movie. And sometimes we talk about the class. (P2)

Emerging from Lockdown

The initial lockdown period in New Zealand was four weeks. This was extended slightly, but on April 28 the country began to move out of lockdown. It was not an immediate change, but a transition that took some adjusting to. At least two of the five participants were clearly reluctant to return to campus, but for different reasons. One had concerns about infection, the other was enjoying the routine she had created. Another admitted to feeling less safe and secure than she had before the lockdown. But at the time of the interviews, all appeared to be happy to return to campus, or at least accepted the change. They ranged in sentiment from 'I love going back' (P2), to agreeing that 'I think I prefer this better, better than staying at home' (P3). At the same time, however, feelings of worry and anxiety had not gone away altogether. These were most explicit on the day that two new cases in the community were reported on the news:

P3: There are two new cases.

JM: I know, I know.

P3: [softly] Bad, bad.

Studying during the Pandemic

The university took the decision to suspend all teaching during the lockdown, at least in part to allow academic staff time to adjust to and prepare for online teaching. Classes did not resume for several weeks and the long delay was generally experienced negatively by these teachers. While, as mentioned earlier, the participants were not wholly focused on studying during their time in New Zealand, being on scholarships they were serious about doing well in their studies. For one participant, a source of anxiety as she entered lockdown was whether she would be able to graduate because of the pandemic.

As shown in Figure 13.1, all the participants had experienced studying in a New Zealand university under normal conditions prior to the lockdown. For most this had been different from prior university learning experiences because of the expectation of independent learning and the lack of 'spoon feeding a little bit'. It was also a catalyst for reflection on the reasons for the teaching here being different from the way they themselves taught.

> Um, it's a bit weird at first, because when I come, like, I came to the class and teacher keep talking. That what I wouldn't do in my, my own class, but back then I admit, to compare the two classes, I was teaching general English to my students and [lecturer], or let's say, other professors are doing their Master's teaching, which is like completely different. And we tend to be like, autonomous learners. So I think my expectation was kind of, like, a little bit different. (P1, interview)

While there was no teaching for several weeks during the lockdown, there were still assignments to do, and reading that could be done. For most, however, this was not a time for an academic focus. The following sums up that experience:

> And during that one month, one month break. Um my habits like have been ruined, more or less, because Oh, that one month I didn't do any academic work at all. I only like, with my friends, we were watching a lot of movies, which is not necessary for our academic journey. And I've been cooking a lot but doesn't help me with anything at school. (P1, interview)

It would be wrong to create the impression that students were abandoned by the university during this period, but the usual routines and structures had vanished. The participants in this study, as noted earlier, tended to either create or fall into new routines and virtual support structures were quickly put in place by the university. However, only one of the five appears to have taken real advantage of these, and even for her it was not always easy. Her account below has all the elements of a good story; the italicized phrases draw attention to the highs and lows she experienced.

> Honestly speaking, *I felt lost* sometimes during the course in trimester 1; however, with the assistance from my course instructors, student learning advisors and a subject librarian, *I could manage* my study properly and found no more obstacles regarding difficulties of studies. It was *stressful at times* studying alone in a room, but when that time came, *I tried to cheer myself up* by exercising, cooking, chit-chatting with families in Cambodia digitally, or just hanging out with friends in NZ. After a month of lockdown, *I could handle* my study well, and then I decided to start a part-time job in a café. (P4, narrative frame)

It is worth mentioning that this teacher was motivated by academic success. She had received a very good grade on her first piece of submitted work, which had made her feel 'very excited inside' and want to repeat the feeling, so she was 'sad' when the next grade was a little lower. She wanted to do well academically because 'I'm so excited to see myself grow'.

Once the university resumed teaching, it remained online for the remainder of the trimester and, with the exception of P3, re-engaging academically posed its challenges. There was a sense of frustration when sitting at the computer screen – 'what do they expect me to learn?' The participants expressed a preference for face-to-face classes because then they could hold discussions with the lecturer and other students, ask questions, and seek clarifications around requirements and expectations. Joining a class online was not the same.

> But when doing the distance learning I felt it's different because people keeping quiet, and you don't really know who actually read [JM laughs]. Yeah, and sometime I, to be honest, I sometime I skipped the one of the Zoom meeting, because I didn't read. And that I think that that's a very bad habit. Yeah, yeah. It shouldn't happen like that. (P2, interview)

One participant very nicely identified another issue that might resonate with many when studying online from home: 'Even if sometimes feel sleepy during session … when you see your bed, when you see your food' (P3, interview). Though, on reflection, that need not apply only to studying online.

Learning through the Lockdown

For all its challenges and mixed emotions, the lockdown provided opportunities for personal learning and individual insights that were possibly unexpected. Perhaps the most mentioned example of learning or self-improvement related to cooking skills; if news reports about shortages of flour and yeast at the time were any indication, then there was a national upsurge in interest in cooking and baking, so the participants were not alone in this.

But there were several other examples of personal learning that received a mention in the interviews. The majority could be classified as coping strategies, often with application to academic study – how to deal with stress, learning to be patient, learning how to motivate oneself, time management skills, the ability to concentrate. At least one admitted to thinking about changes to his teaching practice if he were experiencing Covid-19 lockdown at home, and there were also a couple of comments relating to insights about the self, most memorably:

> Yeah, I think because I think during the Zoom or the weekly Zoom with you I mentioned that I'm quite introvert. Yeah, I enjoy you know, like my alone time but then during the lockdown I realized that no, I'm not actually [laughter] … Like it's very confusing. But yeah, I learned about myself more during that time. I feel like no, actually, I'm not an introvert person. Yeah. (P2, interview)

Discussion

The trajectory that the teacher participants in this study followed during the first half of an extraordinary year was one that began with expectation and excitement as they left Cambodia and arrived in New Zealand to commence their postgraduate studies against the background of a growing Covid-19 threat internationally. This led to disruption of their expectations and experience, marked by feelings of stress and anxiety and of being scared. Such feelings were not conducive to maintaining an academic focus for most during the lockdown. This was then followed by recovery as the pandemic was slowly brought under control in New Zealand, and life returned to normal, more or less. On one level, a similar emotional trajectory was probably experienced by the great majority of people in the country over these months, but the added dimension for these teachers was that they were studying abroad, far from home.

While the circumstances the teachers faced in 2020 were exceptional, in themselves they were similar to those faced by other cohorts of teachers who have studied abroad. When compared with Malaysian pre-service teachers who had also studied in New Zealand, for example, they displayed a similar breadth of goals for their time abroad, including professional, personal and cross-cultural goals (Macalister, 2014), and had a similar relationship to English as a language that can enhance one's life opportunities (Macalister, 2017). Although it was still relatively early in their time abroad, one participant even expressed a similar concern about not being able to meet her personal linguistic proficiency improvement goal, which included making new international friends, because 'we cling together' which she seemed to think would be the case with or without Covid-19 in their lives (see Macalister, 2015, 2017). This issue of social integration is, however, neither unique nor simple (Spencer-Oatey *et al.*, 2017).

Improving language proficiency is a common goal for teachers (and others) when studying abroad, even when the primary focus is on academic or professional learning. In earlier work (Macalister, 2015, 2017), reflecting on the experiences of Malaysian pre-service teachers and with a focus on promoting target language use beyond the classroom, I proposed five principles that could be borne in mind when designing study-abroad programs. These include:

(1) Promoting autonomy through real-world communication.
(2) Fostering positive affect and integrative motivation.
(3) Providing repeated opportunities for real-world communication.
(4) Challenging traditional views of learning and fostering flexibility of learning styles.
(5) Including opportunities for deliberate language learning in the program.

Although these Cambodian teachers were in-service rather than pre-service teachers, these principles still seem to resonate. As one example, in terms of promoting autonomy through real-world communication, one participant had a formal role in the postgraduate program and of this, she said in the interview: 'It's like, the role give me more, more courage. I mean, it's like, even though you you think you shouldn't be doing that, but but it gives you courage. Like, it gives you a job'. The role licenced her to communicate and establish relationships with all other students enrolled in the degree, as well as with academic staff teaching into the degree. As another example, P1's comments about the first experience of university teaching in New Zealand being 'weird' relate to the fourth principle, although it should be noted that 'challenging' is intended to apply to academic staff as well, not just to international students. And as a final example, the regular Zoom meetings during lockdown were a small instance of providing repeated opportunities for real-world communication.

However, what the events of 2020 may have allowed for these teachers is the opportunity for personal growth and development beyond the honing of cookery skills. Whether these would have occurred otherwise, but more gradually, will forever remain unknown; at the very least, however, the lockdown period does appear to have accelerated this development.

The question then might become: what should the host institutions learn from the lockdown and the disruption to normal life caused by the pandemic that could improve the performance and resilience of study-abroad programs like this one? There is no doubt, of course, that host institutions did learn a great deal in 2020, and often responded appropriately and with unusual agility (though, to be clear, it was the actions of individual professional and academic staff, rather than institutions, who probably deserve the credit for this). Much of the institutional response to the pandemic did seem to involve embracing technology, particularly in terms of teaching delivery when face-to-face classes became impossible. What the experiences of these teachers have highlighted, however, is the value of and importance attached to face-to-face teaching. This represents an international student perspective, and perhaps domestic students experienced online teaching differently, but it should not be overlooked. The preservation of face-to-face classes may well end up being an area of contention in universities and other providers if educational institutions regard the forced introduction of online teaching to be a success and see economic advantages in shifting to online spaces.

It is also the case that there will always be scope for making improvements for the benefit of students. Just as the pandemic and the lockdown may have accelerated opportunities for personal growth and development, so they might have heightened awareness of changes needed in study-abroad programs, possibly changes along the lines of the five principles mentioned earlier. To me, those principles extend beyond opportunities for language learning and include elements of pastoral care. With or without a pandemic, we should not lose sight of the fact that study abroad is by definition something that occurs 'in a new country in a foreign country', away from usual support systems. The following extract says all there is to say on the subject.

JM: Okay. Okay. So I was also meaning about what, what to expect in terms of living in New Zealand, that they might not know about.

P4: What to expect? The weather of course, and the weather. And how lonely it is. Because they would expect, I posted a lot of pictures like working, traveling. Yes, it's true out there. But I rarely post about how lonely I am. So I just tell them to, when you come here studying abroad it's the feeling you're gonna encounter. That's the feeling. So if you come with your family, maybe like husband or wife, probably you get you get, you can lessen the feeling. But if you come here alone, even you have friends, you still encounter that problem.

JM: And I guess that's unrelated to Covid-19, that's just the reality of studying abroad.

P4: [quietly] Yeah.

Final Words

When reflecting on the experiences and stories of these language teachers abroad during extraordinary times, what strikes me again and again is the resilience of the human spirit. People find individual ways of coping even when radical disruption occurs, and a global pandemic certainly qualifies as such a disruption. Networks of friends, distractions such as cooking and movies, personal mantras to keep oneself motivated – these are some of the tools the participants in this study employed during Covid-19. But coping and surviving are not necessarily positive endorsements of the study-abroad experience. In the interviews, I was interested in responses to the 'what if?' question, a question along the lines of, 'if you knew then what you know now, would you still have left Cambodia?' P5's response is representative of all: 'Like I said, I don't regret, yeah, having made this choice'. It is reassuring to feel that, despite dealing with the disruption and attendant challenges caused by the pandemic, study abroad for language teachers can still receive a *non, je ne regrette rien* endorsement.

Note

(1) In presenting data, the codes P1, P2, etc. represent the five participants, and JM the author/interviewer. Note that not every extract from the data included in this chapter has been attributed to a speaker; no attribution has been made if this might lead to identification of the speaker.

References

Barkhuizen, G. (2014) Revisiting narrative frames: An instrument for investigating language teaching and learning. *System* 47, 12–27.

Barkhuizen, G. and Wette, R. (2008) Narrative frames for investigating the experiences of language teachers. *System* 36 (3), 372–387.

Macalister, J. (2014) Desire and desirability: Perceptions of needs in a trans-national language teacher education program. In S.B. Said and L.J. Zhang (eds) *Language Teachers and Teaching: Global Perspectives, Local Initiatives* (pp. 303–316). New York: Routledge.

Macalister, J. (2015) Study abroad program design and goal fulfilment: 'I'd like to talk like a Kiwi'. In D. Nunan and J.C. Richards (eds) *Language Learning Beyond the Classroom* (pp. 235–244). New York: Routledge.

Macalister, J. (2017) English and language teacher education in Malaysia: An exploration of the influences on and experiences of pre-service teachers. *RELC Journal* 48 (1), 53–66.

Mann, S. (2011) A critical review of qualitative interviews in applied linguistics. *Applied Linguistics* 32 (1), 6–24.

Mayumi, K. and Hüttner, J. (2020) Changing beliefs on English: Study abroad for teacher development. *ELT Journal* 74 (3), 268–276.

Phakiti, A. and Li, L. (2011) General academic difficulties and reading and writing difficulties among Asian ESL postgraduate students in TESOL at an Australian university. *RELC Journal* 42 (3), 227–264.

Spencer-Oatey, H., Dauber, D., Jing, J. and Lifei, W. (2017) Chinese students' social integration into the university community: Hearing the students' voices. *Higher Education* 74 (5), 739–756.

14 When Teachers Become 'the Other': Studying Abroad in the Dominican Republic

Shondel Nero

Teacher education curricula can therefore be enhanced by providing real opportunities for pre- and in-service teachers and their professors to experience 'otherness', i.e., to engage linguistic and cultural difference first-hand by temporarily living and learning in the countries of their students' origin; reflect upon challenges to their beliefs, values, assumptions and practices; and use that experience to inform their pedagogy.

The teacher just casually said, está bien, dejaré la tarea en su casa de camino a casa *[that's ok, I'll drop off the homework at her house on the way home]. The teacher's simple comment triggered a 45-minute conversation in my class later that afternoon.*

Introduction

In an era where cross-border experiences – geographical, sociocultural and virtual – are normalized, and US classrooms are increasingly populated by culturally/linguistically diverse students, teacher preparation programs are, by necessity, called upon to equip teachers with the requisite dispositions, knowledge, intercultural competence, pedagogical skills and resources to respond equitably to this reality. Among the many approaches to respond to the changing demographics in schools has been an increase in short-term study-abroad programs for pre- and in-service teachers. While many study-abroad programs have historically focused narrowly on language acquisition (Coleman, 2013), programs for teachers have taken a broader view of study abroad with varying goals of developing communication skills in a new language, more globally informed, critical perspectives in education (Baecher & Chung, 2020), empathy for second language learners (Colón-Muñiz et al., 2010; Marx & Pray, 2011; Nero, 2009), critical multilingual language awareness (Lindhal et al., 2020), intercultural competence (Brown & Tignor, 2016; Cushner & Chang, 2015; He et al., 2017) and/or culturally responsive pedagogy (Nero, 2009, 2018; Zhao et al., 2009). These programs foreground the teachers themselves as agentive, reflective participants in a dynamic, cross-cultural experience that includes not only language, but also examines their identities, goals, motivations, emotions, challenges, learning processes and connections to their teaching practice.

In keeping with the goal of this volume to examine 'whole people and whole lives' (Coleman, 2013) in study-abroad experiences for teachers, this chapter describes the conception, goals, design and evaluation of a study-abroad program to the Dominican Republic sponsored by my university that I designed and have led for the past 11 years as one approach to addressing cultural and linguistic diversity in teacher education.

Specifically, the participants' trajectories and voices throughout the program – pre-departure, in the host country and on return home – are foregrounded in order to capture the complexity of the experience and their feelings as they navigate and try to reconcile the goals of the program with their own while becoming 'the other' in a different context.

The Demographic Imperative

According to the US Census Bureau (2012), immigration to the United States has increased significantly since 2000 with the Latino population from the Caribbean, Central and South America leading the way. This demographic shift nationally has translated into a marked increase in English Language Learners (ELLs) in public schools across the country. At roughly 4.4 million (National Center for Education Statistics, 2016), ELLs are the fastest growing segment of the K-12 student population and are predicted to represent 25% of all public school students by 2025. In New York City (NYC) in particular, the most culturally and linguistically diverse city in the country, over 3 million of its 8.4 million residents are foreign born, the largest group of approximately 380,000 or 12.4% hailing from the Dominican Republic. This is directly reflected in NYC classrooms where Dominicans are the largest Spanish-speaking population; therefore, most NYC teachers, regardless of their subject area, are likely to have Dominican children in their classrooms. For this reason, teachers in NYC need a more in-depth understanding of Dominican culture to better serve this population. King and Bigelow (2018) support this argument by noting that pre-service teachers' learning experiences are more meaningful when they are closely aligned with teachers' likely future teaching experiences. Moreover, this program in the Dominican Republic disrupts the overwhelming tendency for students to study abroad in western European countries like the UK, Spain and France, the top destinations for most students from the US (Open Doors, 2017). In so doing, it expands cross-border educational experiences beyond Eurocentric frames, challenging students to rethink White normative majority positioning (Phillion *et al.*, 2009) when confronted with their own minoritized positioning in a developing, non-European country. The program, entitled *Culture and Language Learning in Real Time* (CLLRT), is thus framed within a critical and reflective paradigm of teacher education.

CLLRT was conceived and developed as a collaborative learning experience between New York University's (NYU) Steinhardt School of Culture, Education, and Human Development (hereafter 'Steinhardt') and Pontificia Universidad Católica Madre y Maestra (PUCMM), the leading Catholic University in the Dominican Republic, located in Santiago, the second largest city. The conceptual framework for the program is situated within four interrelated areas of research – critical teacher education, culturally responsive pedagogy, second language acquisition (SLA), and intercultural competence.

Critical Teacher Education

Teacher education programs have too often engaged in superficial and uncritical celebrations of cultural diversity (i.e. the 'food and festivals' approach) in response to changing demographics in schools, leaving out a key component of teacher development, which is to challenge teachers' own understandings of concepts such as culture and diversity in order to address them more equitably in classrooms. Teacher education curricula can therefore be enhanced by providing real opportunities for pre- and in-service teachers and their professors to experience 'otherness', that is, to engage linguistic and cultural difference first-hand by temporarily living and learning in the countries of their students' origin; reflect upon challenges to their beliefs, values, assumptions and practices; and use that experience to inform their pedagogy. Mezirow (1997) characterizes this process as 'transformative learning', namely, becoming aware of invisible frames of reference through a dissonant experience which upsets one's taken-for-granted assumptions, then critically examining and reflecting upon one's beliefs from different perspectives with others.

Hawkins and Norton (2009) argue that a critical approach to teacher education would challenge teachers to explicitly study 'the production and reproduction of power relationships in institutions (such as schools) and society' (2009: 32). This includes how particular groups of students come to be understood as *mainstream* while marginalizing culturally and linguistically diverse *others*. Researchers (Gay, 2000; Ladson-Billings, 2005) have also argued that *culturally responsive pedagogy* (CRP) should be a focal point of teacher education curricula if we are to adequately prepare teachers for the growing diversity in the student population in the 21st century. Gay (2000: 29) defines CRP as 'using the cultural knowledge, prior experiences, and performance styles of diverse students to make learning more appropriate and effective for them; it teaches to and through the strengths of these students'. Such pedagogy requires as a starting point certain dispositions or attitudes towards learners (e.g. empathy, openness, curiosity), foregrounding the psychological and emotional side of teaching, which has been shown to influence both teacher development and pedagogy (Borg, 2003).

Second Language Acquisition and Critical Multilingual Language Awareness

Ever since research in second language acquisition (SLA) has moved beyond the narrow psycholinguistic view of language proposed by Krashen (1982), that is, the well-known, somewhat controversial, distinction between language *acquisition* (learning language by immersion in naturalistic settings) and language *learning* (formal study of language in a classroom), sociocultural and emotional aspects of language learning have been foregrounded for learners, showing their profound effects on learners' motivations and identities (Norton Peirce, 1995).

One way for teachers to experience first-hand the emotional side of language learning is through study-abroad programs, which often include specific learning objectives such as developing communicative skills in a foreign language. Contrary to the focus of most traditional study-abroad programs on measuring growth in target language proficiency based on immersive exposure to the host culture, my goal for this program is focused on the *process* of language acquisition, not the *product*. Specifically, I want pre- and in-service teachers to develop *empathy* for the emotional struggles of language learners they (will) teach, especially those at the beginning level.

An additionally important aspect of language learning, relevant to the present program, is what García (2017) calls critical multilingual language awareness (CMLA), which not only fosters teachers' sensitivity to language, but also 'develops in all teachers a critical understanding of how language use in society has been naturalized', especially by schools reproducing 'dominant ideologies of monolingualism' (2017: 268). García (2017) envisions teachers' enacting CMLA by having their students 'engage in developing a consciousness of language as social practice and a voicing of their own multilingual experiences' (2017: 268–69). In this regard, the present study-abroad program's immersion of pre-service teachers and other participants in Dominican Spanish challenges the naturalized understanding of Spanish as *only* or primarily Castilian, thus changing language attitudes. It also paves the way for teachers to constructively engage in their classrooms the Dominican Spanish/English translanguaging practices of their Dominican immigrant students who live transnational lives between the Dominican Republic and New York City, thereby disrupting perceived homogeneous linguistic and cultural boundaries.

Engaging students' prior knowledge, linguistic and cultural experiences requires intercultural competence, namely, having or seeking in-depth knowledge of students' cultures and languages, and interacting and communicating with students in ways that are contextually appropriate and effective (Lustig & Koester, 2010). Several study-abroad programs for teachers have emphasized intercultural competence as a goal, as stated earlier. Such is the case with CLLRT.

Program Design

CLLRT is a two-part theoretical/experiential study-abroad learning experience developed by me 11 years ago, and offered through my program – TESOL, Bilingual, and World Language Education. The program has been offered each year since 2010 during the January inter-session for a three-week duration in the Dominican Republic. It is open to any graduate student from Steinhardt, other NYU schools, and other universities. As Coleman (2013) notes, study-abroad programs are multifaceted in structure, involving participants from a variety of backgrounds experiencing different phases of the program – pre-departure, in host country, and post-program return – in different ways. This chapter discusses participants' evaluations and experiences from the 2019 cohort.

Participants

The group consisted of 21 students from different programs throughout Steinhardt who registered for the course. Although the majority of students that typically participate in the program are pre-service teachers in my program, several participants were teachers of other subjects such as childhood or special education, or plan to work in other related disciplines like international or higher education, making the group dynamic much richer. An additional graduate student (not registered for the course) served as the course assistant. The course assistant is involved in all phases of the program and plays a strongly supportive role for the students and me during the overseas phase of the program. She assists with logistics in my class, helps to facilitate small group discussion, serves as cultural broker to the host university in coordinating activities, and offers advice and emotional support for students in navigating the host culture.

It should be noted that unlike most study-abroad programs from the US, where participants are born and raised in the US, the majority of my graduate students are international students from mainland China temporarily residing in the US on student visas. Thus, they bring a unique perspective to the study-abroad experience through a different cultural

Table 14.1 Participants' profiles

Name*	Program	Gender	Race/ethnicity	Country of birth
Diana	Higher Education	F	Latina American	U.S.
Eduardo	Bilingual Education	M	Latino	Nicaragua
Maw	TESOL	F	Asian American	Myanmar
Fiona	TESOL & Spanish	F	Latina American	U.S.
Ana	Bilingual Education	F	Afro-Caribbean	U.S.
Alice	TESOL & Spanish	F	European American	U.S.
Leila	Music Education	F	European American	U.S.
Maria	TESOL & Spanish	F	Afro-Latina	Guatemala
Sammy	TESOL	M	Asian	Korea**
Donna	International Education	F	Lebanese American	U.S.
Mona	International Education	F	African American	U.S.
Sheila	TESOL	F	Asian	China**
Zena	TESOL	F	African American	U.S.
Sharon	International Education	F	Lebanese American	U.S.
Sophia	Comm. Sci. & Disorders	F	European American	U.S.
Lily	TESOL & Mandarin	F	Asian	China**
Wendy	TESOL	F	Asian	China**
Stuart	Media, Culture, Comm.	M	European American	U.S.
Laura	International Education	F	European American	U.S.
Karen	Higher Education	F	African American	U.S.
Sue	TESOL	F	Asian	China**
Charlene	Environmental Education	F	European American	U.S.***

*All names are pseudonyms.
**International student.
***Course assistant.

and educational filter. Typical of most study-abroad programs from the US, the majority of the participants were female (18) plus three males; however, unlike said programs where the majority of students are European American, the participants hail from a wide variety of racial/ethnic backgrounds, with six different countries of birth adding diversity to the group (see Table 14.1). The program components are: (a) a three-credit graduate course, (b) a required Spanish immersion class taken at PUCMM, (c) homestay, and (d) tours and activities.

The course

Students take a three-credit graduate course titled, *Intercultural Perspectives in Multicultural Education*, taught by me at PUCMM. Class time in the Dominican Republic serves not only to cover course content but as a reflective space to debrief about their homestay and other Dominican experiences in real time. The course objectives are:

(1) To achieve a deeper understanding of culture, and the relationship between culture and language.
(2) To acquire the ability to critically observe behaviors in order to draw conclusions based on observation rather than preconceptions.
(3) To understand culture membership, enculturation, and the process of becoming socialized into one's culture and subcultures.
(4) To become acquainted with relevant research on culture and cultural behaviors, expectations, values and norms.
(5) To appreciate how culture serves as a filter through which members of a culture assign meanings to social roles, contexts and communicative behaviors and how they perceive, interpret, react or are affected by these.
(6) To develop the knowledge, attitudes and effective cross-cultural communication skills necessary to be interculturally competent.
(7) To develop strategies for constructively engaging cultural differences in multicultural and multilingual classrooms.

Students must attend two pre-departure orientations to obtain background information on PUCMM, discuss program goals, and review the course syllabus. They are also required to read and respond to pre-departure readings and watch videos on differences in values, beliefs and practices across cultures, and the history and current state of the Dominican Republic to provide some context. Schmidt-Rinehart and Knight (2004) note the importance of providing pre-trip knowledge to study-abroad participants on the history, culture and customs of the host country in order to facilitate the adjustment process.

Spanish class

In addition to taking the Steinhardt graduate course, students simultaneously learn Spanish through an immersion model by taking a one-credit undergraduate-level Spanish class offered by PUCMM faculty. All students admitted to the program are required to take the Spanish class regardless of whether or not they know Spanish. The goal for taking the Spanish class is not to become fluent in Spanish (as this is highly unlikely in three weeks) but, rather, for these prospective teachers to experience what it feels like to be a beginning language learner, and hopefully develop empathy for the language learning challenges of ELLs who are new to the US and must learn English for schooling and survival.

Students take a Spanish placement test completely in Spanish upon arrival in the Dominican Republic, and, based on their test results, are assigned to one of two levels of the Spanish class – beginner or intermediate/advanced. This process of diagnostic language testing mirrors what newcomer ELLs are required to do in English in NYC public schools, so participants are immediately able to experience what their future students must feel like when faced with a test in English, a language completely new to them. The Spanish class also provides models of foreign language teaching for prospective language teachers, so they are able to observe best practices as well as challenges in language teaching.

Homestay

The most important experiential component of the program is the fact that students and I stay with Dominican host families for the entire duration of the program, which provides an authentic setting for language and cultural immersion. Studies of study-abroad homestay (Benson, 2017; Di Silvio *et al.*, 2014) have pointed out students' contradictory feelings and perceptions about their homestay experiences, but conclude that the majority of students feel that, on balance, homestay contributes positively to their language and culture learning.

Tours and activities

We also do a number of educational tours and cultural activities across the island, all arranged by PUCMM's Office of International Students. We visit two very differentially resourced Dominican public schools, observe language and other classes in session, and have a debriefing session with teachers to get a better understanding of the Dominican education system. We also visit museums, an orphanage, a binational market at the border with Haiti, and the Colonial Zone in Santo Domingo, among other places. Collectively, the experience of being in Dominican classrooms in different types of schools, the knowledge of Dominican history, culture and art gained from visits to various museums, and the exposure to poverty and structural inequalities at the orphanage and binational market are designed to help paint a rich and nuanced understanding of the intersection of cultural norms, values, practices, social stratification and power. Specifically, the exposure to the Dominican education system, including conversations with current Dominican teachers (albeit brief) is meant to facilitate the intercultural development of pre-service teachers. It provides a space for them to think about their future students' prior educational experiences more critically, how to harness that knowledge to interact with them more empathetically, and to instruct and assess them more equitably when their future students inhabit new identities as immigrants in classrooms.

Evaluation of the Program

The program is evaluated through a combination of quantitative and qualitative measures, which include: (a) the *Intercultural Development*

Inventory (IDI) (Hammer, 1998), a commonly used, highly reliable 50-item survey instrument (rated on a scale from 1 = Disagree to 5 = Agree) for measuring cultural orientations and intercultural development in study-abroad programs. Students complete the same survey pre- and post-program, then items are grouped into subscales representing various dimensions of cultural responsiveness, and means are calculated to assess changes in their intercultural dispositions; (b) a qualitative evaluation form that I developed for the program which asks students to evaluate the Spanish class, my graduate course including the pre-departure orientation and post-program, final post-program wrap-up class, living with a host family, the various educational tours that we do, their overall experience in the Dominican Republic and how they would connect it to their teaching; (c) the regular Steinhardt course evaluation form; and (d) participants' reflective journals. Qualitative data are analyzed inductively for salient and recurring themes. Given the focus on this volume on the psychological and affective aspects of the study-abroad experience, I report only on the qualitative data here.

Findings and Discussion

The qualitative evaluation form asks students to rank their opinions on several aspects of the program on a scale from *Excellent – Very Good – Good – Average – Below Average – Poor.* Fifteen of 21 students completed the evaluation. All students thought the pre-departure readings and materials were helpful in preparing them for their trip to the Dominican Republic. Some commented that the readings were 'long' and 'hard to swallow' but necessary in understanding the country's history. Three comments suggested the use of more videos similar to the Henry Louis Gates Jr. piece on Blacks in Latin America and further justified videos for the 'visual learners'.

Overall, the students' ratings on the Spanish class were mixed. Two rated excellent, 4 rated very good, 7 rated good, 1 rated average, and 1 rated below average. The students who were placed in the beginner class complained that more 'practical vocabulary' would have been useful instead of 'geography'. One student commented that she was unable to evaluate the professor using the online portal because it was in Spanish. Three students asked for an intermediate class, because the beginner class was too easy and the advanced class was too difficult.

With the exception of one native Spanish speaker, all students thought their knowledge and understanding of Spanish had improved. The exposure to Spanish, particularly living with a host family, helped beginners learn 'basic vocabulary' and helped the advanced speakers with 'local slang and Dominican expressions'. One advanced student, who did not feel that their Spanish had improved, recommended a class on 'Spanish literature or Dominican pedagogy'.

Students' opinions for the graduate course ranged from good to excellent. Five ranked excellent, 4 ranked very good, and 6 ranked good. Four students gave specific recommendations for more professor-led classes during the course time to discuss the readings; they also wanted more discussions and debriefs after specific trips. Two students suggested having small group discussions with guided questions to help debrief, as opposed to the full class discussion to 'decrease the amount of social exhaustion'.

Nine of the 15 respondents rated excellent for their host families, 4 rated very good and 2 rated good. Students felt welcomed upon arrival and many still keep in contact with their families. One student commented that the family was 'nice, but the language barrier made things awkward and uncomfortable'.

On a psychological and emotional level, five key themes emerged from the data:

(1) Reconciling program goals and personal goals.
(2) Emotional triggers around racial/ethnic issues and poverty.
(3) Incidents of transformative learning.
(4) Mixed feelings about the Spanish class and language teaching methods.
(5) Appreciation of host family hospitality.

Reconciling program goals and personal goals

An important theme that emerged in the course evaluation and in students' reflective journals is the tension between students' personal goals for participating in the program versus the program goals. During the first pre-departure orientation some students, especially Ana, stated that part of their reason for participating in the program included a personal desire to 'confront Dominicans' about racist attitudes towards Haitians (having prior knowledge of the Dominican Republic's historically fraught relationship with Haiti) while I pointed out to them that the program goals sought to observe and understand the history of the Haiti–Dominican Republic relationship and how constructions of race and anti-Blackness manifest in different contexts. The students' desires set up certain expectations of, and pre-dispositions towards, interacting with Dominicans, which they had to reconcile with course goals while we were there. My class time became the space for sharing their feelings about actual interactions with Dominicans around relations with Haiti, which ranged from 'uncomfortable' (Zena) to 'honest' (Donna) to 'liberating' (Maria). Using strategies we learned in class related to cross-cultural communication on sensitive issues, one participant, Ana, described how she raised the issue of the 1937 massacre of Haitians instigated by Dominican dictator Trujillo (which she read about in her pre-departure readings) with her host mother. She described the interaction as 'testy' but noted, 'I'm glad I did it; we were both uncomfortable, but at least she listened to me, and I listened to her. We still disagree on some things, but we made progress'. By the end of the program, Ana shared that she still had more questions than answers on Dominican Republic–Haiti relations but was glad that she participated in the program. Over the course of the program her personal goals evolved beyond race to finding out more about the history of the Dominican Republic and working more intentionally with *all* of her students around respecting each other.

Emotional triggers around racial/ethnic issues and poverty

Related to the tense relationship with Haiti, issues of race/ethnicity and poverty are salient in the Dominican Republic, which is important for understanding how participants experienced certain activities. The Dominican Republic, like the rest of the Caribbean, has a history of plantation slavery, which left in its wake sharp socioeconomic stratification based on race and color, with darker complexioned Dominicans at the bottom of the socioeconomic ladder. Blackness in the Dominican Republic is equated with being Haitian, and therefore stigmatized. On the other hand, lighter complexioned Dominicans are typically in higher social positions with privilege, and so are light complexioned foreigners.

Against this backdrop, our visit to the binational market at Dajabón became a trigger. Dajabón is a small town on the Dominican side of the Dominican Republic–Haiti border next to a mostly dried-up river that separates the two countries (not-so-coincidentally the site of the 1937 massacre). Despite preparing students for the visit in our pre-departure orientations and readings, and explaining the reason for experiencing poverty first-hand, the sight of poor Haitian vendors, mostly women, desperately trying to sell their goods (second-hand items given to them as 'aid' from the US, like sneakers and bed linens) at low prices in order to buy food to take back to Haiti was emotionally shocking to students. Particularly jarring was seeing poor Haitian children begging for cash near our tour bus. Students returned to the bus silent, many visibly in tears for the entire trip back to Santiago. In my class the next day, they shared their emotions that ranged from 'sadness' at seeing such poverty to 'appreciation for their own privilege' to 'anger' at me, for 'not preparing them properly' for the trip (although I thought I did). Many participants said they felt 'helpless' in the market or felt it was an exercise in 'poverty tourism'. Students from international education raised questions about the purpose of the US sending frivolous items as 'aid' to developing countries when Haitians really needed food and the tools to be agriculturally self-sufficient (an example of critical thinking in action); other students suggested more debriefing time for such an emotional experience. Yet, in our post-program class on campus, and in course evaluations, students ranked the visit to Dajabón market as one of the 'most beneficial' activities for its visceral effect on their consciousness. The candor of students' comments in these instances continually challenges me to rethink my goals for the program.

Another trigger occurred when a group of Chinese female students were walking home from class and heard the catcall 'Chinas' directed at them by two Dominican males. One student, Sue, shared in class that she was visibly upset by this catcall because first she heard it as 'Shinas' (the derogatory ethnic term used by Japanese during the Sino-Japanese war to describe Chinese). Secondly, as females, catcalls are generally perceived as sexist. When she told her host mother about the incident, her host mother said she was sorry about what happened but also dismissed it as simply *piropos* (the Dominican word for catcalls) and implied this was typical behavior by Dominican males and not meant to be hurtful. Sue found her host mother's explanation unacceptable, adding that the incident made her feel immediately sympathetic to African Americans who are called the 'n' word, creating a bond in that moment with the African American students in class. From a single event, Sue and her Chinese peers experienced what they perceived to be a triple insult – racism, sexism, and in the case of Sue's host mother, the tacit acceptance of sexism. Sue's empathy with African Americans based on a shared experience of ethnic stigmatization is reminiscent of Norton Peirce's (1995) study of five immigrant women from different ethnic backgrounds in Canada who shared and fought against their marginalized identities as immigrants, language learners, and the perception that they are not worthy of being 'heard'.

Incidents of transformative learning

Baecher and Chung (2020) describe the potential for transformative learning in moments of dissonance. In 2019, one such moment occurred during our visit to one of the Dominican public schools. We typically break into small groups and observe teachers instructing different class levels and subject areas. During observation of one 5th grade class with three of my students, the teacher was distributing the homework on sheets of paper when a student shouted out that one student was absent because she had a cold. The teacher just casually said, *está bien, dejaré la tarea en su casa de camino a casa* [that's ok, I'll drop off the homework at her house on the way home]. The teacher's simple comment triggered a 45-minute conversation in my class later that afternoon. My students were shocked at the notion that a teacher would take a student's homework to her home. Alice said, 'this would never happen in a New York school'; Eduardo, who is from Nicaragua, noted that this would happen in his country but agreed not in New York (showing that he has already filtered the differences between the educational practices in his country and those in NYC). I acknowledged that the students were right; this would not happen in NYC, but we needed to examine why, to unpack the dissonance. This led to a robust discussion of the cultural differences between the Dominican Republic and the US in terms of school-community relations and values (e.g. in the Dominican Republic, the teacher is more likely to live in the same community as her students; she is treated, and sees herself, as an extension of the students' family; and there is less focus on 'privacy'). In NYC, teachers do not typically live in their students' communities, often exacerbated by racialized settlement patterns. The US culture foregrounds privacy, often encoded in laws; therefore, there is no expectation that a teacher would drop off homework at a student's home on account of her absence, unless a special relationship with the family already exists. Thus, an innocent statement by a Dominican teacher became a moment of transformative learning for my students, as it spawned critical reflection on cultural differences in school-community relations, teacher-student roles and expectations, and values of privacy versus community.

Mixed feelings about the Spanish class and language teaching methods

Students noted that the Spanish class provided models of approaches to language teaching, as well as showing them the pros and cons of an immersion model. All of the international students from China, who had no prior knowledge of Spanish, were placed in the beginner class and felt that the immersion model is not effective for 'true' beginners. Sue and Wendy both expressed feeling 'lost' and 'stupid' during the Spanish placement test, as they knew 'nothing'. They enjoyed the warm and caring atmosphere provided by the Spanish instructor but thought that some English–Spanish translation support would help beginners to build confidence, as was the case when they first learned English in China. This might be a case of students' wanting a familiar teaching style. By contrast, American students placed in the beginner class expressed the opposite sentiment; they preferred the total immersion model. Still, *all* students, especially beginners, expressed empathy for their own ELLs learning English, which is a goal of the program.

The Spanish class also complemented the language and culture learning in their host families, as the course content focused on Dominican culture and exposed students to colloquial and standardized varieties of Dominican Spanish, thereby developing their sociolinguistic competence and countering the tendency in foreign language pedagogy to teach and discuss only the standardized variety of the language. This is a good example of García's (2017) critical language awareness.

Appreciation of host family hospitality

Students stated that the homestay was the best part of their experience, emphasizing it as an authentic engagement with Dominican culture and language simultaneously. Specifically, some shared in their journals that they 'gained a deeper understanding of Dominican cultural values, norms, beliefs, and practices'; those subjective aspects of culture that are subtle, deeply embedded, and often the most difficult aspect of teachers' intercultural work. One noticeable cultural difference in response to the host families was the fact that the international students from China expressed their comfort with, and appreciation of, certain acts of caring within the host family (e.g. the host family's doing their laundry or making their bed). Some students from the US, however, shared that sometimes these acts felt like an invasion of their privacy – another example of how cultural values filter our experiences differently.

Post-program, Pedagogical Implications, and Beyond

Our final class post-program takes place on campus three weeks after our return to NYC. In the three-week interim, I invite students to share their reflections on the program individually with me in my office. This allows a safe space for students to be honest and reflective. Students typically share that the program affected their perception and knowledge of Dominican culture and has impacted their personal and professional life. Specifically, several students mentioned the unexpected and fulfilling bonds they formed with other co-participants from different racial/ethnic backgrounds and disciplines, highlighting the power of a shared experience. They felt the humility of the language learning process, the conflicting emotions of enjoying the hospitality of their host families while simultaneously feeling 'othered' in someone else's space, the heightened awareness of their own identities and cultures while thinking about their future or current students' identity shifts as new immigrants or first-generation Americans, and the highs and lows of the various activities that we did, especially trips to the public schools, the orphanage and Dajabón market. As one student from the 2019 cohort put it, 'Those who can't deal with multiple emotional shifts, may not be a good fit for the program'.

Students saw the knowledge gained about the Dominican Republic through pre-departure readings and our various tours and activities in the Dominican Republic as rich content for teaching. Students who were pre-service teachers doing student teaching and one in-service teacher shared that they plan to teach their students – *all* students – about the Mirabal Sisters (the famous Dominican sisters who valiantly fought against the Trujillo regime). Teachers felt greater awareness of the different cultural expectations of their role and of how to approach their Dominican and other immigrant students with more sensitivity while helping them develop strategies for their own intercultural development. Students in international education planned to raise questions in their program around concepts such as 'aid' and US engagement in the Caribbean.

Several students expressed interest in returning to the Dominican Republic and exploring other Caribbean islands to learn more about the region.

In our final class, students typically share their final projects and debrief on the program. Projects can be individual or collaborative and range from culture portfolios, to traditional research papers, to blogs, or short videos. We also do a poster walk around the room, where students display and describe short versions of their project. It is usually a celebratory affair, but also bitter-sweet. The content of the projects typically mirrors the range of experiences in the Dominican Republic and how they are taken up by students in very personalized ways. While a systematic study of the *actual* effects of the study-abroad experience on students' pedagogy is yet to be done, students all say they would recommend the program to future teachers for the benefits described above.

Conclusion

Studying abroad is one approach to helping teachers better engage with our culturally diverse students today. There are obviously many other approaches that can be constructive to this end, but short-term study-abroad programs such as CLLRT, designed to enhance cultural understanding, create opportunities for critical, transformative learning and culturally responsive pedagogy, offer unique opportunities for pre- and in-service teachers to achieve these goals in a personalized way while inhabiting the other's world. As 21st-century migration patterns continue to change, and students bring new and different cultures, languages and funds of knowledge to our schools, teacher education programs would do well to adjust their dispositions, curricula and practices to a more critical approach in order to engage our students in academically enriching and culturally responsive ways.

Acknowledgments

Thanks to the course assistant for conducting quantitative and qualitative data analysis to evaluate the program. My gratitude to our host university and host families for continuing to graciously host our students. Thanks to NYU for prioritizing and supporting study abroad as an essential part of 21st-century education, and to the participants for their willingness to learn by temporarily becoming the other.

References

Baecher, L. and Chung, S. (2020) Transformative professional development for in-service teachers through international service learning. *Teacher Development* 24 (1), 33–51.
Benson, P. (2017) Sleeping with strangers: Dreams and nightmares in experiences of homestay. *Study Abroad Research in Second Language Acquisition and International Education* 2 (1), 1–20.

Borg, S. (2003) Teacher cognition in language teaching: A review of research on what language teachers think, know, believe, and do. *Language Teaching* 36 (2), 81–109.

Brown, R.K. and Tignor, S. (2016) Preparing culturally competent teachers through faculty-led study abroad. In Information Resources Management Association (ed.) *Teacher Education: Concepts, Methodologies, Tools, and Applications* (pp. 92–108). Hershey, PA: IGI Global.

Coleman, J. (2013) Researching whole people and whole lives. In C. Kinginger (ed.) *Social and Cultural Aspects of Language Learning in Study Abroad* (pp. 17–44). Amsterdam: John Benjamins.

Colón-Muñiz, A., SooHoo, S. and Brignoni, E. (2010) Language, culture, and dissonance: A study course for globally minded teachers with possibilities for catalytic transformation. *Teaching Education* 21 (1), 61–74.

Cushner, K. and Chang, S.-C. (2015) Developing intercultural competence through overseas student teaching: Checking our assumptions. *Intercultural Education* 26 (3), 156–178.

Di Silvio, F., Donovan, A. and Malone, M.E. (2014) The effect of study abroad homestay placements: Participant perspectives and oral proficiency gains. *Foreign Language Annals* 47 (1), 168–188.

García, O. (2017) Critical multilingual language awareness and teacher education. In J. Cenoz, D. Gorter and S. May (eds) *Language Awareness and Multilingualism: Encyclopedia of Language and Education* (3rd edn) (pp. 263–280). Cham: Springer International Publishing.

Gay, G. (2000) *Culturally Responsive Teaching: Theory, Research, and Practice.* New York: Teachers College Press.

Hammer, M. (1998) A measure of intercultural sensitivity: The intercultural development inventory. In S. Fowler and M. Fowler (eds) *The Intercultural Sourcebook* (vol. 2, pp. 61–72). Yarmouth, ME: Intercultural Press.

Hawkins, M. and Norton, B. (2009) Critical language teacher education. In A. Burns and J.C. Richards (eds) *The Cambridge Guide to Second Language Teacher Education* (pp. 30–39). Cambridge: Cambridge University Press.

He, Y., Lundgren, K. and Pyne, P. (2017) Impact of short-term study abroad program: In-service teachers' development of intercultural competence and pedagogical beliefs. *Teaching and Teacher Education* 66 (1), 147–157.

King, K. and Bigelow, M. (2018) East African transnational adolescents and cross-border education: An argument for local international learning. *Annual Review of Applied Linguistics* 38, 187–193.

Krashen, S. (1982) *Principles and Practice in Second Language Acquisition.* Oxford: Pergamon Press.

Ladson-Billings, G. (2005) *Culturally Relevant Teaching: A Special Issue of Theory into Practice.* New York: Routledge.

Lindhal, K., Hansen-Thomas, H., Baecher, L. and Stewart, M. (2020) Study abroad for critical multilingual language development in ESL and bilingual teacher candidates. *TESL-EJ* 23 (4), 3–13.

Lustig, M. and Koester, J. (2010) *Intercultural Competence: Intercultural Communication Across Cultures* (6th edn). Boston, MA: Pearson Education.

Marx, S. and Pray, L. (2011) Living and learning in Mexico: Developing empathy for English language learners through study abroad. *Race, Ethnicity, and Education* 14 (4), 507–535.

Mezirow, J. (1997) Transformative learning: Theory to practice. *New Directions for Adult and Continuing Education* 74, 5–12.

National Center for Education Statistics (2016) *The Condition of Education 2016* (NCES 2016-144). Washington, DC: US Department of Education.

Nero, S. (2009) Inhabiting the other's world: Language and cultural immersion for US-based teachers in the Dominican Republic. *Language, Culture and Curriculum* 22 (3), 175–194.

Nero, S. (2018) Studying abroad in the Dominican Republic: Preparing culturally and linguistically responsive teachers for 21st century classrooms. *Annual Review of Applied Linguistics* 38, 194–200.

Norton Peirce, B. (1995) Social identity, investment, and language learning. *TESOL Quarterly* 29 (1), 9–31.

Open Doors (2017) Institute of International Education, Inc. https://www.iie.org/Research-and-Insights/Open-Doors (accessed April 10, 2021).

Phillion, J., Malewski, E., Sharma, S. and Wang, Y. (2009). Reimagining the curriculum: Future teachers and study abroad. *Frontiers: The Interdisciplinary Journal of Study Abroad* 18, 323–339.

Schmidt-Rinehart, B.C. and Knight, S.M. (2004) The homestay component of study abroad: Three perspectives. *Foreign Language Annals* 37, 254–262.

US Census Bureau (2012) *Statistical Abstract of the United States, 2012.* Washington, DC: Government Printing Office. https://www.census.gov/library/publications/2011/compendia/statab/131ed.html, (accessed April 10, 2021).

Zhao, Y., Meyers, L. and Meyers, B. (2009) Cross-cultural immersion in China: Preparing pre-service elementary teachers to work with diverse student populations in the United States. *Asia-Pacific Journal of Teacher Education* 37 (3), 295–317.

15 Study Abroad as Subjection: Doctoral Students' Emotions during Academic Short Stays

Harold Castañeda-Peña,
Carmen Helena Guerrero-Nieto and
Pilar Méndez-Rivera

> *María thus realizes the struggles of Latin America in relation to its representation in the ELT world. The subjection-emotion interface renders an alternative way of reading community, calling into question its contemporary and modern comprehension.*
>
> *Higher education institutions with doctoral programs could include in their curriculum workshops or seminars focused on researchers' vulnerability ... helping doctoral students deal with research participants' emotional responses (e.g. crying) and their own emotional responses in different stages of the doctoral educational process.*

Introduction

Doctoral students appear to be subjected to an internal-external interaction of identity development that for Schulze (2014: 2) contributes to 'a positioning of the self in the academic space'. Within that interaction, scholars have claimed that 'a deep understanding of what individual doctoral students experience, especially in early candidature, needs more attention in educational research, especially because it is likely to promote greater awareness of the needs of doctoral students' (Creely & Laletas, 2020: 449). This could also help in making curricular decisions to support such needs at the doctoral level in order to strengthen doctoral pedagogies where, for example, 'students act as positive agents in improving their own doctoral experiences' with the aim of 'creating opportunities for collective identity' (McAlpine & Amundsen, 2009: 112). Velardo and Elliott (2018) propose as modes of support for doctoral education the following: (a) workshops to help doctoral students deal with vulnerable research participants, (b) appointing support officers to help doctoral students cope with emotional distress, especially during data co-construction phases, and (c) making institutional ethics boards sensitive to the potential emotional risks doctoral students could face during the research process. In this chapter we intend to make visible the role of emotions in the way doctoral students, in this case experienced language teachers, deal with the pressures, tensions and expectations of taking part in short academic stays abroad.

Feeling vulnerable, that is, 'the possibility of being harmed emotionally' (Ramanayake, 2020: 563) as a result of researching with (not about) others, is part of the doctoral research process (Ballamingie & Johnson, 2011; Laar, 2014). This mirrors 'profound experiences of identity flux, confusion, and transformation' (Phelps, 2016: 7), for example, doctoral students building a cosmopolitan sense of identity (Mu *et al.*, 2019).

Prospective doctoral students who aspire to become doctors are subjected to a complex observation process to fulfill a profile of knowledge production (Hou & Feng, 2019), which is scrutinized. Doctoral students' academic scrutiny while doing internships also tests their character and disposition to embrace new directions, serendipity (Hou & Feng, 2019; Martínez, 2018) and identity formation (Leshem, 2020). Subjection operates in identity formation as a mechanism of validation of some conditions for being and acting within a knowledge community of already established doctors (Frick & Brodin, 2020). What is thought-provoking about subjection is that it works twofold: from outside, examination conducted by the doctoral programs and their actors; and from inside, the demands and pressure doctoral students exercise upon themselves to achieve this aspirational being.

Whilst there is a wealth of literature dealing with doctoral students' identity struggles, the interface between subjection processes and doctoral students' emotions appears to be underexplored in the context of short-term mobility schemes, examined critically (Henderson, 2019), where 'transnational identity capital ... as intimately related to the social process of academics crossing international borders' (Kim, 2017: 982) could be produced or contested. This chapter looks into the narrative experiences of doctoral students studying abroad, focusing on the interface between subjection and emotion. Consequently, this study[1] asks at a general level: What are the narrative experiences of subjection and emotion of doctoral students who spend time studying abroad in short academic stays?

Theoretical Framework

The meaning of subjection

Foucault (2000) claims that subjection operates beyond institutions, that is, in the body itself. The ways in which individuals constitute themselves as subjects are permeated by power relations that act from outside and from inside the individual. Individuals are born in a world full of meanings and rules – socially and historically elaborated – that equip bodies with forms of being and that act aligned to a specific identity to organize society. These meanings constitute what Lévi-Strauss (1949) called the symbolic structure of social relations, which is important for understanding how individuals accept or resist these arrangement practices.

Guattari (2015: 23) explains subjection in semiotic terms to unveil how 'semiotic machines are over-coded components to manipulate, order and subject the individual at the service of power formations'. This is crucially important for understanding the collective desire that guides societies to infuse identities with other semiotic components. Individuals are not totally subjected by external forces, but are also voluntarily subjected by desire, will and personal decisions. Individuals are also subjects of desire that mobilizes actions to achieve their own goals. That is to say, in the words of Goodchild (1996: 196), 'the revolution of desire involves the local development of the means of production of subjectivity'. As a consequence, the analysis of subjection becomes a central element in understanding the construction of one's own subjectivity and the adaptations that one makes to prescribed identities. This goes hand in hand with Foucault's (1997) ideas about the active role of individuals and their creative forces in opposing difference, creation and innovation. Subjection is also a process of accommodation based on the legitimation of a privileged and normalized identity (Castells, 2010). Thus, subjection is the way subjects attach themselves to norms, identities and habits seen as prestigious, visible and hierarchically structured. Therefore, subjectivation corresponds to certain forms of subjection (Balibar, 1994). Although our take on subjection is informed by the philosophical tradition that gave meaning to power and agency in the construction of identities, in this study subjection is understood to be an experiential/emotionally charged device to deal with both personal and social understanding of what it means to be a doctor in education.

Emotion and teacher learning and development

Recent studies have explored emotions and teacher education/development (Johnson & Golombek, 2016; Ruohotie-Lyhty *et al.*, 2018; Song & Park, 2019), emotions as part of power and culture structures (Song & Park, 2019), emotions as part of material teaching contexts (Schmidt & Datnow, 2005; Kelchtermans, 2005) and emotions in relation to identity (O'Connor, 2006; Shahri, 2018).

Teacher education programmes could benefit from investigating teachers' emotions from a relational perspective, for example, with their students. This constitutes a pillar of professional development that allows a better understanding of teaching. Research on the emotions of teachers experiencing short academic stays abroad is scarce, and much less seems to be said about how they might feel subjected, academically speaking. Song and Park (2019: 261) concluded that 'language teacher education that incorporates teacher emotion as an important component of teacher development would encourage teachers to trace their emotion within sociocultural contexts and discuss how social inequalities sustain, reproduce and transfer anxiety'. Additionally, teachers' emotional responses to the implementation of both educational policies and reforms that correlate with the knowledge that they already possess are underexplored; for example, language policies that see teachers from a deficit perspective linguistically and pedagogically. This suggests the need for more research concerned with teachers' emotional commitment framed within their material working conditions. In the professional identities of teachers of English, emotions appear not to be part of the features that constitute such identities. From the critical point of view, then, it is paramount to keep researching teachers' identities and emotions since 'neither the knowledge that teachers teach nor the way to teach it are naive, but are informed by values that must be recognized and criticized for their consequences and effects' (Giroux, 2002: 27). Shahri (2018) found that, in teaching practice, emotional attachments are produced to how one sees oneself as a teacher, which is the basis for identity constructions.

In a complementary perspective, we want to propose that it is necessary to comprehend how doctoral students specializing in ELT education narrate their own emotions and situate them in particular processes of their doctoral education such as academic stays abroad.

Methodology

This is a narrative qualitative study based on the understanding that our interpretations of a particular phenomenon will stem from the ways in which our narrators perceive it. That is, the whole process will privilege their ways of constructing and giving meaning to the subjection-emotion interphase in the doctoral education of teachers of English. In the same epistemological direction, we will take a critical-decolonial perspective by adopting narrative inquiry as our research design.

As a research method, narrative inquiry constitutes a way of knowing that relies on the stories narrators tell about something and about themselves. Narrating implies bringing together characters, time, places and events to make sense of an experience through the eyes of the narrator. As such, narratives become a very useful portal for understanding how people construct their identities, how they understand the self and how they see their existence in the world (Sparkes & Devis, 2007). But, as Barkhuizen (2013) states, stories not only become a referential recalling of events and experiences, but when we tell stories, we also reshape them in a way that allows us to make sense of the world.

The narrators in this study are experienced teachers of English and language teacher educators in Colombia (South America) who participated in a series of narrative interviews. All of them have undertaken doctoral studies since 2016 and 2018 in education, majoring in ELT Education at a state university. As part of the research component of the doctoral program, students have to complete 10 academic credits in an academic short stay either locally or internationally. All the narrators chose the international option, which requires spending at least one month abroad. The narrators fulfilled this requirement by traveling from Colombia to Spain and the UK (María), Mexico (Roberto and Pablo) and Brazil (Pedro). Pedro did his international short academic stay in Brazil virtually, due to the Covid-19 pandemic. Names are fictional to protect the narrators' identities. To guard the identity of the host institutions we will refer to the host countries.

Crying to Resist Subjection: María

> I'm going to tell you something that maybe you don't know … When I listened to Professor One's lecture and Professor Two's lecture, I cried … Why did I cry? Because they talked about the injustices done to Latin America about … and I started to cry and I remember well that Professor One realized that I was crying and he spoke of crying as the first way to protest, so it seemed to me that they understood very well the emotions and the things going on in the classroom. (Narrative interview)

María wrote a doctoral dissertation about communities in ELT drawing on the concept of difference. This defies the canonical understanding of community as something homogeneous. Her initial research topic was transformed in her short academic stay in Spain where she took a course on the decolonial turn. It could be argued that María left behind a traditional paradigm in ELT when she was pushed to the edge by a moment of dissonance (Johnson & Golombek, 2016) through the course abroad content (and through how the professor dealt with her evident emotions), and she was able to read her geopolitical reality differently, connecting it to ELT education. Crying as an emotional manifestation of pain helped her to protest and subvert expected academic behaviors.

In her story, it is also possible to recognize how María's crying was a fruitful emotional response to discourses of political subjugation and coloniality (Kim, 2017). Crying challenges traditional ideas about academics hiding their emotions and confronts forms of knowledge production (geopolitically and body-politically situated otherwise) and, additionally, regimes of subjective representation (Escobar, 1995) supported by systems of power: 'The notion of regimes of representation is a final theoretical and methodological principle for examining the mechanisms for, and consequences of, the construction of the Third World in/through representation' (Escobar, 1995: 10). María thus realizes the struggles of Latin America in relation to its representation in the ELT world. The subjection-emotion interface renders an alternative way of reading community, calling into question its contemporary and modern comprehension.

Negotiating Cultural Immersion and Family Ties: Roberto

> If you go to another country ... you are going to sightsee ... Maybe my wife also had that idea, because obviously Mexico has places to tour, you have to visit places everywhere. So she told me ... first you do your homework and then ... we had planned that they would arrive the last week to stay there at Easter, to be precise ... We were going to be in Mexico ... that was the negotiation that I had with my wife. I was going to study the four weeks, in those four weeks I was going to be locked up. (Narrative interview)

Roberto is a second-year doctoral student who is interested in the untold stories of teachers of English who have attended local and international immersions organized by the Colombian Ministry of Education. Roberto is married with two daughters. It seems that he was very stressed about the idea of meeting up with his family in the host country after finishing his academic stay. However, it is reasonable to infer that he is subjected to family interests contrasting with his own expectation of being immersed in the culture.

There is a negotiation for emotional intimacy mediated by the actual co-presence (Alinejad, 2019) of family members. This raises for Roberto the challenge of either studying and sightseeing or locking himself up until the end of the academic activities planned for a month. According to the literature, 'successful sojourning, defined as adapting psychologically (feeling well) and socioculturally (doing well), maximizes the benefits and minimizes the risks of multicultural experiences' (Geeraert *et al.*, 2019: 333).

Family-shared meanings of short academic stays appear to be connected to family ties and have direct consequences for the well-being of the sojourner. In Roberto's case, he did not want to violate an agreement made with his family in the culture of origin, yet this caused a conflict with his personal desires and beliefs in the culture of destination. The subjection-emotion interface placed him inevitably at a crossroads fueled by emotional dissonance (Johnson & Golombek, 2016).

Mediating a Sense of Self-Realization: Pedro

> The internship was demanding, challenging but at the same time great because of the culture. I know I haven't met them personally [he refers to his short academic stay supervisor and study group in Brazil] but I have friends, we e-mail. Although I did not have the cultural impact because

of the pandemic ... of course, it is totally different to meet virtually instead of meeting face to face ... It was too demanding, it was a month here concentrated in my study room. I was conscious this internship could offer me great opportunities for my research and it did! There were two or three seminars, meetings with the research groups. There were international students in the research group, one girl from Spain ... but we had two meetings weekly and during these meetings they were so nice. We discussed readings, shared reflections, and as I told you it was totally demanding. (Narrative interview)

Pedro is also a second-year doctoral student. His academic stay was placed in Brazil and it was undertaken virtually due to the Covid-19 pandemic. To our question about his experience of a virtual academic stay, he seems to dismiss that he was denied the chance of being culturally immersed. In spite of this emotional dissonance (Johnson & Golombek, 2016) he appears not to have been negatively affected by the demanding workload. He was able to interact with members of Brazilian research groups, where he felt welcomed and where he constructed media routines in home spaces (Alinejad, 2019) to build his own identity as a novice researcher (Leshem, 2020) within an international network (Baker & Lattuca, 2010).

Online mediation gave Pedro a sense of achievement in that he felt he belonged to an academic culture where

> developmental relationships may provide support beyond just career and/ or psychosocial support, to include knowledge development and information sharing. Important to a developmental network approach is the idea of diversity, which is defined as the number of different social systems from which an individual's various connections originate. (Baker & Lattuca, 2010: 811)

He currently corresponds via email with members of the research network, who come from different countries, and with his Brazilian supervisor. He did involve us in a series of webinars in Brazil, thereby widening the developmental network. Pedro addressed the subjection-emotion interface by making the most out of the online interaction within the developmental network to compensate for the disappointment caused by the pandemic, which prevented him from going abroad.

Decentring Applied Linguistics: Pablo

> If I had focused more on a topic of ELT itself, I wouldn't have been in Mexico. I wouldn't have been there with [name of advisor in Mexico], because the work of [advisor's name] is not in ELT but in subjectivity and subject constitution. So I consider that this was my first struggle at the doctoral programme, when you start studying in this doctoral programme, they started to ask your locus of enunciation, your epistemological and ontological positionings and speaking for myself I didn't have that academic profile before starting the program. (Narrative interview)

Pablo is a third-year doctoral student. His research study explores who teacher educators are in language teacher education. This query leads him to interrogate himself regarding the subjection processes of teacher educators. To answer his questions, Pablo turned to a scholar who lives in Mexico. That was a decision with emotional impact in terms of his short academic stay abroad.

Pablo resorts to epistemological foundations that are not traditionally included within applied linguistics and among language teacher educators. This means decentering applied linguistics, unlearning about language teacher education and relearning about it. This also means perhaps undertaking the initial processes of epistemological decolonization. The anxiety that this produces in him demonstrates a profound criticism of the epistemological subjection processes that applied linguistics has undergone throughout its history in relation to language teacher educators and of which Pablo has been a product. For Pablo, in the context of educational research, 'this presents a distinct challenge to the idea of studying and learning from established knowledge systems and then engaging in practice' (Patel, 2016: 12) and defying processes of knowledge subjugation as envisioned by Foucault (1980: 81) as a 'whole set of knowledge that has been disqualified'.

Pablo, wittingly or not, subverts this epistemological subjection by spending his academic stay abroad in a Spanish-speaking country. For Pablo, it is a struggle to think about doing an internship in a program with a different disciplinary field and having to open up to these disciplines to better understand his intellectual pursuit in the doctoral program of origin. The feeling of uncertainty as a result of being exposed to scrutiny surfaces, although not explicitly. However, it is plausible to interpret that Pablo's short academic stay in Mexico, where ELT was not the target discipline and where he is confronted with a course on political theory and semiology, demonstrates how 'the logics of coloniality, which are connected to property and stratification of society, are problematically enlivened through educational research' (Patel, 2016: 12).

This continuous subjection process becomes Pablo's personal struggle. The subjection-emotion interface was confronted by Pablo, while acknowledging how 'unprepared' he was for a doctoral program that posits such epistemological problematization in front of his eyes. In spite of the anxiety and the struggle, he appears determined to embrace the challenge.

Implications and Conclusion

These findings illustrate four narrators' particular experiences of doctoral short academic stays drawing on the subjection-emotion interface. The interpretation of short narrative excerpts illustrates particular responses to serendipity (Hou & Feng, 2019; Martínez, 2018) (e.g. María being exposed to sensitive course content, Roberto juggling family co-presence, Pedro facing off the pandemic, and Pablo navigating in uncharted epistemological waters) and identity formation (Leshem, 2020) (e.g. María affiliating to an alternative epistemology, Roberto weighing decisions about feeling and doing well, Pedro becoming a member of a developmental network, and Pablo daring to enter unknown disciplinary fields to de-center his own discipline).

Identifying external and internal subjection circumstances and mechanisms (Castells, 2010; Foucault, 2000), along with semiotic machines (Guattari, 2015) in relation to emotional dissonances (Johnson & Golombek, 2016), could theoretically contribute to, firstly, comprehending the subjection-emotion interface in different contexts of ELT research (e.g. teaching practices of recently graduated teachers of English) (Shahri, 2018), English teachers' emotional commitment (Kelchtermans, 2005), and teachers' emotional responses to the implementation of policies and reforms (Schmidt & Datnow, 2005).

Secondly, findings reveal that studying abroad can be challenging physically and emotionally. The narrators responded differently according to their personal and academic burden. Crying, negotiating family co-presence, developmental networking and de-centering applied linguistics served the narrators as mechanisms for resisting subjection. These self-developed strategies for coping with subjection-emotion could also inform modes of support for doctoral education (Velardo & Elliott, 2018).

Higher education institutions with doctoral programs could include in their curriculum workshops or seminars focused on researchers' vulnerability (Ballamingie & Johnson, 2011; Laar, 2014), helping doctoral students deal with research participants' emotional responses (e.g. crying) and their own emotional responses in different stages of the doctoral educational process. Our findings reveal that aspects of vulnerability could be extended to the researchers' family members in the case of our mature students who are married with children. Counselling services offered by the institution in this regard could contribute to lessening emotional risks (e.g. learning to negotiate co-presence of family members while abroad).

We agree with McAlpine and Amundsen (2009) that doctoral education could help create opportunities for collective identity. Along this line of thought, institutions could provide opportunities for doctoral students to develop networks as part of the curricular doctoral experience, helping them to foresee subjection-emotion circumstances within the networks. Finally, institutions could qualify doctoral supervisors to critically deal with their students' subjection-emotion manifestations throughout the educational doctoral process (Creely & Laletas, 2020) as part of an emotion-based doctoral pedagogy. The short narrative excerpts of María, Roberto, Pedro and Pablo also make evident that doctoral students need a lot of preparation before embarking on short academic stays to cope with subjection-emotion highs and let-downs. As illustrated, the subjection-emotion interface is present in the narrators' experiences and there should be an institutional response to this. In particular, we also propose appointing officers from the institutions' social services department or welfare offices to support sojourners before, during and after academic stays.

Note

(1) This chapter draws on an ongoing research project titled 'PhD students' emotions after studying abroad: Coping with subjection practices' sponsored by the CIDC (Centro de Investigaciones y Desarrollo Científico) of the Universidad Distrital Francisco José de Caldas. Research Project ID 2460173820.

References

Alinejad, D. (2019) Careful co-presence: The transnational mediation of emotional intimacy. *Social Media + Society* April-June, 1–11.

Baker, V. and Lattuca, L. (2010) Developmental networks and learning: Toward an interdisciplinary perspective on identity development during doctoral study. *Studies in Higher Education* 35 (7), 807–827.

Balibar, E. (1994) Subjection and subjectivation. In J. Copjec (ed.) *Supposing the Subject* (pp. 1–15). London: Verso.

Ballamingie, P. and Johnson, S. (2011) The vulnerable researcher: Some unanticipated challenges of doctoral fieldwork. *The Qualitative Report* 16 (3), 711–729.

Barkhuizen, G. (ed.) (2013) *Narrative Research in Applied Linguistics*. Cambridge: Cambridge University Press.

Castells, M. (2010) *The Power of Identity* (2nd edn). Oxford: Wiley Blackwell.

Creely, E. and Laletas, S. (2020) Transitions, transformations and finding success: A phenomenological analysis of the experiences of a doctoral student in early candidature. *Higher Education Research & Development* 39 (3), 439–453.

Escobar, A. (1995) *Encountering Development: The Making and Unmaking of the Third World*. Princeton: Princeton University Press.

Foucault, M. (1997) Sex, power, and the politics of identity. In P. Rabinow (ed.) *Michel Foucault: Ethics, Subjectivity and Truth. Essential Works of Foucault 1954–1984* (pp. 163–173). New York: The New Press.

Foucault, M. (1980) *Power/Knowledge: Selected Interviews and Other Writings 1972–1977* (Edited by Colin Gordon). Brighton: Harvester Press.

Foucault, M. (2000) The subject and power. In J. Faubion (ed.) *Power* (pp. 326–348). New York: The New Press.

Frick, L.B. and Brodin, E.M. (2020) A return to Wonderland: Exploring the links between academic identity development and creativity during doctoral education. *Innovations in Education and Teaching International* 57 (2), 209–219.

Geeraert, N., Li, R., Ward, C., Gelfand, M. and Demes, K.A. (2019) A tight spot: How personality moderates the impact of social norms on sojourner adaptation. *Psychological Science* 30 (3), 333–342.

Giroux, H. (2002) Los profesores como intelectuales públicos. Paulo Freire. *Revista de Pedagogía Crítica* 1 (1), 21–33.

Goodchild, P. (1996) *Deleuze and Guattari: An Introduction to the Politics of Desire*. London: Sage.

Guattari, F. (2015) *Lines of Flight: For Another World of Possibilities*. New York: Bloomsbury Academic.

Henderson, E. (2019) A PhD in motion: Advancing a critical academic mobilities approach (CAMA) to researching short-term mobility schemes for doctoral students. *Teaching in Higher Education* 24 (5), 678–693.

Hou, J. and Feng, A. (2019) Juggling multiple identities: The untold stories behind a PhD ethnographic study. *International Journal of Qualitative Methods* 18, 1–12.

Johnson, K. and Golombek, P. (2016) *Mindful L2 Teacher Education: A Sociocultural Perspective on Cultivating Teachers' Professional Development.* New York: Routledge.

Kelchtermans, G. (2005) Teachers' emotions in educational reforms: Self-understanding, vulnerable commitment and micropolitical literacy. *Teaching and Teacher Education* 21, 995–1006.

Kim, T. (2017) Academic mobility, transnational identity capital, and stratification under conditions of academic capitalism. *Higher Education* 73, 981–997.

Laar, A. (2014) Researcher vulnerability: An overlooked issue in vulnerability discourses. *Scientific Research and Essays* 9 (16), 737–743.

Leshem, S. (2020) Identity formations of doctoral students on the route to achieving their doctorate. *Issues in Educational Research* 30 (1), 169–186.

Lévi-Strauss, C. (1949) *Las Estructuras Elementales del Parentesco.* Buenos Aires: Paidós.

McAlpine, L. and Amundsen, C. (2009) Identity and agency: Pleasures and collegiality among the challenges of the doctoral journey. *Studies in Continuing Education* 31 (2), 109–125.

Martínez, F. (2018) The serendipity of anthropological practice. *Anthropological Journal of European Cultures* 27 (1), 1–6.

Mu, G.M., Zhang, H., Cheng, W., Fang, Y., Li, S., Wang, X. and Dooley, K. (2019) Negotiating scholarly identity through an international doctoral workshop: A cosmopolitan approach to doctoral education. *Journal of Studies in International Education* 23 (1), 139–153.

O'Connor, K. (2006) 'You chose to care': Teachers, emotions and professional identity. *Teaching and Teacher Education* 24, 117–126.

Patel, L. (2016) *Decolonizing Educational Research: From Ownership to Answerability.* New York: Routledge.

Phelps, J.M. (2016) International doctoral students' navigations of identity and belonging in a globalizing university. *International Journal of Doctoral Studies* 11, 1–14.

Ramanayake, U. (2020) My doctoral journey: An autoethnography of doing sensitive research in a different cultural context. *International Journal of Doctoral Studies* 15, 559–573.

Ruohotie-Lyhty, M., Korppi, A., Moate, J. and Nyman, T. (2018) Seeking understanding of foreign language teachers' shifting emotions in relation to pupils. *Scandinavian Journal of Educational Research* 62 (2), 272–286.

Schmidt, M. and Datnow, A. (2005) Teachers' sense-making about comprehensive school reform: The influence of emotions. *Teaching and Teacher Education* 21, 949–965.

Schulze, S. (2014) Finding the academic self: Identity development of academics as doctoral students. *Koers – Bulletin for Christian Scholarship* 79 (1), Art. #2114, 8 pages.

Shahri, M.N.N. (2018) The development of teacher identity, emotions and practice: Before and after graduation from an MA TESOL program. *System* 78, 91–103.

Song, J. and Park, J.S.-Y. (2019) The politics of emotions in ELT: Structure of feeling and anxiety of Korean English teachers. *Changing English* 26 (3), 252–262.

Sparkes, A. and Devis, J. (2007) Investigación narrativa y sus formas de análisis: Una visión desde la educación física y el deporte. In W. Moreno and S. Pulido (eds) *Educación, Cuerpo y Ciudad: El Cuerpo en las Interacciones e Instituciones Sociales* (pp. 43–68). Medellín: Funámbulos.

Velardo, S. and Elliott, S. (2018) Prioritising doctoral students' wellbeing in qualitative research. *The Qualitative Report* 23 (2), 311–318.

16 Emotional Aspects of Online Collaboration: Virtual Exchange of Pre-Service EFL Teachers

Diana Feick and Petra Knorr

Inspired by intensity profiles of emotional experiences, we asked the participant to draw an emotiogram: a curved line indicating perceived success of the collaboration and experienced emotions.

'At the beginning I had very mixed emotions, and I was a bit desperate. I tried to find reasons for our collaboration not working really well and blamed the time difference and technical problems'.

Introduction

As a result of economic globalization and the internationalization of education, short- or long-term studies abroad are increasingly becoming an integral part of higher education. Pre-service teachers of languages, the focus of our study, in particular benefit from these types of mobilities as they provide an opportunity to experience their target language(s) and culture(s) in authentic contexts.

Due to the increased digitization of education, and recently because of reduced opportunities for physical mobility because of the Covid-19 pandemic, virtual mobility as an alternative has experienced a massive boost. Virtual exchange, similar in ways to studying abroad, allows students to meet and work with people from other parts of the globe, to gain an insight into different cultural practices (supported by constantly advancing technical possibilities) and to develop intercultural communicative competencies. Although it cannot be seen as a substitute for physical mobility, it can induce similar experiences and might pave the way for studying abroad at a later (less restricted) time (Schwieter *et al.*, 2018).

One specific form of virtual mobility is virtual exchange (VE), which, according to O'Dowd (2018: 5), has its origin in telecollaboration within foreign language education:

> Virtual exchange involves the engagement of groups of learners in extended periods of online intercultural interaction and collaboration with partners from other cultural contexts or geographical locations as an integrated part of their educational programmes and under the guidance of educators and/or expert facilitators.

More than 20 years of VE research has revealed a number of potential benefits of VE projects, whether as mere add-ons to a curriculum or firmly established credit-carrying activities. It has, however, also drawn attention to disorienting, critical experiences like communication and language issues, perceived lack of engagement of partners, difficulties in teamwork, variable orientations to task, and negative emotions (O'Dowd, 2020).

This chapter will focus particularly on the latter by investigating how pre-service EFL teachers experience bilingual online collaboration within a VE project from an emotional perspective, and how they deal with dissonant emotions caused by collaborative challenges. These questions were explored using data from two projects with student teachers at a German university, who collaborated with students of German in New Zealand. We analyzed student responses from reflective tasks in a questionnaire and a VE logbook as well as interview data stimulated by an emotiogram. The chapter will present findings in the form of an overview of emotions encountered by all participants as well as one case study.

Student (Teacher) Learning through Virtual Exchange

As opposed to physical exchange programs that rely heavily on learning through exposure to a culture and face-to-face interaction with its members, VE highlights the need for direct engagement and interaction through collaborative online learning scenarios (Duffy et al., 2020). The potential of VE has been shown to be manifold. For example, VE positively contributes to intercultural learning and attitudes towards language use (Helm & Acconcia, 2019). Duffy et al. (2020) showed how VE fosters global competencies (the ability to communicate and collaborate in a global and multicultural context) and critical thinking skills. VEs of future language teachers have also proven to develop critical digital literacy (Hauck, 2019), intercultural communicative competence (Müller-Hartmann, 2012), task-design skills (Kurek & Müller-Hartmann, 2017), telecollaborative competencies (O'Dowd, 2015), discourse facilitation skills (Kurek & Müller-Hartmann, 2017) and (critical) multilingual awareness (Feick & Knorr, 2021a, 2021b).

Grau and Turula (2019) conclude that research on VE in teacher education indicates that the competencies needed to be a VE facilitator are best learnt experientially. Pre-service language teachers engage in experiential learning (Kolb, 1984) during VE, as it is their first-hand experience as both participants and future teachers that forms the basis of critical reflection, experimentation, more abstract meaning-making, and learning. Students are involved holistically in cognitive and emotional ways, and lived experiences are transformed into knowledge by individuals themselves, not through transmission by an educator (Grau & Turula, 2019).

This approach with a strong focus on first-hand experience is similar to the concept of transformative learning, on which various teacher study abroad and VE studies base their research (e.g. Duffy *et al.*, 2020; Trilokekar & Kukar, 2011). Against the backdrop of reports on cultural clashes and miscommunications (Goldoni, 2013) or teacher identity conflicts while studying abroad (Trent, 2011), a focus was placed on these 'disorienting experiences' (Trilokekar & Kukar, 2011: 1141). Transformative learning, which involves the changing or broadening of (teacher) students' perspectives (Trilokekar & Kukar, 2011: 1141), is more likely to happen through the critical reflection of these disorienting experiences. Reflections can focus on (a) content (description of the problem), (b) process (focusing on problem-solving strategies), or (c) premise (questioning the problem itself) of an encountered problematic experience (Trilokekar & Kukar, 2011: 1142). Virtual exchanges, which are a new and unique experience for many participants and therefore might lead to disorienting experiences, could provide a context for transformative learning for future language teachers.

In order to more fully understand the interconnectedness of experienced (negative) emotions and professional development through VE, it seems highly relevant to look more closely at emotions in teacher learning.

Emotions in (Virtual) Language Teacher Education

Emotions have recently become increasingly important in applied language studies and language teacher education. Being labeled the emotional (White, 2018) or affective turn (Pavlenko, 2013), or simply the 'second wave of emotion research' (Prior, 2019: 523), it highlights the interconnectedness of cognition and emotion. This perspective was first introduced to the field within the sociocultural paradigm (Lantolf & Swain, 2019; Prior, 2019) and aims at investigating the 'full spectrum of emotions' (Bigelow, 2019: 515), recognizing them as 'contextual, relational, and the effects of contact among people, ideas, and objects' (Benesch, 2016: 1). Critical approaches to the conceptualization of emotions – as opposed to biological or cognitive ones – see them as 'not innate, not internal psychological states, not universal and not measurable', but rather as cultural constructions that are shaped by our 'lived experiences' (Benesch, 2016: 1) For this, Vygotsky (1935/1994) uses the term *perezhivanie*: the cognitive *and* emotional reciprocal processing of previous and new experience. He describes it as the source that motivates our thinking. Emotions do not just occur but are brought into existence by a reaction to an object or event and are shaped by 'languages, cultures, world views, personal histories, social relationships and affiliations' (Prior, 2019: 524).

From a pedagogical perspective, an increased attention to emotions is important because emotions impact key components such as attention, concentration, cooperation, memory, reasoning and commitment (Prior, 2019). Within emotion research, the focus has mainly been on language learners' positive or negative emotions (see overview in White, 2018), but there is an increased interest in investigating language teachers' emotions (Xu, 2018). Particularly relevant in the context of our study is the finding that teachers' emotional experiences (e.g. in teacher training) may affect their future professional motivation and behaviour (Kong, 2019) and the development of professional identity (Bullogh, 2009). Golombek and Doran (2014) argue that emotional content in student reflections should not be dismissed, but viewed as a functional component of language teachers' cognitive development. Dissonant emotional experiences, often related to a perceived dissonance between the ideal and reality, are seen as growth points and potential sources of novice teacher learning (Golombek & Johnson, 2004). In the VE project (VEP) context, emotional content has also been observed in Duffy *et al.*'s (2020) data on cross-cultural online collaboration, where the authors reflected on the relationships that were built between VE partners.

We assume that it is the experiences at an emotional level in particular that shape pre-service teachers' VE project experience and that influence how they might incorporate VE projects into their own future teaching.

LiLLA: A Virtual Exchange Project in Leipzig and Auckland

The current study of students' emotional responses during VE emerged from two VE projects (VEP 1 and 2) that involved the online collaboration of students of German at the University of Auckland and EFL student teachers at Leipzig University. The two projects were carried out in April–June 2019 (with 21 participants from New Zealand and 39 from Germany) and in September–October 2020 (16 New Zealand/19 Germany). Following a (technology-enhanced) task-based approach, the project's thematic focus was on linguistic landscapes in Leipzig and Auckland (LiLLA) (for a detailed description, see Feick & Knorr, 2021a). After students got to know their partners or teams (they worked in dyads and triads) through a short video clip about themselves, they were asked to:

(1) Plan the project and discuss their preferred ways of working together.
(2) Investigate linguistic landscapes (signs in public spaces) in both cities by collecting photos and further information, analyzing and comparing their findings, negotiating meanings, and developing themes.

(3) Create a joint multimedia presentation about their results.
(4) Present these to their fellow students in an (online) seminar setting.

The bilingual project work was supported by a task frame, background information on linguistic landscapes, workshops on digital tools, and the opportunity to ask for assistance from the instructors. Experiential and (potentially) transformative learning was fostered through various reflective tasks and self-directed work that left room for choices and collaborative decision-making: students were free to choose online tools, working modes, languages, content, and forms of presenting results.

Study Design

The data we used for this study is part of the first and second cycle of a design-based research project. The research questions guiding this study were the following:

(1) How do pre-service teachers of English experience online collaboration within a virtual exchange project from an emotional perspective?
(2) What do their reports reveal about their regulation of dissonant emotional experiences caused by collaborative challenges?

Most of the participants in both projects were in their third year of an EFL teacher education program at a German university. In VEP1, the students were enrolled in a TEFL seminar and the project was part of their course assessment. In VEP2, the participants chose to do the project during their summer break as an extracurricular form of earning credit points for their degree. Students in VEP1 were encouraged to write project diaries, and students in VEP2 were asked to write three entries in a VE logbook at three different points in time. These reflections were prestructured by some guiding questions. Furthermore, both cohorts engaged in more reflective writing at the end of the project, when they answered a set of closed and open questions (Q/VEP1, Q/VEP2) about their perception of various aspects of the project in an online questionnaire. The most relevant open question for this study was added in Q/VEP2: 'How did you feel during the project (at different times) and what might have been reasons for that?' We analyzed the two datasets using qualitative content analysis (Mayring, 2014) coding for themes related to our research questions. For the deductive-inductive coding of emotions, which can be linguistically expressed in very diverse ways (Golombek & Doran, 2014), we used constructs from Cleveland-Innes and Campbell (2012) and expanded them with new emerging inductive codes.

The case study we carried out was based on a retrospective interview (I) with one participant from VEP1 through the video conference software Zoom. Inspired by intensity profiles of emotional experiences

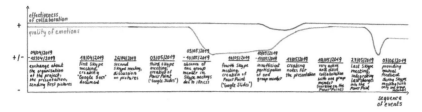

Figure 16.1 Clara's emotiogram (April–June 2019)

(Verduyn *et al.*, 2009), we asked the participant to draw an emotiogram: a curved line indicating perceived success of the collaboration and experienced emotions. This way the student could identify collaboration-related episodes during the project in temporal order (x-axis) and retrospectively rate the quality of her experienced emotion(s) linked to each episode, with ' + ' being the highest intensity of relatively positive emotions (y-axis) and '–' the highest intensity of relatively negative emotions (see Figure 16.1). In contrast to Verduyn *et al.* (2009), the emotiogram included multiple emotions in order to generate an overview of their range related to collaboration-related events over time. We also asked the participant to rate the perceived success of the project collaboration within the same chart by drawing a second graph with ' + ' being the highest intensity of perceived successful collaboration and '–' being the highest intensity of unsuccessful collaboration. The interview focused on explaining and reflecting on the emotiogram and describing the development of the collaboration and the different emotions that were connected to it. The interview was transcribed and the visual data (emotiogram) was triangulated with the interview data in the analysis, so that a narrative for the participants' emotional experience could be reconstructed.

For the purpose of this chapter, German quotes from the logbooks, questionnaire and interview have been translated into English. English quotations were not corrected. In the presentation of the findings, pseudonyms have been used.

Findings

Mixed emotions in VE online collaboration

Data analysis revealed two main patterns of emotional spectra with regard to the VE online collaboration: mixed emotions with a positive tendency, and mixed emotions with a negative tendency. These seemed to be highly influenced by the perceived success of the collaboration of the student teachers with their New Zealand partner(s) during the VEP.

In the majority of cases, the online collaboration was experienced in a positive way and was accompanied by excitement, curiosity, optimism, comfort, confidence, happiness, enjoyment and pride. These positive feelings (over time) mitigated emotions like confusion, feeling over-whelmed or lost, stress, nervousness or insecurity that some of the partici-pants reported having at the beginning or end of the project, so that altogether students valued participating in the VEP as a predominantly positive emotional experience:

> My confusion from the beginning vanished over the time. I felt more secure week by week. I guess it's because of the good group work. (Maria, Q/VEP2)

> I felt a little stressed in the ending as we had different approaches regard-ing our working style: I start early and want it to be done; my AKL part-ner used the last minutes. However, in the end it turned out okay. A reason for that is probably a different work mentality but as we managed to do the tasks anyway, that was perfect. (Mona, Q/VEP2)

On the other hand, one of the students reflected upon how he regulated his initial overly positive emotions, which were a result of expectations being too high:

> I felt okay the entire time, the schedule was not too stressful and manage-able at all times. I might have been too euphoric at the beginning, as I expected VE to be much closer to 'actual' personal exchange but I quickly re-evaluated my expectations, so I would not speak of any disappoint-ment. (Peter, Q/VEP2)

Unsurprisingly, there was also a small number of participants (in VEP2: Cleo, Nadine, Sonja and Markus) who described their collaboration as less or not successful due to what they perceived as different working styles and/or their partners' lack of motivation, investment, engagement, commitment, participation, and even sympathy. This was experienced through, for example, a slower response turnaround time, fewer responses, lack of preparation for online meetings, or missing of deadlines or meet-ings. At the product level, unsuccessful collaboration was attributed to fewer contributions of artefacts, more superficial analysis of artefacts, lack of consultation on creation of the project product, or individual instead of joint product creation. Less successful collaboration was also linked to negative emotions, which these participants referred to as frus-tration, regret, disappointment, anger, annoyance, despair, sadness, unhappiness and helplessness. These stood in stark contrast to their own positive attitude towards the VEP at the beginning, which led to the over-all development of mixed emotions:

> I felt frustrated, as I put a lot of work and interest into the project. (Cleo, Q/VEP2)

> At the beginning I had very mixed emotions, and I was a bit desperate. I tried to find reasons for our collaboration not working really well and blamed the time difference and technical problems. Gradually however, I felt more disappointed, as I realized that our poor collaboration could

be ascribed to a lack of motivation. But at a certain point I decided to stop feeling angry and finish the project as well as possible. (translated by authors, Sonja, Q/VEP2)

Nevertheless, none of these four participants evaluated their overall VEP experience as unsatisfying since most of them still articulated interest, motivation and enjoyment at different stages of the project:

> I was excited most of the times as I thought the project was quite interesting and I was eager to work on it. Towards the end and us having to finish the presentation I became a bit frustrated because of the reasons I stated above. But overall I felt good doing the project, especially seeing all the presentations in our groups was great and very interesting. (Markus, Q/VEP2)

In the survey and logbook data, we observed that these four students not only reported on their less satisfying experience and related negative emotions, but also presented a narrative where they showed how they attempted to deal with the perceived collaborative problems and the dissonant emotions that came with it. One regulation strategy was that of an attitudinal change, which involved lowering expectations in terms of the quality and quantity of exchanges with partners on a personal level, and subsequent emotional detachment.

> I had difficulties to address problems. Initially, I didn't want to be too pushy right from the beginning even though I was pretty annoyed about her not getting in touch at all for 2 weeks. Then we appeared to work together ok and I wasn't angry anymore. I still thought we had different styles due to different cultures but well, this was an exchange project. (German hyper correctness vs. 'Don't worry' in NZ). When I became unhappy again, I felt like it was too late ... So I didn't tell her I wanted us to be more perfectionist as I had no time anymore to do so myself. Especially, as we each had our own presentation I stopped caring about it so much; I probably should have said something right in the beginning and will in my next project works. (Sonja, Q/VEP2)

Sonja makes use of national and cultural stereotypes in her attempt to make sense of the working-style differences she experienced. At the same time, in her second logbook entry she discloses that she decided to adapt this working attitude of 'worrying less' in order to cope with her dissonant emotional experience.

Participants also mentioned that they learned to be more resilient, and realized that collaborative difficulties may be part of VEPs: 'I really do regret that the collaboration with my partner did not work as I had hoped. But it's nobody's fault. I've learned that this is something that can also be part of a VEP' (translated by authors, Nadine, Logbook/VEP2).

In sum, we could observe that disorienting experiences mostly emerge when the participants' expectations of how to collaborate successfully were not reflected in the actual collaborative exchange with the partner.

This led to rather dissonant emotional experiences, mostly in the form of mixed emotions with a negative tendency. Some participants indicated how they successfully regulated these negative emotions; for example, by directly addressing the problem or through attitudinal changes. Others demonstrated, through their successful completion and an overall positive evaluation of the project, that their way of coping with disorienting experiences and dissonant emotions was to reflect on what they had learned from them for their future professional practice.

Clara's case: Collaborative and emotional development over time

To gain an in-depth insight into collaborative and emotional dynamics during the trajectory of a project cycle, we now present Clara's case. It is especially interesting since the project group consisted of three members: Clara and Tina from Leipzig, and Nelly from Auckland. We used Clara's emotiogram and her reflections on it during the interview to reconstruct the collaborative and emotional development during the project from her perspective.

As we can see in Figure 16.1, Clara's emotional state is linked to her perceived collaborative success during different stages of the project. Whenever Clara evaluates the collaboration of her team (upper line) as satisfying (+), her emotional state (lower line) is rated with a + as well. When she felt there were difficulties ('disorienting episodes'), she rated the collaboration with a +/-, and her emotional state declined slightly as well.

In the overall trajectory we can see that her emotions were positive most of the time, and the collaboration with her partners worked well: 'When speaking of positive emotions, it is actually a constantly positive collaboration with Nelly that I associate with it, from beginning to end' (Clara, I/VEP1).

In this context she also highlights the instant sympathy that she felt for her New Zealand project partner, and what effects this had on their collaboration: 'That we were on one wavelength is of course a pleasant side effect, especially for our collaboration and this is something that I can't perceive as separate from the whole project' (Clara, I/VEP1)

She started the project with a mix of emotions (feeling overwhelmed, confusion and positive surprise), which she nevertheless rated with an overall +. At the same time, the collaboration developed in a positive way with an active exchange through a messenger app and two successful video conference group meetings. She experienced a first collaborative challenge during the third and fourth group meetings, when Tina did not participate for health reasons and subsequently reduced her overall participation (see Figure 16.2).

From that point on, the meetings between the three participants turned into meetings only between Clara and Nelly, accompanied by fewer contributions from Tina in the group chat:

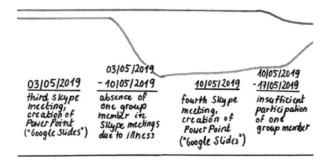

Figure 16.2 Clara's emotiogram: First emotional dissonance

In our chat you can often see that it is more a dialogue between Nelly and myself. And when I asked a question that we directly addressed to Tina, then she replied. But regardless of these questions, she didn't contribute to the same extent. And I think I also noted that sometimes during our Skype meetings, when we discussed our first reflections, that with Nelly it went really well and we would reflect a lot and Tina then seemed to kind of hold herself back a bit. (Clara, I/VEP1)

At this stage, the more proactive collaboration style of Nelly and the more reactive collaboration style of Tina became evident, and Clara experienced them as 'a bit of a contrast': 'This defined the group dynamics, that on the one hand you collaborate very closely and surprisingly productively despite the time difference and on the other hand it sometimes also slows you down a bit' (Clara, I/VEP1).

She further relates that this caused a 'little insecurity' in how to deal with this reactive style. She remembers addressing the issue directly with Nelly, but not with Tina. The imbalanced (i.e. mostly bilateral) collaboration becomes evident one last time on the day of the project presentation on May 29th (not in Figure 16.3, but explained in the interview), when Tina cancelled her participation at the last minute because of health reasons, which turned out to be the last communicative contact between Clara and Tina.

Clara remembers feeling 'taken by surprise' by this, and that she regretted that the group work with Tina ended on a less than positive note: 'But of course it was also a bit sad. At least for me, it didn't feel good to leave this whole working process like that, the group work' (Clara, I/VEP1).

In terms of problem-solving, Clara mentions that she and Nelly directly demanded contributions from Tina with concrete deadlines, which seemed to generate the desired results. On an emotional level, Clara's regulation strategy was one of acceptance:

Well, for me it was okay in the end. I think there was this point when we simply accepted it. But I still thought – and this is what had always been

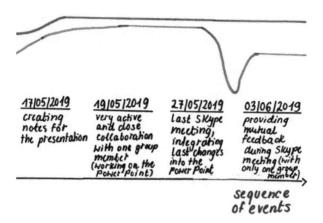

Figure 16.3 Clara's emotiogram: Second emotional dissonance

important to me I think – that it would not be the case that eventually it would be a pair work project, because all three of us were signed up for this group work of three, when we want to look at it from a formal point of view. And it was also important to me that there was a certain balance when it comes to having a fair share of the work that was to be done. (Clara, I/VEP1)

To conclude, in Clara's reflections we can observe how an imbalanced collaboration in a group of three caused positive and negative emotions at the same time. It is an example of mixed emotions, which not only occur at different times of the project but also with regard to different team members. Clara's case also demonstrates that the emotional development during a VEP is not linear but characterized by ups and downs and is closely linked to the perceived collaborative success and possibly disorienting collaborative experiences. She finds different ways of regulating her dissonant emotions: through addressing the issue (even though only with the third team member), through accepting differences in levels of participation, and by being resilient after making sure that her understanding of the project as a collaboration of three is being heard by all her team members.

Discussion and Conclusion

Our findings show that the experience of (mostly mixed) emotions is closely related to how learners experience a VEP and its online collaboration and that the investigation of emotions allows a more complete understanding of online collaboration within a VEP. In the reflective reports, positive emotions dominate and are manifold, but are only partially congruent with the emotional responses to online learning environments described by Cleveland-Innes and Campbell (2012). One reason for this might be that cultural context influences how emotions are directly or indirectly expressed and analyzed. In order to be as context-sensitive as possible, the data in our study was gained through written self-reports and the visualization of emotions through the emotiogram and so allowed for an emic perspective in the exploration and interpretation of emotions and their regulation.

Most participants did not report dissonant emotions. Nevertheless, their overall positive emotional experience was occasionally accompanied by less positive emotions at specific moments of the VEP (e.g. beginning or end), but the satisfying collaboration and project outcomes seemed to mitigate these instances in most cases. The few participants of VEP2 who experienced mainly dissonant emotions, and on whom we focused our more detailed analysis, reported that these were mostly caused by (partly) unsuccessful collaboration with their partner(s). Interestingly, they all managed to regulate these rather negative emotions in ways that allowed them to evaluate the project as a positive experience with opportunities for experiential and transformative learning, especially from the perspective of a future teacher and potential VE facilitator. These students share in their reflections that they learned how important it is to establish a personal relationship with their partner, to be more patient and flexible or tolerant with regard to different working styles, to address collaboration problems when they occur, and to use online-peer support from other participants (if available). With regard to the VEP, in general these students appreciated their improved digital competence and the insight into how to structure a VEP. Consequently, they all felt encouraged to do a VEP again or organize one themselves in the future. Even though this was not the focus of our study, these examples seem to be the first indications of the initiation of experiential and transformative learning opportunities after experiencing disorientation and dissonant emotions during a VEP.

While participants who experienced successful online collaboration might also have learned from their reflections on their positive VEP experiences, we have shown that collaborative challenges and the accompanying mixed or negative emotions provided a particularly rich basis for (transformative) reflection on VEPs for future language teachers.

Disorienting experiences in a VEP can be explained by perceiving collaboration as a culturally bound concept, where different collaborative styles and expectations clash (Duffy et al., 2020). In contrast to this, our data shows that these experiences can also occur with team members from the same cultural context (e.g. Clara's case), so cultural differences might be one but not the only cause for disorienting experiences within a VEP. It has been demonstrated, for instance, that different group decision-making patterns are linked to mixed emotions during project work in foreign language learning (Feick, 2018).

Implications

The findings of this study offer diverse implications for pedagogical practices within the field of language teacher education. VEPs provide an opportunity for experiential learning as students engage in the project as both (language) learners as well as prospective teachers. As learners, students can experience what it 'feels like' to be part of a more or sometimes less successful bilingual collaboration, and what kinds of strategies for regulating dissonant emotions could be used. Following an experiential approach can also help student teachers experiment with different communication or problem-solving strategies in an online environment.

From a future language teacher's perspective, students have the opportunity to learn about how to support bilingual online collaboration, how to empower students to take responsibility, to provide guidance on how to regulate negative emotions, and how to solve possible collaborative challenges in a constructive way. Our data shows that it is the process of dialogic reflection with peers or mentors, or mediating tools like VE logbooks, that support students in their professional development. As educators, we could raise awareness of the role of emotions being 'a valuable resource, rather than a source of incompetence' (Golombek & Doran, 2014: 110) and help students to learn from them, even or particularly if they are dissonant, negative or disorienting.

To deepen the insights of disorienting experiences within a VEP, future research could analyze online communication data between team members to see how their actual bilingual oral or written interaction might have contributed to these disorienting experiences. In addition, the spectrum of experienced emotions during a VEP is not only linked to the success of the collaboration; other aspects like personal attitudes and motivation, expectations and previous VEP experiences, linguistic and digital competency, or familiarity with the partners' cultural context are worth investigating.

References

Benesch, S. (2016) Critical approaches to the study of emotions in English language teaching and learning. In C.A. Chapelle (ed.) *The Encyclopedia of Applied Linguistics* (pp. 1–6). Hoboken, NJ: Wiley.

Bigelow, M. (2019) (Re)considering the role of emotion in language teaching and learning. *The Modern Language Journal* 103 (2), 515–544.

Bullogh, R. (2009) Seeking eudaimonia: The emotions in learning to teach and to mentor. In P. Schutz and M. Zembylas (eds) *Advances in Teacher Emotion Research: The Impact on Teachers' Lives* (pp. 33–53). Berlin: Springer.

Cleveland-Innes, M. and Campbell, P. (2012) Emotional presence, learning, and the online learning environment. *The International Review of Research in Open and Distributed Learning* 13 (4), 269–292.

Duffy, L.N., Stone, G.A., Townsend, J. and Cathey, J. (2020) Rethinking curriculum internationalization: Virtual exchange as a means to attaining global competencies, developing critical thinking, and experiencing transformative learning. *SCHOLE: A*

Journal of Leisure Studies and Recreation Education. https://doi.org/10.1080/19371 56X.2020.1760749

Feick, D. (2018) Social autonomy and decision making in L2 group work. *Studies in Self-Access Learning Journal* 9 (3), 280–305.

Feick, D. and Knorr, P. (2021a) Developing multilingual awareness through German-English online collaboration. In U. Lanvers, M. East and A.S. Thompson (eds) *Language Learning in Anglophone Countries: Challenges, Practices, Ways Forward* (pp. 331–358). Cham: Palgrave Macmillan.

Feick, D. and Knorr, P. (2021b) Erfahrungsbasiertes Lernen in mehrsprachigen Lernumgebungen: Das virtuelle Austauschprojekt 'Linguistic Landscapes Leipzig – Auckland'. *The Langscape Journal*. https://edoc.hu-berlin.de/handle/18452/19672

Goldini, F. (2013) Students' immersion experiences in study abroad. *Foreign Language Annals* 46 (3), 359–376.

Golombek, P. and Doran, M. (2014) Unifying cognition, emotion, and activity in language teacher professional development. *Teaching and Teacher Education* 39, 102–111.

Golombek, P. and Johnson, K. (2004) Narrative inquiry as a mediational space: Examining emotional and cognitive dissonance in second-language teachers' development. *Teachers and Teaching: Theory and Practice* 10 (3), 307–327.

Grau, M.K. and Turula, A. (2019) Experiential learning of telecollaborative competences in pre-service teacher education. *Language Learning & Technology* 23 (3), 98–115.

Hauck, M. (2019) Learning and teaching languages in technology-mediated environments: Why modes and meaning making matter. PhD thesis, The Open University.

Helm, F. and Acconcia, G. (2019) Interculturality and language in Erasmus+ virtual exchange. *European Journal of Language Policy* 11 (2), 211–233.

Kolb, D.A. (1984) *Experiential Learning: Experience as the Source of Learning and Development*. Englewood Cliffs, NJ: Prentice Hall.

Kong, K. (2019) Embracing an integrative approach toward emotion in language teaching and learning. *The Modern Language Journal* 103 (2), 539–544.

Kurek, M. and Müller-Hartmann, A. (2017) Task design for telecollaborative exchanges: In search of new criteria. *System* 64, 7–20.

Lantolf, J. and Swain, M. (2019) On the emotion-cognition dialectic: A sociocultural response to Prior. *The Modern Language Journal* 103 (2), 528–530.

Mayring, P. (2014) *Qualitative Content Analysis: Theoretical Foundation, Basic Procedures and Software Solution*. Klagenfurt. https://www.ssoar.info/ssoar/handle/document/39517

Müller-Hartmann, A. (2012) The classroom-based action research paradigm in telecollaboration. In M. Dooly and R. O'Dowd (eds) *Research Methods for Online Interaction and Exchange* (pp. 56–192). Bern: Peter Lang.

O'Dowd, R. (2015) Supporting in-service language educators in learning to telecollaborate. *Language Learning & Technology* 19 (1), 63–82.

O'Dowd, R. (2018) From telecollaboration to virtual exchange: State-of-the-art and the role of UNICollaboration in moving forward. *Journal of Virtual Exchange* 1, 1–23.

O'Dowd, R. (2020) Reviewing the learning outcomes of virtual exchange in foreign language education. In M. Eisenmann and J. Steinbock (eds) *Sprachen, Kulturen, Identitäten: Umbrüche durch Digitalisierung?* (pp. 15–27). Baltmannsweiler: Schneider Verlag Hohengehren.

Pavlenko, A. (2013) The affective turn in SLA: From 'affective factors' to 'language desire' and 'commodification of affect'. In D. Gabryś-Barker and J. Bielska (eds) *The Affective Dimension in Second Language Acquisition* (pp. 3–28). Bristol: Multilingual Matters.

Prior, M.T. (2019) Elephants in the room: An 'affective turn' or just feeling our way? *The Modern Language Journal* 103 (2), 516–527.

Trent, J. (2011) Learning, teaching, and constructing identities: ESL pre-service teacher experiences during a short-term international experience programme. *Asia Pacific Journal of Education* 31 (2), 177–194.

Trilokekar, R.D. and Kukar, P. (2011) Disorienting experiences during study abroad: Reflections of pre-service teacher candidates. *Teaching and Teacher Education* 27, 1141–1150.

Schwieter, J.W., Ferreira, A. and Chamness Miller, P. (2018) Study abroad learners' metalinguistic and sociocultural reflections on short- and long-term international experiences. *Intercultural Education* 29 (2), 236–257.

Verduyn, P., Van Mechelen, I., Tuerlinckx, F., Meers, K. and Van Coillie, H. (2009) Intensity profiles of emotional experience over time. *Cognition and Emotion* 23 (7), 1427–1443.

Vygotsky, L.S. (1994) The problem of the environment. In R. van der Veer and J. Valsiner (eds) *The Vygotsky Reader* (pp. 338–354). Oxford: Blackwell.

White, C.J. (2018) The emotional turn in applied linguistics and TESOL: Significance, challenges and prospects. In J. de Dios Martínez Agudo (ed.) *Emotions in Second Language Teaching* (pp. 19–34). New York: Springer.

Xu, Y. (2018) A methodological review of L2 teacher emotion research: Advances, challenges and future directions. In J. de Dios Martínez Agudo (ed.) *Emotions in Second Language Teaching* (pp. 35–49). New York: Springer.

Part 4

Relationships and Careers

17 From Language Teaching Assistant Abroad to Language Professional: A Longitudinal Study of Career Entry

Rosamond Mitchell and Nicole Tracy-Ventura

'It [living abroad] really kick started my teaching career, and I never thought that I'd be doing this now to be honest, but I really enjoy doing it and it's all because of what I did in France. It's kind of like I got everything going and I got it all going in the right direction, so it was a really great experience'.

When asked about post-graduation plans, she mentioned not wanting to teach immediately. By 2016, however, she was teaching English in Madrid. She said she had returned to Spain because she felt bored with office jobs and kept thinking about her year abroad.

Introduction

In predominantly English-speaking countries, the promotion of additional language learning among Anglophones conscious of the global reach of English is currently very challenging (British Academy, 2019). The various governments of the UK are taking different initiatives to support foreign languages, such as the promotion of evidence-based languages pedagogy in English secondary schools (https://ncelp.org) and the inclusion of foreign languages in the primary school curriculum (Department for Education, 2013). However, languages education (along with maths and science) is chronically affected by significant teacher shortages (Worth, 2020); in addition Tinsley (2019: 14) notes 'the dependency of English schools on staff who are EU27 citizens', who may be less interested in UK employment post-Brexit.

Against this background, it is important to understand the career paths of UK nationals who choose to study languages at an advanced level and are therefore potentially available as recruits to teaching. There is evidence to suggest that this group of people have developed a distinctive multilingual identity, and an intrinsic attachment to languages, starting from their time at school (Busse & Williams, 2010; Lanvers, 2017; Mitchell *et al.*, 2020). The experience of advanced language study, and in particular of study abroad, in turn reinforces this attachment to languages and the overall international orientation of languages graduates (Mitchell *et al.*, 2020).

However, advanced foreign language competence, intrinsic motivation for language learning, and the development of a multilingual/intercultural identity, need not lead in any straightforward way to a specialist career such as language teaching. In relatively 'open' labour markets such as that of the UK, new graduates have considerable latitude to negotiate their career path, and considerations other than specialist knowledge come into play, such as personal relationships or geographical preferences (Holmes, 2013; Tomlinson, 2010). Additionally, for UK languages students undertaking residence abroad, the option of becoming a language teaching assistant (LTA) as a Native English-Speaking Teacher (NEST) (Keaney, 2016) provides an introduction not only to languages education, but more specifically to the teaching of English as a foreign language. Thus, for those considering teaching, career options are open not only for teaching French etc. in the UK, but also for joining the worldwide industry that is TESOL/ELT, in large part due to their status as native English speakers (Holliday, 2006). It is clear, however, that the motivations of NESTs are highly varied, and may range from a 'backpacker' enthusiasm to see the world, to a desire to settle, integrate and develop a long-term professional career in a new context (Copland *et al.*, 2020).

In this chapter we examine a group of UK languages specialists who became LTAs a decade ago, exploring their motivations for making this particular choice, and its relationship to any longer-term career planning. We then describe a subset of individuals from this group, who have developed over the past 10 years as language education professionals. We address the following questions:

(1) What are the motivations for choosing the LTA role over other study-abroad options, and how do these relate to emergent career identity?
(2) What are the pathways which lead specialist languages graduates into longer-term teaching careers, and how far were these influenced by the sojourn abroad?

The Study

From 2011–2013, the authors ran a research project, tracking the linguistic, social and identity development of 56 undergraduate specialists in

French and Spanish from a UK university, before, during and following their 'year abroad' (Year 3 of a four-year BA program): the *Languages and Social Networks Abroad* project (LANGSNAP; Mitchell *et al.*, 2017). In 2016 and 2019, all participants were invited to participate in follow-up studies to track the longer-term impact of languages study including study abroad on language maintenance and on identity and career development (Huensch *et al.*, 2019; Mitchell *et al.*, 2020).[1] Around half the original participants agreed to meet with us again, n = 33 and n = 28 respectively. During their sojourn, 22 participants worked as LTAs in schools in France and Spain on British Council placements. Ten others worked as LTAs in Mexican universities, through an exchange scheme with the home university; two others undertook workplace internships involving ELT. Thus, a majority of the original LANGSNAP cohort (34/56) gained significant ELT experience during this formative year. A few also undertook LTA roles in the year immediately post-graduation.

In this study, we first examine participants' original motivations to choose the LTA role, and then review the career pathways of those who were actively teaching English, French or Spanish in 2019 (n = 7); we also discuss more briefly those 2019 participants engaged in some form of educational support role (n = 6), and those who had earlier undertaken teacher training but dropped out (n = 2). (Some other participants who were last interviewed in 2013 did declare intentions to teach but we lack evidence on outcomes.)

Our data consists of up to 10 audio-recorded interviews conducted with individual participants over eight years, starting with a pre-sojourn interview in spring 2011, and continuing until summer 2019. Most of these interviews were conducted in French or Spanish and had the dual purpose of providing an extensive L2 speech sample and collecting information about participants' current life experiences, the place of language(s) in their evolving identity and their current language practices.[2] In 2012, 2016 and 2019 additional 'reflective' interviews (RIs) were conducted in English. All interviews were transcribed and entered into an NVivo database. For this study, relevant interviews were coded systematically for comments on motivations and experiences as an LTA (for the original LANGSNAP cohort), and then on motivations and experiences as a language educator or in an educational support role (for relevant 2016 and 2019 participants).

Findings 1: Choosing the LTA Role

In their pre-sojourn interview, participants were asked about their motivations for choosing among different study-abroad options: an Erasmus student exchange, a workplace internship or an LTA role. The most popular reasons for becoming an LTA were, firstly, that it offered a break from formal study, and secondly, that it was financially more advantageous, so that participants could undertake more touristic travel when abroad and/or save some money. The subgroup going to Mexico mainly mentioned the opportunity to experience a non-European setting. The most frequently mentioned potential disadvantages were the lack of access to friends of the same age, if working in a school, and the expectation that the role involved speaking a good deal of English. However, a few participants did mention previous experience with children, and their interest in teaching as a possible future career:[3]

INV: Why did you choose this activity?
180:   It's that I want a change, because I am a student now and I think it is a bit different … I enjoy working with children too, and maybe in future it could be a career option to be a teacher. (Participant 180, pre-sojourn)

During their sojourn, LTAs reported quite variable experiences, concerning the expectations of their schools and mentors, their degree of social integration in the school, and children's engagement and behavior. However, by the end of the sojourn most reported some regret at leaving the role, mainly because of the positive relationships they had established with their students; they offered many descriptions of fond farewells. A few mentioned some impact on career planning, both negative and positive: 'It made me realize that I couldn't be a teacher, I just don't have the patience' (114, RI 2019). And Participant 106 said, 'I think I am going to go on studying to be a teacher, but I am not sure … But all the teachers in France said I am quite (.) at ease with children, and I have done a lot of things with children before and since, so I think I will become a teacher' (post-sojourn 2013).

To sum up, the prospect of a teaching career was not prominent among the motivations of LTAs. When weighing up an LTA-ship over other options, the break from study, the intercultural nature of the experience (especially prominent for those heading to Mexico), financial considerations and possible limitations on social opportunities and opportunity to speak their priority target language, were all more salient than an interest in 'tasting' teaching. However, of those participants who later did actually work in education, almost all had previously been LTAs, either during their year abroad or post-graduation.

Findings 2: UK Schools Careers

Nine participants declared at some point during the longitudinal study their definite intentions of training to become a teacher in UK schools, mostly through the one-year Postgraduate Certificate in Education (PGCE). Of this group, seven had been LTAs when abroad. Three of the nine were not interviewed after 2013, and two completed all or part of the PGCE but then dropped out. Thus, a total of four participants who were tracked post-graduation were working in 2019 as qualified UK languages teachers.

Participant 105 was motivated to specialize in French and German because of family encouragement, extensive time already spent in France, and some good experiences at school. She spent her time as an LTA in a large *lycée* in a depressed post-industrial city in France, with considerable racial tensions, including within the school; she drew on her previous university studies of contemporary France to manage her resulting culture shock. She established good relations with students, teachers and other locals; however, she concluded the year in this testing environment with the thought that 'I don't want to be a teacher' (105, V3).

Upon graduating, Participant 105 spent a year working in the charitable sector, including a three-month placement in West Africa, followed by some months in a London-based educational charity. Her experiences and the influence of London colleagues brought her back to the idea of teacher training, and she did a PGCE at a university in her home area, including teaching practice in both privileged and disadvantaged schools. She then joined a local secondary school as a teacher of French, where she quickly became Head of Languages, and remained in this role in 2019.

Participant 106 studied French at university because of her own very positive school experiences, which developed her intrinsic motivation for languages. For her sojourn abroad she chose the LTA option because of her established liking for children and interest in a possible teaching career, and her experience in France confirmed this choice (see her comment above where she says, 'I am quite (.) at ease with children, and I have done a lot of things with children before'). She undertook a PGCE immediately on graduation, and initially found a job in a state secondary school, where she was the sole full-time languages specialist. In 2016 she moved to join her partner in a different region and found a job in a private school with a larger languages department, which she saw as a great advantage. She had specialized in French at university, but in both settings she found that the schools' priority was for someone who could offer Spanish, and consequently she worked to improve her – initially basic – command of Spanish from her PGCE year onward. In 2019 she was well settled in this second school, teaching only Spanish to students aged 11–16, but hoping to teach French again soon. She summed up her own intrinsic interest in language learning and her enthusiasm for sharing this with students:

> I've always been interested in teaching … I thought it was something that I would possibly do later in life and then I just went with it straight from university. Languages have just always intrigued me … the way that your mind works, the way that you kind of gain languages, the way you acquire them (.) even how your body can produce the sounds I find really fascinating, and so that linguistic side of it really captured my imagination, and then I try and use that when I'm teaching. So it drives some of my students mad, but some of them really enjoy it when I tell them why things work

and why they have a difficulty … making a particular sound or doing things in a different way, how other people might struggle with our language too. That's the side of the teaching that I really enjoy. (106, RI 2019)

Regarding the contribution of study abroad to her teaching abilities, Participant 106 believed that this had given her a greater intercultural perspective, which she could apply to understanding her students. However, her main current focus for self-development was to learn more about mental health and counselling, and to use these skills at work.

Participant 169 had done well in languages at school and found language learning intrinsically interesting; at university she chose to study both French and Spanish. She spent her year abroad in Spain as an Erasmus exchange student, preferring this because of presumed greater access to young people and greater opportunity to speak Spanish, but also because at a Spanish university she could take French language classes. She developed a strong attachment to her study-abroad location, and after doing some multilingual administrative jobs in England post-graduation, she returned to Spain with her British partner for a year, did an online TEFL qualification, and found work in an English language academy. Through this experience she discovered that she enjoyed teaching:

> Actually part of me wanted to know if I wanted to be a teacher at all. It's something that I rebelled against completely, because when I was younger everyone's like 'Oh why are you going to do languages? Like the only thing you can do is teach'. And I was like 'Well I'm not going to teach then' … So I was curious to see whether I'd actually enjoy it, and I do … It was definitely a good experience, because it gave me more of an insight into what I want to do or what I don't want to do. (169, RI 2016)

Participant 169 returned to the UK after one year, and enrolled for a PGCE course. An important factor in her decision was the availability of government grants to support trainees in 'shortage' subjects such as languages; together with her partner she now had a mortgage to pay. When interviewed in 2019, she was teaching both Spanish and French in a secondary school; she felt her time spent in Spain had given her rich cultural knowledge to support her teaching, which she lacked in French. To motivate her students, she talked to them about her own past use of languages at work, and about her own experience of their wider intercultural potential:

> I actually do really enjoy this, it's not just about being able to answer exam questions, and that's what I try and teach the kids as well, like 'This is just so you can have this in your life, you can meet people you never would've met, you can read books you never could've read … and appreciate I don't know, like films and shows, and notice the difference between the subtitles and what they're saying, and things like that', [so] that you start to feel a bit of a sense of achievement about it. (169, RI 2019)

Participant 178 studied Spanish at university because of her love of travel and with the encouragement of an admired teacher. Before going to university, she travelled alone in Latin America for several months, including some time spent working with orphans in Bolivia; for her year abroad, she opted for an LTA-ship in Mexico, working in a private bilingual school. Having graduated, she enrolled on the *Teach First* scheme (a workplace-based alternative to the PGCE). Her LTA experience clearly influenced this decision: 'I don't know if I … would I be a teacher now if I hadn't done it?' (RI, 2019). She worked in a secondary school with many students from immigrant backgrounds and felt she was a role model for them by showing that languages can be learned in school, and can lead to adventure:

> Their concept of learning a language is through your heritage, through your parents, through your family, and you know I've shown them that 'No, I am English, [but] I've learned it, I've learned the language', so that's real, that's nice, and also I think the travel thing, you know going all the way to Mexico, for them is quite interesting as well. (178, RI 2016)

Her experience in Latin America was also helpful in understanding the cultural diversity of the school. However, by 2016 she was experiencing considerable stress because of workload, and was planning to take a year out for volunteer work in West Africa; she spoke of eventual career progression into educational charity work. In 2019, she had returned to become head of languages in another UK secondary school, following a rewarding time in Africa, but was also studying part time for a Master's in international development to further this career aim (though being somewhat conflicted about the financial implications).

As mentioned earlier, two participants (122 and 129) also undertook the PGCE a couple of years after graduating but did not progress to teaching. Participant 122 completed the program successfully but found the challenges of unmotivated learners and heavy workload too stressful; by 2019, she was working for a management consultancy instead. Participant 129 is a talented musician, who did not complete her primary PGCE course, but instead opted for a mix of private music tuition and administrative work.

Overall, the participants who entered school teaching in the UK were motivated partly by a liking for young people, and partly by their own intrinsic motivation to study and enjoy languages, and their intercultural awareness, which had been developed from their schooldays onward, but was then reinforced by their sojourn abroad. Financial considerations were also important, in deciding to train for a particular career in the first place, and then to remain within it. In some form, all those involved with teaching acknowledged the challenges of poor student motivation and of heavy workload, both well-known features of UK language teaching; some drew on their own personal experience and intrinsic motivation to address these challenges in varied ways, while others found them too great and left the profession, or were considering doing so.

Findings 3: ELT Careers

Among those interviewed in 2019, eight participants were working in careers linked to ELT: three were teaching English abroad and five were working in other ELT-related careers. Four of this group had been LTAs during their year abroad, and three others had done so post-graduation.

The three participants who were teaching English abroad in 2019 were Participants 171, 127 and 116. During her year abroad, Participant 171 was an LTA at a Mexican university. She made this choice because she wanted to go to Latin America and did not want to spend the year as a student. At first, she mentioned feeling overwhelmed with the amount of new information she needed to learn but she quickly grew accustomed to her job, and by the end of her stay she was growing tired of its repetitive nature:

> In the end I thought that the classes weren't bad. But I grew tired of doing the classes a little because they weren't like real classes, they were just conversation classes. So you talk about the same topics like 'What you did yesterday', 'What you do in your free time', but all the time. And I think [by] that last month, I had had enough. (171, In-sojourn 3, 2012)

When asked immediately post-sojourn if there was anything she would change if repeating the sojourn, Participant 171 mentioned she would have prepared more activities for her classes or spoken more with other teachers; she felt mentoring had been lacking. When asked what she was going to miss about Mexico, however, she mentioned her Mexican boyfriend. Because of him, she planned on returning after graduation and already had a prospective job teaching English at a private language school. Once back in Mexico she completed a CELTA course[4] and taught first in a private school and later in a state school, also marrying her partner and having her first child in 2017. By 2019 she was also grading students' work for an online university. However, when asked if she felt her year abroad benefited her professionally, she reiterated that she had pursued her ELT career mainly for personal reasons:

> I think it benefited me (.) immensely, personally. I think it probably wasn't great for me professionally because (.) I mean I do like teaching, but I think it's just a job. It's a really great job that I enjoy, and I think I do a good job, but it's not my passion, I have to be honest. And (.) I'm living in a country where the currency is worth a lot less than many other currencies, in a city that's very small, where the salaries are lower than other cities in Mexico as well, so I think professionally and economically (.) … if I had stayed in the UK I'd definitely be earning more and I'd have more of like a professional trajectory … It depends what you value more, right? (171, RI 2019)

Participant 127 originally studied French together with management, intending to work for an international company. For his year abroad, he failed to find a business internship, so he decided to become a LTA to earn some money and 'to live French life'. He was placed in an isolated rural setting but reported himself happy with his year and said he found working in education 'challenging at times but very worthwhile'. After graduation he returned to France for another year as a LTA at a major university, an experience that he found more professionally developmental. On return to the UK, he did CELTA training and taught English in a private language school but was keen to travel. He moved temporarily to Australia, and there again found work teaching English to international students. In 2016, when reflecting on the impact of his two LTA-ships in France, he said:

> It [living abroad] really kick started my teaching career, and I never thought that I'd be doing this now to be honest, but I really enjoy doing it and it's all because of what I did in France. It's kind of like I got everything going and I got it all going in the right direction, so it was a really great experience. (127, RI 2016)

We interviewed Participant 127 remotely again in 2019; he was now working at a private language school in a small town in Japan, where he was living with a Japanese girlfriend he had met in Australia. He described some initial difficulties transitioning to teaching in Japan but said that he 'adapts very well to other situations' (RI 2019) and was enjoying working with children as well as adults, while studying Japanese himself.

Participant 116 spent her year abroad teaching English to the employees of a large French company. She hoped this workplace experience would allow her to speak more French than other placement types. During the year she started a relationship with a local man and returned to France after graduating to join him. She started studying law there but struggled from the beginning with the advanced French required. She soon dropped out and did a CELTA course, later teaching Business English at a private language school. In 2019, she was settled with the same French partner and had been working at the same school for almost five years but was now also working at a major local university, as curriculum expert in a team developing an online English course for their students.

Five participants were working in ELT support roles in 2019. Participant 180 had been an LTA during her year abroad, working in a Basque/English bilingual primary school. She chose the LTA-ship because she wanted a break from studying, liked children and thought of teaching as a possible future profession. While abroad she found the dominance of Basque in the schools was limiting her desired use of Spanish, but still talked positively about her teaching experience. As the year progressed, she was given more responsibility and sometimes taught a group of students on her own, which she enjoyed although discipline was sometimes an issue. Outside school hours she also taught private English classes. After returning to the UK, some of her strongest memories were related to teaching:

INV: What are your strongest memories of living in Spain?
180:   I think those from the last few months there when I had more friends and I was more relaxed because I knew everything, knew everything that I had to do. I think the schools, because they were a big part of my life when I was there. And also the private classes I gave to the children, because I had in the end 10 hours each week, so I was always on the bus going to different classes, talking with the children's parents. (180, post1, 2012)

When asked about post-graduation plans, she mentioned not wanting to teach immediately. By 2016, however, she was teaching English in Madrid. She said she had returned to Spain because she felt bored with office jobs and kept thinking about her year abroad. She took a CELTA course and then moved to Madrid, first as an *au pair* and later as a teacher in a private language school, with both children and adults. She liked her job and hoped to teach more advanced examination preparation classes. She also talked about potentially becoming a CELTA trainer. In 2019 she was still in Madrid but had become an editor with a publishing company working on ELT materials. She said she applied for this job because her teaching schedule at the private school (14:00–22:00 hrs) was wearing her out. She was very happy in her current role although she missed aspects of teaching:

> I miss the funny things that kids say, and I miss the interaction and moving around ... But I wouldn't go back, you know? [In my job now] I get to be creative and I get to go out and do different things, it's not like just sitting at a desk all day. But the part of teaching that I miss is that interaction and working with children, because I really like working with children, and now I do indirectly, but I mean I don't see kids every day. (180, RI 2019)

The remaining participants working in educational support roles are described more briefly. Participants 154, 156 and 166 were exchange students during their year abroad, but all of them took LTA positions after graduation. Participant 154 did so in Quebec, to further improve her French. Once there she met a local partner, and moved with him to Montreal, where she found a university job organizing study-abroad programs, primarily receiving incoming students from the US. In 2019 she held a management position in the same office. Participant 156 returned to Spain (his former study-abroad destination) for a further LTA year, in a desire to improve his Spanish, but also because he was considering doing a PGCE in the future. However, he then spent time traveling around South America where he met a Canadian partner and moved with her to Canada.

There he looked for work teaching Spanish and French but received feedback that his French was not good enough. This inspired him to pursue the British Council LTA scheme once again, and he and his partner spent another year teaching English in France. On their return to Canada he found a university job working on programs in academic English. Participant 166 also wanted to travel again post-graduation, so she did a CELTA course and became an LTA in Mexico. On returning from Mexico, she found a job in the international office at her home university and progressed to a role managing international student exchanges. By 2019 she was working in international student recruitment and undertaking extensive international travel, though she rarely used her Spanish. Finally, Participant 102 was the only person in this group who never taught; she was a workplace intern during her year abroad, and after graduating she studied for a Master's in translation. However, this qualification did not lead to secure employment and, after several short-term jobs, she became a marketing officer for an international English-medium summer school in an English city.

In sum, the data for those pursuing ELT-related careers suggests that personal reasons related to romantic relationships and a desire to travel were strong motivators for their initial entry into ELT and international education more broadly. Their experiences as LTAs during the year abroad or after graduation provided them with confidence that as Anglophones they could always fall back on teaching English abroad, provided they undertook entry-level professional training. Some subsequently showed clear indications of growing professionalism and career progression (e.g. the move of Participant 180 into publishing, or the move of Participant 116 into online materials design); for others, ELT remained a job that enabled their preferred lifestyle (e.g. Participants 127, 171), or was a step toward a career in educational administration. However, almost all of those based abroad had found a partner/chosen to settle in a context where the linguistic and intercultural abilities gained during their university studies and in particular during study abroad were highly relevant. (The exception, Participant 127, was actively applying his language learning skills to a relevant new language, Japanese.) The participants involved in international education also felt that their own experiences of study abroad equipped them well to support the experiences of international students.

Discussion and Conclusion

This longitudinal study demonstrates the complex nature of career decision-making among languages graduates, and its often extended nature, as for other humanities graduates (Clarke, 2018). Thus, the study illustrates the potential impact of personal relationships and geographical moves on career decision-making, alongside the possession of specialist expertise. It also confirms the substantial influence of study abroad in language specialists' decisions to pursue language teaching positions, more broadly by confirming participants' own intrinsic motivation for languages and their sense of self-efficacy as language learners and language users, as well as more narrowly by offering a taste of the professional relationships and skills involved in teaching. In the short term, their first major study-abroad experience, even if it did not involve teaching, inspired several to pursue ELT as a vehicle for living abroad again (Keaney, 2016). Their status as native English speakers (Copland *et al.*, 2020) gave quick access to the profession once licensed through the relatively brief CELTA route. Some who taught English abroad (Participants 154, 156, 166) did so only temporarily to satisfy a continued desire for international travel and improvement of their own language skills, and quickly moved into administrative positions in international education either in the UK or abroad. Some persisted with ELT primarily as a means of sustaining a romantic relationship and desired lifestyle (Participants 127, 171), while others became increasingly professionally engaged in ELT and found higher status and more demanding roles (Participants 116, 180). However, regardless of the particular pathway being followed, it is clear that for those participants who were settling into a long-term life abroad, their personal multilingual identity and intercultural orientation were central to their intertwined personal and professional decision-making (see also the NESTs discussed by Copland *et al.*, 2020).

Regarding the small group who became languages teachers in UK schools, it is clear that their own intrinsic motivation for language learning derived initially from their school career as successful language students, and was then reinforced by their university experiences, with study abroad a key influence. This motivation and their wish to share it with children who might frequently be 'reluctant learners' remained central to their identity as teachers: 'I guess I have to keep my own passion alive to be able to inspire someone else' (178, RI 2019). Their LTA experience allowed them to judge whether they were temperamentally suited to working with children, and gave them some intercultural perspective on education which they found helpful in responding to the diversity of contemporary British schools. However, the heavy workload and accountability pressures also characteristic of contemporary schools, together with the challenge of learner motivation, make this a demanding career pathway to sustain.

One of the distinctive features of this small-scale qualitative study is its longitudinal nature. This has enabled us to document how participants' careers and multilingual identities have evolved since their initial stay abroad as undergraduate languages specialists. Despite some participant attrition, in 2019 we were still able to interview 50% of the original study cohort (n = 28). If funding and other resources allow, our goal is to continue to study the long-term effects of study abroad, including its continuing impact on graduate identity and on teaching careers. A better understanding of career entry and longer-term career development among language educators can contribute usefully to those designing advanced language programs, teacher education programs, and longer-term support systems required to sustain teachers' motivation and professional commitment.

Notes

(1) The original LANGSNAP project was funded by the UK Economic and Social Research Council (Award no. RES-062-23-2996). The follow-up studies were funded by a *Language Learning* Small Research Grant, the University of South Florida, and West Virginia University.
(2) Much of the data reported here is publicly available at langsnap.soton.ac.uk and at talkbank.org.
(3) Interview extracts originally in French or Spanish have been translated by the authors.
(4) The Certificate in English Language Teaching for Adults (CELTA) is a short five-week initial training course for teaching English as a foreign/international language, which is widely accepted internationally as a minimum qualification required to work in the private English language sector.

References

British Academy (2019) *Languages in the UK: A Call for Action*. https://www.thebrit-ishacademy.ac.uk/sites/default/files/Languages-UK-2019-academies-statement.pdf (accessed March 30, 2021).

Busse, V. and Williams, M. (2010) Why German? Motivation of students studying German at English universities. *The Language Learning Journal* 38 (1), 67–85.

Clarke, M. (2018) Rethinking graduate employability: The role of capital, individual attributes and context. *Studies in Higher Education* 43, 1923–1937.

Copland, F., Mann, S. and Garton, S. (2020) Native-English-speaking teachers: Disconnections between theory, research, and practice. *TESOL Quarterly* 54, 348–374.

Department for Education (2013) *Languages Programmes of Study: Key Stage 2*. https://assets.publishing.service.gov.uk/government/uploads/system/uploads/attachment_data/file/239042/PRIMARY_national_curriculum_-_Languages.pdf (accessed March 30, 2021).

Holliday, A. (2006) Native-speakerism. *ELT Journal* 60, 385–387.

Holmes, L. (2013) Competing perspectives on graduate employability: Possession, position or process? *Studies in Higher Education* 38 (4), 538–554.

Huensch, A., Tracy-Ventura, N., Bridges, J. and Cuesta Medina, J.A. (2019) Variables affecting the maintenance of L2 proficiency and fluency four years post-study abroad. *Study Abroad Research in Second Language Acquisition and International Education* 4 (1), 96–125.

Keaney, G. (2016) NEST schemes and their role in English language teaching: A management perspective. In F. Copland, S. Garton and S. Mann (eds) *LETs and NESTs: Voices, Views and Vignettes* (pp. 129–150). London: British Council.

Lanvers, U. (2017) Contradictory others and the habitus of languages: Surveying the L2 motivation landscape in the United Kingdom. *The Modern Language Journal* 101 (3), 517–532.

Mitchell, R., Tracy-Ventura, N. and Huensch, A. (2020) After study abroad: The maintenance of multilingual identity among Anglophone languages graduates. *The Modern Language Journal* 104 (2), 327–344.

Mitchell, R., Tracy-Ventura, N. and McManus, K. (2017) *Anglophone Students Abroad: Identity, Social Relationships and Language Learning.* New York: Routledge.

Tinsley, T. (2019) *Language Trends 2019: Language Teaching in Primary and Secondary Schools in England: Survey Report.* London: British Council.

Tomlinson, M. (2010) Investing in the self: Structure, agency and identity in graduates' employability. *Education, Knowledge and Economy* 4 (2), 73–88.

Worth, J. (2020) *Teacher Labour Market in England: Annual Report 2020.* Slough: National Foundation for Educational Research.

18 Understanding Pre-Service Teachers' Study-Abroad Experiences through Duoethnography: Challenges, Emotions and Developments

Christine Biebricher and Yue You

> *During this dialogic process, we disclosed our personal and emotional experiences openly and discovered that we had many similar feelings about our study-abroad experiences. As we disclosed more, we trusted more and supported each other to venture further into our personal emotional space and our study-abroad experience.*
>
> *'I developed an understanding that there are many different views and perspectives on individual aspects and on life ... I came to realise that two differing opinions could stand side by side and could both be valuable, but I didn't have to agree with both'.*

Introduction

Study abroad has often been researched in terms of language and intercultural gains with a common belief that studying and living in a different country will lead to positive outcomes such as improved linguistic abilities, intercultural sensitivity, resilience, and a stronger motivation to learn languages (Isabelli-García *et al.*, 2018; Róg *et al.*, 2020). Study abroad is also believed to impact on overall personal and identity development (Benson *et al.*, 2013; Kimura & Hayashi, 2019; Kinginger, 2013), but as the experience of studying abroad can be characterized by both positive and negative feelings, such self-formation often involves emotional tensions with differing outcomes based on individual resources so that merely relying on exposure to study abroad will not necessarily result in desired outcomes (Jackson, 2018; Jæger & Gram, 2020).

In this project we chose a duoethnographic approach (Norris, 2008; Norris & Sawyer, 2012) to explore our study-abroad experiences through narratives, as it allowed us to focus on the emotional aspects, the role of identity, and personal positioning through a process of reflexivity in which we critically reflected upon, interpreted and re-interpreted our narratives (Denzin, 2017). By providing thick descriptions of stories and emotions during our lived and subjective experiences, our purpose was to make our individual voices explicit. Through the construction and reconstruction of our stories, we aimed to co-create meaning from our study-abroad experiences and shed light on where our experiences overlapped, but also where they differed. Before we explain our journeys in more detail, in the section below we introduce ourselves as the participants and researchers in this project.

The Researchers and the Researched: Introducing Yue and Christine

Yue is originally from China and currently a PhD student in New Zealand about to submit her thesis. Yue's first study-abroad experience was as a Mandarin Language Assistant (MLA), dispatched by the Chinese government for 10 months to support teachers in New Zealand schools offering Mandarin as a subject. This experience took place six years ago when she was 22 years old. Before coming to New Zealand, Yue had not travelled or lived abroad. Having grown up in an Eastern culture with corresponding value systems, Yue was exposed to the Western world and its values during her study abroad.

Christine is originally from Germany and currently a lecturer at a tertiary institution in New Zealand; she is also one of Yue's supervisors (we elaborate on the ethical implications of this relationship in more detail later). Christine's first study-abroad experience was 10 months in England as part of her initial teacher education degree in Germany, and the study abroad was supported by the Erasmus European Union student exchange program. This first experience was 28 years ago when she was 23 years old. Prior to her first study-abroad experience, she had been on multiple short-term school exchange programs to France, England and the US, ranging from two to four weeks, and had travelled to multiple countries in and outside of Europe. Although she moved to a different country, Christine remained on the same continent and within Western cultures for her study abroad.

Our Research Approach: What We Did and How We Did It

Duoethnography is a collaborative process of compositional research in which two or more researchers engage in collaborative writing to provide multiple understandings of a social phenomenon (Norris, 2008), in our case the study-abroad experience. In the following sections, we explain how we generated and developed our autobiographical narratives, the challenges we encountered, and how we analyzed these narratives.

The iterative data generating and gathering process

We began with writing a reflection on our study-abroad experiences individually, including our thoughts and feelings at the time. Christine had suggested a few prompts to stimulate our reflection, focusing on our thoughts and feelings, expectations, hopes and concerns regarding the study abroad, and reflecting on how those experiences influenced us as teachers. We did not determine a structure for those narratives and did not set ourselves a word limit or any expectations. We gave ourselves a few weeks to write our stories and then sent the result to each other via email. Although our narratives were structured in different ways, they were each between 5000–6000 words long. After reading each other's story, we gave feedback, using comments in the Word documents, mostly asking for clarification. For some aspects of our stories we also prompted each other to provide more detail or to think back to how a particular situation made us feel, for example when recalling a cultural misunderstanding. Each other's feedback stimulated more collaborative reflection, but it also evoked more memories and emotions, which Yue for example tried to elicit further by looking at old photographs taken during her first experience in New Zealand. We each returned to our own writing, attempting to put those newly recovered memories and emotions into words, adding to our original stories, thus increasing the size of our stories to almost double the original length. Several iterations of this cyclical approach across six months allowed us to develop a dialogue and to ultimately transform and expand our understanding of our own and each other's lived experiences. The self-reflections and conversations between the two researchers served as evidence of our collaborative database and helped to expose the similarities and differences of our study-abroad journeys.

Duoethnography is not a fixed blueprint but is emergent and uncertain (Norris & Sawyer, 2012). As both researchers looked back on several study-abroad experiences, we had aimed to make a comparison between those experiences at the beginning of the project. However, as the initial stories developed, it emerged that our first experience was the more impressive for both of us and had a more profound impact on our personal identity development and career trajectories. Thus, we narrowed our focus on this first experience. We continued enriching our reflections to gain an in-depth understanding of this experience.

Writing about emotions

We decided to focus on psychological aspects of studying abroad and to emphasize social, emotional and identity aspects in our reflections rather than only on descriptions of events. We believed that reporting on events would provide concrete examples of our experiences but would lack the depth of how we felt in a particular situation. However, we soon discovered in our writing that it was much easier to write about events than about emotions. For both of us the first study-abroad experience was some years ago, for Christine more than 20, for Yue about 7, and it took some time and effort to delve back into the past and to allow the memories to surface. For both of us the memories triggered emotions, which had not softened over time, and at times it was difficult to relive the impact of those emotions and to deal with the feelings they generated in the present. We also realized during this process that it was important to respect each other's boundaries in regard to how much of those emotions we were willing to share.

In reflecting on our emotions when we were abroad, we experienced additional issues regarding how to express those feelings. One challenge was to find words to describe our feelings in our own language; the other was finding those words in a different language, as we were writing in English. While we are both advanced speakers of English, it was challenging to find words that captured our feelings and had the same linguistic impact and connotation as in our first language. For Christine it felt as if there was a filter between how she would express her feelings in German and what she wrote in English, as her emotional attachment to German was much stronger than that to English. Yue expressed on several occasions that she could not find the appropriate English word to describe the complexity of her emotions and emphasized that Mandarin uses idioms which, in her opinion, are a lot more conducive to explain emotions than individual words.

Incremental data analysis

There was no clear separation between data generation and analysis. While we were writing our own stories, we also commented on each other's experiences so that data collection and analysis occurred concurrently. After our initial stories and comments had emerged, we individually scrutinized both our narratives to identify emerging themes and used online conversations via emails and Zoom (during the Covid-19 lockdown period) to exchange views and to discuss our different impressions. Through our conversations some focal points emerged, and we established themes in our narratives that encapsulated both our experiences.

Aspects that stood out in our narratives focused on challenges during study abroad, but themes also evolved that related to the impact the experience had on our life after study abroad. We then negotiated a structure for how we wanted to report our narratives and our findings. Based on our discussions, we collaboratively mapped our reflections to our recognized themes. Through the construction and reconstruction of our narratives, we aimed to co-create meanings of our study-abroad experiences and to shed light on how psychological and emotional aspects of these experiences influenced our personal and professional identities.

Ethical stance and trust

Trust among co-researchers is one of the tenets of duoethnography, as proposed by Norris and Sawyer (2012). The approach requires transparency and disclosure as well as an openness to learn about self and others (Breault, 2016), so the relationship between the research partners is crucial. Although Christine and Yue's relationship could have been considered an unequal power-relationship, as Christine was also one of Yue's PhD supervisors, Yue, particularly, did not consider this to be an impeding factor. In her opinion, we regarded each other as trustworthy working partners within a foundation of familiarity and trust.

Reflecting back on our deeply personal experiences, writing and sharing our narratives involved a substantial amount of trust. This trust and respect for each other continued to develop over time, allowing us to explore our own and each other's stories gradually in more depth. In the initial stage of writing our self-reflections, we made conscious or subconscious decisions on what stories to include or exclude. After sharing our narratives, we encouraged each other to ask more questions as well as to offer further detail. During this dialogic process, we disclosed our personal and emotional experiences openly and discovered that we had many similar feelings about our study-abroad experiences. As we disclosed more, we trusted more and supported each other to venture further into our personal emotional space and our study-abroad experience. We continued to evaluate and add new aspects to our narratives and made connections to the other's perspectives. We respected each other's stories without judgement and saw both the shared and divergent experiences as valuable sources of the findings. In reporting these findings, we continued to share our writing to ensure that both our perspectives were captured. In the following section, the outcomes of our duoethnographic writing process are presented.

Findings

In this section we focus on each of the themes that emerged from our data analysis. We present the findings according to a timeline, first discussing the themes during our study abroad: (a) emotional challenges and (b) social relationships. This is followed by the post-sojourn theme (c) readjusting to life after study abroad. We conclude this section with themes relating to our study abroad and contributing to our overall personal and professional identity development: (d) critical reflection and self-awareness, and (e) resilience. While our themes indicate how our narratives intersect, the particular emotions and experiences subsumed under a theme also show evidence of divergence.

During study abroad

Emotional challenges

One of the central themes drawn from our written reflections was that of emotional challenge during our study abroad, particularly in the first few months of our experience. Although we could each attribute our negative feelings to different reasons, in our reflections we both concluded that we ended up feeling quite lonely and miserable as a result.

Although Christine felt she was mentally set for an adventure, a lack of organization by the host university soon left her feeling 'forgotten and isolated'. As the host university was not prepared for Christine's and another exchange student's arrival, they both ended up in a newly built, but unfinished hall of residence that was only occupied by a small number of students. For several weeks, the only interaction Christine had was either a coincidental casual conversation in the shared kitchen, small-talk with fellow course students at the university, which usually did not extend beyond 'how are you?', or some short, polite verbal exchange with supermarket staff when she went grocery shopping. Christine felt increasingly isolated and unhappy, and an overall lack of belonging made her feel very anxious: 'I became quite gloomy and started feeling quite sad … I don't think I was necessarily homesick at that stage; I was just very lonely and missed having any social interaction with other people'. The turning point for Christine was when new students moved into her building. The resulting social interactions with peers energized Christine and from then on, she thrived: 'The better I felt, the more people I met; and the more social life became, the happier I became!'

The initial excitement of being in a new country had worn off when Yue was assigned to a homestay after a one-week orientation period with other MLA peers at the university in New Zealand. Staying in a homestay was not as enjoyable as Yue had anticipated. In her reflection she noted that she had moved between three different homestays during her first eight months before she finally got settled in the fourth one. In the first two host families, the feeling of being a token foreigner and feeling like an outsider resulted in a sense of loss and depression. This was particularly the case when Yue was confronted with conflicts with the homestay family that stemmed from a linguistic barrier of not fully understanding or not being able to express herself, and cultural misunderstandings, often without realizing each party had different expectations and values. In contrast, the third homestay treated Yue like a dependent child, controlling most of her activities, for example not giving her a key or not allowing her to do her own washing. The control, coupled with criticism towards her, resulted in Yue losing some of her self-confidence and 'feeling extremely lonely'. As Yue reflected, 'I think those unhappy experiences had affected my mental health, and I always doubted whether I was a nuisance to others'. Such negative feelings disappeared when Yue moved in with the last host family, where she felt understood, cared for and respected as a mature adult.

Social relationships

Another salient theme that emerged from our reflections was that we established social relationships during the year abroad, and we both acknowledged that it was the social relationships that helped us overcome those emotional challenges.

In Yue's case, the immediate working and living context offered the most scope for the formation of new social relationships. The lead teacher (mentor) in Yue's host school was helpful and supportive, and the female host in her last homestay provided her with an immersive experience of local life and culture. Apart from the social relationships with the lead teacher and host, Yue reflected that her social activities were primarily with two other MLA peers who lived and worked in the same area. Yue further highlighted that the study-abroad experience brought them together: 'I think because we supported each other in the new country, and a similar study abroad experience helped us build such solid friendships'.

Unlike Yue, the majority of Christine's new friends were local university members from England and other European countries. Although another German student was in England with Christine, she reflected that they did not spend any time together, and the student's presence did not comfort or help Christine in those challenging times. Christine indicated that the busy social life with new friends from other countries, 'intense discussions' and 'learning about each other's cultures' allowed her to open up to the outside world again. As Christine wrote in her reflection, the social relationships were 'definitely at the centre' of the study-abroad experience where she 'met interesting people and formed life-long friendships' lasting until the present day.

Post sojourn

Readjusting to life

In our reflections, we incidentally recounted the unexpected challenges we experienced when we returned to our home countries after studying abroad. For both of us it was surprisingly challenging to return home, but we attributed those difficulties to the fact that our values had changed in the host countries as we adapted to a different sociocultural environment.

In her narrative, Christine writes how she went through a misalignment stage when she realized her perspective on life had changed significantly as a result of her study-abroad experience, whereas her friends and their surrounding context were still 'stuck in the same old routines'. According to Christine 'it created a feeling of imbalance, of being misunderstood and it created a distance between [her] original context and [herself]'. Christine was taken by surprise by this situation and she felt 'a little bit lost and alone' when she 'should have felt well integrated'. Christine acknowledged that it might have been difficult for her friends to understand her transformative experiences, as they had not experienced what Christine had.

Yue, in a similar vein, indicated in her written reflection that she felt 'being challenged' by the 'old life' after returning. In the following collaborative reflection with Christine, Yue elaborated on the challenges she encountered, which revealed a visible distinction between our readjustment experiences. Yue's feeling of misalignment was mainly due to academic pressure. In contrast to Christine, Yue felt that 'everything had changed a lot' during the time she was away, particularly as she felt she had made no progress in her studies. Her degree had been suspended during the year of study abroad and she had to catch up to her peers. The resulting pressure and stress invoked a sense of helplessness and a loss of professional identity: Yue had to change her role of teaching assistant in a laid-back Western culture to the new one of a postgraduate student in her Eastern, fast-paced culture as quickly as she could to fulfil her academic requirements. 'Life became very busy for me, but I was not well prepared', Yue commented.

In addition to reconciling the experiences abroad with life back home, Christine and Yue both expressed their feelings of missing their study-abroad experience and the new social relationships they had established in the host countries. Christine reflected that she 'felt a little bit sad that … [she] had to say good-bye to [her] new friends and to a social life [she] got used to'. Yue's challenge was to readjust to a different lifestyle back home. She missed the slow pace of life in New Zealand and became frustrated by people's indifference to each other in the busy and crowded city of Shanghai: 'In New Zealand, I smiled and greeted people I met on the street, but when I did the same in China, people treated me as if I suffered from a mental illness'.

Long-term influence of study abroad on our personal and professional identity

Alongside the challenges and learning during and immediately after our study abroad, both our reflections clearly identified that the study-abroad experience had a significant effect on our personal identity, and in turn, had an impact on our professional development as teachers and teacher educators as presented below.

Critical reflection and self-awareness

Living and studying in a new sociocultural environment allowed us to get to know other cultures and value systems. By being exposed to other values and through a continuous process of self-reflection, comparing similarities and differences, we eventually gained greater self-awareness of our own belief and value systems. As Yue reflected, after experiencing some cultural misunderstandings with her host families, for example about the responsibilities and expectations of looking after a child, she became aware that people from different cultural backgrounds had very different expectations, based on their cultural values. Yue realized that neither way was right or wrong and that she could accept the differences between those value systems. Although Christine did not experience significant cultural misunderstandings, socializing and frequent discussions with people from a range of cultural backgrounds exposed her to different perspectives often linked to different value systems. This forced her to reflect on her own opinions and beliefs: 'I developed an understanding that there are many different views and perspectives on individual aspects and on life … I came to realise that two differing opinions could stand side by side and could both be valuable, but I didn't have to agree with both'. Awareness of the study-abroad culture also increased reflection on our own cultural identity, which resulted, to both our surprise, in an appreciation of our cultural heritage.

The increased self-awareness during the period of study abroad was the starting point for an ongoing journey of self-reflection. We both noted that we continuously challenged our beliefs about other people and put ourselves in others' shoes, creating empathy. In our reflections, we both expressed that we transferred our critical reflections and empathy to our professional life as teachers. Yue tried to change her perspective by looking at her learners' challenges from that of a foreign language learner rather than that of a native speaker: 'I completely changed my view of how to be a teacher. I need to think about how to assist New Zealand students from a foreign language learner's perspective'. Christine also indicated that her own study-abroad experience 'created an ability to relate to students who struggle living and adjusting to a different country, culture and context'. When her students struggle to express themselves, particularly their emotions and opinions, Christine can more easily empathize based on her own experience.

Resilience

Another significant development in our reflections was that we found we had become more resilient as a result of the study-abroad experience. Leaving our familiar context forced us to deal with the problems we encountered. In the process, we became aware of our thoughts, actions and emotions and developed a new skillset to cope with challenges, which resulted in a feeling of resilience and higher self-confidence. As Christine reflected, the study-abroad experience taught her what her personal strengths and her challenges were. In reflecting on the negative and positive aspects of her experience, Christine realized that she could rely on herself to find her way in new situations and that she could establish a new social network from scratch. As she concluded, 'The knowledge I have done it [overcome difficulties] before, and that I can do it again, is very reassuring!' In Yue's reflection, she became a more independent and mature adult during her study-abroad experience. Rather than seeking help from parents and friends, Yue learnt to rely on herself in those difficult times. The year abroad gave Yue a sense of confidence in adapting to new environments, which allowed her to be open to her second study-abroad experience.

Studying and living abroad enabled us to discover different options for our lives, which further influenced our career choices. Yue recalled that she discovered her interest in teacher education when she was an MLA in New Zealand. She then decided to pursue a PhD after earning her Master's degree. Christine pursued her career as a secondary-school teacher, but started to look for opportunities to become a teacher educator. Both Christine and Yue indicated that their study-abroad experience triggered a change in their career trajectories because they had built resilience and had become open to exploring other possibilities and opportunities in life.

Implications

Our duoethnographic study has provided evidence that study-abroad experiences are double-edged. Our findings suggest that the study-abroad experience can lead to negative emotions but can also have a positive long-term impact on one's personal and professional identity development. Based on our experience, we make some practical recommendations for teacher education, study-abroad program organizers and study-abroad candidates to support emotional challenges and facilitate the process of all pre-service teachers' and study-abroad participants' individual development.

Pre-departure

Study-abroad participants' adjustment to the new cultural environment could be facilitated by preparatory workshops provided by home universities. Previous study-abroad participants could be integrated into such workshops to provide authentic scenarios for potential misunderstandings, but also to share their experience and learning with pre-service teachers who do not intend to study abroad. Rather than focusing only on transmitting cultural knowledge, we suggest workshops that also include presenting candidates with scenarios or role-plays of intercultural situations to build awareness of the target culture values, but importantly also about the pre-service teachers' own cultural and individual values.

A vital part of the workshops would be to reflect individually on particular situations, but also to become aware of a variety of responses to the same situation by discussing those with members in the bigger group of pre-service teachers.

Christine and Yue recalled feeling isolated in the initial period of their study-abroad sojourn. Pre-departure workshops could provide candidates with strategies to establish social connections and relationships by building social and communication skills through a range of activities and scenarios.

We believe it is important for study-abroad participants to familiarize themselves with their host country, to be open-minded about other cultures and to be aware of a potential readjustment phase upon their return from studying abroad.

During the study abroad

Study-abroad participants cannot be completely prepared for every eventuality in the host country and intercultural learning is a continuous and dynamic process. However, we believe it is important for participants to have ongoing support during their sojourn from their home or host university to soften some of the potential challenges.

Based on our experience, social activities and networks played a significant role in helping us adjust to the new environment, so one way to support candidates is to have individually assigned 'buddies'. Those peers could assist international students to navigate social activities and/or introduce them to some local social settings, for example sports clubs, drama societies or other activities based on the students' different interests.

We both felt quite isolated and alone at the beginning of our study-abroad journey and believe a pastoral care and support person could have helped us significantly. Our recommendation is to assign ongoing pastoral care for study-abroad candidates. This could be in the form of practical support, for example with accommodation or academic issues, but also regular 'check-in' opportunities for candidates to have a sounding board and to share their experience in a small or bigger group. We also suggest that pastoral care includes encouraging study-abroad candidates to keep a regular personal self-reflection log. Ideally, the support person provides changing reflective prompts on a regular basis, for example: 'Think about the last month/week and notice/write down how you have been feeling in your academic/personal context'. 'Think about what the challenges were last week, what went really well, what made you happy?' 'Were there any situations that surprised/confused you last month?' In our opinion, such regular self-reflection raises self-awareness, helps to recognize frustrations as well as positive experiences, and ultimately supports emotional well-being. While the self-reflection log as we recommend it is not meant to be shared with anyone, it can be the springboard for discussions with others or for the 'check-in' sessions in a broader group. Anonymized logs could also be included in teacher education to discuss and analyze candidates' challenges and developments with a view to better support future school students' study-abroad experiences.

Conclusion

It is noteworthy that, despite our very different backgrounds and study-abroad contexts, we experienced very similar emotions and challenges in the different stages of our study-abroad year, which also align, at least in parts, with findings of previous studies (Jackson, 2018; Jæger & Gram, 2020). While the long-term study-abroad benefits in our case clearly were greater than the challenges during the study-abroad experience, the emotional tensions cannot be ignored and some candidates might struggle with coming out stronger 'on the other side'. We believe that every kind of support, including our recommendations above, should be provided to aid sojourners to deal with emotional and psychological aspects of their study-abroad experience.

References

Benson, P., Barkhuizen, G., Bodycott, P. and Brown, J. (2013) *Second Language Identity in Narrative of Study Abroad*. London: Palgrave Macmillan.

Breault, R.A. (2016) Emerging issues in duoethnography. *International Journal of Qualitative Studies in Education* 29 (6), 777–794.

Denzin, N.K. (2017) Critical qualitative inquiry. *Qualitative Inquiry* 23 (1), 8–16.

Isabelli-García, C., Brown, J., Plews, J. and Dewey, D. (2018) Language learning and study abroad. *Language Teaching* 51 (4), 439–484.

Jackson, J. (2018) Intervening in the intercultural learning of L2 study abroad students: From research to practice. *Language Teaching* 51 (3), 365–382.

Jæger, K. and Gram, M. (2020) Enduring not enjoying? Emotional responses to studying abroad among Danish and Chinese students. *Intercultural Education* 31 (1), 1–15.

Kimura, H. and Hayashi, B. (2019) Identity development through study abroad experiences: Storied accounts. *Studies in Second Language Learning and Teaching* 9 (3), 473–493.

Kinginger, C. (2013) Identity and language learning in study abroad. *Foreign Language Annals* 46 (3), 339–358.

Norris, J. (2008) Duoethnography. In L.M. Given (ed.) *The SAGE Encyclopedia of Qualitative Research Methods* (vol. 1) (pp. 233–236). New York: Sage.

Norris, J. and Sawyer, R. (2012) Towards a dialogic method. In J. Norris, R. Sawyer and D. Lund (eds) *Duoethnography: Dialogic Methods for Social, Health, and Educational Research* (pp. 9–40). Walnut Creek, CA: Left Coast Press.

Róg, T., Moros-Pays, Z., Wróbel, A. and Ksiek-Róg, M. (2020) Intercultural competence and L2 acquisition in the study abroad context. *Journal of Intercultural Communication* 20 (1), 76–91.

19 From ESL Student to Teacher Educator: Reflections on Transnational and Transcultural Professional Identity Development

Michael Burri

> *Little did I know that my newly acquired knowledge, pedagogical skills and freshly minted teacher identity were going to be challenged in Japan.*
>
> *My mobility of crossing boundaries and studying abroad as a transnational and transcultural individual also suggests that teacher educators should use their student teachers as resources.*

Introduction

Defined as a practitioner's perception and understanding of themselves as an educator (Murray & Christison, 2011), professional identity is seen as playing an integral role in a teacher's decision making and development (Kanno & Stuart, 2011). Professional identity construction is a complex and continuous process, with the cognitions (beliefs and knowledge), practices, and linguistic and personal background of an instructor being intricately intertwined (Aslan, 2015). My own case presented in this chapter is a reflection of this complexity. I was born on the east coast of the United States (and therefore hold a US passport) but moved to Switzerland – my parents' country of origin – when I was 4.5 years old. Because of this move across the Atlantic, my English began to deteriorate and by the age of 22, I had forgotten most of the language I spoke fluently

245

as a little boy. Bothered by this, I decided to re-learn English abroad and enrolled in a 12-week intensive English as a second language (ESL) course at a private language school in beautiful Christchurch, New Zealand. My studies led me to complete a TESOL certificate in New Zealand, and then obtain, after some initial challenges, my first teaching position in Japan. My time as an ESL student in New Zealand and as a novice (i.e. inexperienced) instructor in Japan proved critical in the formation of my personal and professional identity, while enrolling in a TESOL graduate program in Canada ultimately positioned me to understand my role as an educator better and to construct my professional identity further; eventually preparing me to become an L2 teacher educator and academic in Australia.

For the purposes of studying language and learning to teach abroad, crossing national, cultural and linguistic boundaries on multiple occasions contributed greatly to my transnational and transcultural identity. The objective of this autoethnography is, therefore, to reflect on my mobility and explore three critical time periods that have had a profound impact on the development of my professional identity from a number of perspectives and lenses, including key events, people and formative experiences while (a) studying ESL abroad in New Zealand, (b) learning to teach English in Japan, and (c) being a graduate student in Canada. I hope that the chapter not only contributes to the understanding of effective language learning, pedagogy and second language teacher education, but that it inspires fellow practitioners to make sense of, and perhaps even communicate, their own journey of studying abroad. This is, of course, a personal account, but, given that the majority of English teachers speak English as an additional language (Braine, 2010), I am sure that my sojourn will be recognized in the experiences of many multinational and multicultural practitioners in English language teaching.

Background and Data Source

I had been toying with the idea of documenting my professional trajectory. The thought of 'putting myself out there' and sharing personal information was, however, rather intimidating. A chat with Jonathan Newton over a beer at the 2nd Mekong TESOL Conference in Can Tho City (Vietnam) and then an invitation from Gary Barkhuizen to contribute this chapter, as well as reading one of his latest books on language teacher identity research (Barkhuizen, 2017), convinced me of the merits of communicating my study-abroad experiences. Narratives and personal stories are, after all, some of my favourite papers in TESOL (see, for example, Canagarajah, 2012; Casanave, 2012; McCarthy, 2020) because 'we can experience what happens in the story in a vivid manner, by mentally simulating the content of a narrative' (Martinez-Conde *et al.*, 2019: 8286).

While composing this autoethnography, I spent a considerable amount of time (re)reading my journal that I have been keeping since my departure for New Zealand in 1997. To date, the journal consists of hundreds of entries, sometimes done daily and at other times going months without writing anything. I write when I feel like writing. The initial purpose of journaling was to record my experiences of living, studying and traveling in New Zealand. After about a year of journaling in German, I switched to English with the aim of improving my English writing. As I began my teaching career and then later on during my graduate studies, the journal became an outlet to document challenges at work, insights I gained in the classroom, and new theoretical and practical knowledge I acquired while being a graduate student. At the same time, many of the commentaries continued to be interspersed with various travel entries, world events (e.g. 9/11) and personal experiences (e.g. marriage; birth of my children).

Studying ESL in New Zealand (and Deciding to Become an English Teacher)

The decision to study English abroad proved to be a monumental turning point in my life. Up to my departure for New Zealand, I had little idea of what to do in the future (I had just finished a season as a ski instructor in the Swiss Alps after quitting a full-time electromechanical engineering position). Not having slept for almost two days, I remember getting off the plane in Christchurch and feeling completely exhausted but immediately fell in love with the lush surroundings and fresh winter air (winters in Switzerland are mostly dreary, wet and cold). The fact that I was about to study abroad for the first time in my life certainly contributed to the excitement. That enthusiasm was, however, quickly dampened when I was placed in the lowest level the school offered at that time. Yet, within three months, I moved from the pre-intermediate to the upper-intermediate course. The retrieval of the language I spoke fluently as a four-year-old could, of course, be attributed to this rapid progression, but my journal entries revealed that investment and context both played a much more critical role in facilitating the process of learning English (Norton, 2013).

Having flown halfway around the world, and with my father forking out the tuition costs for my studies, my investment in learning English was considerable. The investment was also due to my desire to 'increase the value of [my] cultural capital and social power' (Darvin & Norton, 2015: 37). I viewed English as a means to connect with my American roots and considered English proficiency to be an opportunity to increase employment opportunities. From the moment I arrived in Christchurch, I began to read English books, watched English TV, and kept a vocabulary notebook (see Casanave, 2012) to record new words I came across in and outside the classroom, in my readings and in my daily interactions with people. After a few weeks, I began to understand the lyrics of songs played on the local radio station and I felt invigorated.

The local context in which I was situated also contributed significantly to my language learning. Research done in Australia has shown that ESL students often have few opportunities to use the language outside the classroom (Benson *et al.*, 2018; Chappell *et al.*, 2018; Kashiwa & Benson, 2018). For me, however, that was not an issue at all. With social media not yet existing and email use just beginning to emerge, I hardly used any Swiss-German and instead spent a great deal of time with my homestay family, to the extent that within a few weeks I became part of the family. Of particular importance was my newly formed friendship with their 17-year-old son (their other children had moved out but frequently visited with their own families). We went skiing and hiking together, had some epic table-tennis battles in the garage, and sporadically enjoyed a late-night pizza in his car. I also joined a church soccer team and got involved in a youth group. After some initial struggles with the Kiwi accent, my confidence in speaking English grew enormously over the course of a few months as a result of my frequent interactions with the host community (Cao & Newton, 2019). Importantly, parallel to my English language development, my identity began to change and be 'reproduced in social interaction' (Darvin & Norton, 2015: 37). Trying to sound like a Kiwi became a source of self-esteem (Cao & Newton, 2019), and I believed that taking on a Kiwi persona would grant me access to the community and to a desired new identity (Norton, 2013). This in turn spurred me on to continue to learn new English vocabulary and work on my pronunciation, which suggests that the processes of language learning and identity development were closely intertwined.

As my personal identity began to evolve, my professional identity also started to take shape. During the 12-week intensive English course I was taught by exceptional teachers. They were skillful and caring, and they showed genuine interest in their students and their learning. Towards the end of my studies, some of the instructors encouraged me to contemplate the possibility of becoming an English teacher. Initially I considered their suggestion to be complete madness given that I was a Swiss ESL student studying abroad, but the idea eventually began to interest me. I could envision myself as a teacher and my desire grew to emulate my instructors' practices and take care of my own students (see Lortie's, 1975, notion of apprenticeship of observation for why instructors often teach the way they were taught themselves). The irony of becoming a teacher was not lost on me, given that a few years earlier I emphatically told my parents that teaching was the worst possible job! After spending six months traveling in Australia and Japan, and another six months doing engineering work in Switzerland to save up money, I returned to Christchurch to complete a four-month TESOL Certificate program offered at the same institution at which I had been an ESL student. Doing the certificate entailed a very steep learning curve as it involved the acquisition of new knowledge and skills as well as content-specific language and vocabulary, but I was excited about the prospect of being an English teacher. Little did I know that my newly acquired knowledge, pedagogical skills and freshly minted teacher identity were going to be challenged in Japan.

Learning to Teach English in Japan

My four years as a novice instructor in Japan turned out to be pedagogically formative with several incidents playing a defining role in the development of my professional identity. In the midst of a slowing economy and widespread concerns about the potential global impact of Y2K, I flew to Japan and arrived in Osaka a week before Christmas in 1999. My mission was to find a teaching job and launch my teaching career as soon as possible. I was confident in my ability to teach English, but securing a teaching position proved to be more challenging than I had anticipated. The language and Japanese culture were foreign to me and my newly formed identity was not proving to be very useful in getting started in Japan.

A week after my arrival, a language school in the south of Osaka invited me to teach a few classes with the prospect of securing a full-time position. I gladly accepted the invitation and enjoyed the experience. A couple of days later, I received an email from the owner saying that he was unable to hire me because I did not speak American English. *Excuse me?* I held a US passport! I was confused and upset at the same time, but the next surprise was just around the corner. A few weeks later, I was offered a job (at a different school) which enabled me to obtain a work visa. With the signed contract in hand, I headed to the immigration office in Osaka only to be asked by the Japanese officer (in flawless but heavily accented English) what on earth a Swiss was doing teaching English in Japan. I instantly knew that he was not going to issue me that much coveted working visa, and so I pulled out my US passport. He looked at it briefly, stamped the document, and muttered something along the lines of 'Welcome to Japan'. If the experience before Christmas did not confuse me enough, this 10-minute encounter with the immigration officer certainly did the trick. *Who was I? Where was I really from? Did this guy have any issues with me having two passports? Did I sound any different when I showed him my US passport?*

The incident bothered me, but the excitement of being able to start teaching abroad made me forget it quickly. I taught various company classes throughout the Kansai area, large communication classes at a business college, children's English classes and several German adult classes. For the English lessons I prepared meticulously, but less so for the German ones. Teaching both languages enabled me to get valuable teaching experience and the confidence in my pedagogical ability grew steadily, but it also made me realize that teaching German was much more challenging than teaching English. My grammatical knowledge of German was limited because I had learned the language more or less incidentally during my time in Switzerland. Teaching these German classes helped me understand that being able to speak the language does not automatically equate to being an effective L2 instructor (Burri, 2015; Moussu & Llurda, 2008).

Two years later, my professional identity was disrupted once again. By now I was teaching at a private high school in Osaka. One morning in the staff room, one of the Australian teachers remarked that my English was good but not quite like a native speaker's. That stung! I had carefully crafted my professional identity over the last few years, but for that comment I was not prepared. *What is a native speaker? Who owns English? Am I belonging to a particular group of teachers? Why am I teaching English? What about my US passport?* These were some of the questions that shot through my mind. I brushed the incident off and continued to prepare for my lesson. I loved teaching and enjoyed a good rapport with my high school students. My time as an ESL student in New Zealand provided me with an insider perspective on acquiring an L2 and so I was able to empathize with some of the struggles my students encountered while learning English. Yet, that rather trivial incident in the staff room bothered me for years to come. In fact, it took me until graduate school in Canada to understand and process the incidents I experienced in Japan.

Being a Graduate Student in Canada

After four years of teaching in Japan, my wife and I moved abroad yet again. This time to Canada for her to pursue ESL studies in Calgary, and a year later I found myself enrolled in the MA TESOL program at Trinity Western University (TWU). Having never written anything formal in English, learning content and academic writing at the same time became paramount for me to excel in my graduate studies. My German proficiency helped me structurally, semantically, and to some extent lexically, but writing those final term papers was daunting and I remember wanting to give up on several occasions (my wife made sure I did not quit). As I progressed through my studies, the confidence in my writing grew gradually, but the first two semesters included a lot of pain, sweat and hard work. Much like in New Zealand, the investment in my studies was considerable. My father once again agreed to cover the tuition costs, we had a newborn at home, and my wife was on maternity leave resulting in some serious financial hardships. A careful read of my journal revealed, however, that the culture of the TESOL program influenced my professional identity development much more significantly than my investment. The professors' knowledge, integrity, patience and passion were truly inspirational. Reflecting strong academic socialization (Morita, 2004) within a sociocultural approach to second language teacher education (Johnson & Golombek, 2020), the graduate students' experiences, backgrounds and identities were seen as resources that contributed to the learning process of everyone involved in the program – including the professors. I felt valued and formed long-lasting friendships with some of my fellow graduate students.

Being Bill Acton's research assistant (RA) contributed substantially to my pedagogical and theoretical knowledge as well as to the formation of my professional identity. As part of the RA job, Bill asked me to be involved in the development of what is now known as haptic pronunciation teaching (Acton *et al.*, 2013; Burri *et al.*, 2019). Bill genuinely viewed my diverse background as an asset in helping him develop the haptic system (for an overview of the system, see Burri & Baker, 2019). Discussing with him how movement and touch could be incorporated into pronunciation instruction was an incredibly enriching and empowering experience. Looking back, I learned a lot about pronunciation instruction, and it eventually led to my very first conference presentation (Acton *et al.*, 2008). In return for being his RA, Bill agreed to supervise my MA thesis. My growing interest in second language teacher education and an ongoing desire to find my place in TESOL led me to explore the training of non-native English-speaking teachers as my thesis topic (Burri, 2018). Working on my thesis augmented my understanding that nativeness was a contested notion and that the boundary between a native and non-native speaker was blurry at best (see Braine, 2010; Huang, 2014; Mahboob, 2010; Medgyes, 1992). These insights helped me process and better comprehend the events I encountered in Japan a few year earlier, and they also nurtured in me a positive view of myself as being a legitimate member of the TESOL community. As such, my graduate studies in Canada profoundly shaped my professional identity, and they prepared me for five years of English for Academic Purposes (EAP) teaching at a postsecondary institution in Vancouver, doctoral studies in Australia, and a subsequent academic position as an L2 teacher educator at my current institution.

Implications for Educators

As the three critical time periods have shown, learning language and learning to teach language abroad does not take place in a vacuum. The different contexts in which I was situated (Ben Said & Shegar, 2013) and the people I met along the way, as well as the reciprocal relationship between my developing beliefs, knowledge and emotions, played an important role in constructing my professional identity (Barcelos, 2015). At times I felt hurt, overwhelmed and inadequate; at other times, I was ecstatic and euphoric about learning English in New Zealand and then learning to teach the language in Japan and in Canada. The point, however, is that this dynamic interplay of a number of internal and external factors within a social ecosystem (Cao & Newton, 2019) has been essential in the development of my professional identity.

Thinking about my own journey of living, studying and working abroad, educators should view their students as multilinguals and multicultural beings with prior learning experiences and a fluid identity. Educators should also keep in mind that language learning and identity construction occur at the same time, and the process often includes struggles, tension and positive as well as negative emotions (Dewaele, 2020; Norton, 2000). Having composed this autoethnography leads me to suggest that novice transcultural and transnational instructors are particularly well suited to empathize with their learners, but their nonlinear and complex identity transformation from imagined to practicing teachers (Jiang *et al.*, 2021) may make them particularly susceptible to factors disrupting the process of professional identity formation, especially if they study or learn to teach abroad in a culturally unfamiliar environment. The incidents in Japan would probably have bothered me less if I had been a more experienced and more educated instructor and therefore more secure in my identity as an English teacher.

My mobility of crossing boundaries and studying abroad as a transnational and transcultural individual also suggests that teacher educators should use their student teachers as resources. This is not a new proposition, but as I personally experienced during my graduate studies at Trinity Western University in Canada, viewing students 'as valuable intellectual and cultural resources and [giving] their unique contributions adequate legitimacy' (Morita, 2004: 598) contributes greatly to prospective teachers' identity formation, their sense of self and their preparation for future teaching endeavors. Now as a teacher educator myself, I often build in time for students to discuss their experiences and thoughts about issues such as discrimination and discriminatory hiring practices, native-speakerism, World Englishes, linguistic imperialism, as well as policy, curriculum and testing constraints. Stories are insightful and empowering (Barkhuizen, 2015) and they allow educators to understand their students' background and to attain insights into their potentially complex life trajectories and change processes that they are undergoing while becoming educators themselves. In the same vein, and with the aim of challenging the status quo and increasing my students' awareness of some of the challenges they may encounter upon the completion of their graduate studies, I occasionally share my own experiences I have had since embarking on that plane trip to study ESL in New Zealand. This not only creates a climate of trust, respect and empathy, as my teachers in New Zealand and my professors did in Canada, but it enables teacher educators to tailor course content to their students' needs and interests. Also, following Bill Acton's model of making student teachers feel valued and asking them to co-present at conferences is empowering and can strengthen their beliefs that they have something positive to contribute to the profession, maximizing their learning potential and subsequent professional identity development.

Creating this type of learning context resonates with Johnson and Golombek's (2020) advocacy for teacher education to encapsulate a socio-cultural approach. That is, the individual's historical background and lived experiences must be taken into account to meet student teachers' diverse needs, which, in turn, prepares them for future teaching contexts. My journey of studying ESL and becoming an L2 teacher abroad suggests that transnational and transcultural teacher educators are in a strong position to follow Johnson and Golombek's proposition. Their professional identity allows them to empathize with their students' needs and challenges, and, as a result, knowledge is not just transmitted but both parties are actively involved in the process of student teachers' professional identity construction and in deep and meaningful learning of subject content. This creates a learning environment in which the native/non-native label is irrelevant and the complex, diverse and evolving identities of student teachers is viewed as a strength (Faez, 2011; Kamhi-Stein, 2014).

References

Acton, W., Baker, A.A. and Burri, M. (2008) *Haptic Approaches to English Intonation Instruction*, 42nd Annual TESOL Convention, New York, United States.

Acton, W., Baker, A.A., Burri, M. and Teaman, B. (2013) Preliminaries to haptic-integrated pronunciation instruction. In J. Levis and K. LeVelle (eds) *Proceedings of the 4th Pronunciation in Second Language Learning and Teaching Conference* (pp. 234–244). Vancouver, BC, Canada.

Aslan, E. (2015) When the native is also a non-native: 'Retrodicting' the complexity of language teacher cognition. *The Canadian Modern Language Review* 71 (3), 244–269.

Barcelos, A.M.F. (2015) Unveiling the relationship between language learning beliefs, emotions, and identities. *Studies in Second Language Learning and Teaching* 5 (2), 301–325.

Barkhuizen, G. (2015) Narrative inquiry. In B. Paltridge and A. Phakiti (eds) *Research Methods in Applied Linguistics: A Practical Resource* (pp. 169–185). New York: Bloomsbury.

Barkhuizen, G. (ed.) (2017) *Reflections on Language Teacher Identity Research*. New York: Routledge.

Ben Said, S. and Shegar, C. (2013) Compliance, negotiation, and resistance in teachers' spatial construction of professional identities. In S. Ben Said and L. Zhang (eds) *Language Teachers and Teaching: Global Perspectives, Local Initiatives* (pp. 273–315). New York: Routledge.

Benson, P., Chappell, P. and Yates, L. (2018) A day in the life: Mapping international students' language learning environments in multilingual Sydney. *Australian Journal of Applied Linguistics* 1 (1), 20–32.

Braine, G. (2010) *Nonnative Speaker English Teachers: Research, Pedagogy, and Professional Growth*. New York: Routledge.

Burri, M. (2015) Student teachers' cognition about L2 pronunciation instruction: A case study. *Australian Journal of Teacher Education* 40 (10), 66–87.

Burri, M. (2018) Empowering nonnative-English-speaking teachers in primary school contexts: An ethnographic case study. *TESOL Journal* 9 (1), 185–202.

Burri, M. and Baker, A. (2019) 'I never imagined' pronunciation as 'such an interesting thing': Student teacher perception of innovative practices. *International Journal of Applied Linguistics* 29 (1), 95–108.

Burri, M., Baker, A. and Acton, W. (2019) Proposing a haptic approach to facilitating L2 learners' pragmatic competence. *Humanising Language Teaching* 3. http://hltmag. ng3.devwebsite.co.uk/june19/proposing-a-haptic-approach (accessed February 22, 2021).

Canagarajah, S.A. (2012) Teacher development in a global profession: An autoethnography. *TESOL Quarterly* 46 (2), 258–279.

Cao, Z. and Newton, J. (2019) Identity construction and language investment by three tertiary level Chinese study abroad learners in New Zealand. *New Zealand Studies in Applied Linguistics* 25 (1), 1–18.

Casanave, C.P. (2012) Diary of a dabbler: Ecological influences on an EFL teacher's efforts to study Japanese informally. *TESOL Quarterly* 46 (4), 642–670.

Chappell, P., Benson, P. and Yates, L. (2018) ELICOS students' out-of-class language learning experiences: An emerging research agenda. *English Australia Journal* 33 (2), 43–48.

Darvin, R. and Norton, B. (2015) Identity and a model of investment in applied linguistics. *Annual Review of Applied Linguistics* 35, 36–56.

Dewaele, J.-M. (2020) The emotional rollercoaster ride of foreign language learners and teachers: Sources and interactions of classroom emotions. In M. Simons and T.F.H. Smits (eds) *Language Education and Emotions: Research into Emotions and Language Learners, Language Teachers and Educational Processes* (pp. 205–220). London: Routledge.

Faez, F. (2011) Reconceptualizing the native/nonnative speaker dichotomy. *Journal of Language, Identity & Education* 10 (4), 231–249.

Huang, I. (2014) Contextualizing teacher identity of non-native-English speakers in U.S. secondary ESL classrooms: A Bakhtinian perspective. *Linguistics and Education* 25, 119–128.

Jiang, L., Yuan, K. and Yu, S. (2021) Transitioning from pre-service to novice: A study on Macau EFL teachers' identity change. *The Asia-Pacific Education Researcher* 30, 11–21.

Johnson, K.E. and Golombek, P.R. (2020) Informing and transforming language teacher education pedagogy. *Language Teaching Research* 24 (1), 116–127.

Kamhi-Stein, L.D. (2014) Non-native English-speaking teachers in the profession. In M. Celce-Murcia, D. Brinton and M.A. Snow (eds) *Teaching English as a Second or Foreign language* (4th edn) (pp. 586–600). Boston: National Geographic Learning/ Heinle Cengage Learning.

Kanno, Y. and Stuart, C. (2011) Learning to become a second language teacher: Identities-in-practice. *The Modern Language Journal* 95 (2), 236–252.

Kashiwa, M. and Benson, P. (2018) A road and a forest: Conceptions of in-class and out-of-class learning in the transition to study abroad. *TESOL Quarterly* 52 (4), 725–747.

Lortie, D. (1975) *Schoolteacher: A Sociological Study.* Chicago: University of Chicago Press.

Mahboob, A. (ed.) (2010) *The NNEST Lens: Non Native English Speakers in TESOL.* Newcastle upon Tyne: Cambridge Scholars Press.

Martinez-Conde, S., Alexander, R.G., Blum, D., Britton, N., Lipska, B.K., Quirk, G.J., Swiss, J.I., Willems, R.M. and Macknik, S.L. (2019) The storytelling brain: How neuroscience stories help bridge the gap between research and society. *Journal of Neuroscience* 39 (42), 8285–8290.

McCarthy, M. (2020) Fifty-five years and counting: A half-century of getting it half-right? *Language Teaching* 54 (3), 1–12. https://doi.org/10.1017/S0261444820000075

Medgyes, P. (1992) Native or non-native: Who's worth more? *ELT Journal* 46 (4), 340–349.

Morita, N. (2004) Negotiating participation and identity in second language academic communities. *TESOL Quarterly* 38 (4), 573–603.

Moussu, L. and Llurda, E. (2008) Non-native English-speaking English language teachers: History and research. *Language Teaching* 41 (3), 315–348.

Murray, D.E. and Christison, M.A. (2011) *What English Language Teachers Need to Know* (vol. 1). New York: Routledge.

Norton, B. (2000) *Identity and Language Learning: Gender, Ethnicity and Educational Change*. London: Longman/Pearson Education.

Norton, B. (2013) *Identity and Language Learning: Extending the Conversation* (2nd edn). Bristol: Multilingual Matters.

20 Transformative Learning and Professionalization through Uncertainty? A Case Study of Pre-Service Language Teachers During a STIE

Anja Wilken and Andreas Bonnet

Teacher professionalism can be defined as possessing functional implicit knowledge and the reflective and emotional abilities to deal with uncertainty and disorienting dilemmas. From its very structure, STIEs have the potential to provide these through experiences that foster transformative learning.

'I was kind of in shock ... because it's it should really should not be about you know thirty students in one classroom and the teacher said "you know this happened this way this happened that way this happened this way", and then "this is the result of it"'. He criticizes this lecturing style based on the theoretical concepts and didactical approaches he is familiar with. Even from this 'negative' example of teaching, he derives his benefit.

Introduction

Language, cultural and aesthetic learning are highly individual and complex processes. Therefore, dealing with the respective uncertainty is a key challenge for foreign language teachers. We theorize in this chapter that a person's dealing with uncertainty is determined by implicit knowledge, shaped by one's biographical experiences. Consequently, successful teacher education needs to impact on this knowledge. We believe that study abroad does this by challenging students' taken-for-granted beliefs and

256

thus initiating transformative learning. This is the essence of our Student Exchange Program (StEP), which offers teach-abroad stays accompanied by academic coursework. This chapter looks at how language teachers in this program experience disruptions and related uncertainty, how they make sense of this, and whether this contributes to their professionalization. Current study-abroad research mainly focuses on explicit knowledge, documents personal growth, language and communication skills, intercultural competences, empathy, dealing with stereotypes, professional competences (Cushner, 2007), and an increased tolerance of ambiguity (Mikulec, 2019). We will expand on this research by focusing on transformative learning and the reconstruction of implicit knowledge.

Student Exchange Program (StEP)

The STIE (short-term international experience) of our study is a teach-abroad program for pre-service teachers that connects the Universität Hamburg and the University of North Carolina at Chapel Hill. Each year 10–12 students from either side participate in the program. About six months before departure to the United States, four seminar sessions provide the German teachers with knowledge about the target country and its school system, and include intercultural orientation and methods of inquiry. During the four-week sojourn, pre-service teachers stay in host families and meet their 'buddy' from the partner university. Participants job-shadow a mentor-teacher, observe and teach classes, and visit special schools (e.g. charter or independent). Their experiences are discussed and reflected upon in weekly seminars.

Once back home, students debrief in a follow-up meeting, before the American buddies come to Hamburg for an identical return visit. The program contains all factors identified by Chwialkowska (2020), namely, academic coursework and cultural immersion, to balance disorienting experiences and supportive interaction. By providing encounters with the unknown, the program echoes a pedagogy of discomfort (Zembylas & McGlynn, 2012), although application and participation are voluntary.

Theoretical Framework

Our research looks at study abroad as part of becoming a foreign language teacher. We conceptualize teacher growth as professionalization and will explain what roles uncertainty and transformative learning play in this development.

Becoming a foreign language teacher

Being a teacher means making myriads of decisions every day. Consequently, teachers need a broad and deep knowledge base. The discourse on teacher knowledge is diverse (see Munby *et al.*, 2001), but there are two overarching rationales. In a top-down approach, teachers are expected to administer set curricula or even scripted instruction based on explicit knowledge; teacher education means acquiring explicit knowledge and training strategies. In contrast to this, a bottom-up model considers schools to be places of transformative learning, which allows for students to pursue individual and collaborative goals and learning trajectories; teacher education means providing opportunities for teachers to become *reflective practitioners*, making their own decisions by moving flexibly between knowledge-in-action, reflection-in-action and reflection-on-action (Schön, 1983).

Both approaches are evident in applied linguistics. Up to the end of the 1970s, the 'process/product paradigm' (Freeman & Johnson, 1998) modeled teacher expertise as putting explicit knowledge directly into practice. Increasingly, constructivist notions of learning were echoed by reflective approaches to teacher knowledge (Freeman, 2002), and critical approaches became influential (Rodgers & Scott, 2008). This sociocultural turn shaped concepts such as 'identity' and 'investment' as sociological categories, which highlight the situatedness and biographicity of knowledge both with respect to K-12 students (Barkhuizen, 2004; Darvin & Norton, 2015) and to teachers (Bonnet & Breidbach, 2017; Cheung *et al.*, 2015). Today, the applied linguistic discourse on teacher identity embraces the notion of reflective practice with its focus on implicit knowledge.

Teacher professionalism: Uncertainty, reflection, habitus

The respective sociological point of view sees professions as:

> the structural, occupational and institutional arrangements for dealing with work associated with the uncertainties of modern lives in risk societies. Professionals are extensively engaged in dealing with risk, with risk assessment and, through the use of expert knowledge, enabling customers and clients to deal with uncertainty. (Evetts, 2003: 397)

Uncertainty is caused by the antinomic structure of teaching; that is, the permanent need for teachers to balance contradictory principles and conflicting norms. For example, teachers need to balance the norm of standardized testing with the norm of individualized and adaptive teaching. Professionalization research assumes that the navigation of uncertainty is based on teachers' implicit knowledge, conceptualized as 'tacit knowledge' (Polanyi, 2009 [1966]), 'knowledge-in-action' (Schön, 1983) or 'habitus' (Helsper, 2018). In what follows we theorize both uncertainty and implicit teacher knowledge, starting with the latter.[1]

Teacher preparation involves an exceptionally long period of socialization (Lortie, 2002). As students, they learn 'to anticipate the teacher's probable reaction to [their] behavior. This requires that the student projects himself into the teacher's position' (Lortie, 2002: 62). In other words, acquiring their student habitus, K-12 students also develop images of and attitudes towards the kind of teacher that matches or contradicts this habitus. This projection is the nucleus of future teachers' knowledge and is subjected to the influence of the fields of teacher education; namely, university and schools involved in internships or probationary teaching.

Professionalization as transformative learning and the potential of STIE

In this sense, the transition from student to teacher involves a change of one's relation to self, others, and the world, which is how Koller (2012) defines his concept of transformative learning; that is, transformative *Bildung*. Thus, becoming a teacher is by definition a process of transformative learning. This is underlined by numerous studies that show how the professionalization as a teacher creates the necessity to rethink, re-evaluate or reframe former practice (e.g. Cammarata, 2010; Hunt, 2011) or 'professional integrity' (Moate, 2011: 343), which can be experienced as an intense 'wrestle' (Palmer & Snodgrass Rangel, 2011).

Combining the theories of reflective practice and transformative learning, being a teacher means acting on one's knowledge-in-action as long as there are no serious problems. If this flow is interrupted, however, teachers need to reassess the situation by reflection-in-action (Schön, 1983), which questions 'the assumptional structure of knowing-in-action' (1983: 28), and 'serves to reshape what we are doing while we are doing it' (1983: 26). This reflection remains unconscious, that is, on the level of implicit knowledge. It is a 'practical reflection' (Bohnsack, 2020), which happens within the boundaries of the habitus and reframes the situation without being cognizant of it. In this case, the interruption is hardly disorienting. Only if the flow of action cannot be re-established, if the disruption has a disorienting quality, subsequent reflection-on-action, that is, 'theoretical reflection' (Bohnsack, 2020), will take place. It involves explicit knowledge, the attempt to reflect on the actual framing of the situation and thus aims at reflecting on one's habitus. If the disorientation remains, the individual may undergo a process of actual change in terms of their relation to self, others, and the world, which means that transformative learning/ *Bildung* is initiated.

In this sense, teacher professionalism can be defined as possessing functional implicit knowledge and the reflective and emotional abilities to deal with uncertainty and disorienting dilemmas. From its very structure, STIEs have the potential to provide these and thus foster transformative learning (Senyshyn, 2018). Students enter foreign social fields and encounter various habitus different from their own, which provides disorienting experiences that necessitate both practical and theoretical reflections and may ultimately lead to transformations of the students' relation to self, others, and the world. On the basis of this theoretical framework, we use teacher professionalization, the notion of the reflective practitioner and the model of transformative learning/*Bildung* as a lens through which to investigate what kinds of uncertainty student teachers encounter, how and to what extent they experience disorientation, what modes of sense-making they use, and to what extent they might even show traces of transformation of their relations to self, others, and the world.

Research Design

The data was collected using episodic interviews (60–80 minutes) which tapped both explicit and implicit knowledge by triggering argumentative answers as well as narrative episodes. All conversations were audio-recorded, transcribed and anonymized. The sample consists of two cohorts of exchange students from Germany:

(1) Twelve students from 2018 were interviewed during their stay in the United States. Two of these interviewees (called Lauren and Marleen) were selected due to maximal contrasts.
(2) Four students from 2020 (Alper, Rita, Karina, Clara), who faced an early end to their stay in the United States due to Covid-19, volunteered for interviews conducted five months after their return to Germany.

Following an interpretative approach, we use the documentary method (Bohnsack *et al.*, 2010). This method aims at reconstructing the perspective from which a situation is experienced by shifting the analytical focus from content ('what' is said) to the structure of the text ('how'). It is based epistemologically on the sociology of knowledge and shares the key assumption of symbolic interactionist theory on humans acting on the basis of their implicit knowledge. Documents are analysed sequentially, and the interpretation gradually proceeds from the textual surface (*formulative* interpretation, which paraphrases the content) to its deep structure (*reflecting* interpretation, which looks, among others, at syntactical, lexical and semantic features of the text). In the following part, we emphasize (a) how and in which field the pre-service language teachers experienced uncertainty, and (b) the different ways they processed it.

Findings on the Experience of Uncertainty

In the cases of Lauren and Marleen from 2018, we can identify the following key dimensions for systematically analyzing ways of dealing with uncertainty and disorientation during a STIE: identity position, mode of experience, mode of sense-making, and mode of reflection (see Table 20.1). Whereas Lauren makes experiences as an observer and from a teacher's perspective, compares the United States with Germany on a

Table 20.1 Overview of all cases and their characteristics along the key dimensions

	Identity position/ role	Mode of experience	Mode of sense-making	Mode of reflection
Lauren	Teacher	Observing	Thinking (on her own)	Circular/stabilizing/ simplifying and generalizing
Marleen	Student	Immersing	Interaction (with family)	Expansive (broadening the frame of references by adding voices)
Karina	Student	Observing	Thinking (on her own)	Circular/stabilizing/ simplifying and generalizing
Rita	Student/ (observer)/ guest	Observing	Writing (on her own)	Collecting (not really reflecting or processing)
Alper	Teacher	Immersing	Thinking/ differentiating/taking various perspectives (mainly on his own)	Expansive (broadening the frame of references by comparison of various/ different cases/situations)
Clara	Teacher	Immersing	Interaction (with teachers and students)	Expansive (broadening the frame of references by adding voices and own experiences)

professional level (teachers' work conditions) and generalizes her observations, Marleen immerses herself in the new environment as a student, attempts sense-making by interacting with locals, and compares her experiences with an assumed 'American normalcy' on a personal level.

In contrast to 2018, the data from 2020 clearly shows uncertainty and disruptions caused by Covid-19 on the personal level and on the program level, with explicit questions evident such as 'how to get back and will there be flights?' (Alper). In the following, we will present two strongly contrasting cases from the 2020 sample. Whereas Rita provides an example of a case whose experience abroad is overshadowed by the disruption, Alper represents pre-service teachers who managed to separate the uncertainty caused by the pandemic on a personal level from their experiences on a professional level during the program.

Rita, *the distanced observer*: Intense disruptions overshadow the STIE

Rita participated in the exchange in the role of a student, who sought comprehension (e.g. of the numerous abbreviations used in her school) without attracting attention. The first example she mentions is the conversations in the evenings with her host family about politics and other topics. Her interview is framed with references to her host family. Instead of immersing herself in family life, she takes the role of a distanced observer: 'I'm sort of being a guest [...] I'm uhm not there to to impose my my opinions and sort of positions on to them but rather sort of tryin' to [...] get a sense of where they stand'. Her outsider position is emphasized by making comparisons with other exchange students who were frequently driven to places by their hosts, as well as by not addressing difficult situations, for example, when not being asked to have dinner together or not being sure whether she was expected to spend time with the host family's children. Therefore, by avoiding negotiating the disorientation she experienced, she missed the opportunity of interactional sense-making and intercultural learning.

This is also significant for the way she dealt with her ultimate disruption: Covid-19. She talks in detail about a situation where she had been suspected of being Covid-19 positive and had to visit a 'mini-clinic'. This not only overshadowed her relationship with her hosts, who didn't drive her to the clinic, but the entire exchange program, because 'It scared me', and prevented her from 'really get[ting] involved' at school. This becomes evident when she talks about school and focuses on the way her mentor talks about the virus rather than on class content. Interestingly, Rita marks the different behavior of her mentor dealing with the virus in front of students and among teacher colleagues:

> I mean she she she meant- she didn't mean any harm by that, she she didn't wanna she didn't want to freak me out and but but she was obviously scared as well sort = of on the- on a grown up level of- sort = of talking, fear was much more openly communicated than it was in the presence of the children.

In this passage, the expression 'freak out' becomes the focal metaphor of her experience. It conceptualizes her school placement as dominated by anxiety. Furthermore, it depicts the mentor as no longer being a superior and helpful facilitator, but a fellow victim of the situation. She depicts neither hosts nor her mentor as scaffolds/supporters for sense-making, but as sources of disorientation and even discomfort. Still, the exchange wasn't fruitless. She states that she started her sojourn with several questions and came back with even more. This emphasizes her mode of uptaking information instead of comparing and analyzing it. Rita's extensive writing in her reflective journal shows that sense-making went on, even if in the self-referential mode of reflection of keeping these thoughts to herself. Thus, by avoiding involvement in extensive negotiations of meaning, Rita limits the intensity of disorientation. This indicates (a) her role as a student or even researcher, and (b) the coronavirus being the lens through which all her experiences were made.

Alper, *the immersed teacher*: Separating disruptive experiences and professional benefit

Whereas Rita participates in the exchange from an observer's perspective, Alper steps into the teachers' shoes. He considers the purpose of the exchange to 'improve myself academically' and participates 'not just for fun'. He also states that gaining insight into the work conditions of teachers in the United States (comparable to Lauren) made him change his mind about becoming a teacher in the United States, calling this a 'life-changing decision'.

Nevertheless, the Covid-19 situation emerges in Alper's first utterance about the program:

> Uh unfortunately what comes to my mind first is (.) the kind of dilemma we had at the end because uh at the end it was it was it was really a shock for us to find a way to get out of there as fast as possible.

He evaluates this first thought negatively ('unfortunately'), although he benefits and learns from the sojourn on a professional level. Talking about Covid-19, he alternates between the 'shock' experienced by the exchange group ('we') and his personal state of being 'afraid'. Furthermore, he uses the metaphoric expression of a 'dark space', which conveys uncertainty:

> I was very uhm (.) a- a little bit afraid also of [...] how to get back and will there be flights and [...] we were (.) constantly uhm in this kind of dark space not knowing the airlines not knowing the you = know (..) the politics who are they going to let in [...] we didn't had any information or clues or everything.

The disruption hit Alper more on the organizational and personal level, for example, the group dynamics and 'panic' within the group. His stammering and more frequent errors in his otherwise eloquent statements indicate uncertainty:

> more and more students became more panic, you = know they were saying <We gotta go now.> <I already rescheduled my flight.> <I'm leaving tomorrow.> So that was-that was a very dynamic situation [...] I did not really panic like that but I I I knew that I had to make a decision (.) uhm but I just didn't know what to do and when to do.

Apart from this and even after explicitly asking him if he recalled situations in which he felt discomfort or disorientation, Alper mentions feeling welcome and 'at ease' in all parts of the program, especially in school. He depicts his most 'valuable' experience as follows:

> and so when we talked about me teaching a lesson, (.) you = know we were very- there was a very communicative and interactive uh discussion [...] I was very free in organizing uhm the materials and the the subject and (.) you = know so there was a time where I- I I really felt it was about me, it was about me getting my experience in an American classroom (.) teaching, [...] I was in a in a space where I could move freely.

The 'shock' and the oblivious 'dark space' (see above) contrasts with 'a space where I could move freely', when Alper talks about his lesson in detail. Additionally, the lesson was planned as a 'free [...] discussion' about students' narratives in the sensitive field of racism. The considerable planning risk he takes underlines his confidence in embracing uncertainty, even if the outcome is unknown.

However, on the professional level, he encounters a 'misunderstanding' about a history teacher who was recommended to him as 'the history guy'. The way he explains the teacher's style ('doing a a monologue, (.) [...] not showing like primary sources') contradicts Alper's norms of problem-centered teaching, which he expresses from the identity position of 'a history teacher':

> I always- for me as a history teacher for me I think it's important to to use primary sources and to make sure everything is you = know is relative, we always have y = know kinda question things.

In the following detailed episode, his disorientation is marked again by being 'in shock':

> I was kind = of in shock (.) [...] because it's it should really should not be about (.) you = know thirty students in one classroom and the teacher said <you = know this happened this way this happened that way this happened this way,> and then <this is the result of it>.

He criticizes this lecturing style based on the theoretical concepts and didactical approaches he is familiar with. Even from this 'negative' example of teaching, he derives his benefit: 'it's important [...] Because now I can see you = know there are different approaches'. Furthermore, he analyzes this situation from various perspectives: 'I saw all the students were very interested (.) the the exams went very well, [...] but the methods, you = know from the didactics or like uh university standpoint [...] could = have been better'.

Modes of sense-making and reflection

After having presented the cases of Alper and Rita in some detail, we now add Karina and Clara summatively to point out contrasts in the sample with respect to their modes of reflection and sense-making (see Table 20.1 above, which provides an overview of the results).

In the sample, the mode of individual sense-making of Rita and Lauren contrasts with Marleen and Clara, who make sense interactively. Alper's processing by weighing his experiences against several perspectives differs from all the other cases. He compares a teaching approach not only to the theoretical point of view he brought from Germany, but also to the approach of his mentor in the United States. Although Karina includes a theoretical perspective too, she quickly draws generalizing conclusions and thus stabilizes her us–them perception:

> when we met [...] [name] [...] Who was like <yeah it's good to see how inclusion works> [...]and I didn't see it working. I think that's like something that is typical for [...] the Americans [...] present themselves <oh yeah this we look and we are great> (.) but actually they don't see that they aren't in a way even though they have lot of more research.

Starting out with her conclusion, Karina forces her theoretical understanding (based on a German discourse) onto practices in the United States. Therefore, even experiences of a disorienting quality do not make Karina review her conclusions. This sharply contrasts with Alper's differentiating approach of making 'intra-American' comparisons.

Another special mode of sense-making is Clara's interaction combined with an expansive mode of reflection (see also Marleen and Alper). She takes into account the teachers' perspective in the context of Covid-19 (see Rita), but is also attentive to the students: 'the students started to freak out, (.) and [...] I was thinking <oh. Maybe there is something happening here that I didn't notice before >'. Furthermore, unlike her peers, she shadows a high school student for a day, and thus gains new perspectives. This becomes evident in the following episode of Clara being uncertain about her level of English.

> I thought it's also a process of learning to show them that even when [...] you learned the language for a long time [...] you always make mistakes and it's not it's not the worst thing in the world because you [...] learn from it and (.) you just go on.

In the course of the sojourn, by switching perspectives, she develops a positive attitude towards making mistakes as a gateway to competence acquisition. Looking at all six cases, the patterns of characteristics in the key dimensions indicate the potential for a complex typology.

Discussion and Practical Implications

The data shows that in both studies (2018 and 2020) the study-abroad school experience is a source of professional disorientation. While this can lead to productive sense-making (Alper, Clara), it can also cause discomfort and block further learning (Rita). Similar to Senyshyn (2018), there is no evidence for complete transformation in the sense of Mezirow (2000) or Koller (2012). However, the students experienced disorienting dilemmas and ways of processing them, which shows that transformative learning and thus professionalization can be initiated by certain elements of study-abroad programs. Furthermore, our results demonstrate that disruptions cause students to notice and focus on uncertainty, which they usually manage to avoid by pursuing cumulative ways of learning, such as collecting information.

Different ways of dealing with disruption (being paralyzed or taking it as a prompt for decision-making) thus call for an analysis of personal causes for these differences, which may include factors such as individual tolerance of ambiguity. Interestingly, those who avoid uncertainty express the need for more reflection and communication (e.g. in seminars). This type of sojourner clearly needs scaffolding to transcend the mode of individual reflection towards transformative learning and to not limit the effects of the exchange if emotional discomfort occurs (see e.g. Rita).

We consider it a key result that the immersing mode of experience concurs with an interactional mode of sense-making. This leads to a mode of reflection we call *expansive*, because it bears the potential for transformative learning as stereotypes and preconceptions are productively challenged. Also, the more different practices within the same field (e.g. classrooms) were encountered, the more substantially existing generalizations were questioned and abandoned. These results clearly suggest intense stays of several weeks framed by academic coursework facilitated the processing of experiences and fostered sense-making and reflection.

As practical implications we firstly suggest that future project teams develop reflection seminars that provide scaffolds for questioning and reviewing the students' observations and conclusions in interactional settings (see also Williams, 2005). Secondly, the return visit (i.e. the exchange) should be emphasized. From evaluations of previous cohorts we know that greater depth of reflection can be reached when the previous observers become objects of stereotyping and generalizations themselves, and their own practice is questioned through the others' perspectives.

For future research, we suggest to triangulate during- and post-sojourn data, because the former provides insight into the students' acts of processing their freshly-made experiences and their emotional responses, while the latter reveals outcomes of reflection and sense-making processes. Analyzing additional group discussions will give insight into interactional modes of reflection.

Our STIE study has shown that participants raised questions, made observations and processed their experiences. Although their dimensions for reflection differ (stereotypes, pedagogical content knowledge, intra-country comparisons), they commonly focus on norms and taken-for-granted perspectives. However, exchange programs and their academic coursework have the potential to empower pre-service teachers to reflect on and challenge their pre-conceived ideas about language, culture and teaching and thus experience transformative learning.

Notes

(1) There are two more aspects of teacher professionalism to consider, which we would like to mention only briefly because they do not immediately help theorize the professionalizing potential of study abroad. While implicit knowledge is the kind of knowledge that predominantly initiates and largely guides teachers' actions, they also rely on explicit knowledge, which includes facts and theories, for example content knowledge and pedagogical content knowledge (Shulman, 2004), as well as methodological or planning skills, which can be verbally expressed. The second aspect is that both types of knowledge are situated in a 'context shared by a community of practitioners' (Schön, 1983: 33).

References

Barkhuizen, G. (2004) Social influences on language learning. In A. Davies and C. Elder (eds) *The Handbook of Applied Linguistics* (pp. 552–575). Malden, MA: Blackwell.

Bohnsack, R. (2020) *Professionalisierung in Praxeologischer Perspektive*. Opladen: Verlag Barbara Budrich.

Bohnsack, R., Pfaff, N. and Weller, W. (eds) (2010) *Qualitative Analysis and Documentary Method in International Educational Research*. Opladen: Barbara Budrich.

Bonnet, A. and Breidbach, S. (2017) CLIL teachers' professionalization: Between explicit knowledge and professional identity. In A. Llinares and T. Morton (eds) *Applied Linguistics Perspectives on CLIL* (pp. 269–285). Amsterdam: John Benjamins.

Cammarata, L. (2010) Foreign language teachers' struggle to learn Content-Based Instruction. *L2 Journal* 2, 89–118.

Cheung, Y.L., Ben Said, S. and Park, K. (eds) (2015) *Advances and Current Trends in Language Teacher Identity Research*. New York: Routledge.

Chwialkowska, A. (2020) Maximizing cross-cultural learning from exchange study abroad programs: Transformative learning theory. *Journal of Studies in International Education* 24 (5), 535–554.

Cushner, K. (2007) The role of experience in the making of internationally-minded teachers. *Teacher Education Quaterly* 34 (1), 27–39.

Darvin, R. and Norton, B. (2015) Identity and a model of investment in applied linguistics. *Annual Review of Applied Linguistics* 35, 36–56.

Evetts, J. (2003) The sociological analysis of professionalism: Occupational change in the modern world. *International Sociology* 18 (2), 395–415.

Freeman, D. (2002) The hidden side of the work: Teacher knowledge and learning to teach. A perspective from North American educational research on teacher education in English language teaching. *Language Teaching* 35 (1), 1–13.

Freeman, D. and Johnson, K.E. (1998) Reconceptualizing the knowledge-base of language teacher education. *TESOL Quarterly* 32 (3), 397–417.

Helsper, W. (2018) Lehrerhabitus. Lehrer zwischen Herkunft, Milieu und Profession. In A. Paseka, M. Keller-Schneider and A. Combe (eds) *Ungewissheit als Herausforderung für Pädagogisches Handeln* (pp. 105–140). Wiesbaden: Springer VS.

Hunt, M. (2011) UK teachers' and learners' experiences of CLIL resulting from the EU-funded project ECLILT. *Latin American Journal of Content and Language Integrated Learning* 4 (1), 27–39.

Koller, H.-C. (2012) *Bildung anders denken. Einführung in die Theorie transformatorischer Bildungsprozesse*. Stuttgart: Kohlhammer.

Lortie, D.C. (2002) *Schoolteacher: A Sociological Study* (2nd edn). Chicago: University of Chicago Press.

Mezirow, J. (2000) Learning to think like an adult: Core concepts of transformation theory. In J. Mezirow (ed.) *Learning as Transformation* (pp. 265–275). San Francisco, CA: Jossey-Bass.

Mikulec, E. (2019) Short-term study abroad for pre-service teachers: Personal and professional growth in Brighton, England. *ij-sotl* 13 (1), 1–12.

Moate, J. M. (2011) The impact of foreign language mediated teaching on teachers' sense of professional integrity in the CLIL classroom. *European Journal of Teacher Education* 34 (3), 333–346.

Munby, H., Russell, T. and Martin, A.K. (2001) Teachers' knowledge and how it develops. In V. Richardson (ed.) *Handbook of Research on Teaching* (pp. 877–904). Washington: AERA.

Palmer, D. and Snodgrass Rangel, V. (2011) High stakes accountability and policy implementation: Teacher decision making in bilingual classrooms in Texas. *Educational Policy* 25 (4), 614–647.

Polanyi, M. (2009 [1966]) *The Tacit Dimension*. Chicago: University of Chicago Press.

Rodgers, C.R. and Scott, K.H. (2008) The development of the personal self and professional identity in learning to teach. In M. Cochran-Smith, S. Feiman-Nemser and D.J. McIntyre (eds) *Handbook of Research on Teacher Education: Enduring Questions in Changing Contexts* (3rd edn) (pp. 732–755). New York: Routledge.

Schön, D.A. (1983) *The Reflective Practitioner.* New York: Basic Books.

Senyshyn, R.M. (2018) Teaching for transformation: Converting the intercultural experience of preservice teachers into intercultural learning. *Intercultural Education* 29 (2), 163–184.

Shulman, L.S. (2004) *The Wisdom of Practice: Essays on Teaching, Learning, and Learning to Teach.* San Francisco, CA: Jossey-Bass.

Williams, T.R. (2005) Exploring the impact of study abroad on students' intercultural communication skills: Adaptability and sensitivity. *Journal of Studies in International Education* 9 (4), 356–371.

Zembylas, M. and McGlynn, C. (2012) Discomforting pedagogies: Emotional tensions, ethical dilemmas and transformative possibilities. *British Educational Research Journal* 38 (1), 41–59.

21 The Impact of a Two-Week Study-Abroad Teacher Development Program on Pre-Service L2 Teachers

Meredith D'Arienzo and YouJin Kim

Benefits of previously researched short-term study-abroad programs can be grouped into four categories: teachers' L2 proficiency, personal changes, cultural or world views, and pedagogical awareness or capabilities. Of particular interest to this study, previous research has found numerous personal benefits of study abroad, such as increased confidence and feeling prepared to be a teacher.

Five months after study abroad, Chobi stated: 'I didn't realize it was going to be such an opportunity for me to grow on my own – not just as a teacher, but as an individual … It was a really good experience for me all around … applying what I learned in school and learning who I am as a person'.

Introduction

Previous studies on short-term study-abroad programs for pre-service L2 teachers have found benefits for pre-service teachers in areas such as their cultural awareness and pedagogical practices, with mixed results for L2 proficiency development (Gleeson & Tait, 2012). However, 'short-term' has been used in the literature to describe immersion experiences ranging from two weeks to one year (Gleeson & Tait, 2012), and there is little research on very brief short-term programs. Given that not all pre-service teachers are able to go abroad for an extended period of time, the current study examined pre-service teachers' experience of a two-week study-abroad teacher development program and its impact on their trajectories as future teachers.

Short-Term Study Abroad

Benefits of short-term study-abroad programs for pre-service teachers

Prior to the Covid-19 pandemic, short-term study-abroad programs (defined here and for this study as eight weeks or shorter) were on the rise for US undergraduates (IIE, 2020), and international experiences for pre-service teachers were increasingly being incorporated into teacher education programs (Barkhuizen & Feryok, 2006; Lee, 2009). Benefits of previously researched short-term study-abroad programs can be grouped into four categories: teachers' L2 proficiency, personal changes, cultural or world views, and pedagogical awareness or capabilities. Of particular interest to this study, previous research has found numerous personal benefits of study abroad, such as increased confidence and feeling prepared to be a teacher (e.g. Yang, 2011). Researchers have reported growth in teachers' cognitive development and adaptability to a foreign culture (Lee, 2009) and in interpersonal awareness (Barkhuizen & Feryok, 2006; Lee, 2009). In addition, study abroad has helped teachers develop self-awareness (Colwell *et al.*, 2019) and impacted their identity construction (Lee, 2009; Trent, 2011).

Additionally, short-term study-abroad research has reported benefits for teachers relating to pedagogy, including enhanced understandings of pedagogy and teaching methods (Barkhuizen & Feryok, 2006; Hepple, 2012; Kabilan, 2013) and of teacher and student roles and relationships (Harbon, 2007). Studies have reported improved teaching skills and strategies (Colwell *et al.*, 2019; Harbon, 2007; Kabilan, 2013; Lee, 2011; Trent, 2011), in particular for lesson planning and classroom management (Yang, 2011). In addition, study abroad has been found to improve teaching characteristics, such as patience, reflectivity, professionalism and reactivity (Willard-Holt, 2001).

Short-term study-abroad characteristics that promote teacher development

In addition to reporting the benefits of study abroad, many studies have highlighted the means by which participants made the reported gains. Nearly all of the studies that included teaching practice emphasized this aspect of study abroad as contributing to teachers' increased pedagogical knowledge and skills and/or personal growth. Reflection was cited frequently as an activity that contributed greatly to teachers' growth. Some programs incorporated self-reflection, such as through blogging (Colwell *et al.*, 2019), while others emphasized the importance of the dialogic nature of reflection (Hepple, 2012) and the ways teachers benefited from the social interaction that took place in group reflection (Barkhuizen

& Feryok, 2006). Still others noted the importance of the recursive nature of reflection (Hepple, 2012) and the benefits that teachers gained from the cyclical process of theorizing and practicing (Trent, 2011). In addition to reflection, teachers benefited from observing experienced teachers (Yang, 2011) and from the relationships they developed with other teachers (Kabilan, 2013; Willard-Holt, 2001). Finally, input from supervisors was valuable for teachers' development, such as through feedback in post-observation discussions (Yang, 2011).

The Current Study

Short-term study-abroad programs have been shown to contribute to pre-service teachers' increased L2 proficiency, personal changes, expanded cultural and world views, and increased pedagogical knowledge and skills. A recent qualitative review of short-term study-abroad research similarly notes, 'short-term international experiences, in fact, can significantly contribute to language teachers' multidimensional development' (Çiftçi & Karaman, 2019: 108). The majority of the study-abroad programs in the studies reviewed above lasted six or eight weeks, while only one study (Harbon, 2007) was as short as three weeks, and one lasted only one week (Willard-Holt, 2001). Thus, there is little in the current literature that indicates the degree to which benefits can be found for pre-service teachers in very brief short-term programs. Given that not all teachers can afford extended periods abroad, and considering the unique foreign language opportunities that short-term programs incorporating teaching practice can offer pre-service teachers, it is worthwhile to further investigate brief stays abroad. In addition, many studies give a snapshot of the influence of study abroad during the experience and shortly afterwards, while few studies take a longitudinal approach or investigate the long-term effects of study abroad (Çiftçi & Karaman, 2019; see Willard-Holt, 2001). Coleman (2013) recognizes the interrelationship of multiple variables in study abroad and argues that research should 'embrace whole people and whole lives' (2013: 33). Thus, this study attempts to gauge the impact of a two-week study-abroad program on pre-service teachers and their future trajectories, examining the topics in depth by taking a comparative case study approach. The current longitudinal study addresses the aforementioned research gaps in the context of a study-abroad program in Mexico and was guided by the following questions:

(1) How do pre-service L2 teachers value a two-week study-abroad program with a teaching component, and do their views change over time?
(2) What is the impact of such a program on pre-service L2 teachers' future trajectories?

Method

Case study approach

To investigate the value of the two-week study-abroad program for pre-service L2 teachers and its impact on those teachers' future trajectories, a qualitative comparative case study was conducted (Casanave, 2015). In order to evaluate whether their views changed over time, data was collected over eight months. In an effort to reduce bias and increase interpretive validity (Onwuegbuzie & Leech, 2007), triangulation was achieved through data sources (e.g. people – participants, researcher observations; times – pre-departure, on study abroad, post-study abroad), data collection methods (interviews, document collection, observations) and data type (e.g. audio recordings, written documents; Miles *et al.*, 2014).

Instructional context and study-abroad program

The study-abroad program was a component of a three-credit Teaching English as a Foreign Language (TEFL) course at a large research university in the United States. The focus of the course was to give the students – pre-service teachers – practice in designing and teaching English as a foreign language (EFL) lessons. The course was open to undergraduate students, Master's students and post-baccalaureate students working to obtain a TEFL certificate. The course took a constructivist approach, starting from students' prior knowledge and promoting explicit analysis of personal practical knowledge and theoretical knowledge (Ogilvie & Dunn, 2010). Learners played a critical, active role in constructing new knowledge.

During the two months prior to going abroad, teachers attended four class meetings and read about and discussed topics such as classroom management, lesson planning, teaching young learners, and teaching approaches and methods. They evaluated the effectiveness of different approaches to TEFL, designed and received feedback on lesson plans, and participated in microteaching sessions with their peers, teaching assistants and professor.

Students then spent two weeks in a large city in northern-central Mexico during the summer semester. They were accompanied by the program director, the first author, who had the role of a teacher-mentor, and two teaching assistants – Master's students from the Applied Linguistics department who had experience teaching EFL/English as a Second Language (ESL) and training teachers. While abroad, participants taught at an English-language summer camp at a non-profit language institute with approximately 300 students. Teachers either stayed in a hotel or with a homestay family. After a half-day orientation upon arrival in Mexico, the teachers taught from Monday through Friday for two weeks. During one of the five weekdays, each teacher acted as a 'floater' and observed other classes. The teachers were responsible for teaching one lesson to four class sections each day, as well as leading a homeroom period. Each teacher was observed daily by the program director, the first author, or a teaching assistant and received brief, oral feedback following the lesson and more comprehensive, written feedback at the end of each day. In addition, after their lessons, the teachers received oral feedback from the program director and participated in small group reflection sessions led by the program director, the first author and the teaching assistants. Thus, the teachers spent from approximately 7:30 am to 2:30 pm each day at school. They were free in the afternoons to spend time with their host families or their peers, explore the local surroundings and prepare subsequent lessons. After returning home, students completed reflection assignments and submitted a teaching portfolio.

Participants

Twenty students (15 female, 5 male) were enrolled in the 2019 TEFL summer course described above. The participants included 11 undergraduate students, seven graduate students and two post-baccalaureate students. The undergraduate students had a variety of majors, including Applied Linguistics (9), Biology (1) and English (1). All seven graduate students were pursuing a Master of Arts in Applied Linguistics, and the two post-baccalaureate students were completing a Master's-level TEFL certificate. The two focal participants in this study, Chobi and John, were selected because they represented the participants' variety in level of education, academic preparation and career plans. Both participants had grown up in the United States, had L1 English, and were 21 years old at the time of the study-abroad program.

Chobi was an undergraduate student whose career goal was to teach English in Japan. During high school, she had tutored peers taking ESL classes but had no other experience tutoring or teaching. While completing her undergraduate degree, Chobi was also completing a TEFL certificate. Chobi had taken a number of upper-level courses in her major (Applied Linguistics), such as Second Language Acquisition (SLA), a TEFL course, and English Grammar in Use. She was excited to see how the principles of SLA might be observable in the classroom. Her main goal for the study-abroad program was to determine whether a career in TEFL, about which she was very passionate, was the right fit for her.

John was a Master's student in Applied Linguistics whose career goals included completing a PhD and conducting research on natural language processing tools. Having recently completed his undergraduate degree in the same department, he had taken a wide range of classes related to applied linguistics and teaching English. John had experience tutoring individuals in ESL. His main goal for the study-abroad program was to find out whether he enjoyed teaching larger classes.

Researcher positionality

In addition to interacting with the participants as a researcher and conducting the individual interviews, the first author acted as a teacher-mentor. She implemented pre-departure class meetings – preparing instructional materials and leading discussions on topics such as approaches to TEFL, classroom management and designing tasks. She provided feedback to some teachers on their lesson plans and microteaching (pre-departure) and on their teaching (abroad). However, she did not provide feedback to those students who were participating in the study (i.e. the focal case participants). By not holding a role that could be seen as evaluative of participants' performance, it was hoped that they would feel more comfortable expressing themselves openly in interviews.

Data collection procedures and materials

As shown in Table 21.1, the study was conducted over a period of eight months, and data was collected during five time periods.

Prior to the TEFL course, teachers completed a needs analysis questionnaire regarding their demographics, academic background and teaching experience. It asked about their experience living or studying abroad, career goals, and familiarity with TEFL approaches and methods. Additionally, teachers participated in a semi-structured interview in order to learn more about their course and career goals. Their second interview prior to departure focused on their expectations for study abroad and their plans to implement course content in their teaching.

During study abroad, each participant had one semi-structured individual interview each week (two in total) and wrote a half- to one-page reflection about their experiences each day. Three weeks after study abroad, participants submitted a final, two-page reflection paper in which they described what they had learned on study abroad and how it had

Table 21.1 Data collection timeline

Phase	Dates	Data Collected
Pre-course	Early May 2019	Needs analysis questionnaire Pre-course interview
During course/ Pre-departure	May – June 2019	Pre-departure interview
Study abroad	June 30 – July 13, 2019	Individual interviews at end of both weeks Daily written reflections
Post-study abroad	July 14 – 31, 2019	Final reflection paper L2 Teaching Philosophy Statement Post-study abroad interview Focus group interview
Delayed post- study abroad	Fall 2019 semester	Delayed post-study abroad interview(s) Revised L2 Teaching Philosophy Statement

impacted them. They also wrote an L2 Teaching Philosophy Statement, in which they described their beliefs about how L2s are learned, the role of the L2 teacher, and opinions about teaching methods and approaches (O'Neal *et al.*, 2007). Subsequently, they had an individual interview in which they were asked to reflect on their overall experience in the course and on study abroad. Lastly, in groups of four, teachers participated in a focus group interview led by a facilitator who was not involved with the study-abroad program. During the focus group, participants discussed topics such as challenges they faced in Mexico, the types of pedagogical activities they found successful, and the impact of study abroad. In the Fall 2019 semester (delayed post-study abroad period), the participants wrote a Revised L2 Teaching Philosophy Statement, in which they evaluated whether and how their beliefs had changed over time, and participated in one to two final individual, semi-structured interviews.

Data analysis

Following the transcription of all audio recordings, the data was analyzed qualitatively through an iterative process using the software NVivo. Some codes from a 2018 pilot study (D'Arienzo & Kim, 2019) served as a starting point, while others emerged from the data. The first author initially assigned descriptive codes to chunks of the data. After defining codes to clarify their meaning (Saldaña, 2009), the second author analyzed several lengthy excerpts of the data. One area of discrepancy arose, and it was resolved through discussion. Next, from the established descriptive codes, pattern codes were developed, using analytical memos to create a chain of evidence and stimulate reflection on the categories of the data (Yin, 2003). Lastly, themes were identified (Miles *et al.*, 2014) that informed an understanding of the value of the study-abroad program for the teachers and its impact on their trajectories. Although the data in this study was largely self-reported, the first author's observations and informal interviews on study abroad helped to triangulate the findings and interpret the data. The following section presents and discusses the findings of the study and is organized according to the themes that emerged through data analysis.

Findings and Discussion

The value of a two-week study-abroad program

The first research question asked about the value of a two-week study-abroad program for pre-service L2 teachers and whether participants' beliefs about it changed over time. The findings are grouped under two broad themes related to the different areas of participants' personal and professional growth and the ways the participants learned and grew on study abroad.

What I learned: From pedagogical to personal

Like the participants in numerous previous studies (e.g. Hepple, 2012; Kabilan, 2013; Lee, 2011), Chobi and John both demonstrated growth related to pedagogical knowledge and skills. Both participants experimented with task-based teaching during study abroad and, as in previous studies (Barkhuizen & Feryok, 2006; Hepple, 2012; Kabilan, 2013), reported having a better understanding of the approach after study abroad. As in previous research (Colwell *et al.*, 2019; Harbon, 2007; Kabilan, 2013; Lee, 2011; Trent, 2011), both participants demonstrated improving skills in implementing task-based lessons over the two weeks, in areas such as increased student participation (observations of John's lessons) and completing task phases (observations of Chobi's lessons).

Similar to Yang's (2011) participants, Chobi and John both felt they had made gains in classroom management during their two weeks' teaching experience. As Chobi noted after study abroad, 'Classroom management is like the key to success because they have the knowledge there, it's just getting them to the point where they can sit still and sit down and produce that language' (post-study abroad interview). Over the two weeks, John began to incorporate classroom management techniques – even ones that he did not feel overly comfortable using, such as clapping – because they proved effective in focusing students' attention (observation notes). Though not greatly discussed in the literature, engaging students was another area that both participants felt was challenging and was also an area in which they had improved. John, in particular, emphasized the importance of choosing topics and designing lessons that engaged students: 'What I learned most is that the lessons have to be somewhat entertaining and related to students' interests, or the lesson will fail to take off' (final reflection). Chobi rewrote nearly all her lesson plans following a survey of students' interests on the first day in order to gear her lessons towards topics that would engage the students (informal conversation). Perhaps since the teachers in this study-abroad program were fully responsible for choosing topics and planning lessons for their students themselves (i.e. there was no assigned curriculum, and they were not given lessons to implement), they were acutely aware of the impact those choices had on student engagement and the success or failure of their lessons. In their revised philosophy statements in the fall, both participants affirmed their belief that student engagement was key.

As in previous studies (e.g. Yang, 2011), many codes that emerged from the analysis related to participants growing into the role of teacher. This study, like numerous others (e.g. Colwell *et al.*, 2019; Lee, 2009, 2011; Willard-Holt, 2001) found that teachers experienced increased confidence as a result of their study-abroad experience. Participants highlighted specific attributes they had learned to embody, such as the need to act as an authority figure, as well as the need to be flexible and think on one's feet (Willard-Holt, 2001). After study abroad, Chobi noted, 'You have to be spontaneous to be a teacher. You have to be able to change your lesson plan if your first class fails ... you just gotta be prepared for that' (post-study abroad interview). Similar to Harbon's (2007) participants, whose understanding of students' needs and characteristics, and the relationship between teachers and students grew on study abroad, John and Chobi highlighted their students' needs and reflected on the desire to promote a student-led classroom that would meet those needs. Overall, the participants described developing a teacher persona (daily reflections) and the ways the experience widened their horizons in terms of how they thought about teaching. After study abroad, Chobi observed that being in the role of the teacher was anxiety-reducing. Five months later, she confirmed this view, saying:

> I enjoyed seeing myself in a totally different light, because I have such bad anxiety when it comes to getting in front of people and talking to people ... But when I get into teacher mode, it's like all of that goes away. (Delayed post-study abroad interview)

Two weeks after study abroad, John reported learning not to expect perfection and that he had to take on unexpected roles: 'I had envisioned being more of a manager or a supervisor of tasks ... but I ended up doing more motivating ... or guiding ... so it was a lot different than I originally thought' (focus group).

A number of topics that emerged from the data analysis related to participants' personal growth. For example, Chobi highlighted strengthened interpersonal relationships with other teachers and students (Barkhuizen & Feryok, 2006; Lee, 2009; Willard-Holt, 2001), and John described developing ties with his host family. The participants also reported enjoying getting to know a foreign culture, although given the study-abroad program's heavy focus on lesson planning and teaching, these experiences remained somewhat limited compared to the findings of other studies. Finally, both Chobi and John reported developing self-awareness, as was true in Colwell *et al.* (2019). Numerous instances in the data related to the ways the participants felt they had challenged and learned about themselves, both immediately after study abroad and later on. Five months after study abroad, Chobi stated:

> I didn't realize it was going to be such an opportunity for me to grow on my own – not just as a teacher, but as an individual ... It was a really good experience for me all around ... applying what I learned in school and learning who I am as a person. (Delayed post-study abroad interview)

As noted in several instances above, overall, the participants' opinions five months following study abroad confirmed their initial beliefs about the value of study abroad and the professional and personal ways they benefited from the experience.

Intensive learning through doing and reflecting in a social context

The second theme that emerged from data analysis related to the different ways the teachers learned on study abroad. The participants noted many positive aspects of their study-abroad experience that related to the intensive nature of teacher training. Thanks to the many hours each day the teachers spent teaching, the immediate feedback they received, and the opportunity to apply that feedback in subsequent lessons, they were able to observe their progress and learn a lot in a short time. After study abroad, John stated, 'You learned an enormous amount in two weeks because you're practically working or thinking about work for 10 hours a day' (post-study abroad interview). One of the biggest benefits of this intensive experience was that participants had the opportunity to figure out whether they liked teaching and whether they could envision themselves pursuing language teaching as a career. John stated, 'The two weeks gives … a good taste of teaching … In two weeks, I can find out, "Well, that's not gonna work", or, "this is great. I want to keep doing this for the rest of my life"' (pre-course interview).

Closely related to the intensive environment of the study-abroad experience was its hands-on nature, reported in previous literature as being one of the most impactful elements of short-term study-abroad programs (Harbon, 2007; Kabilan, 2013; Yang, 2011). This was the participants' first chance to experiment with different teaching roles and approaches with a class of actual students, as opposed to microteaching with peers. As with the participants in Dunn *et al.*'s (2014) study, the teachers were able to experiment in the EFL context first-hand and observe a clear theory–practice connection. John observed that prior to study abroad, he believed task-based teaching was an effective approach but was only able to confirm that after his experience teaching on study abroad (post-study abroad interview). Chobi echoed this sentiment five months later, adding that she hadn't fully understood task-based teaching until she could apply it in her study-abroad classroom (delayed post-study abroad interview). Being in the classroom for the first time also helped the teachers learn to think on their feet and learn from their mistakes. As John noted on several occasions, 'I always think about my first day failure … What I learned is to keep at least one catastrophe in the back of my head so that I understand how to respond to it' (delayed post-study abroad interview 2).

Reflection was also an important means of promoting teachers' development on study abroad. This included both individual reflection, which was incorporated through daily writing tasks, much like the use of blogging in Colwell *et al.* (2019), as well as small- and large-group reflection, which took place at the conclusion of each school day. Similar to studies reporting an increase in participants' reflectivity (Willard-Holt, 2001), in the semester following study abroad, John indicated that during study abroad he had developed the habit of reflecting after teaching and that he continued to implement this after each class he taught.

The participants also benefited from the social nature of the study-abroad experience. They especially emphasized learning from their peers, through peer observation (Kabilan, 2013; Yang, 2011), learning to work together as colleagues, and through group reflection (Barkhuizen & Feryok, 2006; Hepple, 2012). Describing the problem-solving that took place in daily group reflection sessions, John noted after study abroad, 'I think the collaboration was what I learned most from' (post-study abroad interview). The supportive relationships that developed among teachers and the contribution of those relationships to teachers' learning played a key role (Dunn *et al.*, 2014; Kabilan, 2013). These relationships carried over into teachers' free time, during which they planned and critiqued lessons together and did microteaching. Five months after study abroad, Chobi noted, 'Because we had such a small group, and we were able to provide each other feedback ... being able to come together and collaborate ... was really good ... We had a lot of mentors in our group' (delayed post-study abroad interview). The participants also benefited from the sustained support of their leaders, through group and individual feedback, as well as in informal settings, such as breakfast and lunch-time conversations, or even impromptu evening advising sessions (Chobi, informal conversation).

Impact on teachers' trajectories

Chobi: A chance to confirm career goals

Prior to study abroad, Chobi stated that she had wanted to teach EFL for a long time but had never had the chance to try it out. She was anxious to find out if she enjoyed teaching as much as she thought she would. Study abroad affirmed her passion for TEFL:

> This was kind of the determining trip for me, like, 'Am I doing the right thing?' And once I got there, and it felt so natural and so good, I was like, 'it's the right thing. I'm on the right career path'. (Delayed post-study abroad interview)

Just as there is overlap in what researchers may consider personal development, as opposed to professional (e.g. increased confidence), for many teachers (e.g. participants in Dunn *et al.*, 2014; Kabilan, 2013) personal growth was intertwined with professional growth. For Chobi, this was very much the case, as her positive teaching experience prompted significant personal growth:

> I didn't realize it was going to be such an opportunity for me to grow on my own ... not just as a teacher, but as an individual ... I think that those, those two also kind of coincide because ... being a teacher is who I am ... It was a really good experience for me all around ... applying what I learned in school and learning who I am as a person and developing who I am as a teacher. (Delayed post-study abroad interview)

John: An opportunity to develop new skills

John, on the other hand, maintained a solely professional approach, noting that the two intensive weeks on study abroad, in contrast to his undergraduate coursework, had prepared him to teach:

> It's a little bit different when you have six of your American students and co-students in class telling you that, 'Oh, that might work. That might not work', but when you're in a classroom, and it's not working, what do you do? It's one thing to know whether it's a decent idea, but if it's just failing and what do you ... I just think that's the value you don't get from anything else, especially in two weeks. (Delayed post-study abroad interview 2)

After study abroad, John saw teaching as an opportunity he might consider in the future, although it did not alter his overall plans to pursue a PhD. He wrote:

> The time I spent in Mexico teaching was certainly a very positive, professionally enriching experience ... While teaching is not my primary career interest, it is something that I have considered doing abroad after I finish my master's degree next year. It would be a thrill to live in an EFL context and teach students (hopefully, adults or university students). (Final reflection)

Thus, as was true for Harbon's (2007) participants, some teachers may experience personal change after a short-term study-abroad program, but not necessarily all will do so. However, both teachers experienced professional growth after just two weeks abroad, confirming previous research that found positive benefits for pre-service teachers' professional and/or personal growth following short-term study-abroad programs as short as one week (Willard-Holt, 2001).

Implications for Designing Short-Term Study-Abroad Programs for Teacher Training/Development

Considering the elements of the study-abroad program that were found to benefit participants' development, a number of recommendations for future short-term programs can be made. By incorporating a pre-departure training program, the limited time on study abroad can be dedicated to giving teachers more hours of hands-on teaching experience. Combined with immediate feedback, this can lead to a productive theory–practice cycle. The chance to observe other teachers in the classroom can also provide teachers with new ideas for classroom management techniques and pedagogical activities. Including opportunities for reflection, both individual and group, written and oral, can help teachers make the most of their experiences. Social interactions, which the teachers in this study found extremely helpful, can be incorporated both formally (e.g. by including elements such as group reflection) and informally (e.g. by working to create a supportive environment that will encourage teachers to openly accept constructive criticism and to collaborate). Lastly, involving experienced teaching assistants and ensuring that group leaders/mentors are accessible to teachers can facilitate teachers' development in both structured and unstructured moments.

Conclusion

The current study reported the experiences of two pre-service teachers who participated in a two-week study-abroad program in Mexico with daily teaching experience. The program had a positive impact on the participants' pedagogical knowledge and skills, as well as personal growth. These positive changes can be linked to the intensive, daily teaching experience, numerous opportunities for reflection, and social interaction with mentors and peers. In addition, the pre-departure training program prepared the teachers for an intensive study-abroad experience through lesson planning, microteaching and feedback exchanges. The program allowed the participants to either confirm their desired career goals or expand their future career options. The benefits and beliefs reported by participants after study abroad persisted five months later.

As a comparative case study, the findings are limited to an in-depth understanding of two participants, whose experiences may not represent those of all pre-service teachers. Nonetheless, their experiences were fairly representative of other teachers in the program, and similar findings in previous research support the idea that their experiences were not an anomaly. Future research could address this by including greater numbers of focal participants. In addition, analysis of videos of teachers in the classroom could further illuminate the changes reported by participants. Despite such limitations, the current study sheds light on the potential benefits of short-term study-abroad programs in teacher development. In particular, well-designed two-week programs can be extremely beneficial for pre-service teachers who may not be able to go abroad for longer periods due to work or financial restrictions. Although it is not the intention of the authors to promote brief short-term study-abroad programs rather than longer sojourns abroad for pre-service teachers, it is certainly our belief that this type of program is very worthwhile and, with the appropriate planning and implementation, can greatly benefit pre-service teachers, giving them the tools and confidence for teaching and insight into their future trajectories as teachers.

References

Barkhuizen, G. and Feryok, A. (2006) Pre-service teachers' perceptions of a short-term international experience programme. *Asia-Pacific Journal of Teacher Education* 34 (1), 115–134.

Casanave, C.P. (2015) Case studies. In B. Paltridge and A. Phakiti (eds) *Research Methods in Applied Linguistics* (pp. 119–135). London: Bloomsbury.

Çiftçi, E.Y. and Karaman, A.C. (2019) Short-term international experiences in language teacher education: A qualitative meta-synthesis. *Australian Journal of Teacher Education* 44 (1), 93–119.

Coleman, J.A. (2013) Researching whole people and whole lives. In C. Kinginger (ed.) *Social and Cultural Aspects of Language Learning in Study Abroad* (pp. 17–44). Amsterdam: John Benjamins.

Colwell, J., Nielsen, D., Bradley, B.A. and Spearman, M. (2019) Preservice teacher reflections about short-term summer study abroad experiences in Italy. In A.R. Joan and M.M. Tammy (eds) *Pre-Service and In-Service Teacher Education: Concepts, Methodologies, Tools, and Applications* (pp. 1743–1763). Hershey, PA: IGI Global.

D'Arienzo, M. and Kim, Y. (2019, March) *Preservice Teachers' Developing Cognitions about SLA and Task-based Teaching During a Study Abroad Teaching Practicum: A Comparative Case Study*. American Association for Applied Linguistics Conference, Atlanta, USA.

Dunn, A.H., Dotson, E.K., Cross, S.B., Kesner, J. and Lundahl, B. (2014) Reconsidering the local after a transformative global experience: A comparison of two study abroad programs for preservice teachers. *Action in Teacher Education* 36 (4), 283–304.

Gleeson, M. and Tait, C. (2012) Teachers as sojourners: Transitory communities in short study-abroad programmes. *Teaching and Teacher Education* 28 (8), 1144–1151.

Harbon, L. (2007) Short-term international experiences and teacher language awareness. *International Education Journal* 8 (1), 229–243.

Hepple, E. (2012) Questioning pedagogies: Hong Kong pre-service teachers' dialogic reflections on a transnational school experience. *Journal of Education for Teaching* 38 (3), 309–322.

IIE (Institute of International Education) (2020) *U.S. Study Abroad for Academic Credit Trends*. https://opendoorsdata.org/data/us-study-abroad/u-s-study-abroad-for-academic-credit-trends/ (accessed May 3, 2021).

Kabilan, M.K. (2013) A phenomenological study of an international teaching practicum: Pre-service teachers' experiences of professional development. *Teaching and Teacher Education* 36, 198–209.

Lee, J.F. (2009) ESL student teachers' perceptions of a short-term overseas immersion programme. *Teaching and Teacher Education* 25 (8), 1095–1104.

Lee, J.F.K. (2011) International field experience: What do student teachers learn? *Australian Journal of Teacher Education* 36 (10), 1–22.

Miles, M., Huberman, A.M. and Saldaña, J. (2014) *Qualitative Data Analysis: A Methods Sourcebook* (3rd edn). Los Angeles, CA: Sage.

Ogilvie, G. and Dunn, W. (2010) Taking teacher education to task: Exploring the role of teacher education in promoting the utilization of task-based language teaching. *Language Teaching Research* 14 (2), 161–181.

O'Neal, C., Meizlish, D. and Kaplan, M. (2007) Writing a statement of teaching philosophy for the academic job search. *CRLT Occasional Papers, 23*. Ann Arbor, MI: Center for Research on Learning and Teaching at the University of Michigan.

Onwuegbuzie, A.J. and Leech, N.L. (2007) Validity and qualitative research: An oxymoron? *Quality and Quantity: International Journal of Methodology* 41, 233–249.

Saldaña, J. (2009) *The Coding Manual for Qualitative Researchers*. Los Angeles, CA: Sage.

Trent, J. (2011) Learning, teaching, and constructing identities: ESL pre-service teacher experiences during a short-term international experience programme. *Asia Pacific Journal of Education* 31 (2), 177–194.

Willard-Holt, C. (2001) The impact of a short-term international experience for preservice teachers. *Teaching and Teacher Education* 17 (4), 505–517.

Yang, C.C.R. (2011) Pre-service English teachers' perceptions of an overseas field experience programme. *Australian Journal of Teacher Education* 36 (3), 92–104.

Yin, R.K. (2003) *Case Study Research: Design and Methods* (3rd edn). Thousand Oaks, CA: Sage.

Index

agency 44, 75, 79, 124, 131, 193
anxiety 15, 51, 52, 54, 105, 120, 129, 132, 151, 156, 159, 166, 168, 170, 194, 198, 238, 262, 277, 279
Applied Linguistics Association of New Zealand 2
Australia 11, 37, 60–70, 72, 123, 152, 153, 227, 246, 248, 250, 251
(auto)ethnography (*see* duoethnography) 5, 26, 140, 141, 143, 246–247, 252
autonomy 42, 43, 57, 107, 152, 171

Cambodia 7, 12, 47, 49–50, 52, 53, 55–56, 163, 164, 165–166, 167, 169, 170, 171, 173
Canada 8, 11, 35–46, 69, 101, 105, 106, 107, 108, 153, 185, 228–229, 246, 250, 251, 252
careers (*see* career choices, career goals) 6, 13, 15, 26, 41, 47, 78, 82, 94, 102, 197, 219, 220–221, 222, 225–226, 229, 230–231, 235, 247, 249
career choices (*see* careers, career goals) 12, 17, 222, 242
career goals (*see* careers, career choices) 273–274, 279, 281
CELTA (The Certificate in English Language Teaching for Adults) 13, 55, 226, 227, 228, 229, 231
Colombia 9, 195, 196
communicative repertoire 60, 61–63, 64, 65, 66, 67, 68–69
confidence (*see* self-confidence) 6, 7, 12, 35, 40, 49, 51, 52, 53–54, 56, 64–65, 103, 116, 117, 119, 123, 126, 131, 138, 156, 166, 186, 207, 229, 242, 248, 249, 250, 264, 269, 270, 276, 279, 281
Covid-19 2, 3, 6–8, 18, 54–55, 73, 112, 115, 119, 138, 151–162, 163–164, 170–173, 195, 197, 202, 236, 260–265, 270
critical interculturality (*see* interculturality) 87–90, 93, 97
critical internationalization (*see* internationalization) 3–4,
critical multilingual language awareness (CMLA) 177, 203
critical reflection 41, 48, 51, 52, 57, 63, 91, 98, 112, 113, 186, 204, 238, 241
critical reflexivity 6, 14, 27, 30–31, 32, 57, 234
critical thinking 14, 42, 100, 184, 203
cultural identity (*see* identity, professional identity, teacher identity) 15, 89, 94, 145, 220, 241, 246
culture shock 6, 119, 223

doctoral students 191–192, 194–200, 251
decolonial teacher education 6, 90
decolonial ideas (thinking) 14, 89, 93, 95, 97, 194
decolonial turn 195
depression 95, 159, 166, 238
disruption 6–8, 18, 48, 153, 157–158, 161, 164, 170, 171, 172–173, 257, 259, 261–262, 263, 265
Dominican Republic 15, 174–190
duoethnography (*see* (auto)ethnography) 12, 233, 235, 237

Ecuador 13, 87–99
emotiogram 5, 202–213
emotions (*see* negative emotions, emotional distress/challenges) 4, 5, 8, 12, 14, 17, 18, 23–24, 25, 26–27, 28, 33, 49, 92, 126, 131, 138, 144, 156, 170, 178, 191, 193–194, 195, 198, 199, 202, 204–216, 234, 235, 236, 244

emotions and identity 4, 28, 75, 125, 175, 193, 236, 237
emotions and professional learning/ development 8, 23, 24, 30, 31, 48, 138, 177, 199, 204–205, 210, 212, 214, 233, 242, 251, 256, 259
emotional distress/challenges (*see* emotions, negative emotions) 6, 7, 24, 73, 124, 127, 151–152, 169, 183, 184–185, 192, 199, 234, 238–239, 244, 266
emotion work 7, 9, 13, 17
emotional dissonance 6, 187, 196–197, 199, 202, 203, 206–216
emotionality 9, 23, 24, 26, 32, 33
empathy 6, 12, 15, 28, 51, 75, 96, 101, 138, 144, 158, 175, 177, 180, 181, 185, 186, 241, 250, 252, 253, 257, 265
experiential learning 24, 33, 89, 137, 204, 214

feelings 6, 14, 33, 47, 48, 51, 54, 56, 65, 94, 144, 152, 156, 166, 168, 170, 175, 181, 183, 186, 208, 233, 234, 235–237, 238, 239, 240
field trip 23, 25, 26, 27, 29, 31–33, 115

German 203, 205, 206, 207, 223, 236, 239, 247, 249–250, 257
Germany 13, 205, 234, 260
global awareness 93, 135, 143
global studies 1, 153, 157
globalization 131, 151, 158, 160, 202
Guatemala 9, 23–34, 179

Haiti 14, 181, 183–184
homestay 4, 13, 36, 74, 79, 97, 123–134, 179, 180, 181, 186, 238–239, 248, 272
Hong Kong 11, 37, 79, 113, 123, 124, 125, 127, 128, 130, 152

identity (*see* cultural identity, professional identity, teacher identity) 6, 8, 11, 15, 17, 24, 37, 38–39, 44, 47, 50, 57, 61–64, 79, 80–81, 88, 97, 101, 125, 143, 187, 191–192, 193, 194, 197, 199, 221, 233–234, 235, 236, 258, 260–261, 264, 270
identity repertoire 6, 11, 60–70

identity work 7, 8, 9
ideologies 4, 6, 13, 14, 63, 71, 72, 73, 78, 80, 81, 93, 94, 177
independence 12, 47, 51, 52, 54, 56, 58, 81, 168, 242
imagined identity 6, 38, 41
immersion experience 11, 25, 33, 73, 88, 97, 113, 117, 121, 130, 177, 179, 180, 181, 186, 196
immersion program 78, 87, 88, 89, 91, 93, 95, 114–115, 123, 125–126, 127, 131, 133, 257, 269
Indigenous language and culture 79, 92–95, 98
Indigenous worldviews (knowledge) 6, 23, 25, 31, 91, 95
intercultural competence 9, 10, 53, 73, 75, 89, 90, 101, 129, 130, 132, 174, 175, 176, 178, 257
interculturality (*see* critical interculturality) 6, 10, 17, 89–90, 98
intercultural learning 10, 17, 89, 121, 123, 124, 125, 127, 133, 203, 243, 262
international education 8, 14, 164, 179, 184, 187, 229, 230
international program 3
internationalization (*see* critical internationalization) 3–4, 35, 202
internship 2–3, 9, 136, 192, 196–198, 221, 227, 259

Japan 7, 8, 35–46, 151–162, 185, 227, 229, 245–246, 248, 249–251, 252, 273

language teacher educators (*see* teacher educators) 3, 195, 198
language teachers studying abroad 1–19, 47, 81
Language Teaching Assistant (LTA) 14, 15–16, 219, 220–231
lockdown 2, 3, 7, 50, 54, 55, 163, 164, 165, 166–170, 171, 172, 236

Mandarin language assistant (MLA) 72, 74–84, 234, 238, 239, 242
Master of TESOL (MTESOL) 47, 49, 52, 53, 55, 56, 64
media (*see* social media) 6, 72, 73, 74, 75, 80, 81–82, 105, 197

Mexico 13, 16, 195, 196, 197, 198, 222, 225, 226, 229, 271, 272, 275, 280, 281
multicultural education 73, 95, 145, 179, 203
multicultural identity 8, 252
multilingual education 6, 93, 95, 135–136, 180, 196, 246
multilingual identity 220, 230, 252
multilingualism 8, 39, 95, 96, 98, 135, 137, 139, 141–142, 144–145, 177

narrative inquiry 5, 38, 154, 194
narrative knowledging 4
negative emotions (see emotions, emotional distress/challenges) 8, 13, 29, 51, 64, 132, 203, 252
New Zealand 2, 12, 13, 14, 37, 47, 49, 51–52, 53, 54–56, 69, 74, 76, 77–84, 113, 123, 153, 163–173, 203, 205, 207, 210, 234, 235, 238, 240, 241, 242, 246–247, 250, 251, 252

online exchange 3, 17, 113–115, 197, 202–216
online learning (see online teaching) 3, 7, 121, 152, 154, 157, 159, 169, 182, 224
online teaching (see online learning) 6, 7–8, 50, 54, 55, 112, 115, 116–121, 168, 169, 172, 227
Others (see Othering) 24, 25, 93, 96, 104, 174, 175–176
Othering (see Others) 104, 187

pastoral care 56, 172, 243
pedagogy of discomfort 257, 262, 263, 265
personal growth 6, 12, 17, 48, 57, 101, 112, 171, 172, 257, 270, 277, 279, 280, 281
political awareness 13, 14
positivity 41, 102, 117
postcoloniality 6
professional learning/development 3, 5, 8–13, 15, 17, 35–46, 48, 50, 52, 74, 79, 101–102, 105–109, 111–122, 123, 171, 193, 204, 214, 241, 280
professional knowledge 48, 51, 52, 54, 76, 79, 116

professional identity (see cultural identity, identity, teacher identity) 14, 38, 50, 54, 57, 72, 75, 76–77, 78, 79, 80–81, 112, 164, 205, 238, 240, 242, 245–246, 248, 249–255
professionalization 6, 7, 256–260, 265
program administrators 109
program leaders 5, 97

reflective writing 5, 36, 37, 39, 42, 43, 44, 49, 98, 102, 141, 182, 206
relationships, professional 11, 12–13, 17, 18, 48, 55, 76, 88, 90, 97, 98, 99, 102, 106, 107, 108, 113, 171, 176, 197, 205, 222, 230, 234, 237, 277, 279
relationships, romantic 227, 229, 230
relationships, social 6, 12–13, 17, 94, 113, 123, 125, 130, 131–132, 186, 205, 213, 238, 239, 240, 243, 262
remote-area schools 111–112, 113
resilience (see teacher resilience) 12, 33, 54, 75, 171, 172, 233, 238, 241–242

self-awareness 6, 12, 40, 144, 224, 238, 241, 244, 270, 277
self-confidence (see confidence) 6, 12, 113, 239, 242
self-efficacy 6, 49, 53, 55, 113, 124, 230
self-esteem 54, 248
short-term programs 13, 25, 113, 123, 174, 188, 234, 257, 269–271, 280–281
social media (see media) 73, 91, 126, 127, 248
sociopragmatic knowledge 123, 128, 129, 130, 131–132, 133
South Africa 10, 135–147
Spain 9, 176, 195, 197, 219, 221, 224, 228
stereotypes 24, 29, 33, 73, 77, 209, 257, 266
subjection 192–193, 195, 198, 199, 200
subjection-emotion interface 191, 194, 196, 197, 198, 199
Sweden 7, 151–153, 156–157, 159, 160
Switzerland 245, 247, 248, 250

Taiwan 10, 111, 113–115, 116, 117, 118, 121, 122, 152, 154, 156–158, 159, 160

teacher educators (*see* language teacher
     educators) 4–5, 18, 24, 57, 81, 89,
     109, 113, 198, 241, 245, 252–253
teacher identity (*see* cultural identity,
     identity, professional identity)
     5, 6, 9, 36, 39–41, 48, 61, 67–69,
     75–76, 204, 220, 230, 245,
     246, 258
teacher resilience (*see* resilience) 6
transformative learning 6, 7, 25, 47,
     48–51, 54–55, 57, 112, 176, 183,
     185–186, 188, 204, 206, 213,
     256–260, 265–266
translanguaging 91, 92, 96, 98, 177
trust 51, 97, 167, 233, 237, 252

United Kingdom (UK) 9, 11, 64, 75,
     123–134, 153, 176, 195, 219–221,
     222–223, 224, 225, 226, 227, 228,
     230–231

United States (US) 9, 10, 13, 14, 15, 24,
     25, 30–31, 37, 54, 64, 72, 76, 87,
     88, 91, 93, 95–97, 111, 113–114,
     117–119, 121, 135–137, 140, 144,
     152, 154, 159, 174–190, 228, 234,
     245, 249–250, 257, 260, 263, 264,
     265, 270, 273

Vietnam 11, 60, 63, 68, 246
virtual exchange/study abroad 13, 17,
     113–114, 115, 119, 120–121, 151,
     169, 174, 195, 197, 202–216
volunteer teaching 101
vulnerability 81, 151, 155, 191, 192, 199

well-being 7, 12, 75, 196
work abroad 3, 76

Zoom 5, 36, 50, 112, 164–165, 169–171,
     206, 236